D0463502

Elementary Theoretical Psychology

JAMES G. GREENO
Indiana University

Elementary Theoretical Psychology

ADDISON-WESLEY PUBLISHING COMPANY
Reading, Massachusetts · Menlo Park, California · London · Don Mills, Ontario

This book is in the

Addison-Wesley Series in

BEHAVIORAL SCIENCE: QUANTITATIVE METHODS

FREDERICK MOSTELLER

Consulting Editor

and

FOUNDATIONS OF SCIENTIFIC PSYCHOLOGY

DOUGLAS ELLSON

Consulting Editor

Printed in the United States of America.
Published simultaneously in Canada.
Library of Congress Catalog Card No. 68-9756.

This book is dedicated to Noreen, my wife.

Preface

The purpose of this book is to present some ideas about people. There are many ways to try to understand people, and this book uses one set of methods. The main approach here is theoretical, in that general ideas are used to try to understand psychological processes. I have tried to emphasize those aspects of psychological theory in which the ideas have been developed to a relatively high degree of clarity and precision.

The theories presented in this book represent attempts to answer several fundamental questions about people. One question is how people receive information about situations and arrive at judgments. A second question involves values and motives and the way in which they influence choices that people make. A third question is how individuals change the choices they make in order to adjust to the conditions around them. A fourth question is how people memorize information, and related questions involve forgetting and the effect that material learned in one situation can have on learning in a new situation. And a fifth question is how people use information in solving problems. These five questions are discussed in the first six chapters, and the seventh chapter also includes a section dealing with processes of choice and judgment. The eighth chapter deals with a different kind of question; there we will consider concepts that are useful in understanding psychological tests.

Previous course work in psychology is not assumed. At the same time, much of the content of this book is not included in other introductory texts and students who already have had a beginning course in psychology probably will find new material and ideas that are worked out in new ways. A minimum of mathematical preparation is required; it is assumed that the student can solve a linear equation, use exponents and logarithms, and understand what a probability is in an elementary way.

Additional mathematical ideas are developed as they are used. Chapter 1 introduces the idea of a measurement scale, and develops the Power Law and the log scale for psychophysical judgments. It notes the importance of ratios in these scales and applies them in an elementary analysis of some constancies and illusions. Chapter 2 presents an analysis of the concept of response strength. Elementary probability theory is used to analyze the selection of an action from a set of alternatives. The concept of conditional probability is used to compare choices made from different sets of alternatives. The analysis in terms of response strength is extended to provide an introduction to the standard decision-theory treatment of choices in conditions of uncertainty. Chapter 3 gives an analysis of instrumental conditioning from the point of view of choice theory. The notion of response strength is used to show a connection between the concepts of motivation and reinforcement. Psychological expectations are analyzed to understand the role of discriminative cues and partial reinforcement. Some situations involving simple social interactions are examined.

After a brief introduction to descriptive statistics in Chapter 4, Chapter 5 analyzes the learning of an association as a simple waiting-time system. It also uses the idea of simple waiting times in discussion of short-term retention and forgetting. And it considers positive transfer based on stimulus generalization in relation to the idea of common elements, applying a standard set-theoretical analysis. Chapter 6 develops the idea of a waiting-time system based on selection from a set of possibilities; the application is to problem solving. The chapter uses simple concept identification as the main example to develop the idea of a trial-and-error process in problem solving and to analyze the influence of distracting irrelevant factors and of readiness or set in problem solving. It attempts to show the generality of these concepts through informal comments about standard problem-solving experiments other than concept identification. Then there is a brief discussion of relational properties connecting the issues of relational transposition and productive thinking to the general treatment given for problem-solving situations.

Chapter 7 presents the normal distribution, and uses it to develop a theory of choice based on variable response strengths, and the corresponding theory of judgments leading to an introduction to the theory of signal detectability. The concept of covariance is also introduced. Chapter 8 presents the idea of measurement error and uses it in a discussion of test reliability and predictive validity. Construct validity is also discussed.

Like any text emphasizing mathematical ideas, this book is intended to be studied, rather than merely read. The examples in the text are meant to provide illustrations of concepts and to fix ideas. In order to understand the material, most students will have to work through each example, even on first reading. Many of the problems at the ends of chapters are simple exercises; others extend the material in the text. Problems of the second kind are marked with arrowheads. A few problems have answers given at the end of the book; these problems are marked with asterisks.

I am grateful to many people who contributed criticism and suggestions during the development of this book. The thoughtful editorial work done by Frederick Mosteller and Douglas Ellson provided many helpful and stimulating suggestions.

Others who read all or part of the manuscript include David LaBerge, David Premack, Wesley Salmon, and John Milholland. All of these men contributed comments and suggestions that helped me in clarifying issues and ideas. I also am indebted to Clifford Gillman who read the final version of the manuscript with great care, suggesting many clarifications of the presentation.

Bloomington, Indiana
February, 1968

J. G. G.

Contents

CHAPTER ONE

Judgment and Perception

Sometimes when you start to read, you decide that you need more light. Then when you turn on another lamp, you judge that the light is bright enough so that you can read comfortably. Or perhaps you sit down to read and notice that the record player in the next room is loud enough to be distracting. You get up and close the door, and judge that the sound in your room is now soft enough so that you will be able to concentrate.

People make judgments all the time. A person driving a car on a two-lane highway comes up behind a slow truck and wants to pass; he has to judge whether the road is clear far enough ahead so that he has time to pass safely. A boy who has climbed into a tree wants to jump down; he judges the distance from his branch to the ground to decide whether he will get hurt when he lands. When a violinist tunes his instrument, he judges whether the pitch of his violin agrees with that of the oboe. A photographer makes a judgment about the quality of light in a situation in deciding what filter to use.

A judgment involves a kind of measurement. When you judge whether you have enough light to read comfortably, you are measuring the amount of light, in a way. When you judge whether you can pass a truck safely while driving, you are measuring the distance between your car and the nearest oncoming car.

A psychologist who wants to know how people judge things has the problem of finding out how people arrive at measurements. When a person makes a perceptual judgment, he acts as a kind of measuring instrument, and the theory of perceptual judgments is an attempt to understand how these measurements are produced.

Imagine that you are given a mechanical instrument like the one in Fig. 1 and your job is to find out what it does. The instrument has a dial, and a plate on which you can set things. When you place different objects on the plate, different numbers appear on the dial, and the numbers seem to be larger for heavier objects. You consider the possibility that the instrument measures weight. Now you set a one-pound weight on the plate and the dial reads 454. A two-pound weight produces the reading 907. A one-half-pound weight produces the reading 227. You find that you can set any object on the plate and if you then add a one-pound weight, the reading on the dial increases by 454. After a few more experiments, you conclude that the instrument measures weight, and the dial readings are measures of weight in grams.

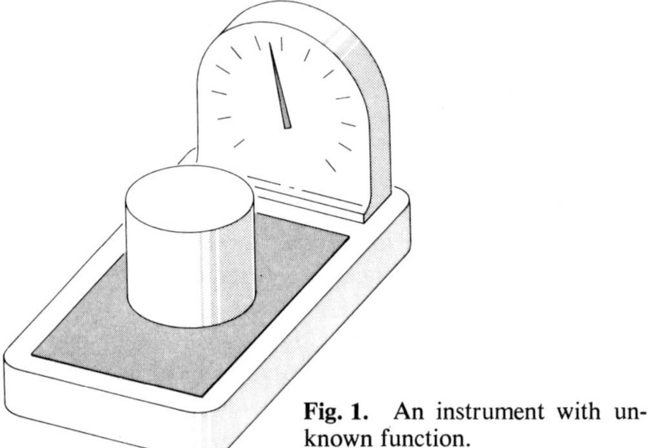

Fig. 1. An instrument with unknown function.

We know that the weight of an object can be given either in pounds or grams. Figure 2 shows the relationship between the pound scale and the gram scale.

Another way in which the relationship can be understood is by a graph, shown in Fig. 3. If we know the weight of an object in pounds, we find the point along the base line of the graph corresponding to that weight. Then the height of the line above that point is the object's weight in grams.

Still another expression of the relationship is given by a formula. Let g stand for the weight of an object in grams, and let b be its weight in pounds. Then if b is known, we find that g is b multiplied by 453.6. In other words,

$$g = 453.6b.$$

The experiments leading to the formula tell us what the unknown measuring instrument does. The method is quite general. We can get informa-

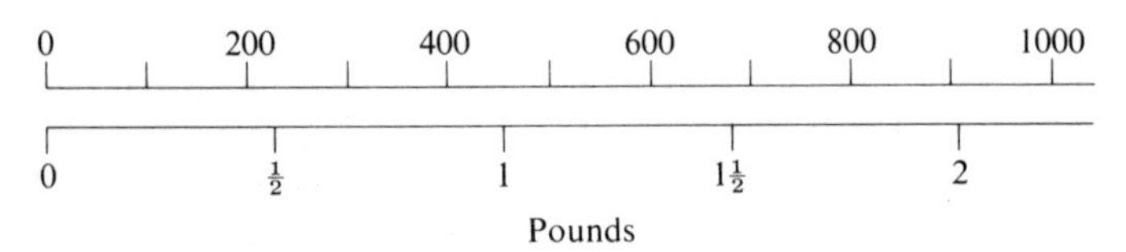

Fig. 2. Relationship between weight in pounds and reading on unknown instrument.

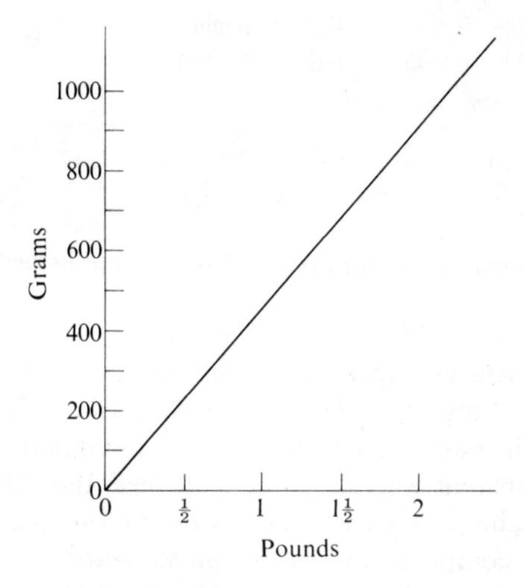

Fig. 3. Graph showing relationship between pounds and grams.

tion about an unknown measuring instrument by finding out what readings are obtained when we use it to measure different objects. We will consider situations like the one described above, but the unknown measuring instrument will be a person, and his measurements will be perceptual judgments. The experimenter measures some objects using a known system; this system is a part of physics. Then the measurements given by the unknown instrument are related to the measurements in the known system, and we find out how psychological judgments about objects are related to the physical properties of objects. Work of this kind is given the name *psychophysics.*

1A JUDGMENTS OF MAGNITUDE[1]

Three kinds of judgments will be discussed here—judgments of weight, area, and brightness. The general principle shown in these three cases seems to apply whenever people judge stimulus properties having to do with magnitudes or intensities.

In an experiment, stimuli are presented to a person who gives judgments of magnitude. The judgments represent the magnitudes as they are perceived by the person; thus, the judgments represent the psychological magnitudes or apparent magnitudes of the stimuli. The experimenter often gives a number for one stimulus as a standard, and then other stimuli are judged in relation to the standard.

[1] The general idea in this section was developed by S. S. Stevens, and presented in an article entitled, "On the Psychophysical Law," *Psychol. Rev.*, 1957, **64,** 153–181.

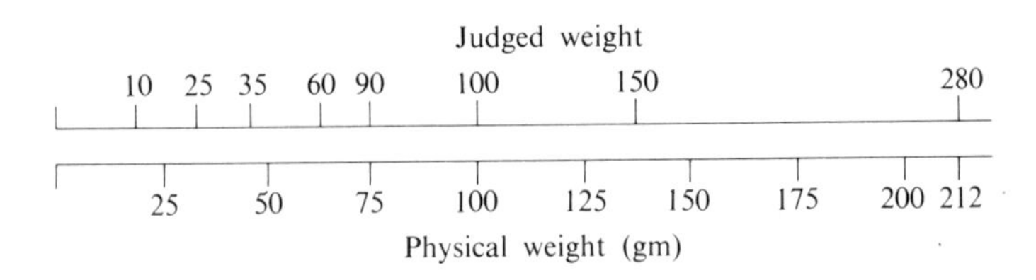

Fig. 4. Relationship between physical weight and judged weight.

We will begin with an experiment where subjects judged the apparent weights of some small objects.[2] The objects weighed 19, 33, 45, 63, 74, 98, 136, and 212 gm. The 98-gm weight was used as a standard, and the subject was told that its apparent weight should be called 100. Then the subject lifted the other weights and gave numbers to say how heavy each of the other weights felt in comparison to the 98-gm standard.

Table 1 shows the results. For example, when the subjects lifted the 33-gm weight, the average number given was about 25. In other words, the 33-gm weight felt about one-fourth as heavy as the 98-gm standard, which had been assigned the number 100. The 136-gm weight felt about one and one-half times as heavy as the 98-gm standard. Figure 4 shows the data in the same form as Fig. 2, and Fig. 5 shows the data as a graph.

Now remember the hypothetical experiment about the unknown mechanical instrument for measuring weights. Here the "instrument" is a person, and we can see that his measurements and the physical weights are not related in the same simple way as grams and pounds are.

In comparing pounds and grams, whenever we add a certain amount of weight in pounds, there is a corresponding constant increase in grams. If we start with 500 gm and add one pound, the grams increase by 454 to 954 gm. If we start with 2500 gm and add one pound, the grams again increase by 454 to 2954. The simple rule of addition did not appear in the relationship between grams and judged weights. For example, when the physical weight was increased by 73 gm from 63 to 136, the judged weight increased by 90. But when the physical weight changed almost exactly the same amount from 136 to 212 gm, the judged weight increased by 130. We do not find that a constant amount is added to judged weight when we add a constant amount to physical weight.

However, we can think about the results in a different way. There are quite a few cases in which we can compare the judgments of two objects where one has about twice the physical weight of the other. When we start

[2] The data are taken from a graph presented by S. S. Stevens and E. H. Galanter in "Ratio Scales and Category Scales for a Dozen Perceptual Continua," *J. Exp. Psychol.* 1957, **54,** 377–411.

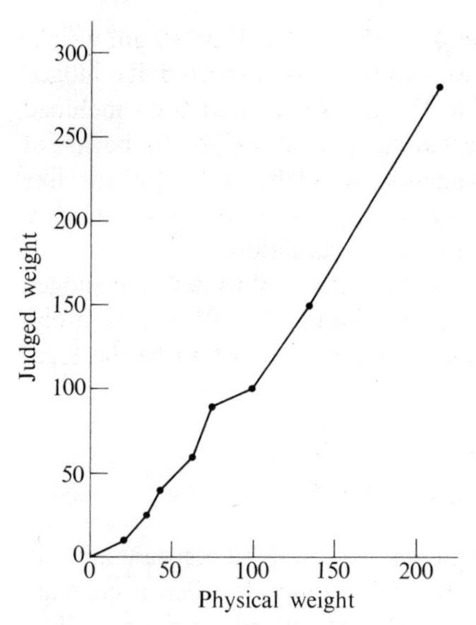

Fig. 5. Graph of the relationship between physical weight and judged weight.

Table 1

Relationship between Physical Weight and Judged Weight in an Experiment

Physical weight (gm)	Judged weight
19	10
33	25
46	35
63	60
74	90
98	100*
136	150
212	280

**Note:* The 98-gm weight was given the number 100 as the standard.

with an object weighing 33 gm and double its physical weight ($63 \approx 2 \times 33$), we find that the judged weight is multiplied by about 2.4 ($60 = 2.4 \times 25$). Multiplying a 46-gm weight by about two ($98 \approx 2 \times 46$) multiplies the judged weight by about 2.8 ($100 \approx 2.8 \times 35$). When we multiply by about two from 63 gm to 136 gm, the judgment is multiplied by 2.5 ($150 = 2.5 \times 60$). And when we multiply by about two from 98 gm to 212 gm, the judgment is multiplied by 2.8 ($280 = 2.8 \times 100$). The multipliers 2.4, 2.8, 2.5, and 2.8 are not exactly equal, but the small differences could easily be produced by minor inconsistencies in the judgments. Doubling the physical weight does not double the judgment, but it does seem to have a consistent effect on the judgment, multiplying it by a nearly constant amount.

The regularity that we have just noticed is quite general in these data. Whenever the ratio of physical weights is about 2:1, the ratio of judged weights is about 2.6:1. If we chose a different ratio of physical magnitudes (say, 3:1 or 5:2), we would find a corresponding ratio of judged magnitudes which would remain approximately constant for all pairs of stimuli with the selected ratio of physical magnitudes. Comparing the 98-gm weight and the 33-gm weight ($98 \approx 3 \times 33$), we see that the judgment for the 98-gm weight is four times as great as the judgment of the 33-gm weight. Let H be the physical weight of one stimulus, and let J be the judged weight of that stimulus. If we compare a stimulus physical weight $3H$, the judged weight should be approximately $4J$. For example, the judgment about the 136-gm weight ($136 \approx 3 \times 46$) should be about $4 \times 35 = 140$. If a 190-gm weight had been included ($190 \approx 3 \times 63$), we would have expected its judged weight to be about $4 \times 60 = 240$; if a 220-gm weight had been included ($220 \approx 3 \times 74$), we would have expected its judged weight to be about $4 \times 90 = 360$. The results of experiments show that relationships like this hold quite generally; that is, *equal ratios of physical magnitude produce equal ratios of judged magnitude*, to a close approximation.

There is a convenient way to express the relationship between judged magnitude and physical magnitude, using logarithms. Recall that multiplying a number by a constant corresponds to adding a constant to the logarithm of that number. That is,

$$\log (KH) = \log K + \log H,$$
$$\log (MJ) = \log M + \log J.$$

This means that the ratio rule can be restated as follows: if a constant amount ($\log K$) is added to the logarithm of physical magnitude, then a constant amount ($\log M$) will be added to the logarithm of judged magnitude. This means that $\log J$ and $\log H$ will be related by a linear function.

Table 2 shows how this works out for the weight-judging experiment described earlier. The numbers in the second and third columns of Table 2 are quite close to the relationship

$$\log J = -0.7 + 1.4 \log H,$$

where J is the judged weight and H is the physical weight. This function is drawn in the left-hand panel of Fig. 6. Note that every time the log of physical magnitude increases by 0.10, the log of judged magnitude increases by about 0.14.

Table 2

Relationship between Physical Weight and Judged Weight, and Logarithms of Both Quantities

Physical weight (gm)	log Physical weight	log Judged weight	Judged weight
19	1.28	1.00	10
33	1.52	1.40	25
46	1.66	1.54	35
63	1.80	1.78	60
74	1.87	1.95	90
98	1.99	2.00	100
136	2.13	2.18	150
212	2.33	2.45	280

In the preceding formula, we can replace -0.7 by log (0.2). Now recall that in general,

$$\log H^p = p \log H.$$

Then

$$\log J = \log (0.2) + 1.4 \log H$$
$$= \log (0.2) + \log (H^{1.4});$$

$$J = 0.2H^{1.4}.$$

This gives a relationship which is approximated by the first and fourth columns of Table 2, in the form of a power law. It is drawn as a graph in the right-hand panel of Fig. 6.

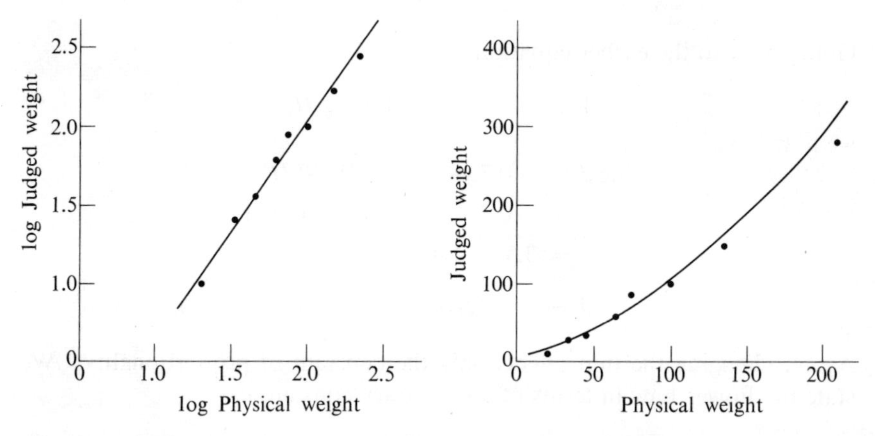

Fig. 6. Graphs showing the theoretical relationship between physical weight and judged weight.

In the formula, the constant of proportionality is arbitrary. For example, if we assigned the number 10 to the 98-gm weight, we probably would obtain judgments of the other stimuli of about 1, 2.5, . . . , 15, 28. Then the relationship between judged weight and physical weight would be

$$J = 0.02H^{1.4},$$

because we would only change the units on the scale of judged magnitudes, dividing each judgment by 10. Another arbitrary feature is the unit of physical weight. Suppose that we used kilograms instead of grams. Then the physical weights would be 0.019, 0.033, . . . , 0.212. Let H' be these new quantities. Of course,

$$H = 1000H'.$$

Table 3

Relationship between
Judged Area and Physical Area
in an Experiment

Judged area	Physical area (cm^2)
2.5	16
5	52
10	130
20	400
40	900
80	3300

Going back to the earlier equation

$$\log J = -0.7 + 1.4 \log H,$$

we now have

$$\begin{aligned} \log J &= -0.7 + 1.4 \log (1000\, H') \\ &= -0.7 + 1.4(3.0 + \log H') \\ &= 3.5 + 1.4 \log H'; \end{aligned}$$

$$J = 3162(H')^{1.4}.$$

Again, changing the unit affects only the constant of proportionality. We state the Power Law in terms of an arbitrary constant c,

$$J = cH^{1.4}.$$

The value of c depends on the units of measurement of physical magnitude, and on the sizes of the numbers used in making judgments.

On the other hand, the value of the exponent is not arbitrary. The value 1.4 comes from the results of the experiment. It should be the same regardless of the units used for either physical weight or judged weight. The value of the exponent depends on experimental procedure, and judgments of other properties such as brightness and loudness will determine different values for the exponent. In general, we can state the Power Law relating judged magnitude and physical magnitude as

$$J = cH^{p}, \tag{1.1}$$

where p depends on the kind of judgment we are talking about and the experimental conditions, but where c is chosen arbitrarily so the values of J will be in a convenient range. A verbal statement of the Power Law is the

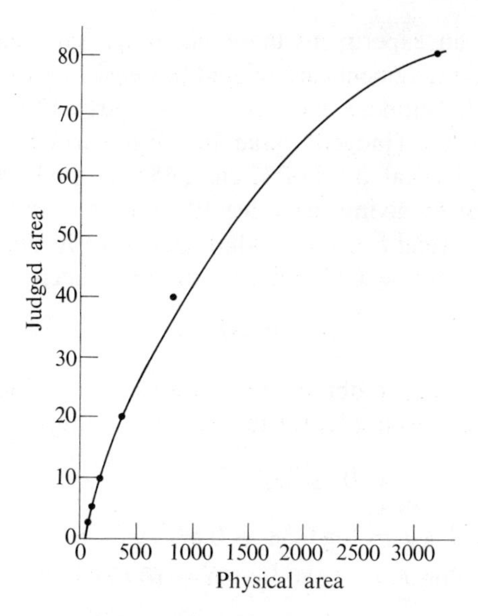

Fig. 7. Relationship between physical area and judged area.

following: *the judged magnitude is proportional to the physical magnitude raised to a power.*

The judgment of weights has been discussed in considerable detail to explain the Power Law and the kind of experimental result on which it is based. Now two other kinds of judgment will also be discussed, but more briefly.

First we consider judgments about area, in a slightly different kind of experiment.[3] An experimenter read numbers, and the subject was asked to adjust the area of a square to correspond to the numbers. The square was projected on a screen, and the subject controlled the size by turning a knob. The results are given in Table 3 and Fig. 7.

Note that when the physical magnitude increased by a factor of about three the judged magnitude increased by a factor of about two. In this case, increasing the physical magnitude by a certain factor increased the judged magnitude by a smaller factor. However, the factors again remained fairly constant throughout the range. The data are quite close to the curve, drawn in Fig. 7, which corresponds to the formula

$$J = 0.38H^{0.67}.$$

[3] Data are from S. S. Stevens and M. Guirao, "Subjective Scaling of Length to Loudness and Brightness," *J. exp. Psychol.*, 1957, **66,** 177–186.

Example 1.1. For an experiment involving judgments about the areas of squares, assume that judgments are related to physical areas as in the experiment just described. Suppose that a square with area 130 cm^2 is used as the standard and given the (judged) value 10. What will be the judged areas of squares having physical areas of 32 cm^2, 65 cm^2, and 520 cm^2?

First, note that by giving the value 10 to a 130 cm^2 figure we have set the units of judged weight equal to what they were in the data of Table 3. Assume that the power $p = 0.67$ holds for this experiment. Then the formula

$$J = 0.38H^{0.67}$$

will hold. It is quite easy to obtain the results using logarithms. Use Table A of the Appendix. For example, for the 32 cm^2 square,

$$J = 0.38(32)^{0.67};$$

$$\begin{aligned} \log J &= \log 0.38 + 0.67 \log 32, \\ \log J &= (9.580 - 10) + (0.67)(1.505) \\ &= -0.420 + 1.008 = 0.588; \end{aligned}$$

$$J = 3.9.$$

The student should carry out the necessary calculations to verify the following results.

For $H = 65$, $J = 6.2$.
For $H = 260$, $J = 15.8$.
For $H = 520$, $J = 25.1$. ▮

The two kinds of judgment discussed thus far both follow the same kind of rule—the Power Law—but with different values of the exponent. In the case of weight, the exponent is greater than one—if we double the physical weight, we more than double the judged weight. In the case of area, the exponent is less than one—if we double the physical area the judged area is multiplied by less than two.

Now we shall mention an experiment involving judgment of brightness.[4] In this study, judged brightness of lights was found to be related to physical brightness by a power law with an exponent of about 0.5. That is, for brightness,

$$J = cH^{0.5},$$

where H is luminance. A subject was seated in a dark room, one meter away from a Plexiglas® screen. Light was shone on the screen through a pinhole,

[4] This experiment was reported by Stevens and Galanter, *op. cit.*
® Plexiglas is a registered trademark of Rohm & Haas Co.

and the intensity of the light was controlled by filters. The subject's task was similar to judging the brightnesses of stars.

The dimmest "star" presented in the experiment had a physical brightness of 0.01 lamberts, and was given a judged brightness of 2. We can consider this as fixing the units of the judgment scale.

$$2 = c(0.01)^{0.5};$$

$$\log 2 = \log c + 0.5 \log 0.01;$$

$$0.30 = \log c - 1.0,$$
$$\log c = 1.30;$$

$$c = 20.$$

Another "star" presented in this experiment had a luminance of 0.04 lamberts. Its brightness should have been judged equal to

$$J = 20(0.04)^{0.5}.$$

Using logarithms, we have

$$\log J = \log 20 + 0.5 \log (0.04) = 1.30 + 0.5(-1.4) = 0.60;$$
$$J = 4.0.$$

The subjects gave this "star" a judged brightness of about 4.5.

Example 1.2. Using the formula $J = 20H^{0.5}$, how bright must a light be in lamberts to be judged five times as bright as a 0.01-lambert light? In other words, if we give the judgment 2 for a light of 0.01 lamberts, what will be the luminance of a light which has a judged brightness of 10?

Here the value of J is fixed by the problem, and we need to solve for H.

$$J = cH^p;$$

$$10 = 20H^{0.5}.$$

Using logarithms,

$$\log 10 = \log 20 + 0.5 \log H;$$

$$1.0 = 1.301 + 0.5 \log H;$$

$$-0.301 = 0.5 \log H,$$

$$\log H = \frac{-0.301}{0.5} = -0.602;$$

$$H = 0.25 \text{ lamberts}.$$

In other words, a light which is 25 times as bright as the standard in physical units will be judged five times as bright as the standard in psychological terms. ▮

1B DETECTION OF DIFFERENCES

In the first section we discussed experiments where a person judges the amount of the difference between two different stimuli. In another kind of experiment, two very similar stimuli are presented, and a person has to judge whether they are different at all. The idea of the experiment is to find out about the sensitivity of our perceptual measurements.

Different kinds of measuring instruments are sensitive to different degrees, and the sensitivity of a particular kind of instrument is one of its important characteristics. For example, consider different instruments for measuring weight. The scales that people use to weigh themselves need to be accurate only to about the nearest pound. However, a grocer's scale should be somewhat more accurate—perhaps to the nearest ounce. And a pharmacist's scale, used to weigh drugs for medical prescriptions, needs to be considerably more accurate than a grocer's scale. As another example, consider different thermometers. Thermometers used to measure room temperature usually are accurate to about the nearest degree. But clinical thermometers usually are accurate to about the nearest 0.1 degree.

We want to know about the sensitivity of perceptual judgments, and the way we study this is by a detection experiment. It should be clear that with a very sensitive measuring instrument very small differences would be detected consistently; but with an insensitive instrument larger differences would be required. Suppose that you had two jars of water, one at 99.5°F and the other at 99.6°F. This small difference could be detected quite reliably with a good clinical thermometer, but not with an ordinary room thermometer.

In one procedure for a detection experiment, pairs of stimuli are presented and the subject judges whether they seem to be the same or different. Over a series of trials a standard stimulus is compared with several different comparison stimuli, and for each comparison stimulus the subject says "different" on a certain proportion of the trials. If there is practically no difference between the standard and a comparison stimulus, the person says "same" most of the time. If there is a large difference between the standard and comparison stimulus, the person says "different" on all or nearly all of the trials. We can show the results of the experiment in a graph, where the proportion of times the person says "different" is plotted against the amount of physical difference between the stimuli. Such a graph is called a *psychometric function*, and one is given in Fig. 8. The data are hypothetical, but results like those shown are easily obtained. The base line has

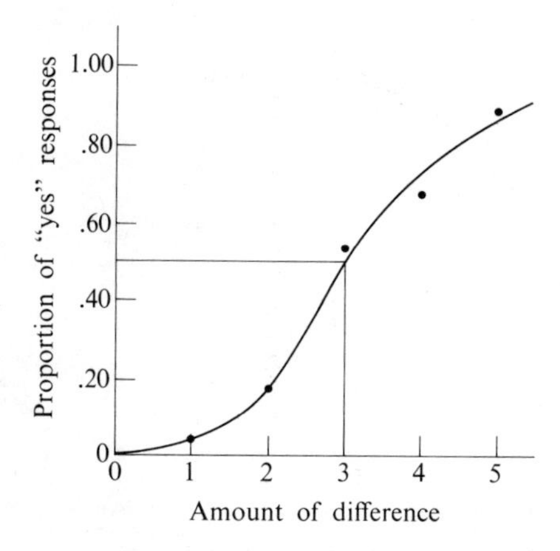

Fig. 8. A hypothetical psychometric function, showing determination of the threshold.

the amount of difference, and the curve plots the proportion of times the subject said "yes," thus indicating that the stimuli seemed different.

It is conventional to find the amount of difference that is detected 50% of the time, and call that difference the *threshold*, or the *just noticeable difference*, abbreviated *jnd.* In Fig. 8, a smooth line has been drawn close to all the data points, and a line has been drawn at a height of .50 to meet the data line. Then the line is dropped to the base line, and it turns out that a 50% detection level corresponds to a difference of about 3 units. This means that the threshold is about 3 units.

Before going on, a procedural point should be mentioned. We have talked about the presentation of two stimuli, and the judgment "same" or "different." It often happens that a person shows a bias in his responses. If he is anxious to detect every difference that is presented, he will say "different" on some trials when he is not sure there is a difference; he may even say "different" on some trials when the two stimuli are actually the same. The effect of this would be to raise the whole psychometric function and to lower the apparent threshold, as shown on the left in Fig. 9. In other situations, the person might be extremely careful not to say "different" unless he were sure that he detected a difference. This would produce a lowering of the whole psychometric function and an increase in the threshold, as shown on the right in Fig. 9. This variability is undesirable, since we are really interested in how sensitive the perceptions are, rather than how strict or lenient the person is when he decides whether to say "yes."

This difficulty is partly overcome if we present stimuli sometimes larger than the standard, and sometimes smaller, and force the person to say

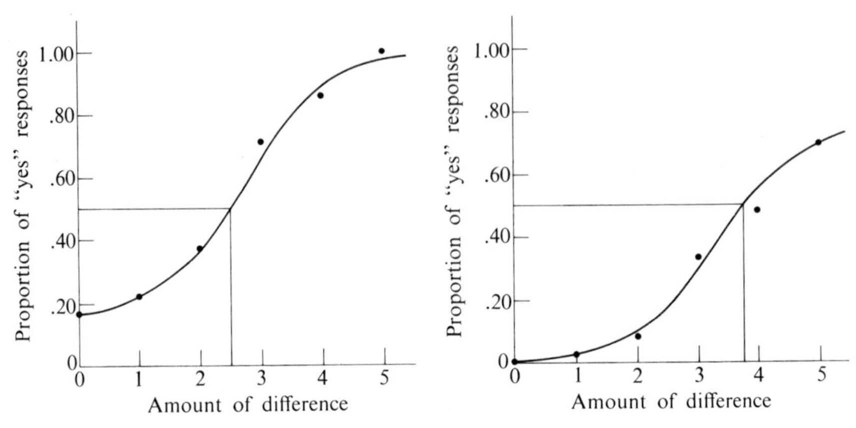

Fig. 9. Psychometric functions and "thresholds" resulting from different response biases.

"larger" or "smaller," even when he does not think there is a difference. It is useful to have larger and smaller stimuli occur equally often, and to instruct or train the person to say "larger" and "smaller" with equal frequency. Then the psychometric function is like Fig. 10, with the data given as proportions of "larger" judgments.[5]

We are still interested in calculating a threshold, or *jnd*, and we need to know how to do this using the results of a forced-choice experiment. In the "same–different" experiment, we use the stimulus which the person judges "different" 50% of the time. The idea is to find the stimulus which is discriminated from the standard on one-half of the trials. In the forced-choice experiment, we can apply the same idea. Consider a certain stimulus which is being compared with the standard. Suppose that on some proportion of the trials *d*, the comparison stimulus is noticeably different from the standard, and the rest of the time the two stimuli seem the same. Further, suppose that when the two stimuli seem to be the same the person says "larger" on one-half of the trials and "smaller" on the other trials. Then the proportion of correct responses will be

$$P(C) = d + (1 - d)(\tfrac{1}{2}).$$

By convention, we say a *jnd* is a difference that is detected one-half of the time. In that case

$$P(C) = \tfrac{1}{2} + (1 - \tfrac{1}{2})(\tfrac{1}{2}) = 0.75.$$

[5] Data taken from R. S. Woodworth and H. Schlosberg. *Experimental Psychology*, (Revised Edition). New York: Holt, 1954, p. 216. The experiment cited was done by W. Brown in 1910.

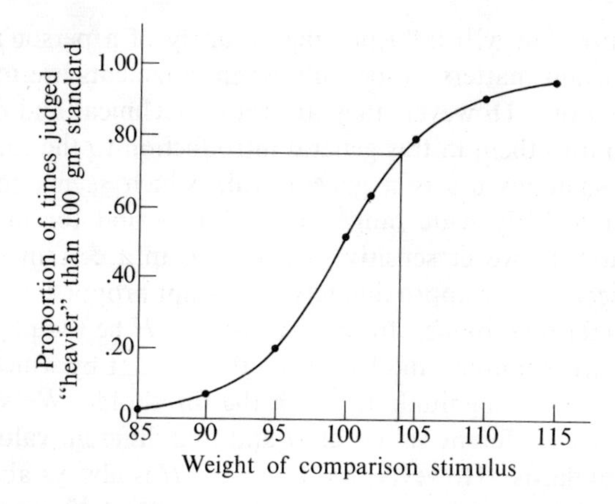

Fig. 10. A psychometric function obtained by using the forced-choice procedure.

Therefore, the threshold stimulus is one for which the person gives the correct judgment 75% of the time in a forced-choice experiment. We find the threshold stimulus above a standard by drawing a line across at a level of "larger" judgments equal to 0.75 until it meets the forced-choice psychometric function.

In the rest of the present discussion, we will be concerned with the size of the *jnd*—the difference between a standard and a stimulus that is enough larger so that the difference is detected about one-half of the time. This is best thought of as a stimulus for which a person has 75% correct judgments in a forced choice experiment.

By now, the student should have a good idea of what it means to say that the threshold difference (or just noticeable difference) is a certain amount. But recall that the reason for carrying out a detection experiment is to find out something about how people make perceptual measurements. We are trying to understand something about the sensitivity of our judgments.

We shall not say very much here about just how sensitive a person's judgments are for specific kinds of stimulus differences. As you may expect, the ability of a person to detect a difference depends heavily on the conditions of the experiment. Suppose, for example, that you are trying to detect differences between the weights of objects. In one situation you might be permitted to compare weights for an unlimited time, holding the two weights simultaneously, shifting them from hand to hand, and so on. In another situation you might be required to make your judgment after just lifting each object once. Certainly you would be able to show better accuracy in the first of these situations than in the second. And no matter what kind of judgment we consider, there are many technical aspects of the experimental procedure that will influence the accuracy of a person's judgments. These are important matters—especially when judgments are to be made in a practical situation. However, they are rather technical and detailed, and we shall not go into them in this general introduction to the topic.

What we shall discuss is a general rule which seems to hold quite accurately over a fairly wide range of conditions and for many different kinds of stimuli. However sensitive a person is in a certain situation, the size of the *jnd* seems to be approximately a constant proportion of the magnitude of the standard stimulus. In other words, let H be the physical magnitude of a standard stimulus, and let ΔH be the amount by which we have to increase the stimulus magnitude to reach the threshold. We shall measure ΔH at a number of different values of H and find different values of ΔH for the different standards. However, the value of ΔH is always about the same fraction of H. An example is given below in Table 4, showing results for detection of differences between weights.[6] The value of $\Delta H/H$ is not exactly constant, but it is not a bad approximation to say that the amount of change needed to reach threshold is about 8% of the weight of the standard.

This general feature seems to apply for quite a number of different situations. Figures 11, 12, and 13 present graphs of the size of a just noticeable difference plotted against the magnitude of the standard, for experiments involving judgments about the lengths of lines, the brightness of lights, and the loudness of tones.[7] In all three cases, as in the case of judgments about weight, the size of the threshold is approximately proportional to the magnitude of the standard stimulus.[8]

The data tell us something quite important about the sensitivity of our perceptual measurements. For any measuring instrument, the accuracy of the instrument tells us how small a difference could be detected reliably. For example, if a balance is accurate to the nearest 0.01 gm, we should expect to detect a difference of 0.01 gm without appreciable error. But the statement suggests that the accuracy of the balance is about equal throughout the scale. In other words, the balance will permit us to detect the difference between objects weighing 0.50 and 0.51 gm, and also to detect the difference between objects weighing 5.00 and 5.01 gm.

Another way to describe the accuracy of a measuring instrument is in terms of a percentage. We might say that a balance was accurate to the nearest 2%. Then the balance should allow us to detect the difference be-

---

[6] G. Fechner, *Elements of Psychophysics*. The book was published in German in 1860. It has been translated into English by H. E. Adler, New York: Holt, Rinehart and Winston, 1966. The data in Table 4 are from p. 154 of the translation.

[7] The data on line lengths are from Fechner, *op. cit.*, p. 179. Those on brightness and loudness are taken from Woodworth and Schlosberg, *op. cit.*, pp. 223–224.

[8] This general rule is called Weber's Law.

Table 4

Standard Weights and Amounts of Increase that Result in Threshold Differences

Standard weight (H)	*jnd* (ΔH)	$\Delta H/H$
300	31	.103
500	54	.108
1000	90	.090
1500	111	.074
2000	133	.067
3000	198	.066

tween objects weighing 0.50 and 0.51 gm, and also to detect the difference between 5.0 and 5.1 gm.

Now consider the data in Table 4 and in Figs. 11 through 13. One possibility is that judgments are accurate within a fixed number of units. Then the range of error would be a certain number of grams, or a certain number of millimeters, or a certain number of millilamberts. But if that were true, the *jnd* should be approximately constant, and the curves should be horizontal lines. A second possibility is that judgments are accurate within a

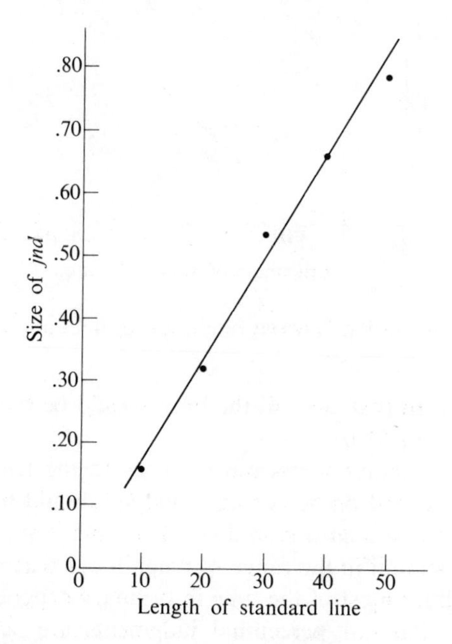

Fig. 11. Relationship between physical line length and size of *jnd*.

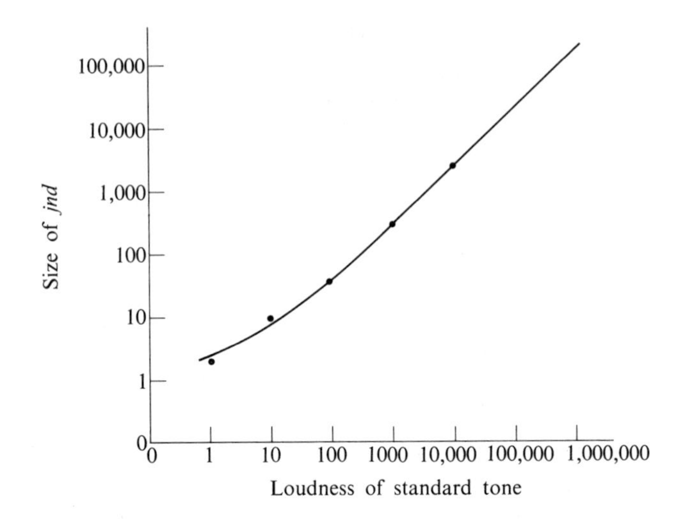

Fig. 12. Relationship between loudness of tone and size of *jnd*.

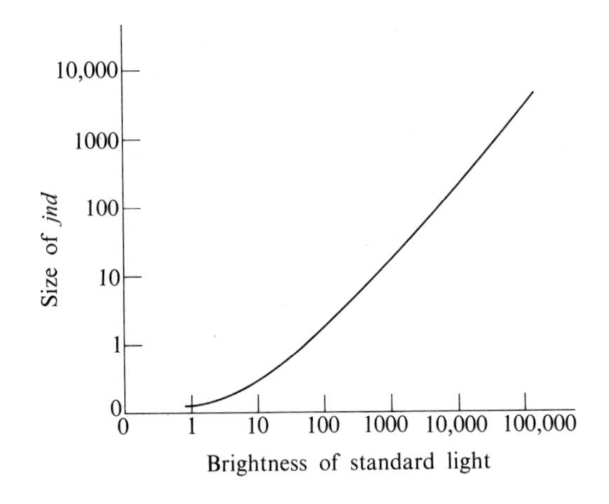

Fig. 13. Relationship between brightness of light and size of *jnd*.

certain percentage. In that case all the lines should be straight, and should pass through the point (0, 0).

The second possibility seems much closer to the truth than the first. To have accuracy depend on percentages, the *jnd* should be proportional to the magnitude of the standard stimulus. This rule is quite accurate if we consider standard stimuli in the range of magnitudes that we perceive easily and that we encounter most of the time in ordinary experience.

We conclude that our perceptual judgments are accurate to a percentage rather than to a fixed unit. The size of the percentage will vary depending on the experiment, as well as on the kind of stimulus. In the data presented here, judgments of weight were accurate to about 8%, judgments of length to about 3%, judgments of brightness to about 2%, and judgments of loudness to about 9%.

This relationship can be stated in another way. Let H_0 be the physical magnitude of a standard stimulus, and let H_1 be the magnitude of a comparison stimulus that is just enough larger (heavier, longer, or whatever) so that H_1 is judged larger on 75% of the trials of a forced-choice experiment. In other words, the difference between H_0 and H_1 is one *jnd.* According to Weber's Law, the ratio of the two magnitudes is a constant. This can be seen quite easily. First, the magnitude of the comparison stimulus, H_1, is equal to H_0 plus ΔH, the size of the *jnd.* But then the ratio

$$H_1/H_0 = (H_0 + \Delta H)/H_0 = 1 + \Delta H/H_0.$$

We have seen already that $\Delta H/H_0$ is approximately constant; this is the rule that says the size of the *jnd* is a constant fraction of the standard stimulus. But if $\Delta H/H_0$ is a constant, then $1 + \Delta H/H_0$ also is a constant. Therefore,

$$H_1/H_0 = k, \tag{1.2}$$

where k is a constant.

Example 1.3. In one experiment it was found that lights with brightnesses in the ratio 1.016 were just noticeably different. In this situation, using a standard of 10 millilamberts, how bright should a comparison stimulus be to be judged "brighter" 75% of the time? What if a standard of 300 millilamberts were used?

We use the simple formula given as Eq. (1.2), where H_0 is the physical magnitude of the standard, and k is 1.016. We need to solve for H_1 with two values of H_0. For a standard of 10 millilamberts,

$$H_1/10 = 1.016;$$
$$H_1 = 10.16.$$

For a standard of 300 millilamberts,

$$H_1/300 = 1.016;$$
$$H_1 = 304.8. \blacksquare$$

Now we shall develop another scale of psychological magnitude. In the first section we found a formula relating physical magnitudes to judged magnitudes of stimuli. Think of the judged magnitudes as constituting a scale where every unit seems to be about equally large to a person. However, the units on that scale are not necessarily equally easy to discriminate. It also is interesting to develop a scale with units that are equally easy to tell apart.

We can have a scale with units that are equal to *jnd*'s.[9] We work with logarithms of the physical magnitudes. By Eq. (1.2), if H_1 and H_0 are just noticeably different with H_1 larger, then

$$H_1/H_0 = k;$$

$$\log H_1 - \log H_0 = \log k.$$

That is, the difference between the logarithms of two stimuli that are different by a *jnd* equals $\log k$. We want this difference to equal one scale unit. Therefore, we obtain the desired scale values if we take logarithms and divide by $\log k$. Let D be the value of the stimulus magnitude on the new scale. Then

$$D = \log H/\log k,$$

or, since $1/\log k$ is a constant,

$$D = b \log H, \tag{1.3}$$

where

$$b = 1/\log k.$$

Here, b is a constant which determines the scale units just as c does in Eq. (1.1).

Example 1.4. To see how the scale of discriminability works, we do some calculations for judgments of weights. If an experiment permits very fine discrimination of weights then objects weighing 51 and 50 gm are about just noticeably different. In other words,

$$k = \tfrac{51}{50} = 1.02.$$

The logarithm of 1.02 is 0.0086, so the value of b is

$$b = 1/\log k = 1/0.0086 = 116.$$

Therefore, if H is the weight of an object in grams, the weight of that object on the discriminability scale is

$$D = 116 \log H.$$

---

[9] The log scale was proposed by Fechner, *op. cit.* An important discussion regarding the mathematical derivation of the scale was given by R. D. Luce and W. Edwards, "The Derivation of Subjective Scales from Just Noticeable Differences," *Psychol. Rev.*, 1958, **65,** 222–237.

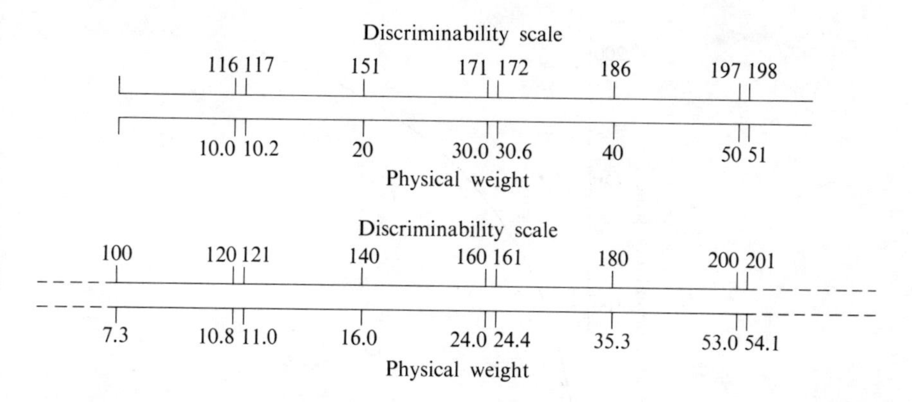

Fig. 14. Two representations of the relationship between physical weight and scale values where units are equally discriminable.

The scale values of stimuli are found easily. For example, for a 50-gm weight,

$$D = 116 \log 50 = (116)(1.699) = 197.$$

For a 51-gm weight,

$$D = 116 \log 51 = (116)(1.708) = 198.$$

Note that the difference between the scale values is one unit, which was what we designed the scale for. Similarly, as the student can easily show, the scale values of 500- and 510-gm weights will be 313 and 314, again with a difference of one unit. ▌

Figure 14 has two representations of the scale for discriminability of weights, based on the calculations of Example 1.4. The picture at the top is scaled to physical weights. Note that the discriminability scale values go up rapidly at first, and then less quickly. For example, there are 116 *jnd* units between 0 and 10 gm, but only 11 *jnd* units between 40 and 50 gm. Also notice that the size of the *jnd* increases in physical units. The picture at the bottom is scaled to units of the discriminability scale. In these units, physical weight increases slowly at first, and then more rapidly. This corresponds to the fact that a single *jnd* has to include a larger physical interval for larger stimulus magnitudes. Figure 15 has the scales plotted as a graph.

Example 1.5. Using the information given in Example 1.3, find the value of b for the scale of equal discriminability for brightness of lights. Find the scale values of lights having brightnesses of 10 and 300 millilamberts.

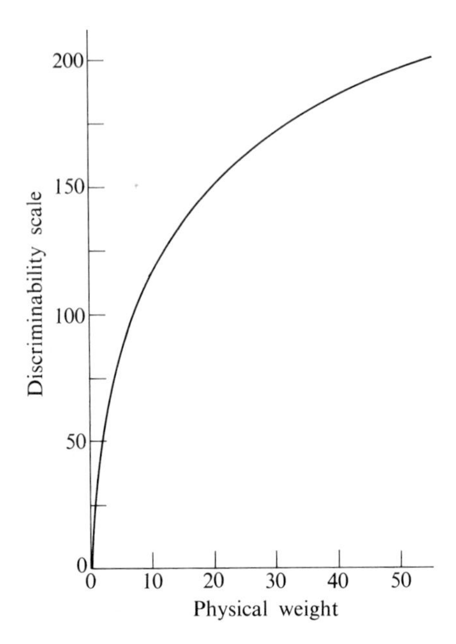

Fig. 15. Graph of relationship between physical weight and equal-discriminability scale values.

The value of k is given as 1.016. Therefore

$$b = 1/\log k = 1/0.0069 = 145.$$

The scale value for a 10-ml light is

$$D = 145 \log 10 = 145.$$

For a 300-ml light, the scale value is

$$D = 145 \log 300 = 333.6. \blacksquare$$

Equation (1.3) which gives the discriminability scale values of stimuli has two constants, k and b. The value of k is determined by an experiment, and it shows how sensitive the person is to small differences between stimuli. The value of b determines the units of the discriminability scale. When we set b equal to $1/\log k$ we obtain a scale where each unit equals one *jnd*. If we set b equal to $0.1/\log k$, we would obtain a scale where each unit would equal 10 *jnd*'s. The size of the unit can be chosen for convenience; changing the value of b would not change the basic relationship between stimulus magnitudes and the scale values. (See Problem 14.)

In these two sections we have worked with two different psychophysical scales. The scale of judged magnitudes and the discriminability scale involve relationships between physical magnitudes and numbers that have psychological significance. The two scales do not assign psychological numbers in the same way, as we can see by comparing the two equations:

$$D = b \log H, \qquad J = cH^p.$$

We can see how the two scales relate by transforming each equation into a formula for log H.

$$\log H = D/b;$$

$$\log H = (1/p) \log (J/c).$$

Then the psychological values on the two scales are related by the equation

$$D = (b/p) \log (J/c).$$

Recall that the units on the discriminability scale are equally easy to tell apart, and that the units on the scale of judged magnitudes represent equal differences between magnitudes as the subject judges them. The equation shows that the ease of discriminating between pairs of stimuli is proportional to the difference between the logarithms of their judged magnitudes, rather than to the difference between their judged magnitudes. For example, two stimuli with judged magnitudes of 10 and 11 might be quite easy to discriminate, but stimuli with judged magnitudes of 100 and 101 could be very hard to tell apart.

How should we interpret these two sets of scale values? Certainly we should not suppose that when a person sees a stimulus of some magnitude he has anything like two mental dials that register numbers corresponding to the values of J and D on the two scales. It is important to remember that these sets of numbers are used by psychologists to describe the judgments that are made in special experimental situations. The numbers used for the two kinds of judgment are different because the situations are different and the judgments turn out to have different properties.

Although the two kinds of judgment are different, we can see how they probably arise from a single system of perception. The responses a subject gives when he is asked to judge magnitudes and when he is asked to detect differences both depend on ratios of physical stimulus magnitudes in a fundamental way. This suggests that the information used in making simple perceptual judgments is in the form of ratios of magnitudes rather than magnitudes themselves. This idea is consistent with the kinds of judgments made in both the magnitude-judging experiments and the detection experiments. In judgments of magnitude, stimuli with equal ratios of physical magnitude are judged to be equally different. And in detection experiments, the ability to distinguish between two stimuli also depends on the ratio of their physical magnitudes. Specifically, if two stimuli are different by one *jnd*, their ratio is equal to a quantity that is approximately constant.

1C SOME PERCEPTUAL CONSTANCIES AND ILLUSIONS

It is reasonable to conclude that one way we obtain quantitative information about the world is by perceiving ratios of stimulus magnitudes. This idea will now be used to analyze a few cases of perceptual constancy and one kind of perceptual illusion.

Perceptual constancy refers to the fact that people generally can maintain constant judgments about objects even when the conditions of perceiving the objects are changed significantly. By a change in the conditions of perceiving we mean a change in some important aspect of the physical input to a receptor organ.

It is possible to make quite an interesting psychological mistake about perception, and if the mistake is made, even simple cases of perceptual constancy are hard to understand. The mistake is to suppose that judgments about objects depend in a simple way on the absolute magnitudes of physical properties of the objects. For example, consider judgments about the lightness of an object. A person's judgment must depend in some way on the amount of light reflected from the object into his eyes. If the amount of light falling on the object is changed then the amount of light reflected by the object will change accordingly. If our judgment depended on just the amount of reflected light, then objects would appear to become darker when the amount of light was decreased.

You can do a simple experiment that shows that this theory is false. You need to have two lamps in the room. Preferably one of the lamps should be near your study desk or table and the other some distance away so that if only the distant lamp is on the light on your desk is dim, but if both are on, the light is quite bright. Start with both of the lamps on. Now place a book on your desk and think about how dark or light it is. Then turn off the lamp near your desk and consider whether the book seemed to change so as to appear darker. Ordinarily, there will be no change in a person's judgment about the lightness of the object, even though the amount of light reflected from the object to his eyes changes a great deal.

Another important case involves judgments about the sizes of objects. When a person judges how large an object is, his judgment must depend in some way on the size of the image reflected by the object on his retina. Of course, the size of the retinal image varies greatly depending on whether the object is near or far from the person. If judgments about the size of an object depended on just the size of the retinal image, then objects would appear to shrink when we move away from them and to expand when we approach them.

Again, a simple experiment disproves the theory. Take the same book that you used for the lightness experiment and place it upright on your desk. Consider how large the book seems to be when you are standing close to your desk. Now step a few feet away from the desk and consider how large the book seems to be. Ordinarily, there is very little change in a person's judgment about the size of an object when he changes his distance from it in this normal way.

These simple cases of perceptual constancy show that we do not judge objects simply on the basis of absolute magnitudes of physical stimulus properties. However, in the cases mentioned here, constancy will result if the perceptual system works rather simply with ratios of physical magnitudes.

In the case of lightness constancy, it is convenient to use the concept of *reflectance* or *albedo.* Any illuminated surface reflects some fraction of the light that falls on it. A dark surface has low reflectance.

Now suppose that we judge the lightness of an object by comparing the amount of light coming from the object with the amounts of light coming from the background and other objects that are nearby. Suppose that you are looking at a gray book with reflectance of about 0.50, against a dark background with reflectance of about 0.20, and near a white sheet of paper with reflectance of about 0.80. If an equal amount of light falls on all three objects, the ratio of the amounts of light coming from them will be 5:2:8, and this will be true whether the overall illumination is bright or dim. Therefore, if the judgment about an object depends on the ratios of its lightness to the lightness of other objects, the judgment should not change when there is a change in overall illumination.[10]

Similar reasoning applies to judgments of object size. When a person is near an object, the image that it casts on his retina is quite large; so are the images of other objects around it. When the person is farther away, the retinal image of the object is smaller; and the objects near it also project smaller images on the retina of the distant viewer. It may be assumed that judgments about size depend on comparisons of the retinal-image sizes of objects which are judged to be equally far from the viewer. If we move closer to or farther from an object, we also move closer to or farther from all the other objects near it, and the ratios of retinal image sizes are all

[10] Although perception of simple ratios would produce simple constancy of the kind we are discussing, other facts about judged brightness make it more probable that a more complicated relation is actually perceived. See D. Jameson and L. Hurvich. "Theory of Brightness and Color Contrast in Human Vision." *Vision Research*, 1964, **4,** 135–154.

preserved. If these ratios are the basis of judgments about object size, then judgments of size should not change when we move closer to or farther from the objects.

We have seen the way in which the perception of ratios can help explain some perceptual constancies under normal changes in viewing conditions. The same idea can help us understand why certain kinds of illusions occur.

One dramatic effect that can be obtained involves apparent brightness. A black disk is shown against a gray background with overall dim illumination. When the illumination of the entire field is increased, a viewer still judges the disk to be black. But if a bright light is turned on so that it shines only on the disk and does not produce visible shadows or increased illumination anywhere else, the disk seems to change from black to white.[11]

The change that produces the illusion is one which alters the ratio of magnitudes between the judged object and the background. Unlike a normal change in illumination, the light shining on the disk alone causes the ratio of brightnesses to increase so that the low-reflectance disk now has more light reflected from it than does the surrounding background and objects. This change makes the disk seem to change color. Even when a person knows about the apparatus, he reports that the change seems to involve the lightness of the disk, rather than the amount of illumination.

An analogous illusion can be created involving judgments about size. Recall that judgments about size probably involve comparisons of the retinal-image size of objects which seem to be about equally far from the person. Then if a person has to judge the sizes of objects in a situation where he cannot judge their distance, the constancy of his judgments will disappear and instead he will have to judge on the basis of the sizes of retinal images. This is consistent with experimental results. If circular disks are shown to a subject at various distances under normal viewing conditions, he can judge their relative sizes quite well. However, if his vision is limited by having to view the disks through a small hole (an artificial pupil or a reduction screen), he can no longer judge the distances between himself and the objects. Then his judgments of size are no longer constant. With distance information taken away, the person has to use the sizes of retinal images to make judgments, and his judgment about a disk will vary as the disk is placed nearer to or farther from him.[12]

When we view disks through a reduction screen, we make judgments without the benefit of any information about distance. In this situation, our

---

[11] The experiment was carried out by A. Gelb and reported in German in 1929. Discussions are available in many textbooks; e.g., Woodworth and Schlosberg, *op. cit.*, pp. 441–442.

[12] A. H. Holway and E. G. Boring. "Determinants of Apparent Visual Size with Distance Variant." *Amer. J. Psychol.* 1941, **54,** 21–37.

judgments apparently are made as though all objects were equally distant from us, so that the relevant physical magnitudes are ratios of retinal image sizes. In another situation, judgments about size are distorted in a different way—by providing information about distance and perspective that is misleading.

A room can be constructed so that the distance from floor to ceiling is much greater at one end than another. The angles at which windows are cut and the illumination of the room are carefully arranged. There is a place from which a viewer with one eye closed sees the distorted room as being normal. The various distortions cancel each other so that smaller distances are on closer surfaces with brighter illumination and thus appear to be equal to larger distances in other parts of the room. Now two people of the same height stand at opposite ends of the room. The person at the short end stands with his head against the ceiling. The person at the tall end of the room is only half the height of the room at that point. The impression is that the persons are of different heights. The person who is as tall as the room appears to be about twice as tall as the person at the other end.[13]

Clearly, our perception in this situation is based on judging the height of a person in relation to the heights of a wall, window, and other features of the room. There are two men of about equal height. However, one man is judged to be twice as tall as the other when the ratio of his height to his surroundings is twice that of the other.

Another example of a size illusion is drawn in Fig. 16.[14] The circle surrounded by large circles appears to be smaller than the circle surrounded by small circles, although the two inner circles are the same size. Again, the figure that appears to be larger is larger relative to other figures in its neighborhood. Unlike the case of the men in the distorted room, though, the illusion is not complete. The ratio of the area of the inner circle to its smaller neighbors is about 4:1. The ratio of the area of the inner circle to its larger neighbors is about 4:9. But the circle surrounded by smaller circles certainly does not appear to be nine times as large as the other inner circle. In this case the viewer's judgment probably takes into account the size of the page and other background factors that are common to the two inner circles. Therefore, while constancy is not perfect and a distortion of judgment occurs, a tendency toward constancy is maintained due to common

---

[13] The demonstration was developed by A. Ames, *Some Demonstrations Concerned with the Origin and Nature of our Sensations.* Dartmouth Eye Institute, 1946. It was described by W. H. Ittelson and F. P. Kirkpatrick, "Experiments in Perception," *Sci. Amer.*, 1951, **185,** 50–55.

[14] This is shown in E. R. Hilgard, *Introduction to Psychology*, Third Edition, New York: Harcourt, Brace and World, 1962, p. 199.

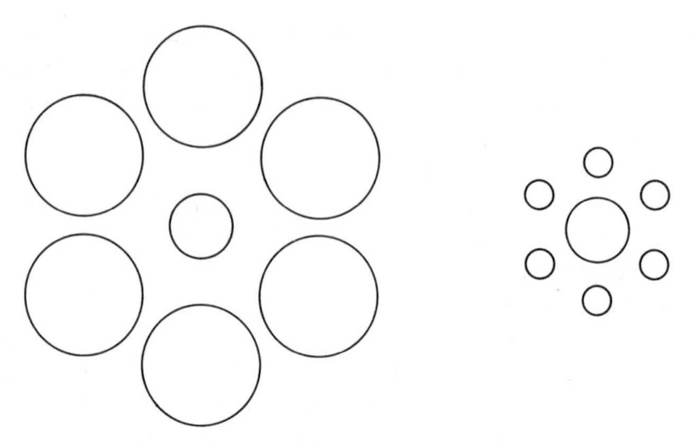

Fig. 16. A simple example of size illusion.

factors. In fact, the situation illustrated in Fig. 16 is typical of many interesting perceptual situations, where perceptual constancy usually is approximated, but variable background factors produce some distortion in judgments of objects.

PROBLEMS

1. Suppose that you are given an object which looks like a thermometer, and asked to find out what it does. You place it in liquids of various temperatures, and obtain different readings, as follows:

Known Temperature (°F)	30	50	72	90	150	200
Reading on Unknown Instrument	−0.9	10.0	22.2	32.2	65.5	93.3

Find the relationship between the two sets of magnitudes. Do the readings on the unknown instrument obey the ratio rule?

2. From the data of Table 3, construct a graph of $\log J$ vs. $\log H$. What is the appropriate theoretical formula for $\log J$, corresponding to the formula

$$J = 0.38\, H^{0.67}?$$

3. Suppose that the following results are obtained in an experiment on judgments of weights.

Physical Weight (gm)	50	100	200	300	400
Judged Weight	$3\frac{1}{2}$	10	$27\frac{1}{2}$	50	75

a) Take logs of these quantities and compare them with the formula

$$\log J = -2.0 + 1.5 \log H.$$

b) Show that if the formula is accepted, the relationship between physical weight and judged weight is

$$J = 0.01\,H^{1.5}$$

c) Calculate the judged weight that should be expected for objects weighing 250 gm and 500 gm.

* **4.** Suppose that a 0.10-lambert light is given the number 5. Assume that the exponent of the Power Law for judged brightnesses is 0.5. What number will be given to a light which has a physical brightness of 0.05 lamberts? What will be the physical brightness of a light which has a judged brightness of $2\frac{1}{2}$?

5. The exponent of the Power Law for judgments of loudness has been measured to be about 0.3.[15] Suppose that we present a standard tone with a sound pressure level of 2×10^4 dynes/cm^2 (80 db). The standard is given the judged value 10. (a) What is the value of c in the formula $J = cH^p$? (b) What will be the judged loudness of a tone with physical intensity of 20 dynes/cm^2 (50 db)? of 10^6 dynes/cm^2 (97 db)? (c) What would be the physical intensity of a tone which was judged to have loudness of 5? of 20?

* **6.** Use the data of Tables 1 and 2, but transform the physical weights to pounds. In this case, what is the relationship between judged weight and physical weight? What would be the judged weight of an object weighing one-eighth pound? an object weighing one pound?

7. There are about 6.45 cm^2 in 1 in^2. Suppose that instead of the data in Table 3, we had areas of squares in in^2 rather than cm^2. What would be the formula relating judged size and physical size?

▸ **8.** Let H denote any dimension of physical magnitude, and consider any transformation of the physical magnitude

$$H' = mH^r.$$

Prove that if judged magnitudes follow the Power Law in H,

$$J = cH^p,$$

then judged magnitudes also follow a power law in H'.

9. Suppose that in the data of Table 1 subjects lifted wooden cubes with density 0.8. Let H' be the length of an edge of a cube. Assuming that

$$J = 0.2H^{1.4},$$

where H is physical weight, find the Power Law relating judgments to H'.

---

* The asterisk is used to indicate problems for which answers are given at the end of the text.

[15] S. S. Stevens. "The Direct Estimation of Sensory Magnitudes—Loudness." *Amer. J. Psychol.*, 1956, **69**, 1–25.

▸ This symbol is used to indicate problems which are extensions of the text.

* **10.** The ratio of two 1000-cycle tones just noticeably different in loudness is about 1.09. If a standard of 100 dynes/cm^2 is used, what physical intensity will be required for a comparison tone to be judged "louder" 75% of the time? What if the standard is 10^{50} dynes/cm^2?

* **11.** Using the information in Problem 10, find the value of b required for the scale of discriminability. Find the scale values for tones of 100 dynes/cm^2 and 10^{50} dynes/cm^2, and for the stimuli that are just noticeably different from each of these.

12. Find the value of b for a situation where the ratio of lengths of two just noticeably different lines is 1.03. Find the scale values of lines with physical lengths of 10 cm and one meter. Find the physical lengths of lines just noticeably longer than standards of 10 cm and one meter.

13. Since we have constructed the D scale so that one unit always corresponds to one *jnd*, the scale values of objects will depend on the physical units used for H. Consider objects weighing 50 and 500 gm, but convert their weights to pounds. Calculate their scale values using the formula

$$D = 116 \log H,$$

as before. Show that the unit on the scale still corresponds to one *jnd*.

▸ **14.** As an alternative to fixing the scale so that one unit equals one *jnd*, consider fixing the discriminability scale so that a certain stimulus has a fixed scale value. For example, find the value of b which would give the value $D = 10$ for an object with physical weight $H = 100$ gm. With this value of b, how large would a *jnd* be in units of the D scale?

▸ **15.** Suppose that instead of being proportional to the magnitude of the standard stimulus, the *jnd* were proportional to the square of the standard stimulus; that is,

$$\Delta H/H^2 = \text{constant}.$$

Construct a counterexample to show that the scale

$$D = b \log H$$

would not give equally discriminable units.

16. Suppose that there is perfect perceptual adjustment to the background in each of the following situations.

a) You are viewing two figures, each contained in a separate frame. You are told that the frames are of equal size, but one appears larger than the other because it is closer to you. The apparent height of one frame is 24 in. and of the other frame is 48 in. Each of the figures has an apparent height of 12 in., when the frames are ignored. What will be your judgment of the real height of the figure in the 48-in. frame, as compared to that of the figure in the 24-in. frame?

b) You are viewing two backgrounds each with a light shining on it. Both backgrounds reflect 70% of the light that falls on them. Light 1 is twice as bright as light 2. Now the background for light 1 is changed to reflect only 40% of the light falling on it; however, the change seems to be in the brightness of the light. You are asked to adjust light 1 so that you judge it to be as bright as it was before. After your adjustment, how much brighter will light 1 be than it was before? How much brighter will it be than light 2?

17. In a situation where cues for distance are inadequate, a subject made the following judgments about the height of a single block of wood. The subject is told that the block that appears largest is $7\frac{1}{2}$ in. tall.

Distance from viewer	12 in.	24 in.	26 in.
Judged height	$7\frac{1}{2}$ in.	6 in.	5.4 in.

Compare these judgments with those which would occur with perfect constancy, and also with judgments which would occur if only the retinal image were controlling the judgment.

CHAPTER TWO

Choice and Preference

This chapter is about the process of choosing among alternative objects or actions. Typical situations involving choice include selecting a dinner from a restaurant menu, deciding which courses to take next semester, or deciding whether to travel somewhere by car or airplane.

2A PREFERENCES, RESPONSE STRENGTHS, AND CHOICE FREQUENCIES

If a person always chooses a lobster dinner when he can have either steak or lobster, we suppose that he prefers lobster to steak. Or if a person always decides to travel by airplane when he can go by plane or by car, we suppose that he prefers flying to driving.

In different situations, a person has to choose among different sets of alternatives. In one restaurant the menu might include steak, lobster, and squab; while in another restaurant the menu might include steak, fried shrimp, and chicken. Suppose that a person strongly prefers lobster over squab or steak, but that he strongly prefers steak to fried shrimp or chicken. Then when he eats in the first restaurant, he usually will order lobster, and in the second restaurant, he usually will order steak.

Whenever a person makes a choice, he selects from sets of alternatives. We will use the letter $\mathcal{A}$ to refer to the set of alternatives in a general way. Two sets of alternatives were considered in the example just above. In the first case, the members of $\mathcal{A}$ were steak, lobster, and squab. In the second case, the members of $\mathcal{A}$ were steak, fried shrimp, and chicken.

The set $\mathcal{A}$ is really a subset of a larger class of things which can be alternatives for choice in different situations. In a restaurant we make choices among different things to eat. Then the set $\mathcal{A}$ is a list of alternative meals. The list of all the possible alternative meals would be very long; it would certainly include lobster, squab, steak, fried shrimp, and chicken, as well as hamburger, pork chops, filet of sole, and turkey. We will use subscripted letters like $A_1, A_2, \ldots$ to refer to choice alternatives in a general way.

Example 2.1. Denote a list of meals as A_1: steak; A_2: lobster; A_3: squab; A_4: fried shrimp; A_5: chicken; A_6: hamburger; A_7: pork chops. If a menu offers steak, lobster, and squab, we say that

$$\mathcal{A} = \{A_1, A_2, A_3\}.$$

If a menu offers steak, fried shrimp, and chicken, then the set of alternatives is

$$\mathcal{A} = \{A_1, A_4, A_5\}. \blacksquare$$

If a person prefers A_1 to A_2, we suppose that he likes (or wants, or values) A_1 more than A_2. We can assume that a person has a certain amount of liking or attraction for each single alternative. In other words, a person's liking or desire or value for various objects involves a set of quantities, and these quantities are the basis of the person's preferences and choices. We will use the notation $v(A_i)$ to refer to the person's liking for alternative A_i.

The idea that we are using here has several names. We have used the common-sense terms "liking," "wanting," and "value." Economists speak of the *utility* of an object. Our use of the idea here is mainly to help understand the process of making choices. When a person has a strong liking for an alternative, then he will have a strong tendency to choose that alternative when it is offered. Therefore, for our purposes it is convenient to think of $v(A_i)$ as the *response strength* of choosing alternative A_i.

We have thought of a certain set of alternatives $\mathcal{A}$ available to a person. Now, in addition, we suppose that the person has a certain response strength for each alternative A_i that is included in $\mathcal{A}$. Then, of the alternatives in $\mathcal{A}$, the alternative with the greatest strength will be the one chosen most of the time.

Example 2.2. Suppose that a person's response strengths for choosing various dinners are

steak: $v(A_1) = 6$; lobster: $v(A_2) = 10$;
squab: $v(A_3) = 5$; fried shrimp: $v(A_4) = 3$;
chicken: $v(A_5) = 3$; hamburger: $v(A_6) = 1$;
pork chops: $v(A_7) = 2$.

If we offer the set of alternatives

$$\mathcal{A} = \{A_1, A_2, A_3\},$$

then A_2 will be chosen more than A_1 or A_3 because $v(A_2)$ is higher than $v(A_1)$ or $v(A_3)$. In fact, for any set of alternatives that we could form by selecting from the listed items, A_2 would be chosen more than the other alternatives because $v(A_2)$ is the highest response strength in this list.

If we offer the set of alternatives

$$\mathcal{A} = \{A_1, A_4, A_5\},$$

then the alternative chosen most frequently would be A_1 since $v(A_1)$ is greater than $v(A_4)$ or $v(A_5)$. ▮

Up until now we have asked a vague question; which alternative will be chosen most often? Now we would like to be more precise. One theory says that the probability of each choice response is proportional to the strength of that response.[1] Let $P(A_i \mid A_i, \ldots, A_k)$ be the probability of choosing alternative A_i when $\mathcal{A} = \{A_i, \ldots, A_k\}$. Then the theory says that

$$P(A_i \mid A_i, \ldots, A_k) = \frac{v(A_i)}{\sum_{A_x \in \mathcal{A}} v(A_x)} . \tag{2.1}$$

The denominator is the sum of the strengths of all the alternatives in $\mathcal{A}$.

Example 2.3. Use the assumptions from Example 2.2, and consider the alternatives

$$\mathcal{A} = \{A_1, A_2, A_3\}.$$

Calculate the probabilities of the three alternatives.

We use Eq. (2.1).

$$P(A_1 \mid A_1, A_2, A_3) = \frac{v(A_1)}{v(A_1) + v(A_2) + v(A_3)} = \frac{6}{6 + 10 + 5} = \frac{6}{21} = .29.$$

$$P(A_2 \mid A_1, A_2, A_3) = \frac{v(A_2)}{v(A_1) + v(A_2) + v(A_3)} = \frac{10}{6 + 10 + 5} = \frac{10}{21} = .48.$$

$$P(A_3 \mid A_1, A_2, A_3) = \frac{v(A_3)}{v(A_1) + v(A_2) + v(A_3)} = \frac{5}{6 + 10 + 5} = \frac{5}{21} = .24.$$ ▮

We are using two sets of numbers, $P(A_i)$ and $v(A_i)$. The value of $P(A_i)$ is equal to the proportion of times that a person would choose alternative

[1] This idea has been used frequently. A thorough and systematic investigation and application to several kinds of experimental situations was given by R. D. Luce, *Individual Choice Behavior*, New York: Wiley, 1959. A different choice theory assumes that response strengths vary from time to time, and that the alternative with the higher strength at the moment will be chosen with probability one. The two assumptions do not lead to very different calculated choice probabilities, at least in the situations that have been studied thus far. The basic idea of the variable-response-strength theory will be presented in Chapter 7, after some necessary statistical ideas have been developed.

A_i if he had a large number of chances to select from the same set $\mathcal{A}$. To calculate $P(A_i)$, we use the response strength of choosing A_i and the strengths for the other alternatives in the set $\mathcal{A}$. The response strengths stand for the amount of a person's liking or attraction for alternative A_i. Different people will have differing values for objects, and an important question is how we can measure a person's liking for various alternatives.

The most direct measurement would be to observe a person's choices many times. Suppose, for example, that a man has to go several blocks from his office to eat lunch every day. He can walk, drive his own car, take a taxi, or ride a bus. The proportions of times that he did each of these could be used as a measurement of the relative response strengths for choosing these alternatives

Example 2.4. Suppose that a man walks to lunch 0.50 of the time, drives his own car 0.05 of the time, takes a cab 0.25 of the time, and rides a bus 0.20 of the time. Find a set of response strengths that are consistent with these choice frequencies.

The main thing to understand is that we need to keep the ratios of response strengths equal to the ratios of the choice frequencies. For example, the choice frequencies show that the response strength of walking is twice as great as the response strength of taking a taxi. However, we have to make an arbitrary decision about what units to use.

For notation, let A_1, A_2, A_3, and A_4 be the alternatives, so we know that

$$\begin{aligned} P(A_1 \mid A_1, A_2, A_3, A_4) &= .50, \\ P(A_2 \mid A_1, A_2, A_3, A_4) &= .05, \\ P(A_3 \mid A_1, A_2, A_3, A_4) &= .25, \\ P(A_4 \mid A_1, A_2, A_3, A_4) &= .20. \end{aligned}$$

These probabilities are consistent with the response strengths

$$\begin{aligned} v(A_1) &= 50, & v(A_2) &= 5, \\ v(A_3) &= 25, & v(A_4) &= 20. \end{aligned}$$

The probabilities are also consistent with the response strengths

$$\begin{aligned} v(A_1) &= 10, & v(A_2) &= 1, \\ v(A_3) &= 5, & v(A_4) &= 4. \ \blacksquare \end{aligned}$$

In general, if we could observe a person's choices many times from the same set of alternatives $\mathcal{A} = \{A_i, \ldots, A_k\}$, we could use the frequencies of his choices to measure his response strengths, and use the formula

$$v(A_i) = KP(A_i \mid A_i, \ldots, A_k), \tag{2.2}$$

where K is an arbitrary constant.

An important insight into this theory of choice comes through consideration of changes in the set of alternatives $\mathcal{A}$. If we find out about the strengths of a person's choice responses using one set of alternatives, we will know how that person will react when he has a reduced set of alternatives. To accomplish this, we would need to observe a set of choice frequencies to obtain a set of response probabilities. We would use Eq. (2.2) to obtain response strengths. Then we would use Eq. (2.1) to calculate choice probabilities for the new situation.

Example 2.5. Consider the man described in Example 2.4. Suppose that the bus company changes its routes so that he can no longer ride a bus to lunch. What will be his choice probabilities for the remaining alternatives?

We already have used Eq. (2.2) to obtain the response strengths. We can use either of the sets of values given in that example. Now we want the response probabilities for the set of alternatives

$$\mathcal{A} = \{A_1, A_2, A_3\}.$$

Using Eq. (2.1), we obtain

$$P(A_1 \mid A_1, A_2, A_3) = \frac{v(A_1)}{v(A_1) + v(A_2) + v(A_3)} = \frac{10}{10 + 1 + 5} = .62,$$

$$P(A_2 \mid A_1, A_2, A_3) = \frac{1}{10 + 1 + 5} = .06,$$

$$P(A_3 \mid A_1, A_2, A_3) = \frac{5}{10 + 1 + 5} = .31. \blacksquare$$

An alternative method can be used to solve problems like the above, and in most problems it provides a short cut. The shortening consists of not having to find a set of values for the response strengths. Instead, we work with ratios of choice frequencies which give us ratios of response strengths directly without the need for setting an arbitrary constant. Suppose that we want to know the ratio of two response strengths, $v(A_i)$ and $v(A_j)$. We can observe choices from a set $\mathcal{A}$ containing both A_i and A_j, although other alternatives may be included also. If $\mathcal{A} = \{A_i, A_j, \ldots, A_k\}$, we use Eq. (2.2) and see that the ratio of their strengths is

$$\frac{v(A_i)}{v(A_j)} = \frac{KP(A_i \mid A_i, A_j, \ldots, A_k)}{KP(A_j \mid A_i, A_j, \ldots, A_k)} = \frac{P(A_i \mid A_i, A_j, \ldots, A_k)}{P(A_j \mid A_i, A_j, \ldots, A_k)}. \tag{2.3}$$

In words, *the ratio of two response strengths equals the ratio of the choice probabilities, provided that the alternatives are both present in the same set* $\mathcal{A}$.

Ratios of response strengths can be used to calculate choice probabilities. The method is illustrated in the next example.

Example 2.6. We work with the problem of Example 2.5, but we use a different method. Instead of assigning response strengths on an arbitrary scale, we first calculate ratios of response strength from the choice probabilities. The ratios we use are $v(A_1)/v(A_3)$ and $v(A_2)/v(A_3)$. These ratios give us the choice probabilities. For example, if we take the expression for $P(A_1)$ and divide the numerator and denominator by $v(A_3)$, we obtain

$$P(A_1 \mid A_1, A_2, A_3) = \frac{v(A_1)}{v(A_1) + v(A_2) + v(A_3)}$$
$$= \frac{v(A_1)/v(A_3)}{v(A_1)/v(A_3) + v(A_2)/v(A_3) + v(A_3)/v(A_3)}.$$

We calculate the ratios using Eq. (2.3). (The probabilities were given in Example 2.4.)

$$\frac{v(A_1)}{v(A_3)} = \frac{P(A_1 \mid A_1, A_2, A_3, A_4)}{P(A_3 \mid A_1, A_2, A_3, A_4)} = \frac{.50}{.25} = 2.0;$$

$$\frac{v(A_2)}{v(A_3)} = \frac{P(A_2 \mid A_1, A_2, A_3, A_4)}{P(A_3 \mid A_1, A_2, A_3, A_4)} = \frac{.05}{.25} = 0.20.$$

Then

$$P(A_1 \mid A_1, A_2, A_3) = \frac{2.0}{2.0 + 0.2 + 1.0} = .62;$$

$$P(A_2 \mid A_1, A_2, A_3) = \frac{0.2}{2.0 + 0.2 + 1.0} = .06;$$

$$P(A_3 \mid A_1, A_2, A_3) = \frac{1.0}{2.0 + 0.2 + 1.0} = .31. \blacksquare$$

When we calculate the probability of choice using ratios of response strength, we choose some alternative A_j as the denominator of all the ratios. Then, instead of Eq. (2.1), we have

$$P(A_i \mid A_i, A_j, \ldots, A_k) = \frac{v(A_i)/v(A_j)}{\sum_{A_x \in \mathcal{A}} [v(A_x)/v(A_j)]}. \tag{2.4}$$

We have been considering a case where we know choice probabilities from a large set of alternatives, and then calculate choice probabilities for a reduced set of alternatives. Sometimes we are interested in working the other way—from smaller sets of alternatives to larger ones. We need to know choice probabilities in different situations where at least one choice alternative in each set is also present in another set. The common alternative will have different probabilities in the different sets, but in each set the ratios of the other probabilities to that of the common alternative can be obtained. Then the ratios can be used to calculate choice probabilities when alternatives from the different sets are combined.

Example 2.7. Consider two situations where a man reads magazines. Suppose that when he goes to his barber shop he can read *Life*, *Sports Illustrated*, or *The New Yorker;* call these A_1, A_2, and A_3. Suppose that in his doctor's waiting room he can read *Life*, *Newsweek*, and *Saturday Review;* call these A_1, A_4, and A_5. Now suppose that he has the following choice probabilities in the two situations: in the barber shop,

$$P(A_1 \mid A_1, A_2, A_3) = .50,$$
$$P(A_2 \mid A_1, A_2, A_3) = .20,$$
$$P(A_3 \mid A_1, A_2, A_3) = .30;$$

and in the doctor's waiting room,

$$P(A_1 \mid A_1, A_4, A_5) = .20,$$
$$p(A_4 \mid A_1, A_4, A_5) = .10,$$
$$P(A_5 \mid A_1, A_4, A_5) = .70.$$

Now suppose that on an airplane the man is offered the magazines *Sports Illustrated*, *The New Yorker*, *Newsweek*, and *Saturday Review*. Calculate the choice probabilities for this new situation.

We use ratios of response strengths. Alternative A_1 appears in both of the situations where we know the probabilities. Therefore, we can obtain the ratios of the other response strengths to the response strength of A_1. To find the ratios of $v(A_2)$ and $v(A_3)$ to $v(A_1)$, we use the probability of A_1 from the set $\mathcal{A} = \{A_1, A_2, A_3\}$. We use Eq. (2.3).

$$\frac{v(A_2)}{v(A_1)} = \frac{.20}{.50} = 0.40,$$

$$\frac{v(A_3)}{v(A_1)} = \frac{.30}{.50} = 0.60.$$

To find the ratios of $v(A_4)$ and $v(A_5)$ to $v(A_1)$, we use the probabilities from the set $\mathcal{A} = \{A_1, A_4, A_5\}$.

$$\frac{v(A_4)}{v(A_1)} = \frac{.10}{.20} = 0.50,$$

$$\frac{v(A_5)}{v(A_1)} = \frac{.70}{.20} = 3.50.$$

Now we can calculate the choice probabilities for the new situation where $\mathcal{A} = \{A_2, A_3, A_4, A_5\}$.

Using Eq. (2.4), we have

$$P(A_2 \mid A_2, A_3, A_4, A_5)$$

$$= \frac{v(A_2)/v(A_1)}{v(A_2)/v(A_1) + v(A_3)/v(A_1) + v(A_4)/v(A_1) + v(A_5)/v(A_1)}$$

$$= \frac{0.40}{0.40 + 0.60 + 0.50 + 3.50} = \frac{0.40}{5.00} = .08;$$

$$P(A_3 \mid A_2, A_3, A_4, A_5) = \frac{0.60}{5.00} = .12;$$

$$P(A_4 \mid A_2, A_3, A_4, A_5) = \frac{0.50}{5.00} = .10;$$

$$P(A_5 \mid A_2, A_3, A_4, A_5) = \frac{3.50}{5.00} = .70. \blacksquare$$

Thus far we have discussed choice probabilities in relation to response strengths, and we have seen how the probabilities in one situation can be related to other situations where the set of alternatives is changed in certain ways. All of these calculations were based on Eq. (2.1).

Equation (2.1) works quite well in describing choice frequencies in many situations. However, there are other situations where it involves a serious mistake. In closing this section, we shall consider one example of a weakness of the theory, and then take up briefly a means of correcting the weakness.

The problem involves choices between very similar alternatives. Suppose, for example, that a boy can choose between two bicycles that are identical except that one has a bell and the other does not. We suppose that the boy does not have a bicycle and wants one very much. The boy's feeling about the bell is mildly positive, but he does not care very much about the bell. We should suppose that the boy will have about equal response strengths for choosing the two bicycles—perhaps $v(A_1) \approx 100$ for the bicycle with the bell and $v(A_2) \approx 99$ for the bicycle without the bell. Then according to Eq. (2.1) his probability of choosing A_1 would be

$$P(A_1 \mid A_1, A_2) \approx \frac{100}{199} = .503,$$

barely over one-half.

The result is contradicted by experience. Given two alternatives, where one includes every aspect of the other and something else in addition, we should expect the alternative containing the "extra" to be chosen every time. Certainly, if the boy likes the bell at all, he will choose the bicycle with the bell, and the probability should be 1.0.

It is likely that in many situations calling for a choice among alternatives, people ignore the aspects that are common to all the alternatives.[2] In the example, the boy will get a bicycle regardless of his choice; therefore, his choice is really between having a bicycle with a bell and having a bicycle without a bell.

Then we have to reformulate the situation to apply the theory; we need to know the response strength for choosing to have a bell, and the response strength for choosing not to have a bell. With the problem phrased in this new way, the theory leads to a realistic prediction.

The example shows something quite important about the theory given as Eq. (2.1). The theory probably is accurate only when the common attributes of objects do not enter into judgments about them. For example, in choosing a meal at a restaurant, a person probably decides by considering the items' differences. The items share an important quality—they are all edible—but the person has already decided that he wants to eat so his choice of a dinner probably is made without considering the common quality. However, if we consider a person's choice among the alternatives eating steak, eating chicken, and going to a movie, then the shared quality of two of the alternatives certainly will enter into the choice, and the simple theory presented here will not be correct.[3]

2B SUBJECTIVE JUDGMENTS OF VALUE

This section is about the measurement of a person's liking or attraction for various choice alternatives. In the preceding section we discussed the method of observing choice frequencies, where the response strength of choosing an alternative is measured by observing how often the alternative is chosen. That method probably gives the best information about a person's true motives and values; however, it is very hard to use. To obtain reliable information about a person's choice probabilities, we must observe his choices from the same set of alternatives many times. This is always difficult and sometimes impossible. For example, if we want to study the process of selecting a career, it is not possible to observe an individual's choice more than once or twice.

---

[2] This idea is an extension of the "sure thing" principle which was contributed to statistical decision theory by L. J. Savage, *The Foundations of Statistics*, New York: Wiley, 1954. The implications of this idea for several kinds of psychological experiment are discussed by F. Restle, *Psychology of Judgment and Choice*, New York: Wiley, 1961.

[3] In cases like the one described, it seems likely that the person will not make a simple choice but will decide in "stages," first choosing between eating and the movie, and then choosing between the meals if he decides to eat. Then, as F. Restle has pointed out in *Psychology of Judgment and Choice*, the theory of choice has to include assumptions about the sequence of subchoices that lead to a final selection.

A natural way to measure a person's liking for something is to ask him how much he likes it. This is not quite as easy as it sounds, because many of the kinds of answers that a person might give would not help us understand his feelings about things. The amount of a person's liking for an alternative is "within the person" in a way, and our problem is to have the person tell us something that will give us useful information about his internal state.

The psychological problem here is similar to the problem of understanding a person's perceptual judgments, discussed in Chapter 1. The mechanism that produces perceptual judgments is in the person, and we use the person's judgments to gain some understanding of how that mechanism works. Now we are interested in another state of affairs in the person—the amount of his liking for an alternative.

Recall that the main method used for understanding perceptual judgments is to present stimuli with known physical properties and have the person tell us his judgments. In this way, we find out about relationships between the judgments and the physical magnitudes. In studying a person's attitudes and values, we can present objects and ask the subject to tell us how much he likes or values each one. However, there is an important difference between this situation and the psychophysical experiment. Here we do not have a system for assigning nonpsychological values to objects which would correspond to the system we have for assigning nonpsychological (physical) stimulus magnitudes.

From Chapter 1, recall that two kinds of perceptual judgments can be obtained. One kind involves judgments of relative magnitudes where the person assigns a number to a stimulus to show how much larger or smaller it seems when compared with another stimulus. Another kind of judgment occurs when we ask a subject to decide *whether* one stimulus is larger or smaller than another stimulus. We will consider both kinds of judgment.

Suppose that we conduct an experiment like the one used to obtain judgments of magnitude. One procedure would be to present one choice alternative and give it a number, and have the subject assign numbers to all the other alternatives using the first one as a standard of comparison. We would ask the subject to use numbers that indicated how much he liked the alternatives, compared to the standard.

We assume that for each object presented, the subject has a certain value which we have called the response strength of choosing alternative A_i, or $v(A_i)$. We might suppose that when the subject gives his judgment of how much he likes alternative A_i, it is related to $v(A_i)$ in the same way that judgments of physical magnitude relate to physical magnitude. If that were true, then the judgment of each alternative would be related to the response strength for the alternative by the formula

$$J_i = c[v(A_i)]^p, \tag{2.5}$$

where c is an arbitrary constant, but p is a property of the judgment process.

What we want is information about $v(A_i)$. Therefore, we want to work backward from the judgment, J_i.

$$[v(A_i)]^p = J_i/c,$$
$$v(A_i) = \sqrt[p]{J_i/c}.$$

Since c is an arbitrary constant, we can define a new constant

$$c' = \sqrt[p]{1/c}$$

which gives the simpler formula

$$v(A_i) = c'\sqrt[p]{J_i}.$$

This shows that we cannot measure $v(A_i)$ without knowing both p and c'. However, we do not need to know the absolute value of $v(A_i)$ to use it for calculating choice probabilities. Recall from Eq. (2.4) that the needed quantities are ratios of response strengths. We could calculate choice probabilities if we could obtain values like

$$\frac{v(A_i)}{v(A_j)} = \frac{c'\sqrt[p]{J_i}}{c'\sqrt[p]{J_j}} = \sqrt[p]{\frac{J_i}{J_j}}.$$

The result is that we cannot use the judgments to calculate choice probabilities unless we know the value of p. However, in the situation where values rather than magnitudes are being judged, we cannot determine the value of p.

Another possibility would be to conduct an experiment similar to those used to study detection of differences between stimuli. A common procedure is to present choice alternatives in pairs, and ask the subject to judge which alternative he prefers. The procedure is called the method of paired comparisons.

As in the previous case, we suppose that for each alternative presented, the subject has a value $v(A_i)$. We might assume that the subject makes his judgment of preference based on that alternative he thinks has the higher response strength. If we presented alternatives with nearly equal response strengths, the subject probably could not consistently discriminate between them. We could then say that two objects were just noticeably different if the subject chose one of them as the one he liked more on 75% of the times the two were presented. For these judgments we also could make an assumption by analogy with judgments about physical stimuli. Consider two alternatives A and A' that differ by one *jnd*—that is, the subject says he likes A' better than A on 75% of their paired presentations. Then a natural assumption would be that the ratio of the response strengths of A' and A equals a constant. That is,

$$\frac{v(A')}{v(A)} = k,$$

where k is the same for all pairs of stimuli that differ by one *jnd*.

In Chapter 1 we showed that when *jnd*'s are proportional to stimulus magnitudes, we can develop a scale where alternatives that differ by one unit are just noticeably different. The scale values are called D and are related to the response strengths by the formula

$$D = (1/\log k) \log v(A_i). \tag{2.6}$$

The data from a paired-comparison experiment can be used to assign scale values to objects, based on the idea of a just noticeable difference.[4] Therefore, we can obtain values of D in Eq. (2.6), and we now ask whether we can work back to values of $v(A)$, which we are mainly interested in measuring. From Eq. (2.6)

$$\log v(A_i) = D_i \log k = \log (k)^{D_i};$$
$$v(A_i) = (\mathrm{k})^{D_i}.$$

Here, as with magnitude estimation, the judgments given in an experiment do not permit us to calculate $v(A_i)$. We would also need to know k, the ratio of two values that are just noticeably different, and the judgments given in the experiment do not give us the value of k.

Again, we recall that we do not need to know absolute values of response strengths to calculate choice probabilities; ratios of response strengths would do. However,

$$\frac{v(A_i)}{v(A_j)} = \frac{(k)^{D_i}}{(k)^{D_j}} = (k)^{D_i - D_j}.$$

We still need to know the value of k, and therefore the judgments do not give us enough information to calculate choice probabilities.

We have found that subjective judgments of value or preference do not tell us what we need to know about response strengths to give an analysis of choice behavior. However, questions about the judgments still are interesting, since we may want to know what kinds of processes operate when a person tells us how much he likes something. In the analysis here we assumed that people make judgments about value in the same way that

[4] One method is based on a theory by L. L. Thurstone, "A Law of Comparative Judgment," *Psychol. Rev.*, 1927, **34,** 273–286. An extension of the idea for pair-comparisons permits the determination of scale values when subjects classify stimuli into categories (for example, *very good*, *good*, *medium*, *poor*, *very poor*).

they make judgments about physical magnitude, except that the source of the value judgment is in the person instead of being a property of a physical object. This assumption leads to Eqs. (2.5) and (2.6), with the two equations applying to different kinds of judgments.

We can derive a result from Eqs. (2.5) and (2.6) that allows us to see whether the assumption is reasonable.[5] From Eq. (2.5).

$$\log J_i = \log c + p \log v(A_i);$$

$$\log v(A_i) = (1/p) \log J_i - (1/p) \log c.$$

Then by substituting in Eq. (2.6)

$$D_i = \frac{1}{\log k}\left[\frac{1}{p}(\log J_i) - \frac{1}{p}(\log c)\right].$$

For purposes of abbreviation,[6] let

$$\alpha = -\frac{\log c}{p \log k}, \qquad \beta = \frac{1}{p \log k}.$$

The abbreviations give us

$$D_i = \alpha + \beta \log J_i, \tag{2.7}$$

a linear relationship between D and $\log J$.

What we have just found is that if we ask subjects for two kinds of judgments, we can perform a check between the two in order to see whether our assumption about the judgments might be correct. The two kinds of judgments are: pair comparisons (which of these do you prefer?), and judgments of relative magnitude of liking or value (how much better or worse is this one than that one?). If our assumption is correct, then the first kind of judgment can be used to give a scale based on the discriminability of values, and the second to give a scale based on the judged magnitudes of values. And then the scale values should be related according to Eq. (2.7).

The idea is sketched in Fig. 1. We are considering assumptions about relationships between $v(A)$ and J, and between $v(A)$ and D. These are shown as dashed lines in the figure, and the assumed relationships are given. But

---

[5] This was pointed out by S. S. Stevens, "A Metric for the Social Consensus," *Science*, 1966, **151,** 530–541.

[6] Since c is an arbitrary constant, α will have no empirical meaning. However, both p and k are psychologically meaningful so we should think of β as a property of a situation that we could measure.

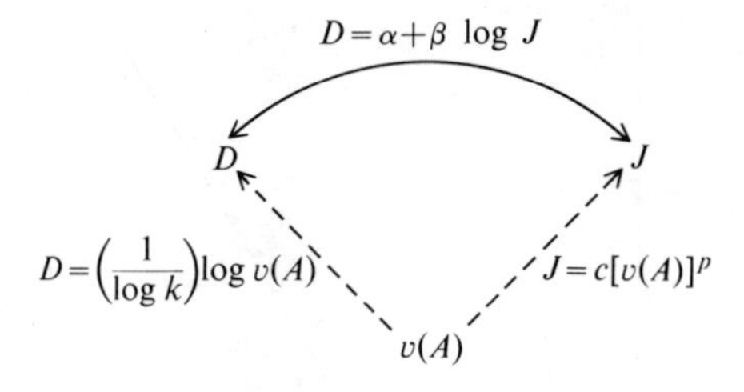

Fig. 1. Theoretical relationship between two scale values obtained for object A.

we have seen that these two assumptions imply a relationship between D and J, which is shown as a solid line in the figure because we can observe values of D and J and check the formula to see whether it is acceptable.

In one experiment,[7] students were given pictures and descriptions of 16 different wristwatches. They were shown the material for two wristwatches at a time, and asked to give two judgments. The first was a preference judgment—which watch seemed better. The other was a judgment of the magnitude of preference. The subject marked a point on a line to show how much better he thought one watch was than the other. The marks on the line can be considered as ratio judgments. For example, if the mark was three-fourths of the way across the line, that indicated that the student thought one watch was three times as good as the other.

The judgments were translated into scale values for each watch, with the judgments of preference used to obtain a scale of discriminability (based on the consistency of judgments) and the judgments of amount of preference used to obtain a scale of judged magnitude. Figure 2 shows a graph of the two sets of judgments, with the values of D plotted against the logarithms of the values of J. The straight line fits the data quite well, consistent with Eq. (2.7).

The result is a nice confirmation of the idea that subjects' judgments of value may be based on their true response strengths for choosing the judged objects. However, if the present analysis is correct, a subject's judgments of value do not provide enough information to predict his choice probabilities. It seems, then, that to understand the choices a person makes, we must obtain some information about his actual choice probabilities; we cannot rely only on his stated judgments of value.

---

[7] The experiment was conducted by T. Indow, "An Example of Motivation Research Applied to Product Design," published in Japanese in *Chosa to gijutsu*, 1961, No. 102, pp. 45–60. The data and reference were taken from the article by S. S. Stevens, cited in footnote 5.

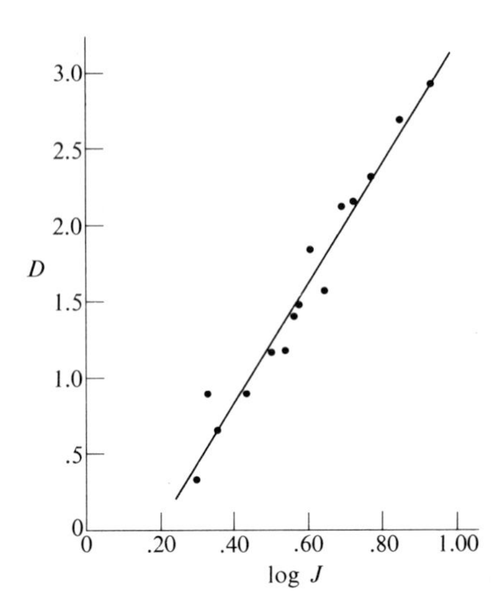

Fig. 2. Relationship between D and $\log J$ obtained in an experiment.

2C MEASURING PREFERENCES IN ANIMALS

We usually are not able to observe a person's choices many times from the same set of alternatives, because in ordinary life the choice situations presented to a person are always changing. One advantage of studying choice processes in animals is the possibility of setting up reasonable choice situations where the alternatives remain the same.

In one kind of experiment animals are offered repeated choices between different foods, and we find out about their preferences by counting the number of times each food is chosen. In one experiment[8] rats were studied in order to find out about their liking for sucrose, wheat powder, and casein. The foods were presented two at a time. In one condition the rats chose between sucrose and wheat powder, in a second condition they chose between sucrose and casein, and in a third condition they chose between wheat powder and casein. Four tests were given between each pair of foods, with each test consisting of 30 choices.

The data are shown in Fig. 3. The animals tended to choose the preferred food more frequently in later tests, as they became more acquainted with the situation.

In Fig. 3 a single line is drawn connecting the proportions of choice of sucrose rather than casein, and of sucrose rather than wheat powder. The

[8] The experiment was done by P. T. Young, "Studies of Food Preference, Appetite, and Dietary Habit: VII. Palatability in Relation to Learning and Performance." *J. Comp. Physiol. Psychol.*, 1947, **40,** 37–72.

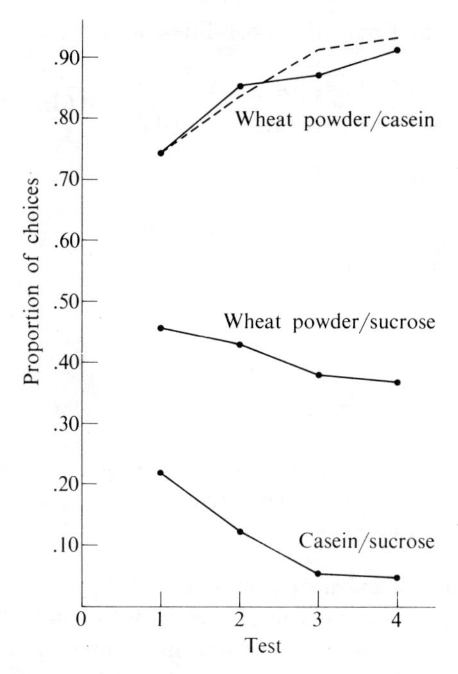

Fig. 3. Proportions of choices between three pairs of foods.

proportions of choice of wheat powder rather than casein have two lines. The solid line connects the points that were actually obtained in the experiment. The dashed line connects four theoretical proportions, where the proportion of choice between wheat powder and casein is predicted from the proportions between sucrose and wheat powder, and between sucrose and casein. The prediction for Test 4 is worked out in the example that follows: the student has the task of working out the calculations for the first three tests. (See Problem 11.)

Example 2.8. Denote the three foods A_1: sucrose; A_2: wheat powder; A_3: casein. Then for the rats offered sucrose and wheat powder,

$$\mathcal{A} = \{A_1, A_2\}.$$

On the fourth test,

$$P(A_1 \mid A_1, A_2) = .62, \qquad P(A_2 \mid A_1, A_2) = .38.$$

For the rats offered sucrose and casein, $\mathcal{A} = \{A_1, A_3\}$. On their fourth test,

$$P(A_1 \mid A_1, A_3) = .95, \qquad P(A_3 \mid A_1, A_3) = .05.$$

We want to predict $P(A_2 \mid A_2, A_3)$. We use the method of ratios of response strengths. From the first pair of probabilities, we obtain

$$\frac{v(A_2)}{v(A_1)} = \frac{P(A_2 \mid A_1, A_2)}{P(A_1 \mid A_1, A_2)} = \frac{.38}{.62} = 0.61.$$

From the second situation, we have

$$\frac{v(A_3)}{v(A_1)} = \frac{P(A_3 \mid A_1, A_3)}{P(A_1 \mid A_1, A_3)} = \frac{.05}{.95} = 0.053.$$

Then when $\mathcal{A} = \{A_2, A_3\}$,

$$P(A_2 \mid A_2, A_3) = \frac{v(A_2)/v(A_1)}{v(A_2)/v(A_1) + v(A_3)/v(A_1)} = \frac{0.61}{0.61 + 0.05} = .92.$$

In the experiment, the proportion of choices of wheat powder rather than casein was .91 on the fourth test. The prediction of .92 agrees very well with the results of this experiment. ▌

In a second kind of experiment for measuring preferences in animals, two substances are made available continuously and the experimental measurement is the amount of each substance that is taken. Usually two liquids are available in bottles equipped with drinking tubes, and it is easy to note the amounts taken from the two bottles during a given period of time.

This method can be used easily to study the attractiveness of different kinds of sugar, salt, and other substances that can be dissolved in water or given in liquid form. For example, when rats are offered a choice between plain water and salt water, they prefer the salt water if the salt concentration is very low, but they prefer plain water if the salt concentration is high.

In one experiment[9] several different concentrations of salt were presented, and each was compared with plain water. When the concentration was about 0.1%, rats took an average of 18 cc per day of the salt water and 11 cc per day of the plain water. When the salt concentration was about 0.9% (the concentration of salt in body fluids), the rats took about 34 cc per day of the salt water and 9 cc per day of plain water. When the concentration was higher than 1%, the preference for salt water declined sharply; with a concentration of about 1.6%, the average daily intake of salt water was 15 cc, compared to 17 cc of plain water.

A third kind of experiment is closely related to the second, but extends the method to alternatives that cannot be measured in amounts of substance

[9] J. K. Bare, "The Specific Hunger for Sodium Chloride in Normal and Adrenalectomized White Rats." *J. Comp. Physiol. Psychol.*, 1949, **42**, 242–253.

consumed. As an example, consider the problem of measuring a rat's preference for eating food relative to being near another rat. We could measure the amount of food eaten but there is no measure of the attractiveness of the other rat that can be compared with an amount of food. It is convenient, then, to compare the two alternatives by offering them both continuously and measuring their relative attractiveness in terms of the time spent with each one.

In one set of experiments[10] measures were taken of rats' preferences for eating food, being near another rat, and playing on a metal step. Alternatives were presented two at a time, in different compartments. On a test, a rat was offered the two alternatives for 10 min and during that time it could move back and forth between the compartments. The measure of preference was the amount of time spent in each compartment.

In one experiment each rat was tested once on each pair of alternatives. In another experiment the rats were tested twice on each pair; between the tests the rats were trained to run in a straight alley to obtain a food reward. The results are given in Table 1. Note that in all cases, eating was preferred to being near another rat and also to playing on the step. Playing was preferred to being near another rat.

Table 1

Proportions of Time Spent in Compartments Containing Different Alternatives

Alternatives	First experiment	Second experiment Test 1	Second experiment Test 2
Food, rat	.69	.62	.70
Food, play	.57 (.66)	.53 (.57)	.69 (.63)
Play, rat	.53	.55	.58

Note: The proportions are given for the underlined alternative in each pair.

Example 2.9. We can test the idea that time spent in each compartment is proportional to the response strength of choosing the alternative that is in the compartment. Denote the alternatives A_1: food; A_2: play; A_3: rat. Use the probabilities when $\mathcal{A} = \{A_1, A_3\}$ and $\mathcal{A} = \{A_2, A_3\}$ to calculate theoretical choice probabilities for the case where $\mathcal{A} = \{A_1, A_2\}$.

[10] J. Allison, "Strength of Preference for Food, Magnitude of Food Reward, and Performance in Instrumental Conditioning." *J. Comp. Physiol. Psychol.*, 1964, **57,** 217–223.

The calculations will be given here for the second test of the second experiment. When $\mathcal{A} = \{A_1, A_3\}$,

$$\frac{v(A_1)}{v(A_3)} = \frac{P(A_1 \mid A_1, A_3)}{P(A_3 \mid A_1, A_3)} = \frac{.70}{.30} = 2.33.$$

When $\mathcal{A} = \{A_2, A_3\}$,

$$\frac{v(A_2)}{v(A_3)} = \frac{P(A_2 \mid A_2, A_3)}{P(A_3 \mid A_2, A_3)} = \frac{.58}{.42} = 1.38.$$

Then the theoretical probability of A_1 when $\mathcal{A} = \{A_1, A_2\}$ is

$$P(A_1 \mid A_1, A_2) = \frac{v(A_1)/v(A_3)}{v(A_1)/v(A_3) + v(A_2)/v(A_3)} = \frac{2.33}{2.33 + 1.38} = .63.$$

This value, as well as those calculated for the other tests, is in parentheses in Table 1. In this situation the agreement between theoretical and obtained values is not as good as it was in the case described earlier involving three kinds of food. ▮

One more method of measuring response strengths will be mentioned. The main new feature of this last method is that we measure the animal's response strength for some activity without specifying any particular alternative activity. An alternative A_i is offered continuously, and the animal will spend some amount of time in that activity. The rest of the time the animal will be doing other things. The amount of time spent on A_i can be used as a measure of the strength of A_i.

The idea of this measure is that the set of alternatives is not specified in an exact way. We know that it includes A_i and some other activities in addition. In the experiment that will be described here, the subject was a monkey. A_i was playing with a mechanical gadget, and the other alternatives were eating, drinking, grooming, climbing on the walls and ceiling of the cage, and whatever else the monkey might do in the cage. We will use the letter M to stand for this vague set of miscellaneous alternative responses, and $v(M)$ to indicate their combined response strengths. When one alternative A_i is offered, we say that the set of alternatives is $\mathcal{A} = \{A_i, M\}$, and the probability of A_i is

$$P(A_i \mid A_i, M) = \frac{v(A_i)}{v(A_i) + v(M)}.$$

We assume that the subject is either engaged in A_i or with some other activity at all times. In other words, whenever the subject is not performing the response alternative A_i, we assume that he is performing one of the response alternatives included in the set M. In that case

$$P(M \mid A_i, M) = 1.0 - P(A_i \mid A_i, M).$$

And from Eq. (2.3),

$$\frac{v(A_i)}{v(M)} = \frac{P(A_i \mid A_i, M)}{P(M \mid A_i, M)} = \frac{P(A_i \mid A_i, M)}{1.0 - P(A_i \mid A_i, M)}. \qquad (2.8)$$

We can present different responses to a subject in separate tests at different times in the same situation. That means that the set of miscellaneous alternatives M is the same for all tests, but the presented response A_i is changed from one test to another. We assume that in each test the probability of A_i is equal to the proportion of time spent performing A_i.[11] Then Eq. (2.8) tells us how to obtain a comparison between the strengths of the responses used in the different tests.

A monkey named Chicko was tested on three playthings: a handle that could be moved horizontally, a door that could be opened and closed, and a plunger that could be pushed up and down.[12] During a test period, one of the playthings was attached to the door of Chicko's cage so that he could use it. Except for the introduction of the test plaything, Chicko's living conditions were not altered during the tests. For example, food and water were available at all times, including test periods.

Chicko was tested with each of the three choice alternatives for one hour. A record was kept of the number of times he played with the toy, and this number was multiplied by the average time that it took to manipulate the toy once; the result gives the approximate amount of time that Chicko spent with each toy during an hour. The times were 13.4 min for the handle, 8.7 min for the door, and 2.6 min for the plunger.

Example 2.10. Estimate the probability of each response by converting the amounts of time to proportions. Then from these results calculate the ratios of response strengths $v(A_i)/v(M)$.

---

[11] It is convenient to use the proportion of time spent performing a response as the estimate of its probability, since this permits direct comparisons between different responses. A discussion of this matter is given by D. Premack, "Reinforcement Theory," in M. Jones (Ed.) *Nebraska Symposium on Motivation.* Lincoln: Univ. of Neb. Press, 1965. Pp. 123–180. A number of interesting mathematical questions that arise are presented in a mimeographed paper by W. Kintsch and D. Premack, "On Some Problems in the Description of Steady State Behavior."

[12] This is part of an experiment done by D. Premack, "Rate Differential Reinforcement in Monkey Manipulation." *J. exp. Anal. Behav.*, 1963, **6,** 81–89. Actually, four monkeys were tested, but the other three did not show as much difference between the objects as Chicko did, and their data were not reported in sufficient detail for us to apply the present analysis. A fourth plaything was also used, and the reported data for its tests are mentioned in Problem 15.

We denote the responses A_1: handle; A_2: door; A_3: plunger. When $\mathcal{A} = \{A_1, M\}$,

$$P(A_1 \mid A_1, M) = \frac{13.4}{60} = .22;$$

when $\mathcal{A} = \{A_2, M\}$,

$$P(A_2 \mid A_2, M) = .15;$$

and when $\mathcal{A} = \{A_3, M\}$,

$$P(A_3 \mid A_3, M) = .043.$$

Now we obtain ratios of response strengths using Eq. (2.8).

$$\frac{v(A_1)}{v(M)} = \frac{P(A_1 \mid A_1, M)}{1.0 - P(A_1 \mid A_1, M)} = \frac{.22}{.78} = 0.28;$$

$$\frac{v(A_2)}{v(M)} = \frac{.15}{.85} = 0.18;$$

$$\frac{v(A_3)}{v(M)} = \frac{.043}{.957} = .05.$$

This gives us a set of measures that are comparable, since each alternative is measured relative to the same set of other responses, M. It appears that $v(A_1)$ is about $1\frac{1}{2}$ times as great as $v(A_2)$, and about $5\frac{1}{2}$ times as great as $v(A_3)$, and that $v(A_2)$ is about $3\frac{1}{2}$ times as great as $v(A_3)$. ▮

The results found in Example 2.10 should tell us what to expect if more than one of the alternatives are offered at the same time. In the experiment that led to the results given above, there were tests in which two of the play-things were attached to Chicko's cage. In other respects, these tests were just like those described earlier. Each test lasted one hour, and Chicko still had food and water available and could move about in the cage when he was not playing with test alternatives.

In the test with two specified responses A_i and A_j, the whole set of alternatives is $\mathcal{A} = \{A_i, A_j, M\}$. Therefore we have

$$P(A_i \mid A_i, A_j, M) = \frac{v(A_i)}{v(A_i) + v(A_j) + v(M)}.$$

We do not need to know the absolute values of all three quantities to calculate $P(A_i)$, because we can use ratios of response strengths.

$$P(A_i \mid A_i, A_j, M) = \frac{v(A_i)/v(M)}{v(A_i)/v(M) + v(A_j)/v(M) + v(M)/v(M)}$$

$$= \frac{v(A_i)/v(M)}{1.0 + v(A_i)/v(M) + v(A_j)/v(M)}.$$

Therefore, we can calculate the theoretical probabilities for the situation with two choice alternatives using the results of the tests where single alternatives were presented.

Example 2.11. Use the results obtained in Example 2.10 to obtain theoretical probabilities for A_1 and A_2 when $\mathcal{A} = \{A_1, A_2, M\}$.

$$P(A_1 \mid A_1, A_2, M) = \frac{v(A_1)/v(M)}{1.0 + v(A_1)/v(M) + v(A_2)/v(M)}$$

$$= \frac{.28}{1.0 + .28 + .18} = .19.$$

$$P(A_2 \mid A_1, A_2, M) = \frac{v(A_2)/v(M)}{1.0 + v(A_1)/v(M) + v(A_2)/v(M)} = \frac{0.18}{1.46} = .12.$$

According to these calculations, we expect Chicko to spend about 19% of a test period playing with the handle, about 12% of the test period playing with the door, and the remaining 69% of the time doing other things. ▮

The experiment included test periods with all three pairs of playthings. For example, in a 60-min test with both the handle and the door, Chicko spent 11.3 min playing with the handle and 6.3 min playing with the door. The results of all three tests are given in Table 2, in the form of proportions of time spent with each plaything. The numbers in parentheses are the theoretical probabilities, calculated as in Example 2.11. The theoretical calculations agree quite well with the data in all these cases.

Table 2

Proportions of Time Spent with Alternatives in Two-Choice Tests

Alternatives	Handle	Door	Plunger
Handle, door	.19 (.19)	.10 (.12)	—
Handle, plunger	.24 (.21)	—	.04 (.04)
Door, plunger	—	.14 (.15)	.05 (.04)

In this section we have discussed four methods of measuring animals' response strengths for a set of alternatives. In one method, food substances are presented in pairs and each animal chooses between them a great number of times. The relative frequencies of choice are used to measure the relative strengths of the choice responses. In a second method, liquid food substances are presented continuously, and relative response strengths are measured by observing the amount of each liquid that is consumed. A third method is to present alternative incentives in two different compartments. The relative response strengths for choosing the two incentives are measured by noting the proportions of time the animal spends in the compartments. Finally, we studied the method of presenting choice alternatives continuously and measuring response strengths by observing the amounts of time actually spent performing the alternative responses.

In the discussion here, we have been especially interested in testing whether the methods of measuring response strength are valid. If just two alternatives are used, the methods can be applied, but the results can be checked only when there are three or more alternatives. With three alternatives, say A_1, A_2, and A_3, we use the results from the choice between A_1 and A_2 and from the choice between A_1 and A_3 to predict what should happen for the choice between A_2 and A_3. In the data used here, best results were obtained using the method of discrete choices and the method of measuring the actual time spent performing alternative responses. The good agreements between the predictions and the results are encouraging in two ways. First, the results support Eq. (2.1), suggesting that we are using a fairly accurate idea about the relationship between response strengths and choice probabilities. Secondly, the results support the successful methods of measurement. With these techniques, the measurements of response strength probably permit calculations of choice probability that are accurate to within .02 or .03.

2D TESTS OF GENERAL MOTIVATIONAL TENDENCIES

We have discussed several situations involving choices of specific objects from sets of alternatives that do not change. For these simple situations the theory of choice provides a reasonably accurate statistical account of the responses that are made. However, we do not yet have a satisfactory theory about the way that different choice alternatives interrelate when a person notices similarities among them, and we do not have good ways of measuring response strengths for specific choices when we cannot observe those choices in a constant context of choice alternatives. In other words, our present theories do not include satisfactory ways of dealing with the complexity and variability of choice situations that occur frequently in everyday life.

While we cannot give an exact account of all the choices that a person makes, it is possible to obtain information of a general kind that tells us something about the nature of the person's preferences and motives. The situation for a psychologist predicting an individual's choices is a little like a meteorologist trying to predict the weather two or three months in advance.

There are too many unknown factors to permit exact predictions of each day's weather far in the future. However, it is possible to make predictions of a fairly general kind. The weather at a particular place and season tends to be fairly consistent from year to year, and we can have quite a bit of confidence in approximate predictions based on observations taken in earlier years. For example, we have fairly high confidence in statements like: "The temperature in Minneapolis will go below zero several times during January," "In San Francisco the high temperature will be below 80° almost every day all year," and "In Southern Indiana the high temperature will be above 90° several times during August." General statements like these do not tell us exactly what kind of weather to expect on any certain day, but they do help greatly when we have to decide about clothing to take on a trip.

In a similar way, it is possible to obtain information about a person so that his choice behavior can be compared with other persons' choices in a general way. For example, there are some people who frequently choose political articles and books to read, who choose to join political organizations, and whose conversations often deal with political events and issues. Other persons are much less interested in politics, but are very interested, say, in economic matters and tend to choose their reading and activity accordingly. We can make general statements about a person's interests and values, and these are a little like the general statements that we can make about the weather in a certain city.

The best way to obtain general information about a person's interests and values probably is to observe his choices over a long period of time and in many different situations. However, it is possible to obtain reasonably good information in a much shorter time by asking a person a series of questions that are selected carefully so that the answers contain information about the person's general tendencies in choice situations. These tests represent one kind of personality test.[13]

One test that deals with human motivation is called "A Study of Values."[14] In taking this test a person answers many questions, each involving a preference or a choice. Sample questions are: "Would you prefer to watch an educational television program about (a) English poetry in the eighteenth century or (b) early developments in physics?" or, "If you could match the accomplishments of any person in history, which of the following would

[13] Many different kinds of personality tests are used. We are talking here about tests of a person's values or motives. Other tests deal with a person's emotional adjustment, his attitudes toward social situations and other people, his tendencies toward certain neurotic and psychotic disorders, and other things.

[14] The most recent version of this test is by G. W. Allport, P. E. Vernon, and G. Lindzey, *A Study of Values: a Scale for Measuring the Dominant Interests in Personality*. Boston: Houghton Mifflin Company, 1960.

you prefer most to emulate: (a) Andrew Carnegie, (b) Peter the Great, (c) Helen Keller, (d) Albert Einstein?" The questions are selected so that a person's answers show the relative strengths of seven values or motives: religious, political, social, aesthetic, economic, and theoretical. For example, if a person consistently chooses answers having to do with how things work and with scientific matters, he receives a high score on the theoretical scale. If a person makes many choices indicating preference for activities involved in religious practice, he receives a high score on the religious scale, and similarly with the other categories used in scoring the test.

Now recall the discussion given earlier about measurements of preference. Remember that to measure the relative strengths of two choice responses, the alternatives are presented many times, or are presented continuously for a long time. We find out about the response strength of choosing an alternative by observing the proportion of choices of that alternative or the proportion of time spent with it.

In a test like "A Study of Values," each specific set of choice alternatives is presented only once. Therefore, we do not obtain reliable information about a person's probabilities of choice between specific alternatives. For example, we would not be able to predict how often a person would actually choose to watch a television program about English poetry rather than about physics.

However, the test is intended to measure the person's general interests rather than his specific preferences. And since a large number of different alternatives is presented, a general picture of the person's values and interests can be obtained. Of course, the information is based on what the person says he likes, rather than on choices which we actually observe between real alternatives available to the person. Therefore, we may obtain erroneous information—the person may say he likes to do certain things even though he never does them. On the other hand, the information is rather easy to obtain, and the problem of obtaining truthful answers can be at least partly solved by using the test in situations where the person who is taking it is motivated to give an accurate impression of his interests and values.

A rather different type of test has been developed and used successfully to measure motives like the need for achievement and the need for affiliation. The problems of measuring such general motives are quite complicated; in fact, the question of what these motives are is not especially easy to answer. Speaking in a general way, the amount of a person's need for achievement is the extent to which his choices are aimed toward accomplishing things, succeeding in competition with others, and maintaining high standards of excellence in hard tasks. The amount of a person's need for affiliation is the extent to which his choices are aimed toward having friendship and warm, congenial relationships with other persons. Similar definitions could be

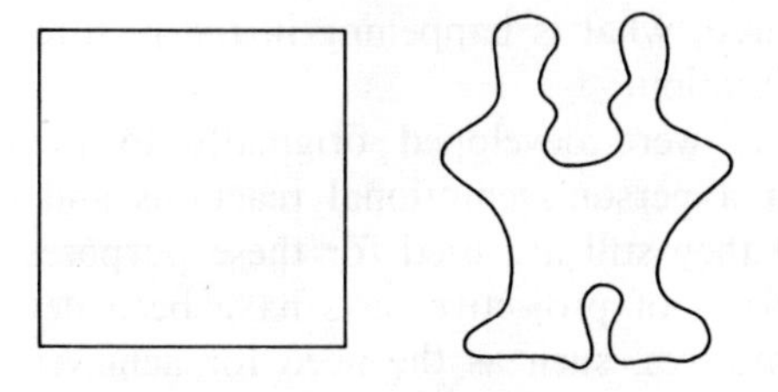

Fig. 4. A stimulus that determines a response, and an ambiguous stimulus.

given for other general social motives, such as the need for power, the need to be dependent, etc.; however, the needs for achievement and affiliation have been studied most successfully at this time.

The tests for affiliation and achievement motivation that will be described here use the method of projective testing. In general, a projective test uses a person's reaction to an ambiguous stimulus—a stimulus which does not completely determine an appropriate response. The principle can be understood by thinking about reactions that different people would have to two pictures, shown in Fig. 4. Suppose that you asked a number of people, "What do you see in these two pictures?" Almost everyone would give the same answer for the picture on the left: "a square." However, the responses to the picture on the right would be much more varied. Some people might say, "a butterfly," others might say, "two witches," and there would almost certainly be a wide variety of other reactions. The response to the picture on the left is almost completely determined by the picture itself. But the response to the picture on the right is not determined nearly as completely by the picture. The responses to stimuli in a projective test are determined by factors other than the stimuli themselves. Therefore, the responses may indicate something about the person, such as the strengths of certain motives.

One projective test[15] uses ambiguous stimuli actually made from ink blots. In another type of projective test the stimuli are pictures rather than blobs, and the person is asked to tell a story based on the picture, rather than tell "what he sees."[16] The pictures usually have a person or two in some relatively ambiguous situation. For example, there might be a man and a boy apparently engaged in conversation. The person taking the test tells a story for each picture, including things that have happened leading up to

[15] The test was developed by H. Rorschach, *Psychodiagnostics*. Berne: Hans Huber, 1942.

[16] This test is called the "Thematic Apperception Test." It was presented by E. D. Morgan and H. A. Murray, "A Method for Investigating Fantasies: the Thematic Apperception Test," *Archives of Neurological Psychiatry*, 1935, **34,** 289–306. Several studies using the test were presented by H. A. Murray and others, *Explorations in Personality*, New York: Oxford University Press, 1938.

the situation pictured, what is happening in the picture, and what will be the result of the situation.

Projective tests were developed originally to provide very general information about a person's emotional reactions and relationships with other people, and they still are used for these purposes. However, more recently special forms of projective tests have been developed specifically to study certain motives, such as the need for achievement and the need for affiliation.[17]

To understand the way in which the tests work, consider two stories that might be told by different people about a picture of a man and a boy talking. One person might tell a story about a father and son discussing school grades, plans for college, and what the son should do to have the best possible chance of going to graduate school. Another person could look at the same picture and tell a story about a boy and his dad planning a fishing trip or an afternoon at a baseball game.

To score these tests for a certain motive, a count is made of the number of ideas or themes in the stories that have to do with that motive. For example, in evaluating a person's need for achievement, a count is made of the number of themes involving accomplishment, success in competition with other people, and behavior that satisfies a high standard of excellence. A story involving school and grades and hopes for future admission to graduate school would be scored as showing a high need for achievement. In evaluating a person's need for affiliation, a count is made of the number of themes involving friendship, congeniality, and warm feelings between people. A typical story about two people planning some entertainment would be scored as showing a high need for affiliation.

The measurement of general motives using a projective test is a little like the method of measuring a specific response strength by making the response possible and observing the amount of time that the response is carried out. The stimuli used in a projective test make it possible for a person to express ideas about achievement, or about affiliation, or about something else. The measure taken is the frequency of expressions that relate to a particular kind of motive. The interpretation of these scores depends on the reasonable assumption that people who think a lot about achievement, or affiliation, or whatever tend also to make choices that relate to that motive in real situations.[18]

---

[17] One representative collection of research is by J. W. Atkinson (Ed.), *Motives in Fantasy, Action, and Society*. Princeton: Van Nostrand, 1957.

[18] Of course, this is an assumption of fact, and it can be tested in experiments. Some illustrative experiments involving the achievement motive are described in Chapter 8, along with other matters about the validity of psychological tests.

2E CHOICES WITH NEGATIVELY VALUED OUTCOMES

All the choice situations we have discussed thus far have outcomes that are liked by the person or animal making the choice. Therefore, our discussion is badly incomplete. The theory that we have developed would be satisfactory in a world where choices were offered without cost and nothing unpleasant ever happened. However, in real choice situations we do not get what we choose for nothing, and we are sometimes in situations where even the best available choice has outcomes we would prefer to avoid.

Almost every choice alternative a person considers has some aspects that he likes and other aspects that he dislikes. For example, a person might be deciding whether to buy a certain car. He would like to own the car, but he would dislike having to pay a large amount of money each month. Or a student might be deciding whether to go out and see a film on the night before an examination. The student would like the entertainment of seeing the film but would dislike getting a low grade in the examination.

Assume that a person likes some aspects of an alternative A_i, and the amount of his liking is some quantity $g(A_i)$. Also, the person dislikes some aspects of A_i, and the amount of his dislike is another quantity $b(A_i)$. Finally, assume that the person's response strength for choosing A_i is the difference between these quantities,[19]

$$v(A_i) = g(A_i) - b(A_i). \tag{2.9}$$

A problem arises when Eq. (2.9) is used in connection with the choice theory where response probabilities are calculated from response strengths by

$$P(A_i \mid A_i, \ldots, A_k) = \frac{v(A_i)}{\sum_{A_x \in \mathcal{A}} v(A_x)}$$

because if $b(A_i)$ is greater than $g(A_i)$, then $v(A_i)$ is negative, and we get a negative number when the probability is calculated. Several suggestions have been made for handling this problem, but we do not have enough experimental evidence about choices involving costs to decide on an acceptable theory. In this book we will not try to solve this problem.

---

[19] The idea of treating the net response strength as the difference between positive and negative tendencies is found in most theories of choice. Perhaps the most widely known version is C. L. Hull's theory, given in *Principles of Behavior*, New York: Appleton-Century, 1943. In that theory the positive tendency is called "reaction potential" and the negative tendency is called "inhibition." The idea of analyzing a choice alternative by considering its liked and disliked aspects is due to F. Restle, *Psychology of Judgment and Choice*, cited previously.

Example 2.12. Suppose that a person is choosing a dinner from a menu with two items: steak and chicken. The dinners differ in flavor and cost. Suppose that the person likes steak a lot so that $g(A_1) = 8$, and that he likes chicken less so that $g(A_2) = 4$. However, the person dislikes the higher cost of steak; suppose the difference in cost[20] gives him $b(A_1) = 6$. Calculate the probability of choosing A_1.

We have

$$v(A_1) = g(A_1) - b(A_1) = 8 - 6 = 2$$

and

$$v(A_2) = 4.$$

Therefore,

$$P(A_1 \mid A_1, A_2) = \frac{v(A_1)}{v(A_1) + v(A_2)} = \frac{2}{2 + 4} = .33. \quad \blacksquare$$

The effect of monetary costs on choices is an important problem in economics, and leads to the idea of a demand curve. If a high price is charged for some commodity, people will not buy much of it. However, if a lower price is charged, people will buy more. In a psychological theory, we are interested in the strength of a tendency to choose a certain alternative. But the amount of a commodity that a person buys should be quite a good measure of his response strength for choosing that commodity, given the price that he has to pay for it.

Figure 5 shows some illustrative economic data.[21] The figures show the average family egg consumption per week in 1935–36 in different cities where the price of eggs varied. The data are given separately for different income groups. If we suppose that the response strength for choosing to buy eggs is measured by the amount purchased, then we see that the response strength is greater in situations where the price is lower, as we would expect.

In many experiments hungry animals receive food after they perform some response. In one kind of experiment a rat has to run down an alley to obtain food. The distance the rat has to run may be like a price that he

[20] Note that we do not assign a value $b(A_2)$ and another value $b(A_1)$ based on the separate prices of the two meals. We are applying the idea, mentioned in Section 2A, that the choice will depend on the difference between the alternatives. If the prices of chicken and steak are $3.50 and $5.00, we assume that the person chooses by considering the fact that steak costs $1.50 more. The $3.50 that he would have to spend for chicken might make him decide to leave the restaurant and get his meal somewhere else, but it should not influence his choice between chicken and steak.

[21] These data are taken from G. J. Stigler, *The Theory of Price* (Rev. Ed.) New York: Macmillan, 1952, p. 58. Stigler obtained the data from Bureau of Labor Statistics, *Family Expenditures in Selected Cities*, 1935–36, Bulletin 648, Vol. II, Food (Washington, 1940), Table 5.

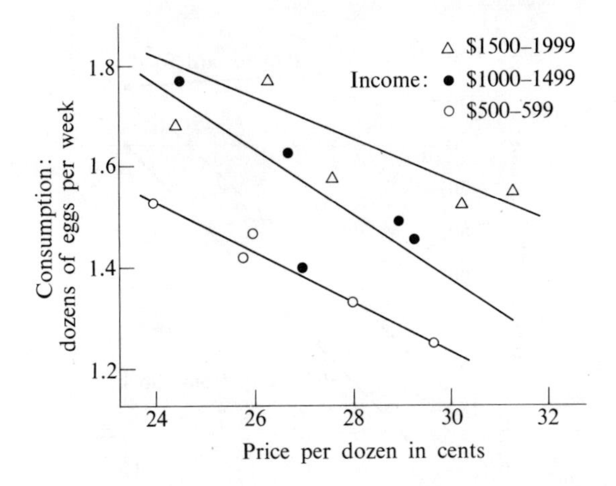

Fig. 5. Relationship between price and amount purchased.

has to pay to obtain the food. In one experiment[22] rats were trained to run in an alley and then were stopped at different distances from the food. This was accomplished by having the rat run in a light harness, and having a block that kept the harness from moving past a certain point above the alley. This arrangment also permitted a measurement of how hard the rat pulled on the harness when he was blocked. The idea is that when the rat still has a short distance to go to the food his response strength will be greater than it will be when he has a long distance to go. Then we expect the rat to pull harder on the harness if he is stopped close to the food than if he is stopped a long distance away. A small difference in the expected direction was obtained. When the animals were stopped 30 cm from the food, the average pull was 56.5 gm. When they were stopped 170 cm away from the food, the average strength of pull was 40.9 gm.

We have spoken of one kind of negative value—the price that is paid for something that is desired. Another kind of negative value is important in psychology. This involves aversive situations that a person or animal would avoid if it were possible. We can think of a person as having a response strength for choosing to avoid a certain situation, or we can think in terms of a negative response strength for choosing that situation. The idea is to represent a person's tendency to stay away from situations that are painful, embarrassing, or boring to him.

In experiments with rats, a common procedure is to set up avoidance tendencies by shocking the animal. In the experiment described above where the strength of approach was measured for food, the same technique was

[22] J. S. Brown, "Gradients of Approach and Avoidance Responses and Their Relation to Level of Motivation." *J. comp. physiol. Psychol.*, 1948, **41**, 450–465.

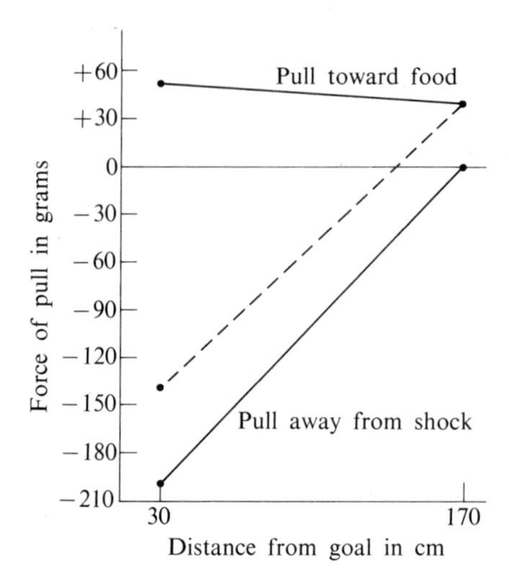

Fig. 6. Relationship between distance from goal and measures of approach and avoidance responses.

used with a different group of rats to measure the strength of avoidance for shock. First, the animals were shocked at one end of an alley. Then they were placed there in the same harness arrangement as was described before, but this time they ran away from shock instead of toward food. When they were stopped 30 cm away from the end of the alley, the average strength of pull on the harness was 198.4 gm. When the situation was set up to prevent the rats from running farther than 170 cm away, most of the rats did not run far enough to be stopped by the block. The four animals (out of 20) that ran to the block pulled with an average strength of only 10.0 gm.

Clearly, the strength of a tendency to go away from an unpleasant situation decreases as the distance from the situation increases. The reason is obvious; if a person or animal is a safe distance away from something that is disliked, then there is no need to go further. But while this is obvious in itself, it has interesting implications when we remember that the strength of an approach response also decreases as the distance from the goal increases.

Many situations in life involve some aspects that are pleasant and others that are unpleasant. In other words, our reactions to many situations involve both positive and negative feelings. Choices that involve these situations involve a kind of conflict.

Suppose that a rat has been both fed and shocked at one end of an alley. Then when he is hungry he has a tendency to go to that place because he has been fed there, but he also has a tendency to stay away from it because it has been painful. In Fig. 6 this is illustrated with the data from the experiment where response strengths were measured with the harness. (Recall, however, that these measurements were taken using different animals.) The strength of the pull toward food is shown as a positive response strength, and the strength of the pull away from the shock is shown as a negative response strength. In the figure, the points where the measurements were taken are connected by straight lines to make the ideas easier to understand.

We might suppose that if a rat had been both fed and shocked in the same place, his response strength would be the sum of the negative and positive response strengths associated with the two experiences. This would be like the dashed line in Fig. 6. Note that beyond a certain point the response strength is positive; however, near the goal the response strength is negative. The behavior that is sometimes observed is a vacillation between approaching the goal and going away from it. As the animal approaches the goal, his fear of the shock increases and the negative response strength dominates. He goes away from the goal, but then the fear is reduced and the positive response strength for food dominates. The result can be that the animal is caught between these two tendencies. His hunger can keep him from getting far enough away from the goal to be comfortable, but the fear of shock keeps him from getting close enough to the goal to satisfy his hunger.

Situations like this are not restricted to animal experiments. Consider a person who has an invitation to dinner where he expects a good meal but a dull group of people. Because of his attraction to good food and his desire to be polite he will have a tendency to accept the invitation, but because of his wish to avoid being bored he will have a tendency to decline. Sometimes a person will just postpone making such a decision, hoping that something will happen so that it will be impossible for him to go.

Quite a few conflict situations are more serious. Consider a student who wants to earn a college degree but who does not like to study. The situation can develop so that his dislike of studying keeps him from working effectively, but his desire for a degree keeps him from leaving school and doing something he would really like to do. This kind of conflict can arise in a man's job where he may find his work unpleasant but he stays in the job to earn money, or in an unhappy family situation where one of the persons is afraid or resentful of the other person, but is also attracted to or dependent upon the person.

Logically, there are two ways to resolve the kind of conflict that is pictured in Fig. 6. One is to reduce the negative response strength associated with the goal so the person can approach the situation and obtain the desired goal. This is especially reasonable when the negative tendency is due to unwarranted fear or anxiety. For example, a student may be afraid to study hard because he would damage his pride more by failing than by not trying. Or a person may be afraid of approaching other people in a close personal way because of a fear of being rejected. One goal of psychological counseling and psychotherapy is to reduce the strength of anxieties which prevent a person from engaging in useful and enjoyable activities. Through a variety of methods, the therapist or counselor tries to change the picture given in Fig. 6 by raising the lower line so that the negative response strength does not cancel the positive response strength. The methods include helping the person to understand his own feelings, encouraging a friendly relationship, and setting the occasion for conditioning to change the person's emotional reactions to feared situations.

The other way to resolve this kind of conflict is to reduce the relative importance of the positive response strength so that the person can leave the situation. This might involve a student who is unhappy in his present course of study and finds another field he enjoys, or it might involve a man who dislikes his present job and finds a different line of work that satisfies him. In cases like this, the person is fortunate enough to find an alternative choice that provides satisfaction without the accompanying displeasure.

This section has taken up choice alternatives with negatively valued aspects. If an alternative has aspects which are unpleasant to a person or animal, his response strength for choosing that alternative will be lower than it would be without those aspects. And in some cases the presence of positively and negatively valued aspects produces conflict that can prevent effective action.

2F CHOICES WITH UNCERTAIN OUTCOMES

We have discussed situations where a set of alternatives is offered to a person or animal and one of the alternatives is chosen. In the real choice situations we have dealt with, the person or animal receives whichever alternative he selects. However, choice situations often involve a complicating factor. Sometimes we make a choice because of what we expect to happen later, rather than what is available at the moment. And when we cannot know with certainty what is going to happen, our expectations are important factors influencing our choices and decisions.

For example, consider the choice of whether to carry an umbrella on a cloudy morning. Suppose that a person strongly dislikes getting wet so that he would never choose to be in the rain without an umbrella. In other words, if it were raining outside, he would choose to take an umbrella with probability one. However, it is not raining, and the person cannot know with certainty whether it will rain later when he has to be outside. If it does rain, this person will be in a situation where he would choose to have an umbrella. If it does not rain, then the person would choose not to have the inconvenience of carrying an umbrella.

The alternatives for the person are taking the umbrella or leaving it at home. But the choice is not based simply on the person's preference for taking or leaving the umbrella; the choice also depends on the person's expectations and feelings about what will happen to him later after he decides whether to take the umbrella.

We suppose that when a person makes a choice with uncertain outcomes he is influenced by the amount that he likes or dislikes different outcomes, and by his expectations about how likely the different outcomes are. Let $u(O_j)$ be the amount of the person's liking for outcome O_j, and let $s(O_j \mid A_i)$ be the person's expectation that outcome O_j will occur if he chooses alternative A_i. Think of $u(O_j)$ as a response strength for choosing outcome O_j; in fact, if O_j were offered as a choice alternative which was certain to occur, the response strength for choosing it would equal $u(O_j)$. A positive value of $u(O_j)$ indicates a liking for outcome O_j; a negative value indicates that O_j is disliked by the person. If the person is completely indifferent about O_j, then the value of $u(O_j)$ is zero.

The expectation $s(O_j \mid A_i)$ can be considered as a kind of probability; in fact the term "subjective probability" is used in the economic theory of decisions. If the person is almost sure that outcome O_j will not occur if he chooses alternative A_i, then $s(O_j \mid A_i)$ will be close to zero. If the person is almost sure that outcome O_j will occur if he chooses A_i, then $s(O_j \mid A_i)$ will be close to one.

Now return to the example about the umbrella. The possible outcomes of the choice are

O_1: getting wet;

O_2: having to carry the umbrella.

Suppose that the person has a small dislike of having to carry an umbrella, but a great dislike of getting wet. For an illustration,

$$u(O_1) = -12;$$
$$u(O_2) = -1.$$

The choice alternatives are

A_1: take the umbrella;

A_2: leave the umbrella at home.

Suppose that the person thinks there is a 40% chance of rain. Then if he leaves the umbrella home, he has a 40% chance of getting wet; that is,

$$s(O_1 \mid A_2) = 0.40.$$

However, if he takes the umbrella, he will not get wet; that is,

$$s(O_1 \mid A_1) = 0.0.$$

If he takes the umbrella, he has to carry it during the day whether it rains or not.

$$s(O_2 \mid A_1) = 1.0; \qquad s(O_2 \mid A_2) = 0.0.$$

Now we assume that these quantities combine in a certain way to produce response strengths for choosing the alternatives. The rule of combination is that the like or dislike of each outcome is multiplied by the expectation of that outcome and the products are added. For the present case,

$$\begin{aligned} v(A_1) &= u(O_1)s(O_1 \mid A_1) + u(O_2)s(O_2 \mid A_1) \\ &= (-12)(0.0) + (-1)(1.0) = -1.0. \end{aligned}$$

$$\begin{aligned} v(A_2) &= u(O_1)s(O_1 \mid A_2) + u(O_2)s(O_2 \mid A_2) \\ &= (-12)(0.40) + (-1)(0.0) = -3.0. \end{aligned}$$

As we have formulated the situation, the person has negative response strengths—he would prefer to avoid both alternatives. However, it is likely that the only way to avoid leaving the umbrella home is to take it, and vice versa. Then this person might have a probability of about .75 of choosing alternative A_1—that is, of taking the umbrella.

In general, suppose that in considering a choice, a person is influenced by n different possible outcomes. Then the response strength for choosing alternative A_i is

$$v(A_i) = \sum_{j=1}^{n} u(O_j)s(O_j \mid A_i). \tag{2.10}$$

Example 2.13. How low would the person's expectation for rain have to be to make his dislike of alternative A_2 equal his dislike of alternative A_1?

The response strength $v(A_1)$ is unaffected by the expectation for rain. Thus, we want

$$v(A_2) = -1.0 = (-12)s(O_1 \mid A_2) + (-1)(0.0).$$

$$s(O_1 \mid A_2) = -1.0/-12.0 = 0.067.$$

Presumably, then, on a day when the chance of rain was between 6% and 7%, the probability of the person's carrying his umbrella would be about .50. ▮

We have been discussing situations where a number of outcomes are possible following a choice, and a person's expectations regarding the outcomes influence response strengths. In many situations, a person's expectations about outcomes of choices are based on his experience. For example, a child might learn that if he chooses to walk on the living room carpet wearing muddy shoes, he should expect his mother to be angry with him. He would develop this expectation because in most cases when he tracked mud onto the carpet, his mother became angry. Generally, we have the strongest expectation for the outcome that we have experienced most often.

The development of expectations is studied in experiments in which subjects are asked to predict which of two lights will flash on each trial in a series. The prediction is made by pressing a lever, and one of the lights is flashed. The experimenter flashes the lights in a random sequence, with some constant probability of each light. Subjects in this experiment probably try to discover some pattern in the sequence of lights; this means that they probably have higher expectations for the right-hand light on some trials than others. However, on the average, the expectation for a light should be equal to the probability that the experimenter flashes that light. The choice alternatives are:

A_1: predict right-hand light,
A_2: predict left-hand light.

The outcomes for the subject are:

O_1: prediction is correct,
O_2: prediction is wrong.

There is a fixed probability π that the right-hand light will go on, regardless of the subject's response. Therefore, over a series of trials, the subjects probably learn to expect[23]

$$s(O_1 \mid A_1) = \pi, \qquad s(O_2 \mid A_1) = 1 - \pi,$$
$$s(O_1 \mid A_2) = 1 - \pi, \qquad s(O_2 \mid A_2) = \pi.$$

If this is true, then

$$v(A_1) = \pi u(O_1) + (1 - \pi)u(O_2),$$
$$v(A_2) = (1 - \pi)u(O_1) + \pi u(O_2).$$

The probability of choosing to predict the right-hand light will be

$$P(A_1 \mid A_1, A_2) = \frac{v(A_1)}{v(A_1) + v(A_2)} = \frac{\pi u(O_1) + (1 - \pi)u(O_2)}{u(O_1) + u(O_2)}. \tag{2.11}$$

We expect $u(O_1)$ to be a positive number, and $u(O_2)$, the feeling about being wrong, to be either negative or zero. The value of $P(A_1 \mid A_1, A_2)$ will

[23] The assumption that subjects' expectations equal the true probabilities is rather arbitrary. However, special techniques are needed in order to find out about expectations and subjective values separately. One technique for doing this is described in Section 2G.

equal π if $u(O_2)$ is zero; and $P(A_1 \mid A_1, A_2)$ will be between π and 1.0 if π is greater than one-half and $u(O_2)$ is negative.[24] When experiments are run with subjects instructed to be correct as often as they can, the most frequent result is that $P(A_1 \mid A_1, A_2)$ is quite close to π. This indicates that in these experiments the subjects are not very unhappy when they make wrong predictions; that is, $u(O_2) \approx 0$. However, in other experiments subjects are given points or money for correct predictions and may have penalties when they are wrong. In these latter experiments when $\pi > \frac{1}{2}$, $P(A_1 \mid A_1, A_2)$ is usually greater than π, which is consistent with the idea that $u(O_2)$ should become negative when there is a specified payoff for correct responses.[25]

Example 2.14. In one experiment[26] with $\pi = .60$, some subjects were just told to be correct as often as they could, others were given one cent for each correct prediction and penalized one cent for each error, and a third group was given ten cents for each correct prediction and penalized ten cents for each wrong prediction. The proportions of A_1 choices for the three groups were .62, .65, and .71. Calculate the ratios of the utilities $u(O_1)/-u(O_2)$, using Eq. (2.11).

We use .60 for π in Eq. (2.11) and substitute the obtained values for $P(A_1 \mid A_1, A_2)$. First, for the condition with instructions only,

$$.62 = \frac{.60u(O_1) + .40u(O_2)}{u(O_1) + u(O_2)};$$

$$.62u(O_1) + .62u(O_2) = .60u(O_1) + .40u(O_2);$$

$$.02u(O_1) = -.22u(O_2);$$

$$\frac{u(O_1)}{-u(O_2)} = 11.$$

[24] However, if $u(O_2)$ is a very large negative number, the formula will not give a positive probability. The restriction that must be satisfied for $P(A_1 \mid A_1, A_2)$ to be a probability is

$$u(O_2) \geq -\frac{(1-\pi)}{\pi} u(O_1).$$

The student can easily show that $P(A_1 \mid A_1, A_2) = 1.0$ when this minimum value is substituted into Eq. (2.11).

[25] Results from 16 experiments without specific payoffs, and from seven experiments using payoffs are given in R. D. Luce and P. Suppes, "Preference, Utility, and Subjective Probability," in R. D. Luce, R. R. Bush, and E. Galanter, (Eds.), *Handbook of Mathematical Psychology, Vol. III.* New York: Wiley, 1965. Pp. 249–410. The results that are referred to here are given on pp. 390–396.

[26] Results are from J. L. Myers, J. G. Fort, L. Katz, and M. M. Suydam, "Differential Monetary Gains and Losses and Event Probability in a Two-Choice Situation." *J. Exp. Psychol.*, 1963, **66**, 521–522.

In words, the positive value of being correct seems to have been about eleven times as great as the negative value of being wrong. Similar calculations for the other two cases give

$$\frac{u(O_1)}{-u(O_2)} = 5$$

for the group with one-cent rewards and penalties, and

$$\frac{u(O_1)}{-u(O_2)} = 2.8,$$

for the group with ten-cent rewards and penalties. ▮

When a person's choice could lead to several different outcomes and the person cannot tell which will occur, the response strength for that choice will be influenced by the person's expectations about how likely the various outcomes are, as well as his values for the outcomes. Equation (2.10) is one idea about how expectations and values combine to produce the response strength of choosing an alternative. We have applied Eq. (2.10) to some hypothetical situations and also to the results of some prediction experiments.

2G MEASURING VALUES AND EXPECTATIONS FOR UNCERTAIN OUTCOMES

Much of the discussion of this chapter has involved the problem of measuring how much a person likes or dislikes an alternative. In this final section we will consider the problem of measurement again, with our attention on choices that have uncertain outcomes. We have considered two factors which influence these choices: expectations and values. First, we will consider an experiment in which expectations were assumed to equal the true probabilities of events, and values were measured. Then we will consider an experiment in which both values and expectations were measured.

In the first of these experiments[27] the subjects decided whether or not to play on each of a series of bets. Each subject was given one dollar at the beginning of each session and a session included about 100 trials. Each trial of the experiment was a hand of dice poker, with the dice contained in a wire cage. On each play, the experimenter offered an amount of money, and specified a hand that the subject would have to beat in order to win. If the subject decided to play and then beat the hand, he received the money that was offered. If he decided to play and then failed to beat the hand, he had to give the experimenter five cents. Seven different hands were used, ranging

[27] The experiment is by F. Mosteller and P. Nogee, "An Experimental Measurement of Utility." *J. Pol. Econ.*, 1951, **59**, 371–404.

from 44321 where the subject had a 2/3 chance of winning to 44441, where the subject had only a 1/101 chance of winning.

For each trial, let A_1 be the alternative of playing and A_2 be the alternative of not playing. Let x be the amount of money offered by the experimenter on that trial; let O_1 be the event of winning and O_2 be the event of losing, if the subject plays. If O_1 occurs, the subject wins the amount of money x. If O_2 occurs, the subject loses five cents. Then using Eq. (2.10), the response strength for playing should be

$$v(A_1) = u(+x)s(O_1) + u(-5¢)s(O_2).$$

The response strength for not playing should be

$$v(A_2) = u(0¢),$$

the subject's value or liking for holding the money he has, rather than increasing it or decreasing it.

In this experiment, quite a bit of attention was given to instructing the subjects and giving them experience about the odds for winning against the different hands. In later experiments it has been found that instructions do not guarantee that the expectations and the probabilities will agree; however, it was assumed that they would. Therefore, instead of $s(O_1)$ and $s(O_2)$, we have p and $1 - p$, where p is the true probability of winning against the hand that the experimenter specified. Then we have

$$v(A_1) = u(+x)p + u(-5¢)(1 - p).$$

The value of $u(0¢)$ was arbitrarily set at 0 and the value of $u(-5¢)$ was arbitrarily set at -1. These values provide scale units and a zero point that are convenient. Then

$$v(A_1) = u(+x)p - (1 - p), \qquad v(A_2) = 0.$$

During the experiment, several different values of x were used for each value of p (that is, for each of the seven hands that were specified). The idea was to find a value of x where the subject would choose to play the bet on one-half of the trials. Suppose that the desired value of x is found. Then since $P(A_1 \mid A_1, A_2) = .50$, we know that $v(A_1) = v(A_2)$ for that particular value of x. But we have also set $v(A_2)$ equal to zero. Therefore,

$$v(A_1) = 0.0 = u(+x)p - (1 - p);$$

$$1 - p = u(+x)p;$$

$$u(+x) = (1 - p)/p. \tag{2.12}$$

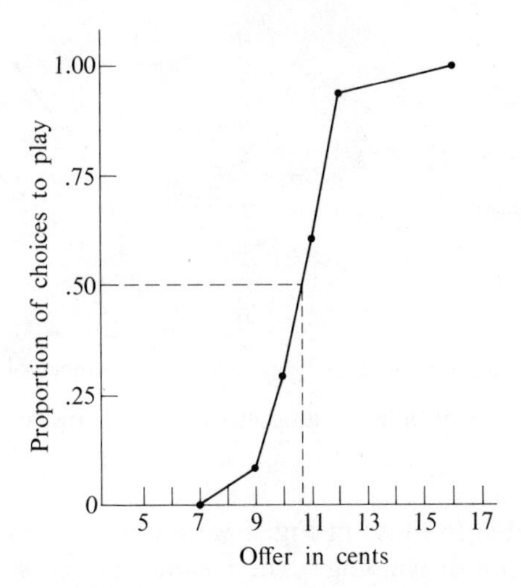

Fig. 7. An illustration of proportions of plays for various amounts offered when the probability of winning was .33.

What we have is a way to measure the psychological value of an amount of money. When we find that a certain number of cents produces

$$P(A_1 \mid A_1, A_2) = .50,$$

we know that the psychological value of that number of cents is equal to $(1 - p)/p$ (assuming that the subject's expectation of winning equals p).

The method of finding the desired value of x is like the method used to measure a threshold in a psychophysical experiment. Remember in measuring a threshold that different stimuli are presented, involving several amounts of difference between the standard and comparison stimuli. In the present experiment, several different amounts of money were offered, and all were compared with the standard bet of 5¢ with a fixed chance of winning. If the amount offered was very small, the subject would never accept the bet. If the amount offered was very large, then the subject would always accept the bet. By offering several different amounts, the experimenter found an amount where the subject chose to accept the bet on one-half of the trials. In Fig. 7 there is a graph of one subject's choice frequencies for several different amounts of money, when the hand he had to beat was 55221. The probability of beating this hand is .33. The value of x that produced $P(A_1 \mid A_1, A_2) = .50$ was evidently about 10.6¢.

Example 2.15. From the data graphed in Fig. 7, calculate the subject's subjective value of winning 10.6¢.

Using equation (2.12), with $p = .33$,

$$u(+10.6¢) = .67/.33 = 2.0. \blacksquare$$

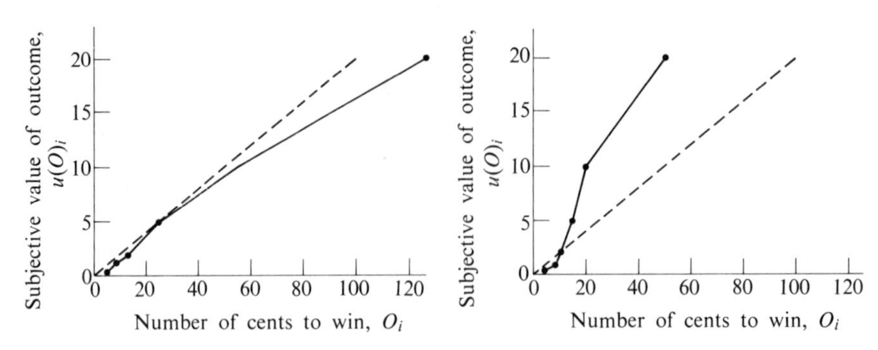

Fig. 8. Subjective values of different amounts of money, measured for two groups of subjects.

Data comparable to those in Fig. 7 were obtained for each subject for all seven probabilities of winning. The results can be used to give a table or graph showing the psychological value of different amounts of money for each subject. The subjects included 10 students and five members of the Massachusetts National Guard. The left-hand panel of Fig. 8 shows the average amount of money for each probability of winning that produced $P(A_1) = .50$ for the students. The right-hand panel shows the same data for the Guardsmen. In each panel, the dashed line shows the amounts that would apply if the subjects had a value of winning five cents to exactly balance the negative value of losing five cents, and had a value of winning ten cents that was exactly twice their value of winning five cents, and so on. The two groups of subjects reacted quite differently to the low-probability bets. With probabilities of .05 and .01, the students required offers above those that would make "fair" bets, while the Guardsmen were willing to bet for much smaller offers with small chances of winning. Note that this is interpreted as a relatively higher utility of moderate amounts of money on the part of the Guardsmen. This can be seen by comparing the inferred utilities for the two groups for amounts of money in the range 20¢–50¢.

It is important to keep in mind that the unit of the utility scale is arbitrary. For these data the unit was chosen to be equal to the difference in value to the subject between staying even and losing five cents. Using these units, it appears that amounts of money won between 20¢ and 50¢ were two or three times as valuable to the Guardsmen as to the students. However, there are other equally valid interpretations. Another possibility is that losing a nickel was only between one-half and one-third as important to the Guardsmen as it was to the students. (See Problem 20.)

There is a second problem in interpreting these results. An assumption of the analysis is that the expectations $s(O_1)$ and $s(O_2)$ were equal to the true probabilities of winning and losing, p and $1 - p$. However, that need not have been the case. The two groups might have had quite different feelings about how likely they were to win for a given stated probability. For example, the students might have felt that a .10 or a .05 probability of winning represented quite a slim chance, whereas the Guardsmen's attitude might have been that a .10 or a .05 probability gave them a fairly reasonable chance of winning. In other words, the Guardsmen's greater willingness to bet a nickel against moderate sums of money at low odds might be the result of their having higher expectations, rather than higher values. (See Problem 21.)

The results of the experiment just discussed show that there was some difference between a group of students and a group of National Guardsmen in the way that they made bets involving small amounts of money. However, we have to conclude that we cannot determine just what kind of difference was involved. Unfortunately there are no further experimental data to help us decide which of the possible kinds of difference really existed. However, there has been some further work on the technical problem of separating the factors of value and expectation.

The main innovation in the next experiment[28] involves the use of a random event O^* for which we know the subjects have expectation $s(O^*) = .50$. We know that when a coin is tossed, the probability of a head is very close to .50, or that when a die is tossed, the probability of an odd number of spots is very close to .50. However, we do not always act that way.

Suppose that you are offered a choice between the following bets involving the toss of a coin. You can bet on heads, and if you take that bet and win you will receive five cents and if you lose you will have to pay five cents. Or you can bet on tails, and if you take that bet and win you will receive six cents but if you lose you will have to pay five cents. This can be summarized in a table,

	Heads	Tails
Win	5¢	6¢
Lose	−5¢	−5¢

Clearly, if a person knew that heads and tails were equally likely, he would always choose to bet on tails. However, people do not always choose to bet on tails in this kind of situation. We conclude that people do not have equal expectations for heads and tails. The same thing seems to be true for dice; the behavior indicating unequal expectations also occurs when the choices are between betting on an odd number of spots or an even number of spots when a die is tossed.

[28] D. Davidson, P. Suppes, and S. Siegel. *Decision Making: an Experimental Approach.* Stanford: Stanford University Press, 1957, Chapter II.

The experimenters needed an event that had expectation $s(O^*) = .50$, and they found one. A special die was made with nonsense syllables printed on the faces. One die had ZEJ on three faces and ZOJ on the other three. Two other dice were made with QUG and QUJ, and WUH and XEQ. Then a number of tests were run, in which the subjects tested chose between bets like

	ZOJ	ZEJ
Win	5¢	6¢
Lose	−5¢	−5¢

and

	QUJ	QUG
Win	17¢	17¢
Lose	−9¢	−10¢

Each subject made about 12 choices of this kind, with different amounts of money and with other bets (not having an obvious best choice) also presented. Of 19 subjects tested, all of them made appropriate choices on all trials, with the exception of a few trials at the beginning that probably were due to confusion about the task or the situation.

The experimenters capitalized on the event with .50 expectation in the following way. Suppose that we have amounts of money v, w, x, and y, and offer two bets

	O^*	$\overline{O^*}$
Win	v	x
Lose	w	y

where O^* and $\overline{O^*}$ are both events with expectations of one-half. Further, suppose that a subject finds the two bets equally attractive. (This might mean that he would choose them equally often. Or, as in the case of the present experiment, the smallest possible change in one of the values caused the subject to switch his preference.) The alternatives are to bet on O^* or to bet on $\overline{O^*}$. Call these A_1 and A_2. If the response strengths of A_1 and A_2 are equal, then

$$\tfrac{1}{2}u(v) + \tfrac{1}{2}u(w) = \tfrac{1}{2}u(x) + \tfrac{1}{2}u(y),$$

which means that

$$u(v) - u(y) = u(x) - u(w).$$

The important fact is that the differences are equal. This means that we can use the betting situation to find amounts of money that are equally different in value to the subject. This method solves one of the problems raised in connection with the preceding experiment. The subjective values are being measured without the necessity of assuming that the subject's expectations are equal to the true probabilities of winning. However, the problem of arbitrary units is not solved by this method.

In the experiment, two amounts of money were selected as fixed points, and four more amounts were located on a scale of subjective value. The amounts used to begin were +6¢ and −4¢. These were used in choices between bets of the form

	O^*	$\overline{O^*}$
Win	+6¢	−4¢
Lose	a	−4¢

Different amounts of money were used for *a* until the subject showed that he was indifferent between the two bets.[29]

The subject's value of *a* is lower than his value for −4¢ by the same amount that his value for +6¢ is greater than his value for −4¢. That is,

$$u(+6¢) - u(-4¢) = u(-4¢) - u(a).$$

The amounts determined for different subjects ranged between −6¢ and −15¢.

After a value of *a* was determined, this was used along with +6¢ and −4¢ in a new choice between bets.

	O^*	$\overline{O^*}$
Win	+6¢	b
Lose	−4¢	a

Different values were used for *b* until one was found that made the subject indifferent between the bets. Then

$$u(+6¢) - u(a) = u(b) - u(-4¢).$$

We determined *a* so that it was as far below −4¢ in value as −4¢ was below +6¢. Now we have a new amount *b* that is just that far above +6¢ in subjective value. In other words, we can think of +6¢, −4¢, *a* and *b*, as being on a line

•	•	•	•
a	−4¢	+6¢	b

where the distances between the points are all equal.

[29] Actually, two amounts were found that differed by just one cent, where the subject chose O^* with the higher amount, and chose $\overline{O^*}$ with the lower amount. For this discussion, we will ignore this important technical matter and assume that an amount *a* was actually found. The amounts that we will present are midway between the bounds that were determined in the experiment.

The next choice of bets used both a and b.

	O^*	$\overline{O^*}$
Win	b	$+6¢$
Lose	c	a

Different values of c were tried until the subject was indifferent between the bets. This means that a value of c was determined so that

$$u(b) - u(a) = u(+6¢) - u(c).$$

Therefore, we have another amount of money located on our scale of equal spacing:

•	•	•	•	•
c	a	$-4¢$	$+6¢$	b

The final choice of bets used the value determined for c.

	O^*	$\overline{O^*}$
Win	d	$+6¢$
Lose	c	$-4¢$

with d determined as before. Then

$$u(d) - u(-4¢) = u(+6¢) - u(c).$$

Therefore, d is as far to the right of $-4¢$ as c is to the left of $+6¢$, and we have the scale

•	•	•	•	•	•
c	a	$-4¢$	$+6¢$	b	d

The experimental procedure described here was carried out using 19 student subjects. Each subject was tested for about two hours. He was given two dollars to bet with during the session. For 15 of the subjects, amounts of money were found corresponding to the positions c, a, b, and d on the scale drawn above. We know that the amounts of money determined for each subject are equally spaced on his scale of subjective value. We are then able to assign numbers corresponding to the subjective values of these amounts of money. The amount of money corresponding to zero value is arbitrary, and the size of the unit also is arbitrary. For this situation, it is convenient to assign the values

$$u(+6¢) = +1, \qquad u(-4¢) = -1.$$

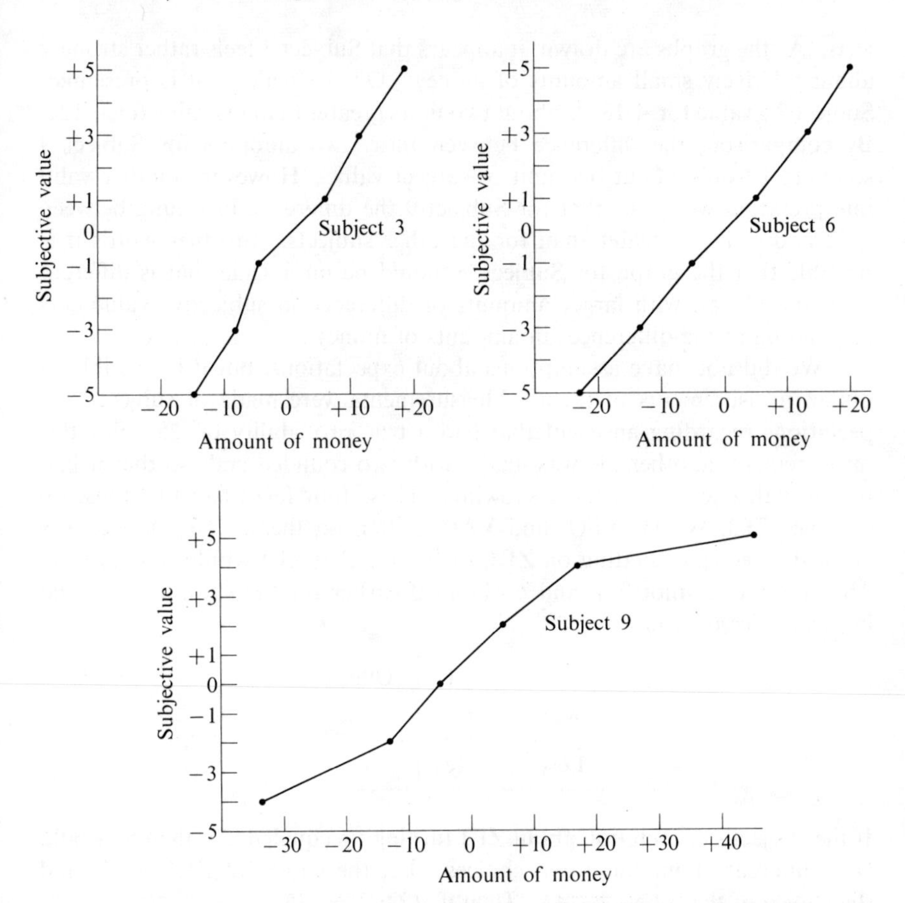

Fig. 9. Subjective values of different amounts of money, measured for three individual subjects.

This means that the distance between two points on our scale is two units of subjective value. Therefore,

$$u(b) = 3, \quad u(d) = 5, \quad u(a) = -3, \quad u(c) = -5.$$

Figure 9 shows the subjective values of the amounts of money obtained for three of the subjects in the experiment. The subjects were selected mainly to show the variability in the reactions of the subjects. For Subject 3, the points of equal spacing in subjective value involved relatively small differences in amounts of money; for Subject 9, the intervals involved relatively large differences in amounts of money.

In interpreting the results, keep in mind that the unit of measurement is arbitrary, and it may not be appropriate to use the same unit for all subjects. As the graphs are drawn, it appears that Subject 3 feels rather strongly about relatively small amounts of money. On the scale as it is presented, Subject 3's value for +18¢ is about two units greater than his value for +12¢. By comparison, the difference between these two amounts for Subject 9 seems to be only about one unit of subject value. However, another valid interpretation would be that for Subject 9 the difference in feeling between +6¢ and −4¢ is greater than for the other subjects. In other words it is possible that the graph for Subject 9 should be on a scale that is different from the others, with larger amounts of difference in subjective value corresponding to the differences in amounts of money.

We did not make assumptions about expectations, but it is possible to obtain measurements of them. Measurements were made of subjects' expectations regarding an event that had a true probability of .25. For this measurement, another die was made, with two rounded ends so that it had to fall with one of four faces showing. These four faces had the nonsense syllables ZEJ, WUH, XEQ, and VAF written on them. The subject was given the choice of betting on ZEJ, or betting that ZEJ would not turn up. The amounts of money a and b obtained earlier for the subject were used in this choice of bets.

	ZEJ	Others
Win	b	+6¢
Lose	−4¢	a

If the subject's expectation about ZEJ turning up equaled .25, then he would be indifferent about these two choices. Let the choice of ZEJ be A_1 and the choice of the others be A_2. Then if $s(\text{ZEJ}) = .25$,

$$v(A_1) = .25u(b) + .75u(-4¢),$$
$$v(A_2) = .75u(+6¢) + .25u(a).$$

But using the scale values we decided on earlier,

$$v(A_1) = (.25)(3) + (.75)(-1) = 0.0,$$
$$v(A_2) = (.75)(1) + (.25)(-3) = 0.0.$$

(Any other permissible scale values for the subjective values would also give the result that $v(A_1) = v(A_2)$, although we could choose a set of scale values for which these would not be zero.)

Many of the subjects were not indifferent between these two choices, and since the subjective values were based on measurements, we conclude that the expectations of the subjects for ZEJ did not equal .25. To find what it did equal, the experimenters substituted different values in place of the amount $-4¢$ until they found a combination for which the subject was indifferent. Let e stand for the amount of money that was determined in this way, and let O_1 be the occurrence of ZEJ.

$$v(A_1) = s(O_1)u(b) + \big(1 - s(O_1)\big)u(e),$$
$$v(A_2) = \big(1 - s(O_1)\big)u(+6¢) + s(O_1)u(a).$$

The values of $u(b)$, $u(+6¢)$, and $u(a)$ were known from the previous data. A value for $u(e)$ was obtained by looking at the graph drawn for the subject in the manner of Fig. 9 here, and reading off the subjective value corresponding to the amount determined in the experiment. Then we have

$$s(O_1)(3) + \big(1 - s(O_1)\big)u(e) = \big(1 - s(O_1)\big)(+1) + s(O_1)(-3),$$
$$s(O_1) = \frac{1 - u(e)}{7 - u(e)},$$

whatever $u(e)$ turned out to be. For the three subjects whose subjective values are shown in Fig. 9, the values of $u(e)$ turned out to be about -1.0, -0.27, and -0.74; the values that we infer for their expectations about ZEJ are .25, .18, and .22.

SUMMARY

In this chapter, we have developed a theory of choice behavior and used the theory to analyze several situations. The basic concept in the theory is the idea of response strengths that determine probabilities of choosing among available alternatives. In Section 2A we analyzed some simple cases where all the alternatives have positive value. Sections 2E and 2F extended the ideas to cases where some aspects of an alternative have negative value, and then to situations where a person cannot be certain which of several outcomes will follow his choice of an alternative.

An important problem in the theory of choice is the measurement of a person's values or response strengths for choosing various alternatives. We have studied measurement of response strengths that animals have for various alternatives in experiments where the same choice situation can be presented many times or can be made available continuously. In measuring human values and response strengths, we considered some of the difficulties in using a person's stated values to find out about his response strengths. We also described two kinds of test that can be used to measure a person's general motivational tendencies. Finally, we discussed two experiments where choice situations involving uncertain outcomes have been used to measure persons' values for various amounts of money.

PROBLEMS

1. Continue Example 2.1. In set notation, what would be the set for a situation where the alternatives were fried shrimp, hamburger, and pork chops? Where the alternatives were steak, lobster, chicken, and hamburger?

2. Use the assumptions of Example 2.2. Find a set including fried shrimp and two other alternatives where fried shrimp would be chosen most often. Find three sets each containing chicken and two other alternatives where chicken would be chosen least often. Find two sets, each containing squab and two other alternatives, so that in one set squab would be chosen most often, and in the other set squab would be chosen least often.

* **3.** Use the assumptions of Example 2.2 and Eq. (2.1). How often should we expect the person to choose steak, when his alternatives are steak, lobster, fried shrimp, and hamburger? How often would he choose hamburger from those alternatives?

4. Using the assumptions of Example 2.2 and Eq. (2.1), find sets of alternatives satisfying each of the following:

* a) $P(A_4 \mid A_4, \ldots) = .50$.
b) $P(A_4 \mid A_4, \ldots) = 1/3$.
c) $P(A_1 \mid A_1, \ldots) = \frac{1}{2}$.
d) $P(A_6 \mid A_6, \ldots) = .10$.

5. Suppose that a person has the following choice probabilities for entertainment: Stage play, .15; Opera, .15; Ballet, .20; Film, .15; Basketball game, .10; Concert, .20; Television, .05.

(a) Find a set of response strengths that are consistent with the choice probabilities.
(b) Calculate this person's choice probabilities for a different situation where his only choices are film, basketball game, and television.

6. On one trip that a businessman takes frequently, he can fly or take a train. He flies .70 of the time. On another trip involving the same distance, his alternatives are a train or a bus. He takes the train .80 of the time. Calculate the choice probabilities for a third situation where the alternatives are flying, taking a train, and taking a bus.

7. Suppose that for a certain student the response strength for choosing mathematics is twice that for physics, the response strength for physics is three times that for astronomy, and the response strength for astronomy is one-half as great as that for chemistry. If he has to choose a course from one of the four fields to fulfill a requirement, what will the choice probabilities be?

8. Show that Eq. (2.1) implies the following theorem, called the Product Rule. For any three alternatives A_1, A_2, and A_3,

$$\frac{P(A_1 \mid A_1, A_3)}{P(A_3 \mid A_1, A_3)} = \frac{P(A_1 \mid A_1, A_2)}{P(A_2 \mid A_1, A_2)} \times \frac{P(A_2 \mid A_2, A_3)}{P(A_3 \mid A_2, A_3)}.$$

9. A man chooses to fly rather than drive with probability .60. He chooses to drive rather than ride a bus with probability .70. Calculate the probability that he will fly rather than ride a bus.

▸ **10.** Suppose that four beverages are rated by a person by the method of magnitude estimation. Call the beverages A_1, A_2, A_3, and A_4, and suppose that the numbers given as judgments of preference are 10, 5, 20, and 30, respectively. Now suppose that you have additional information. When the person chooses from the alternatives $\mathcal{A} = \{A_1, A_2\}$, the probability of choosing alternative A_1 is

$$P(A_1 \mid A_1, A_2) = .80.$$

Assume that the judgments are made according to Eq. (2.1). What is $P(A_3)$ for each of the following sets of alternatives? (a) $\mathcal{A} = \{A_1, A_3\}$; (b) $\mathcal{A} = \{A_2, A_3\}$; (c) $\mathcal{A} = \{A_1, A_2\}$; (d) $\mathcal{A} = \{A_3, A_4\}$.

* **11.** For the experiment with sucrose, wheat powder, and casein, calculate the theoretical probability of choosing wheat powder rather than casein for the first three tests. For those tests, the probabilities of choosing wheat powder rather than sucrose were .46, .44, and .39. The probabilities of choosing casein rather than sucrose were .22, .12, and .06.

12. Consider the hypothesis that in a continuous preference test, amounts of substances taken are proportional to the response strengths for choosing those substances. Denote plain water as A_1, 0.1% salt as A_2, and 0.9% salt as A_3. Recall that when $\mathcal{A} = \{A_1, A_2\}$, the rats took 18 cc per day of salt water and 11 cc per day of plain water; when $\mathcal{A} = \{A_1, A_3\}$, the rats took 34 cc per day of salt water and 9 cc per day of plain water. If the ratios of response strengths equal the ratios of substance taken, calculate the probabilities of choice for $\mathcal{A} = \{A_1, A_2\}$ and for $\mathcal{A} = \{A_2, A_3\}$.

* **13.** Continue Example 2.9 by calculating theoretical choice probabilities when $\mathcal{A} = \{A_1, A_2\}$ for the first experiment, and for the first test of the second experiment, using the data in Table 1.

14. Use the results given in Example 2.10 and calculate the choice probabilities for test situations where $\mathcal{A} = \{A_1, A_3, M\}$ and where $\mathcal{A} = \{A_2, A_3, M\}$.

15. In addition to the three objects mentioned in Section 2C, Chicko was also tested with a fourth plaything—a lever that could be moved up and down. During a 1-hr test with just the lever present, Chicko played with the lever for a total of 6.3 min. Use this to estimate the ratio of the response strength of playing with the lever relative to the nonspecific set of other response alternatives. Calculate theoretical response probabilities for tests in which the lever is present, along with (a) the handle, (b) the door, and (c) the plunger. (These tests were carried out in the experiment, but only partial results were reported. When the handle and the lever were present, Chicko played with the lever .13 of the time. When the door and the lever were present, Chicko played with the lever .09 of the time. And when the plunger and the lever were present, Chicko played with the plunger .02 of the time.)

16. Suppose that a young man has just tried to phone a girl he likes and she did not answer the telephone. He knows that she sometimes goes out for coffee with some other girls from her dormitory, so there is some chance that he will see her if he goes to the coffee shop. His choice alternatives are:

A_1: go out for coffee,
A_2: stay in his room.

The possible outcomes are:

O_1: meet his girl,
O_2: have coffee,
O_3: get some studying done,
O_4: get involved in a card game.

Assume the following expectations and values:

$$u(O_1) = 20, \quad u(O_2) = 2, \quad u(O_3) = 12, \quad u(O_4) = 8.$$
$$s(O_1 \mid A_1) = .80. \quad s(O_2 \mid A_1) = 1.0. \quad s(O_3 \mid A_1) = s(O_4 \mid A_1) = 0.0.$$
$$s(O_1 \mid A_2) = s(O_2 \mid A_2) = 0.0. \quad s(O_3 \mid A_2) = .70. \quad s(O_4 \mid A_2) = .30.$$

Calculate $v(A_1)$ and $v(A_2)$ using Eq. (2.10). Calculate the choice probabilities using Eq. (4).

17. Assume the quantities given in Problem 16, except assume $s(O_1 \mid A_1) = .20$. Calculate $v(A_1)$ and the choice probabilities.

18. Find a value of $s(O_1 \mid A_1)$ for Problem 16 that would make the probability $P(A_1 \mid A_1, A_2)$ equal to .50.

19. Another condition in the experiment described in Example 2.14 had $\pi = .70$. With instructions only, $P(A_1 \mid A_1, A_2)$ was .75. With one-cent or ten-cent rewards and penalties, $P(A_1 \mid A_1, A_2)$ was .87. [$P(A_1)$ was about equal for the two amounts.] Calculate the ratios $u(O_1)/-u(O_2)$ implied by these results and Eq. (2.11).

▸ **20.** In the experiment that included students and Guardsmen subjects, suppose that the outcome of losing five cents was only four-tenths as important to the Guardsmen as it was to the students. Then for the students we could set the value of $u(-5¢)$ at -1, but then for the Guardsmen we would set the value of $u(-5¢)$ at -0.4.

a) Show that this different assumption would lead to a formula

$$u(+x) = (0.4)(1 - p)/p$$

instead of Eq. (2.12).

b) The average offers producing $P(A_1) = .50$ for the Guardsmen were 4.0¢, 6.0¢, 8.5¢, 15.4¢, 20.1¢ and 52.5¢ for probabilities of winning equal to .67, .50, .33, .20, .10, and .05, respectively. Calculate inferred utilities from the data using the new formula given just above, and compare with the inferred values for the group of students.

▸ **21.** For the experiment involving students and Guardsmen, the analysis given before assumed that the subjects' expectations equaled the true probabilities of winning, and the data were used to infer the subjective values. It is also possible to assume that the subjective values for winning or losing money are equal to the amounts of money, and then to use the data to infer the subjects' expectations. Recall the assumption that when $P(A_1 \mid A_1, A_2) = .50$, $v(A_1) = v(A_2)$, and $v(A_2) = 0.0$. Then

$$v(A_1) = s(O_1)u(+x) + s(O_2)u(-5¢) = 0.0,$$
$$s(O_1)u(+x) = -s(O_2)u(-5¢),$$

where $s(O_1)$ is the subjective probability of winning $u(+x)$ is the subjective value of the amount of money to be won, and $u(-5¢)$ is the subjective value of losing the nickel that had to be bet if the subject chose to play.

Now we adopt the assumption suggested above, namely

$$u(+x) = x, \qquad u(-5¢) = -5.$$

Also, we assume that the subjects' expectations added to one, so

$$s(O_2) = 1 - s(O_1).$$

Then we have

$$s(O_1)(x) = (1 - s(O_1))(5), \qquad s(O_1) = 5/(x + 5).$$

Using this formula, estimate the expectations of winning that corresponded to the true probabilities of winning in the experiment. The data for the Guardsmen are given in Problem 20. For the students, the average offers producing $P(A_1) = .50$ were 4.1¢, 6.2¢, 11.8¢, 24.4¢, 54.6¢, and 128¢, when the true probabilities of winning were .67, .50, .33, .20, .10, and .05.

CHAPTER THREE

Motivation and Conditioning

In any situation a person or an animal can choose from a number of alternative responses. Each response A_i has a strength $v(A_i)$. The choices made by the person or the animal are assumed to be determined by the response strengths, so that the strongest response occurs most often and the weaker responses occur less frequently. In Chapter 2 we worked with a specific rule about response probabilities; namely,

$$P(A_i \mid A_i, \ldots, A_k) = \frac{v(A_i)}{\sum\limits_{A_x \epsilon \mathcal{A}} v(A_x)}.$$

In this chapter we consider situations that produce changes in response strength. One of these involves deprivation, where a response becomes more probable because it has been unavailable for a time. An example is when an animal is not allowed to have food for several hours. When food is finally made available, the response of eating is unusually strong.

Another kind of change in response strength can be called conditioning. This term will be used here to refer to changes in response strengths that occur as an animal or person adjusts to conditions in his environment.[1] An example, taken from animal experiments, is when a hungry rat learns to press a bar in order to obtain food. Another example, involving human behavior, is when two persons learn to work cooperatively in a certain way to accomplish something they both want.

[1] The present use of the term "conditioning" is broader than that found in most texts. Many psychologists use the term only when they believe that a behavior is being strengthened in an automatic, nonvoluntary way. In the discussion here, there will be no distinction between automatic, nonvoluntary adjustments to the environment and cases where a person consciously decides to change his behavior. I think it is very hard to tell which is happening, and it may be that in many situations the difference between conscious and unconscious conditioning has very little effect on choice behavior anyway.

3A DEPRIVATION AND RESPONSE STRENGTH

In ordinary circumstances an animal or a person goes from one activity to another, performing quite a variety of responses. Some kinds of responses occur rather frequently; other responses occur much less often. For example, eating is an important and regular response for any animal. In one experiment[2] rats were given continuous access to food and water, and they responded by eating fairly regularly every three to four hours. In addition to responses like eating and drinking which involve consuming a needed substance, animals also have reasonably high probabilities of responses to exercise, explore their surroundings, play, interact with other animals, and touch soft, comfortable objects.

If an animal is prevented from making a high-probability response for a period of time, that response will have an increased probability when it is finally made available. The most obvious examples involve deprivation of food or water. If a person or animal is unable to eat at a time when he usually has food, then when food is finally available he usually will eat more than at a normal meal.

A good example of this is shown in Fig. 1.[3] The graph represents a count of small food pellets eaten by a rat. Each pellet eaten caused a pen to move up the paper by a fixed amount, and the paper moved under the pen from right to left at a fixed rate. Therefore, if no pellets were eaten, there would be a horizontal line. If pellets were eaten at some constant rate, there would be a straight line and the line would have a steep slope if the rate were high, or it would increase slowly if the rate were low. A graph like this is called a *cumulative record.*

The rat that gave the data for Fig. 1 got his food only at one time each day, in a special box. When food was put into the feeding box, the rat ate pellets at quite a high rate. The graph shows that he ate about 90 pellets during a 90-min period. Note that there is a slightly higher rate at the beginning than there is later in the period, but after the first 10 min or so the rat was eating about one pellet per minute. When the rat had been eating for about 20 min, the food box was locked for 13 min so he could not eat. Note that when the food box was first reopened the rat ate about 15 pellets in about 5 min—three times as much as in the 5 min just before the box had been locked. After a short period at the higher rate, the rat went back to eating about one pellet per minute again for nearly another hour.

---

[2] Reported by C. P. Richter, "Animal Behavior and Internal Drives." *Quart. Rev. Biol.*, 1927, **2,** 307–343.

[3] These data were presented by B. F. Skinner, *The Behavior of Organisms*, New York: D. Appleton-Century, Inc., 1938, p. 348.

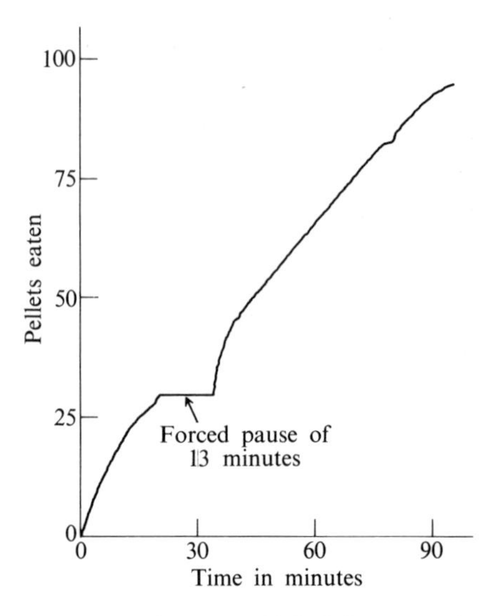

Fig. 1. Compensatory increase in rate which fails to reach extension of original curve.

Another example comes from a preference experiment where rats were tested in a box with two compartments.[4] In one condition, food was placed in one of the compartments and a hardware-cloth step was placed in the other. In a second condition, food was put in one compartment and in the other compartment was a window with a second rat on the other side. The relative strengths of choosing the alternative objects were measured by counting the proportions of time spent in each compartment.

Sometimes a rat was placed in the boxes just after he had eaten. At other times the rat was placed in the boxes after he had not eaten for 11 hours or 22 hours. (There was very little difference between the 11-hr and the 22-hr condition in these data.) Just after eating, the rats spent 59% of the time with food rather than the other rat, and 39% of the time with food rather than the hardware-cloth plaything. When hungry, the rats spent 88% of the time with food rather than the other rat, and 80% of the time with food rather than the plaything.

The effect of deprivation on response strength was also studied in the experiment where the rats were put in a harness and the strength of their pulling as they ran was measured when they were blocked from approaching

[4] The experiment was reported by J. Allison and M. Rocha y Silva, "Time Spent with Food and Nonfood Incentives as a Function of Food Deprivation." *Psychonomic Sci.*, 1965, **2,** 63–64.

a goal.[5] Rats in one group were tested sometimes when they had eaten one hour previously. The block was placed 30 cm from the goal where they usually found food. The average pull by the rats when they were 46-hr hungry was 48.7 gm. When they were one-hour hungry, the average pull was 16.5 gm.

A fourth way of studying the effect of deprivation on response strength uses a situation where attractive choice is opposed by something painful. From Chapter 2 recall that if an alternative A_i is attractive to some extent $g(A_i)$ and is unpleasant to some extent $b(A_i)$, we suppose that its value is the difference between these, or

$$v(A_i) = g(A_i) - b(A_i).$$

The obstruction method for testing the strength of responses uses this idea to study rats.[6] In the test, a rat is put on one side of an electrified grid; food, water, another rat, or some other attractive object is put on the other side of the grid. To reach the incentive object, the rat must cross the grid. Of course, this means that the response of going to the goal is partly positive and partly negative. In the procedure that was used, the strength of the shock was not varied; therefore the amount of unpleasantness $b(A_i)$ did not change very much. However, deprivation was used to change the attractiveness of the object; that is, $g(A_i)$ was made large or small by depriving the animal for a long or short time before the various tests. Another purpose was to compare the strengths of several different responses.

In a test, an object or substance was placed in the incentive compartment, and the rat was placed in the starting compartment. The rat was allowed to approach the incentive four times without being shocked; then the grid between the rat and the incentive was electrified for the remainder of the test. Each time the rat moved across the grid and approached the incentive it was picked up and replaced in the starting compartment. The strength of the approach response was measured as the number of crossings in a 20-min test period.

In a series of experiments, male and female rats were tested with food, water, and a sex partner as incentives; female rats were tested with pups as an incentive, and male rats were tested with an interesting and complicated box for exploration as an incentive. The results for hunger, thirst, and

---

[5] This was a part of an experiment by J. S. Brown, "Gradients of Approach and Avoidance Responses and their Relation to Level of Motivation," *J. comp. physiol. Psychol.*, 1948, **41,** 450–465. Other parts of this experiment were discussed in Chapter 2.

[6] The experiments discussed here are described in *Animal Motivation, Experimental Studies on the Albino Rat*, by C. J. Warden. New York: Columbia University Press, 1931. The data presented here are on pp. 383–384.

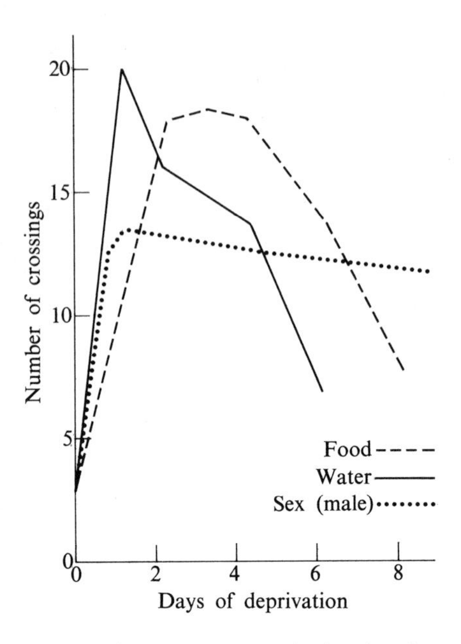

Fig. 2. Measurements of response strengths by the obstruction method.

male sex drives are shown in Fig. 2. Note that hunger and thirst produce up to 20 crossings—an average of about one per minute during the test period. The number of crossings by a male rat to reach a female in oestrus is 12 to 13 at the high levels. Females in oestrus were tested to see how many times they would cross to approach a male; the average number was 14. Females were also tested to see how many times they would cross a grid to reach a litter of their pups. This number was about 25—the highest number of crossings for any condition in the experiments. The interest of male rats in exploring a complicated enclosure was much smaller; they crossed the grid an average of six times.

When a response is impossible for a time and then is made available, it may be very strong at first, which gives it a very high probability. Then after it has been performed quite a bit, its strength decreases to a more moderate level. This is shown in Fig. 1 where the rate of eating at the very beginning was high and then decreased somewhat; the rate after the forced pause was high again, and then the rate leveled off.

In a situation like the one depicted in Fig. 1, the reason for the high initial rate and the later decrease may seem obvious. Certainly one thing that helps produce a high probability of eating is an empty stomach. And when the rat eats, his stomach is not as empty; therefore it is not surprising that the probability of eating goes down. However, this same pattern of responding occurs in other situations where the cause is not as obvious.

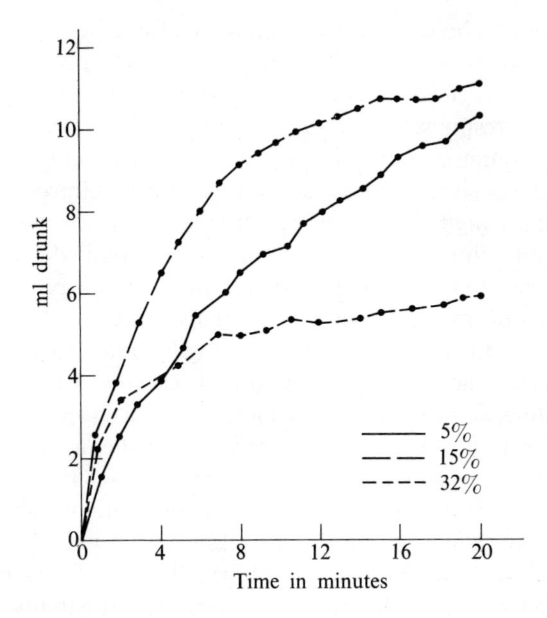

Fig. 3. Cumulative records of drinking different concentrations of glucose.

Figure 3 shows cumulative records of the intake of three concentrations of glucose, by rats who had not been deprived of food or water.[7] However, they did not have access to sugar-water all the time; and when sugar-water was offered there was a high probability of drinking it. After a time, this probability decreased. Another experiment involved a measure of preference between sucrose and wheat powder.[8] In Chapter 2 we saw that rats prefer sucrose to wheat powder when both are offered. However, when rats were given sucrose alone for 15 min before the preference test, they developed a preference for the wheat powder.

This discussion leads to a general idea about the effect of deprivation on the strength of a response. Imagine a person or animal in a constant environment with everything available to satisfy all his needs for survival. Many different responses would occur. Some of the responses would occur quite often, and others would occur rarely. Many responses, like eating, would show periodic increases and decreases in probability. We can consider the behavior of a person or animal in a constant environment as a con-

[7] The experiment was by E. H. Shuford Jr. "Palatability and Osmotic Pressure of Glucose and Sucrose Solutions as Determinants of Intake." *J. comp. physiol. Psychol.*, 1959, **52,** 150–153.

[8] This was by P. T. Young, "Reversal of Food Preferences of the White Rat through Controlled Prefeeding," *J. genet. Psychol.*, 1940, **22,** 33–66.

tinuous stream of choices, with the strength of each choice response relatively constant, or varying in a fairly regular, periodic fashion.

When an experiment involves deprivation, the environment is not constant. Some response that would be fairly probable is made impossible for a time. A common result of a deprivation experiment is to increase the strength of the deprived response so that when it is reintroduced its probability is unusually high. Then that response is performed quite frequently—it may be the only thing the person or animal does for a while. Subsequently the behavior tends to return to the normal state where the previously deprived response has its normal range of varying probabilities.

This general idea about response strengths and deprivation probably gives a satisfactory account of the important features of many experiments. At the same time, some complicating factors need to be mentioned, to avoid too much oversimplification. First, deprivation that eliminates one response also has effects on the probabilities of other responses. One example involves food and water. If water and other liquids are made unavailable, the obvious effect is to make drinking impossible. However, a person or animal will not eat as much when he is thirsty as he normally does. Thus the deprivation of the drinking response indirectly decreases the probability of the eating response.

In other situations, the deprivation of one response may increase the probability of another response. Suppose that a constant environment permits two eating responses—say, hamburger and chicken—and the two responses are about equally probable for the person. If one of these becomes impossible, then the effect will surely be to increase the probability of the other. For example, deprivation of the response of eating hamburger would increase the probability of the response of eating chicken.

The example of chicken and hamburger involves responses that substitute for each other in an obvious way. The same general relationship applies in other cases where the responses do not seem to be substitutes for each other. An example involves laboratory rats that are maintained on a regular once-a-day feeding schedule. At the time when food is offered the rats have a high probability of eating. However, other responses also become more probable. For example, rats show an increase in restless movement and general activity as their feeding time approaches.

We need to keep in mind that deprivation of one response can increase or decrease the probabilities of other responses during the time of deprivation. Similarly, when a response is made available, the effect may be to increase or decrease the probabilities of other responses.

Examples of this can be taken from the situations just mentioned, when looked at conversely. If the normal environment has a very limited supply of water, the probability of eating dry food would be quite low. Then if the water supply increases, the probability of eating would also be likely to increase. If the constant environment of a person only permitted eating chicken, the probability of that response would be quite high. Then if the response of eating hamburger became possible, the probability of eating chicken would decrease.

An example of the last kind of interaction was shown in an experiment on cats.[9] There were four different food mixtures used in the experiment. The cats were only able to eat at one time during the day. One food mixture was offered until the cat stopped eating it; then a second food mixture was offered. At the beginning of the feeding period, the probability of eating the available food was very high. For example, when milk was offered first, one cat took between 114 and 166 gm on different days. However, when the same food was offered second, the probability of eating that food was much lower. When plain milk was offered after the cat had eaten his fill of a mixture of ground beef-kidney and milk, or a mixture of raw ground beef, cooked oatmeal, and milk, no milk was taken; when plain milk was offered after a mixture of ground fish and milk, 36 gm were taken.

This experiment shows that offering one response can decrease the probability of another response. The responses do not have to be as closely related as they were in the experiment. The same kind of thing happens between eating and general activity. After a period of deprivation, the probability of eating is high, but so is the probability of moving about. After food is offered and eaten, the probability of eating decreases significantly, and so does the probability of moving about. In fact, for many animals the probability of sleeping is quite high immediately after a meal.

Now we have quite a general idea of the effects of deprivation. We still suppose that in a constant environment with a fixed set of response alternatives, a person or animal would have a response strength for each alternative that was fairly constant or varying in a regular, periodic way. When some response becomes impossible, this has an effect on the strengths of the other responses. Some of the remaining responses may increase in strength and others may decrease. Similarly, when a response is introduced that was not available, its strength will be high for a time and then decrease, and consequently the strengths of some other responses may also increase or decrease.

3B CHANGES DUE TO CONTINGENCIES[10]

Deprivation changes response strengths by removing some alternative from the set of possible responses. In the situations discussed in the last section, the response alternative is taken away or reintroduced at times decided on

---

[9] The experiment was done by W. A. Bousfield, and the data are given by B. F. Skinner, *The Behavior of Organisms*, p. 370.

[10] The ideas in this section are based on a theory by D. Premack. A good summary is available in his chapter, "Reinforcement Theory," in the *Nebraska Symposium on Motivation*, 1965.

by the experimenter, and the subject's behavior does not influence the availability of alternatives.

In a different kind of experiment, a response with fairly high probability is unavailable most of the time, but the subject's behavior determines or at least influences the times that the response will be available. The experimenter picks out some response alternative that is always available, and when the subject performs that response a certain amount, or at a certain time, the experimenter reintroduces the response that he has been withholding.

Consider two responses that might be available for a young boy after he comes home from school in the afternoon. The alternatives are watching television and practicing his piano lesson. The boy's mother might say, "You can't watch television until five o'clock." This would be a deprivation situation, where a response is unavailable and will become possible at a certain time regardless of what the boy does in the meantime. Or the boy's mother might say, "You can watch television after you practice the piano for 20 minutes, but not before." This would be a contingency situation, where the unavailable response will become possible after the boy gives a certain amount of performance on some other response.

A contingency experiment involves a base response B and a contingent event C, usually a response of higher probability than the base response. In the simplest experiment, the subject has the base response available all the time, and is allowed to perform the contingent response once each time he performs the base response once. In other words, each time the subject performs B once, he is rewarded by being allowed to perform C once.

In one common type of contingency experiment, an animal is made hungry by deprivation so that the response of eating has a high probability. Then a response with relatively low probability is made available; for example, the animal may be put into a box where it can press on a bar. No food is given to the animal until it makes the low-probability response of bar pressing. But each time the bar is pressed, a small bit of food is given. In this experiment, the bar press serves as B, the base response. The response of eating is C, the contingent response.

When the contingent response C has higher probability than the base response B, we expect that the performance of B will increase so that C can be performed. Without the contingency, C would be performed much more than B. The contingency forces the subject to perform B in order to be able to perform C. Therefore an increase in performing B represents a sort of compromise. B is performed more than the subject would prefer, so that the opportunity to perform C can be somewhat higher, and therefore closer to the subject's preferred rate.

Many experiments show that animals and people do adjust their behavior in ways that give more opportunities to perform high-probability contingent responses. A thirsty rat can be trained to run down an alley to be permitted to drink water. A hungry pigeon can be trained to peck at a disk to be permitted to eat food. A dog can be trained to roll over to receive food or hear his master praise him. A seal can be trained to walk on its flippers to be permitted to eat fish. In each of these cases, a response that would normally have a very low probability is performed reliably in a situation where performance of the weaker response permits the animal to perform a stronger response.

It may seem to some readers that the discussion of response probabilities here is an unnecessary technicality. After all, it is when an animal is made hungry that food can be used successfully as a reward. It might be thought that animals—and people, for that matter—change their behavior as a result of contingencies just because this leads to satisfaction of needs or drives. However, sometimes a low-probability base response will increase when a high-probability response is contingent on it, even when the contingent response does not involve the satisfaction of any obvious need.

In an experiment[11] where first-grade children were subjects, each child had a test on two responses: eating chocolate bits and playing a pinball machine. Each child was tested twice. In the first test, the child sat in front of the pinball machine and a candy dispenser and was allowed to eat and play the machine as often as he wanted to. For 19 of the 32 children the number of plays on the machine was greater than the number of candies eaten. The larger frequency of playing means that the strength of playing was greater than the strength of eating for these children. (It took about as much time to eat a piece of candy as to play the machine.) For the remaining 13 children, the frequency (strength) of eating was equal to or higher than the frequency (strength) of playing the pinball machine.

In the second test, each group of children was divided into two smaller groups to see what they would do when there was a contingency. One-half of the children had a contingency where playing the pinball machine was the base response and eating candy was the contingent response. These children were rewarded by a piece of candy for playing the pinball machine, somewhat as a hungry rat may be rewarded by a food pellet for pressing a bar. For the other children, the contingency was set up the other way. Eating was the base response and playing the pinball machine was the contingent response. Remember that playing the machine had higher strength than eating for a few more than one-half of the children. At this stage the experiment really had four groups: for ten children the first test showed that playing was stronger than eating, and playing was made the contingent response. For nine children the first test showed that playing was stronger than eating, and eating was made the contingent response. For a third group of seven children

[11] By D. Premack, "Toward Empirical Behavior Laws," *Psychol. Rev.*, 1959, **66,** 219–233.

Table 1

Increases in Responding over Test Session

Contingency	Children with higher probability of eating	Children with higher probability of playing
If Play then Eat	9.4	5.0
If Eat then Play	2.0	25.5

the first test showed that eating was equal to or stronger than playing, and eating was made the contingent response. And in the last group, with six children, eating was equal to or stronger than playing in the first test, and playing was made the contingent response in the second test.

The idea tested in the experiment is that a response with higher probability can be used as a reward for a response with lower probability; and the probabilities are what matter, rather than what the responses are. This means that for children with a higher frequency of eating than playing, the probability of playing should increase when eating is made contingent on playing. It also means that for children with a higher probability of playing than eating, the probability of eating should increase if playing is made contingent on eating. Both of these things happened. For children with a higher probability of eating, the contingency "if-play-then-eat" increased the frequency of playing by an average of 9.4 responses for a 15-min session. For the children with a higher probability of playing, the contingency "if-eat-then-play" increased the frequency of eating by an average of 25.5 responses for a 15-min session. By comparison, for the nine children with higher probabilities of playing, the contingency "if-play-then-eat" produced an average increase in eating of only five responses per 15 min, and for the six children with higher probabilities of eating, the contingency "if-eat-then-play" produced an average increase in playing of only two responses. (See Table 1.) The conclusion is that a high-probability response can be used in a contingency situation to increase the probability of a weaker response, and it does not matter very much whether the contingent response is one that satisfies some need for the subject. In fact, the probability of a need-reducing response like eating can be increased in a contingency situation by a response that does not reduce a need, if the contingent response has a higher probability.

The remainder of this section will present a tentative analysis of simple conditioning. The main goal is to develop connections between the main facts about conditioning and the theory of choice given in Chapter 2.

Think about a situation involving a pair of responses. We will use the letters *B* and *C* to refer to the responses in a general way; *C* will ordinarily be used to stand for the response with higher probability. Suppose, for example, that a rat lives in a cage with a drinking tube and an activity wheel. If the rat is made thirsty by having the drinking tube taken away for a time, then when the tube is put back in the cage, the response of drinking will be stronger than the response of running. In that case, we would use B to refer to the running response, and C to refer to drinking. On the other hand, the rat may have had access to the drinking tube for a long time, but not have been able to use the activity wheel. In that case, the response of running would be stronger than drinking, and we would call drinking B and running C. Putting this in a general way, we will use the letters B and C to stand for responses in a situation so that

$$v(C) > v(B),$$

when both are freely available. This means that if both B and C were offered, the animal or person would spend more time performing C than B.

Now suppose that the situation is changed so that B has to be performed before C is made available. In other words, C is made contingent on performing B. One effect of this is to increase the performance of B. The amount of this increase will depend on the strength of C. It also will depend on the amount of performance required on B and the amount of time that C is given after B is performed. We do not know enough now to say just how these several factors combine, so we give a rather general but simple formula to express the idea. Let $v_0(B)$ be the strength of the base response when there is no contingency, and let $v_1(B)$ be the strength of the base response after conditioning has occurred. Let $v_1(C)$ be the strength of contingent response after conditioning has occurred. We will use an illustrative equation and assume that conditioning increases the strength of response B according to the following formula:

$$v_1(B) = bv_0(B) + cv_1(C). \tag{3.1}$$

In words, Eq. (3.1) says that the initial strength of B is multiplied by a constant b, and a quantity is added that depends on the final strength of C. Equation (3.1) will be called the *reinforcement equation*, because it describes an increase in the strength of B produced by the contingency of C on B, and this is commonly called reinforcement of B.

In a contingency situation, the contingent response is kept unavailable most of the time. We know that when a response is kept unavailable its strength increases; therefore we expect the strength of C to be higher in the contingency situation than it is when there is no contingency. Again, we will use an illustrative equation to express the idea. Let t be the proportion of time that the contingent response is available in the contingency situation, and let $v_0(C)$ be the strength of C in a free response situation. Then we suppose that

$$v_1(C) = v_0(C) + h(1 - t), \tag{3.2}$$

where h is an empirical constant. Equation (3.2) will be called the *deprivation equation.*

Equations (3.1) and (3.2) are expressed in terms of response strengths. The measures that we take in an experiment do not give absolute values of response strengths, but only relative values. For example, we can permit the base response in a certain situation and measure the ratio $v_0(B)/v(M)$, where $v(M)$ is the combined strengths of the other responses that are available. Different experiments will require slightly different modifications of the equations; however, the probabilities of responses are often observed in relation to a reasonably constant set of alternatives so we consider that case here. If all responses are measured relative to the same set of other miscellaneous responses, called M, then we can apply the reinforcement equation (3.1) in the form

$$\frac{v_1(B)}{v(M)} = b\,\frac{v_0(B)}{v(M)} + c\,\frac{v_1(C)}{v(M)}.$$

Similarly, the deprivation equation (3.2) can be applied in these situations:

$$\frac{v_1(C)}{v(M)} = \frac{v_0(C)}{v(M)} + \frac{h}{v(M)}(1 - t).$$

Since h and $v(M)$ are both constant, we can define a new constant

$$h' = \frac{h}{v(M)},$$

giving

$$\frac{v_1(C)}{v(M)} = \frac{v_0(C)}{v(M)} + h'(1 - t).$$

Example 3.1. Suppose that in an experiment the base response B is running in a wheel and the contingent response C is drinking. Suppose that when wheel running is measured with drinking unavailable the probability of running is

$$P_0(B) = \frac{v_0(B)}{v_0(B) + v(M)} = .01.$$

And when drinking is measured with no wheel present, the probability of drinking is

$$P_0(C) = \frac{v_0(C)}{v_0(C) + v(M)} = .091.$$

Suppose that a contingency is introduced and, after conditioning occurs, the animal runs enough so that the drinking tube is available 8% of the time. Assume that $h' = 0.7$ and calculate the value of $v_1(C)/v(M)$. Then assume that $b = 1.0$ and $c = 0.1$ and calculate the value of $v_1(B)/v(M)$. What will be the probability of response B after conditioning occurs?

First we need to translate the given response probabilities into ratios of response strength. We have

$$\frac{v_0(B)}{v(M)} = \frac{P_0(B)}{1 - P_0(B)} = \frac{.01}{.99} = 0.01,$$

$$\frac{v_0(C)}{v(M)} = \frac{P_0(C)}{1 - P_0(C)} = \frac{.091}{.909} = 0.10.$$

Now, using the assumed value of $h' = 0.7$, and the value of $t = .08$ in the modified form of Eq. (3.2),

$$\frac{v_1(C)}{v(M)} = 0.10 + (0.7)(0.92) = 0.10 + 0.64 = 0.74.$$

Using the assumed values of b and c in the modified form of Eq. (3.1),

$$\frac{v_1(B)}{v(M)} = (1.0)(0.01) + (0.1)(0.74) = 0.08.$$

Now we can calculate the probability of B,

$$P_1(B) = \frac{v_1(B)}{v_1(B) + v(M)} = \frac{v_1(B)/v(M)}{[v_1(B)/v(M)] + 1} = \frac{.08}{1.08} = .074. \blacksquare$$

In an experiment a number of different contingent responses were compared.[12] There were two different wheels, one heavy and hard to turn, and the other light and easy to turn. There were also three different solutions of sugar and water—64%, 32%, and 16%. The responses of running in these wheels and drinking these solutions were measured in test sessions, and the probabilities ranged from .16 for the heavy wheel to .46 for drinking the 16% sugar solution. The probabilities are translated into ratios of response strengths with the formula

$$\frac{v_0(C)}{v(M)} = \frac{P_0(C)}{1 - P_0(C)}.$$

These results are in Table 2, in the column labeled $v_0(C)/v(M)$. The values are average strengths over the total session. The strength of drinking 64%

[12] By D. Premack, "Prediction of the Comparative Reinforcement Values of Running and Drinking," *Science*, 1963, **139,** 1062–1063.

Table 2

Results of Varying Strength of Contingent Response

Contingent response, C	$v_0(C)/v(M)$	Number of bar presses	t
Run: Heavy Wheel	0.19	21	.18
Drink: 64% Sugar	0.23	23	.19
Run: Light Wheel	0.39	27	.22
Drink: 32% Sugar	0.67	30	.25
Drink: 16% Sugar	0.89	36	.30

sugar is below the others probably because it decreases faster during this session.

In a contingency situation, one of the C responses was used. A rat was given a bar to press, and each time it was pressed three times, the contingent response was offered for 15 sec. Suppose that it took a rat about 1 sec to press the bar once.

We expect that the stronger contingent responses will produce higher probabilities of bar pressing than the weaker ones. This is what happened; the average number of bar presses during 10-min contingency sessions ranged from 21 (when the contingent response was running in the heavy wheel) to 36 (when the contingent response was drinking 16% sucrose). The results are also given in Table 2, along with the proportions of time in the 10-min sessions that the contingent responses were available. These proportions were calculated using the formula

$$t = \left(\frac{\text{number of bar presses}}{3} \times 15 \text{ sec}\right) \Big/ 600 \text{ sec}.$$

We can use the modified forms of Eqs. (3.1) and (3.2) to work with these data. Bar pressing is a response that has practically zero strength for a rat when there is no contingency. In other words, we can assume that

$$\frac{v_0(B)}{v(M)} = 0.0.$$

In that case, Eq. (3.1) becomes

$$\frac{v_1(B)}{v(M)} = c\,\frac{v_1(C)}{v(M)}.$$

But we can substitute, using Eq. (3.2), and obtain

$$\frac{v_1(B)}{v(M)} = c\left[\frac{v_0(C)}{v(M)} + h'(1 - t)\right].$$

To obtain values of $v_1(B)/v(M)$, we need to remember several things. First, we remember that for each three bar presses, the contingent response was made available for 15 sec. We shall assume that while the contingent response was available, the rat did not press the bar. In other words, the time available for bar pressing was $600(1 - t)$ sec. Then we calculate the probability of bar pressing as the number of seconds spent bar pressing divided by $600(1 - t)$. Finally, remember our supposition that it took about 1 sec to press the bar. The values obtained for $P_1(B)$, based on the number of bar presses per session, are .042, .047, .056, .067, and .088. Finally, we obtain values of $v_1(B)/v(M)$ by using the formula

$$\frac{v_1(B)}{v(M)} = \frac{P_1(B)}{1 - P_1(B)}.$$

Therefore we obtain a value of $v_1(B)/v(M)$ for each of the five contingency situations of the experiment. We also have a value of $v_0(C)/v(M)$ for each of the five contingent responses, as well as a value of t. The outcome is that we have five equations involving c and h', based on the experimental results.

$$\begin{aligned} .044 &= c(.19 + .82h'), \\ .050 &= c(.23 + .81h'), \\ .061 &= c(.39 + .78h'), \\ .071 &= c(.67 + .75h'), \\ .094 &= c(.89 + .70h'). \end{aligned}$$

We use the first and last equations to obtain values of c and h', and then use these estimated values to calculate theoretical values of $v_1(B)/v(M)$ for the other three cases to see whether they agree with the data.[13] To obtain our estimates,

$$.044/c = .19 + .82h', \qquad .094/c = .89 + .70h'.$$

If we multiply all terms of the first equation by 2.14, we have

$$.094/c = .41 + 1.75h'.$$

Therefore,

$$\begin{aligned} .41 + 1.75h' &= .89 + .70h'; \\ 1.05h' &= .48; \\ h' &= .45. \end{aligned}$$

[13] The values of c and h' obtained in this way will not give the best possible agreement with the results. Better values would be obtained if all the data were combined in the estimation. Various methods for this are possible, but they involve statistical ideas that are beyond the scope of this book.

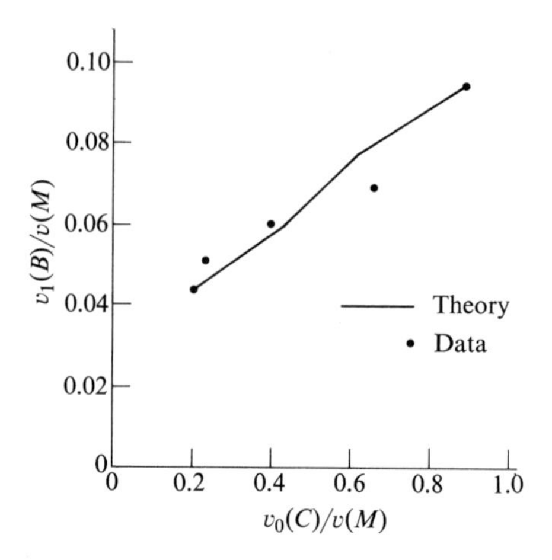

Fig. 4. Relationship between strength of contingent response and strength of base response in a contingency experiment.

But then from

$$.094/c = .89 + .70h',$$

we obtain

$$.094/c = .89 + .31 = 1.20;$$

$$c = .094/1.20 = .078.$$

Now we substitute these values in the equation for $v_1(B)/v(M)$ in the three cases not used for estimation.

$$.078(.23 + .81h') = .046,$$
$$.078(.39 + .78h') = .058,$$
$$.078(.67 + .75h') = .080.$$

The results are shown in a graph in Fig. 4. The predictions are not perfect, of course, but they seem to give quite a good approximation. The important fact here is that the same values of the constants c and h' can be used in all cases, even though the contingent responses were different in kind (drinking and running) and differed widely in their strengths.

In another experiment there were several different base responses and just one contingent response.[14] Again, the subjects were white rats. The contingent response was wheel running, and the rats were allowed to run only during two 10-min sessions each day. In preliminary training, the rats

[14] R. W. Schaeffer, "The Reinforcement Relation as a Function of the Instrumental Response Base Rate," *J. exp. Psychol.*, 1965, **69**, 419–425.

were trained with drinking water as the base response. After experience with plain water, different groups of rats had four different base responses. Two groups had sugar added to the water so that the strength of drinking was higher than it had been with plain water. One of these groups drank a 4% solution of sugar, and the other had a 32% solution. A third group had plain water, as before. A fourth group had the drinking tube, but it had no water in it. This last group licked the tube as a base response, but of course the response was much weaker than it had been with water.

In each group, the contingency between the particular base response and the contingent running response was set up in two ways. One contingency required the rat to give five licks in order to run for 10 sec. In the other condition the rat had to lick 41 times to earn 10 sec of running.

Initial strengths of licking for plain water and of running were obtained in the preliminary part of the experiment. In sessions with both water and the wheel available and without a contingency, the rats drank for about 15 sec during a 10-min test session and they ran for about 150 sec during the same interval. Let B_3 be the response of drinking plain water. We have

$$P_0(B_3) = \frac{v_0(B_3)}{v_0(B_3) + v_0(C) + v(M)} = \frac{15}{600} = .025.$$

$$P_0(C) = \frac{v_0(C)}{v_0(B_3) + v_0(C) + v(M)} = \frac{150}{600} = .25.$$

We want to calculate values of $v_1(B_3)/v(M)$ and $v_1(C)/v(M)$, as before. Our information here is in somewhat different form from that in earlier cases. However, the techniques of calculation here are almost the same as those used before. From the information given above, we can calculate

$$\frac{v_0(B_3)}{v_0(C) + v(M)} = \frac{P_0(B_3)}{1.0 - P_0(B_3)} = \frac{.025}{.975} = .026;$$

$$\frac{v_0(C)}{v_0(B_3) + v(M)} = \frac{P_0(C)}{1.0 - P_0(C)} = \frac{.25}{.75} = .333.$$

Now we divide the numerators and denominators by $v(M)$.

$$\frac{v_0(B_3)/v(M)}{1.0 + [v_0(C)/v(M)]} = .026; \qquad \frac{v_0(C)/v(M)}{1.0 + [v_0(B_3)/v(M)]} = .333.$$

Then we have two equations

$$\frac{v_0(B_3)}{v(M)} = .026 + .026\,\frac{v_0(C)}{v(M)}; \qquad \frac{v_0(C)}{v(M)} = .333 + .333\,\frac{v_0(B_3)}{v(M)}.$$

The second equation can be changed to read

$$-\frac{v_0(B_3)}{v(M)} = 1.0 - 3.0\,\frac{v_0(C)}{v(M)}.$$

This is combined with the first equation from before:

$$\begin{aligned} 0.0 &= 1.026 - 2.974\,v_0(C)/v(M); \\ v_0(C)/v(M) &= 0.345. \end{aligned}$$

Then we can solve for $v_0(B_3)/v(M)$:

$$\begin{aligned} v_0(B_3)/v(M) &= .026 + .026\,v_0(C)/v(M) \\ &= .026\big(1 + v_0(C)/v(M)\big) = .026 \times 1.345 \\ &= 0.035. \end{aligned}$$

The other three base responses were also measured in situations where the wheel was available. During 10-min test sessions the rats spent an average of 128 sec drinking the 4% sugar solution, 93 sec drinking the 32% sugar solution, and 4 sec licking at the empty tube. Converting these to probabilities, if we let B_1 be drinking the 4% solution, let B_2 be drinking the 32% solution, and B_4 be licking the empty tube, we have

$$\begin{aligned} P_0(B_1) &= \frac{v_0(B_1)}{v_0(B_1) + v_0(C) + v(M)} = \frac{128}{600} = .213; \\ P_0(B_2) &= \frac{v_0(B_2)}{v_0(B_2) + v_0(C) + v(M)} = \frac{93}{600} = .155; \\ P_0(B_4) &= \frac{v_0(B_4)}{v_0(B_4) + v_0(C) + v(M)} = \frac{4}{600} = .007. \end{aligned}$$

These equations can be modified in the way just shown above for B_3. For example,

$$\frac{v_0(B_1)}{v_0(C) + v(M)} = \frac{v_0(B_1)/v(M)}{1 + [v_0(C)/v(M)]} = \frac{P_0(B_1)}{1 - P_0(B_1)} = .271.$$

We know that

$$1 + v_0(C)/v(M) = 1.345.$$

Therefore,

$$v_0(B_1)/v(M) = .271 \times 1.345 = 0.364.$$

Using the same procedures in the other cases, we obtain

$$\begin{aligned} v_0(B_2)/v(M) &= 0.246. \\ v_0(B_4)/v(M) &= 0.009. \end{aligned}$$

Table 3

Results of Varying Initial Strength of Base Response

Base response	Five licks for 10-sec running		41 licks for 10-sec running	
	Time on B	Time running	Time on B	Time running
B_1: 4% Sugar	175	127	200	202
B_2: 32% Sugar	133	124	158	119
B_3: Plain water	22.5	111	46.7	67
B_4: Empty tube	12.5	107	16.7	29

Note: All times given in seconds.

The results obtained with the two contingency situations are summarized in Table 3. The amounts given as time running were the actual measured times during which the wheel was free so that the rats could run.

We need to convert these results into values of $v_1(B)/v(M)$. As an example, consider the base response B_1 in the five-lick contingency. During a total of 473 sec the rat could not run in the wheel. We assume that the 175 sec of licking took place in these 473 sec. Then

$$P_1(B_1) = \frac{v_1(B_1)}{v_1(B_1) + v(M)} = \frac{175}{473} = .370.$$

But then

$$\frac{v_1(B_1)}{v(M)} = \frac{P_1(B_1)}{1 - P_1(B_1)} = 0.587.$$

Using the same procedure in the remaining cases, we obtain the results in Table 4 and Fig. 5. The results for the five-lick contingency seem to lie

Table 4

Response Strengths in Experiment with Different Base Responses

Base response	$v_0(B)/v(M)$	$v_1(B)/v(M)$	
		Five-lick contingency	41-lick contingency
B_1: 4% Sugar	0.364	0.587	1.010
B_2: 32% Sugar	0.246	0.387	0.489
B_3: Plain water	0.035	0.048	0.096
B_4: Empty tube	0.009	0.026	0.030

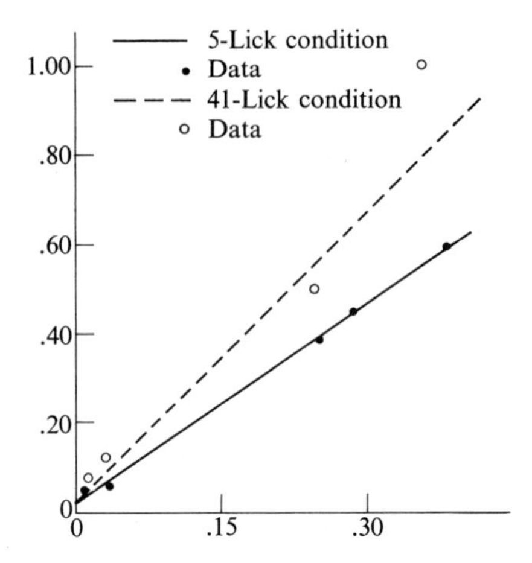

Fig. 5. Relationships between initial and final strengths of base responses in two contingency conditions.

quite close to a straight line that goes through the origin and has a slope of about 1.6. The results for the 41-lick contingency are less close to a straight line; however, if the best-fitting straight line were chosen, it apparently would go near the origin and have slope of about 2.3. Recall the reinforcement equation:

$$\frac{v_1(B)}{v(M)} = b\,\frac{v_0(B)}{v(M)} + c\,\frac{v_1(C)}{v(M)}.$$

Apparently the values of b in the two contingency situations here were about 1.6 and 2.3, respectively, and these values were much larger than the respective values of c. (This is reasonable, since in the previous calculation we obtained a value of c on the order of .08.) The lines in Fig. 5 were drawn assuming these values of b and neglecting the apparently small values of

$$c\,\frac{v_1(C)}{v(M)}.$$

We have worked with the results of two experiments. In the first study a single base response was used, and there were five different contingent responses. After conditioning occurred, the probability of the base response was different, depending on the probability of the contingent response, and the results agreed reasonably well with Eqs. (3.1) and (3.2). The second experiment had one contingent response, and there were four base responses. The amount of increase produced by conditioning depended on the initial strength of the base response, approximately as assumed in Eq. (3.1).

The assumptions about reinforcement [Eq. (3.1)] and deprivation [Eq. (3.2)] seem reasonably accurate for these two experiments. However, we need to view the present analysis as a tentative first step toward a theory linking conditioning experiments to the general theory of choice. Further research may substantiate these ideas, or it may show that quite a different relationship is more accurate.

While we cannot say exactly what equation is most accurate for describing conditioning, we can be quite confident in the general idea that conditioning depends on the initial strength of the base response and on the strength of the contingent response. In the next three sections we will use this general idea as a framework for some further general facts found in conditioning experiments.

3C ROLE OF EXPECTATIONS IN CONDITIONING

In a conditioning experiment, we begin with a contingent response that has high strength and a base response that has low strength. The experimenter permits the contingent response after each performance of the base response. At the beginning of the experiment there is no connection between the two responses for the subject, but after enough experience in the situation, the animal develops the expectation that the contingent response will follow the instrumental response. In the preceding section we discussed the main effect of this expectation, which is to increase the strength of the base response. At the beginning of a conditioning experiment, the strength of the base response is $v_0(B)$, and we used Eq. (3.1) as one possible way in which the strength of B might increase from $v_0(B)$ to its final value. This increase occurs because of the subject's growing expectation that he will be able to perform the contingent response after the base response.[15]

The idea of expectation was used earlier in Section 2F, where we studied choices that have uncertain outcomes. Recall that if there are two outcomes that are considered possible by the subject, the response strength for a choice alternative B was given by

$$v(B) = s(O_1 \mid B)u(O_1) + s(O_2 \mid B)u(O_2). \tag{3.3}$$

[Cf. Eq. (2.10).] This can be compared with Eq. (3.1) of this chapter, for the strength of a base response

$$v_1(B) = bv_0(B) + cv_1(C).$$

We can see the relationship between these two equations as follows. We suppose that two outcomes are relevant—O_1 is the outcome of being able to perform the contingent response, and O_2 is the outcome of not being able to perform C. We can reasonably assume that the subjective value of O_2 is

---

[15] This way of talking about animal conditioning is due to E. C. Tolman, *Purposive Behavior in Animals and Men*, New York: Century, 1932. F. Restle has recently used the idea using mathematical techniques of linear algebra, and the main results are very similar to those obtained here. Restle's article is "Linear Theory of Performance," *Psychol. Rev.*, 1967, **74,** 63–69.

zero; that is,

$$u(O_2) = 0.$$

Then the second term of Eq. (3.3) is zero. In the first term, we should suppose that the value of outcome O_1 is the response strength of performing the contingent response.

$$u(O_1) = v_1(C).$$

And then the expectation of O_1 following response B corresponds to the constant c;

$$s(O_1 \mid B) = c.$$

The two equations now fit together if the first term of Eq. (3.1) is zero. This was the case, for example, in the first experiment we considered in Section 3B. In that case, recall that $v_0(B)$ was zero; in other words, the base response had no strength other than that resulting from its association with the contingent response.

These remarks provide a connection between our discussion of expectations in uncertain choice situations and our discussion of conditioning. They also increase our understanding of the equations used in both situations. We now may conclude that the equation used in Chapter 2 for choices with uncertainty will be correct only when the choice response itself has no particular value. For example, if a person enjoys betting on long shots, a term like $bv_0(B)$ would have to be included in the analysis of his betting behavior. On the other hand, the analysis also shows us something about the analysis we used earlier for simple conditioning. We now may conclude that the constant c is related to the strength of the subject's expectation that the contingent response will be permitted after he performs the base response. (In this connection, the apparently small values obtained for c in experiments using rats are surprising and interesting. There may be something about averaging the results of complete sessions that causes c to be artificially low. On the other hand, it may just be difficult to teach a rat a strong expectation between such unrelated responses as bar pressing and drinking, or drinking and running.)

In many situations there are a number of alternative responses, and a subject learns to select the alternative that leads to a desired outcome. In a simple *T*-maze experiment, a rat is made hungry so the response of eating has high strength. On each trial of the experiment the rat is placed in the starting alley of the maze and allowed to run down the alley and then to one side or the other of the "*T*." The experimenter selects one of the sides and always places food at that side. Suppose that the positive side is to the left. Then if the rat chooses the left arm of the maze he is permitted to eat. If he chooses the right arm, there is no food—usually the rat is kept at that end of the maze for a few seconds and then removed.

In the experiment, there are two outcomes—eating (E), and reaching the end of the maze and finding no food (N). The response strength of eating, $u(E)$, is high. The response strength for running to the end of an empty maze, $u(N)$, is low—it probably is zero or negative. There also are two response alternatives which we call B_1 and B_2. We use B_1 to refer to choosing the side on which the experimenter puts food. Then the response strengths for the choice alternatives are

$$v(B_1) = s(E \mid B_1)u(E) + s(N \mid B_1)u(N),$$
$$v(B_2) = s(E \mid B_2)u(E) + s(N \mid B_2)u(N).$$

Whenever the rat chooses B_1, he can eat; whenever he chooses B_2, he gets no food. We suppose that the rat then learns to expect eating following B_1 —that is, $s(E \mid B_1)$ will become large and $s(N \mid B_1)$ will be small. On the other hand, the rat should learn that he will receive no food following B_2— that is, $s(N \mid B_2)$ should become large and $s(E \mid B_2)$ should be small. Since $u(E)$ is large and $u(N)$ is small or negative, the result will be to have $v(B_1)$ large relative to $v(B_2)$, and the rat will eventually choose B_1 consistently (or at least on most of the trials).

A more refined experiment can be conducted by permitting the rat to eat at one side of the maze on some trials and at the other side on other trials. This experiment can be run in two ways. One method is called the correction procedure. On each trial the experimenter decides on which side of the maze eating will be permitted and locks a door on the other side. Then if the rat goes to the wrong side, he can turn around and go to the side where he can eat. Thus, in the correction procedure, the rat is allowed to eat on every trial. The side where eating is permitted is determined by a preset schedule with one of the sides, B_1, having an unlocked door on a fixed proportion π of the trials.

The other method is the noncorrection procedure. Again, the experimenter decides on which side of the maze eating will be permitted, but if the rat goes to the side where he cannot eat, he is not permitted to turn around and go to the positive side. Instead, the rat is held in the empty end of the maze for a few seconds and then removed. Thus, in the noncorrection procedure, the rat can eat only if he chooses the side that is positive on that trial. Again, the positive side is selected on each trial by a preset schedule with B_1 positive on a proportion π of the trials.

The two procedures give different results for the experiment. In the noncorrection procedure, rats eventually choose consistently whichever side has food more often.[16] But in the correction procedure rats do not develop such a strong preference for the side that is positive more often. After many trials in the situation, the proportion of choices of side B_1 is about equal to π, the proportion of trials when B_1 was positive.[17]

---

[16] A. Parducci and J. Polt, "Correction vs. Noncorrection with Changing Reinforcement Schedules," *J. comp. physiol. Psychol.*, 1958, **51,** 492–495.

[17] W. K. Estes, "Of Models and Men," *Amer. Psychologist*, 1957, **12**, 609–617.

One possible reason for the difference comes from the different outcomes that follow choices in the two procedures. In the correction procedure, after the rat chooses one side or the other, the outcomes are either to eat right away (E), or to have to run back to the choice point and then to the other side, thus obtaining food after some delay (D). In the noncorrection procedure, the outcomes are to eat (E), or to be held at the end of the maze (H). Then if we apply Eq. (3.3) in the correction procedure, we assume the response strengths for choosing the two sides are

$$v(B_1) = s(E \mid B_1)u(E) + s(D \mid B_1)u(D),$$
$$v(B_2) = s(E \mid B_2)u(E) + s(D \mid B_2)u(D).$$

However, in the noncorrection procedure we should have

$$v(B_1) = s(E \mid B_1)u(E) + s(H \mid B_1)u(H),$$
$$v(B_2) = s(E \mid B_1)u(E) + s(H \mid B_2)u(H).$$

Now suppose that rats learn to expect the two outcomes accurately—that is, assume that on the average the conditional expectations eventually equal the proportions used by the experimenter. Then, after a sufficient number of trials in the correction procedure,

$$s(E \mid B_1) = s(D \mid B_2) = \pi, \qquad s(E \mid B_2) = s(D \mid B_1) = 1 - \pi;$$

and in the noncorrection procedure,

$$s(E \mid B_1) = s(H \mid B_2) = \pi, \qquad s(E \mid B_2) = s(H \mid B_1) = 1 - \pi.$$

Now recall that in the correction procedure rats choose side B_1 about as often as the experimenter makes B_1 the positive side. This should happen if $u(E)$ is some positive value, and $u(D)$ is zero. In other words, the rats have some positive response strength for eating right away, but this is just neutralized by having to retrace and go to the other side. If $u(E)$ is positive and $u(D)$ is zero, then the probability of choosing B_1 should be

$$P(B_1) = \frac{v(B_1)}{v(B_1) + v(B_2)} = \frac{s(E \mid B_1)u(E)}{s(E \mid B_1)u(E) + s(E \mid B_2)u(E)} \cdot$$

Then, by the assumption about expectations,

$$P(B_1) = \pi,$$

which is typically what happens.

Also recall that in the noncorrection procedure, the rats will consistently choose the side that is positive more often. This suggests that there is a negative response strength associated with being held at the end of the maze. In other words, $u(H)$ is negative, which means that being held in the maze is something the rat would just as soon avoid. For example, suppose that

$$u(E) = +1, \qquad u(H) = -1.$$

Then the equations for the noncorrection procedure give the following results.

$$v(B_1) = \pi(+1) + (1 - \pi)(-1) = 2\pi - 1,$$
$$v(B_2) = \pi(-1) + (1 - \pi)(+1) = 1 - 2\pi.$$

If B_1 is positive more often than B_2, this means that $\pi > .50$. In that case $v(B_1)$ would be positive and $v(B_2)$ would be negative. Our equation for computing choice probabilities does not apply in such a case (see footnote 18 in Chapter 2); however, we should expect that in such a situation rats would choose B_1 all the time, which is what happens typically with the noncorrection procedure.

A kind of experiment closely related to the *T*-maze experiments just discussed uses responses like bar pressing by rats or pecking at disks by pigeons. There are two response alternatives (for rats, two bars; for pigeons, two disks). The experimental subject is made hungry, and the experimenter gives some food after responses on either alternative. However, the animal is not fed after every response; instead, reinforcement is given according to some specified schedule in which reinforcement occurs only at certain times or after certain numbers of responses occur. Procedures like this are called partial reinforcement schedules. In the experiments that we discuss here, the schedule used is called a variable interval schedule. First consider a situation involving a single response *B*. There is an interval of time during which responses will not be followed by food. At the end of the interval, the schedule "sets up," which means that the animal's next response on that alternative will be followed by an opportunity to eat. For example, at some point in the experiment the schedule might call for a 1-min interval. A timer starts and no responses on *B* will be followed by eating until 1 min has elapsed. As soon as the time period ends, the animal's next response on *B* will be followed by an opportunity to eat. The length of the interval varies during the experiment, and we describe a schedule by specifying the average length of the interval needed to obtain a reinforcement. For example, VI(3 min) refers to a schedule with varying intervals, where the average length of the intervals is 3 min. Obviously, if the average interval is short, the animal can eat relatively often; if the average interval is long, the chances to eat will come less often and the number of opportunities to eat will be smaller.

In experiments involving two responses different schedules can be used for the two alternatives. For example, in one situation where the subjects were pigeons and the responses were pecking two different disks,[18] the

[18] R. J. Herrnstein, "Relative and Absolute Strength of Response as a Function of Frequency of Reinforcement." *J. exp. Anal. Behav.*, 1961, **4,** 267–273.

schedule for one of the disks (B_1) was VI(2.5 min) and for the other disk (B_2) the schedule was VI(4 min). This means that if the pigeon started making response B_1, he would be able to eat after a shorter time, on the average, than if he started making response B_2. Frequently (though not always) there is a procedure which keeps the subject from switching from one response to the other between reinforcements. In the pigeon experiments this is done by giving a penalty of a second or two before he gets a chance to eat when the bird begins on one alternative and switches. An alternative procedure that has been used in rat experiments is to wait until the animal starts pressing on one of the bars and then remove the other bar until the time period on the chosen bar ends and the animal has had a chance to eat.[19]

During an experimental session, the animal will make some B_1 responses and some B_2 responses. He will also have some chances to eat; sometimes eating will follow B_1 responses and sometimes it will follow B_2. If B_1 has a schedule with short intervals and B_2 has a schedule with long intervals, then eating will follow B_1 responses more often than it will follow B_2. In that case, the animal's expectation of eating following B_1 should be higher than his expectation of eating following B_2. In fact, the data suggest a particularly simple relationship between the subject's expectations and the frequencies with which opportunities to eat follow the two base responses. If eating follows B_1 k times as often as it follows B_2, then the expectation of eating, given B_1, will be k times the expectation of eating given B_2. Or, putting this in another way, *the ratio of the conditional expectations of reinforcement following the two responses will equal the ratio of the frequencies of reinforcement following the two responses.* If we let $n(B_1, E)$ and $n(B_2, E)$ stand for the numbers of reinforcements that are given following the two responses, then the rule says that[20]

$$\frac{s(E \mid B_1)}{s(E \mid B_2)} = \frac{n(B_1, E)}{n(B_2, E)}. \tag{3.4}$$

The data of the experiments that we will consider here involve the frequency of performing response B_1 relative to the total frequency of performing B_1 and B_2. The data are obtained by counting the number of B_1

[19] J. T. Miller and D. Premack, "Possible and Actual Reinforcement Times as Determinants of Choice." Cited by D. Premack, "Reinforcement Theory," *op. cit.*

[20] Note that the rule talks only about the relative values of the expectations. The animal's overall expectation for eating apparently is determined in a fairly complicated way by the overall frequency of eating responses in the situation. One suggestion regarding this problem is made by A. C. Catania, "Concurrent performance: reinforcement interaction and response independence," *J. exp. Anal. Behav.*, 1963, **6**, 253–264. Catania's suggestion involves a power law relationship between the total frequency of base responding (for example, pecking) and the total frequency of eating.

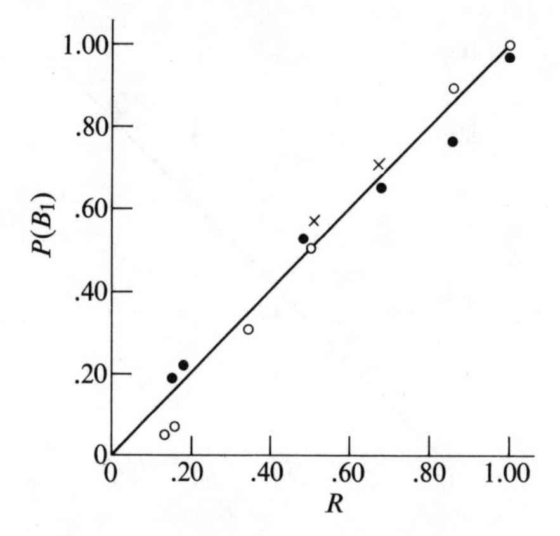

Fig. 6. Relationship between proportion of reinforcements following a response and proportion of choices of that response.

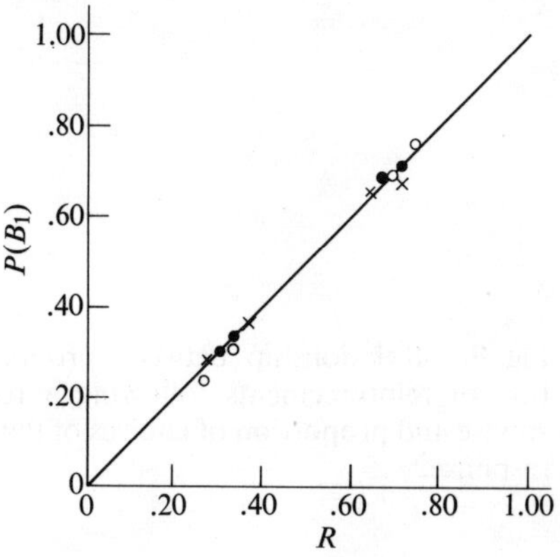

Fig. 7. Relationship between proportion of reinforcements following a response and proportion of choices of that response.

and B_2 responses [$n(B_1)$ and $n(B_2)$] and calculating

$$P(B_1) = \frac{n(B_1)}{n(B_1) + n(B_2)}.$$

The relative frequency of eating following B_1 is also calculated. The numbers of reinforcements following B_1 and B_2 are counted and the fraction

$$R = \frac{n(B_1, E)}{n(B_1, E) + n(B_2, E)}$$

is calculated. The results of the experiment regarding $P(B_1)$ and R are as simple as they could be. In at least three experiments, the data have been consistent with the relationship

$$P(B_1) = R.$$

Figures 6, 7, and 8 show the data from three experiments[21] in which the prediction was supported by the results.

Equation (3.4) gives a good prediction for the data if we use Eq. (3.3) and assume that the animal has zero response strength associated with an outcome of not eating. Then we have

$$v(B_1) = s(E \mid B_1)u(E), \qquad v(B_2) = s(E \mid B_2)u(E). \tag{3.5}$$

[21] The data in Fig. 6 are from Herrnstein, *op. cit.;* in Fig. 7, from C. S. Reynolds, "On Some Determinants of Choice in Pigeons," *J. exp. Anal. Behav.*, 1963, **6,** 53–62; and in Fig. 8, from Miller and Premack, *op. cit.* The data labeled ×, ○, and ● are from different experimental subjects.

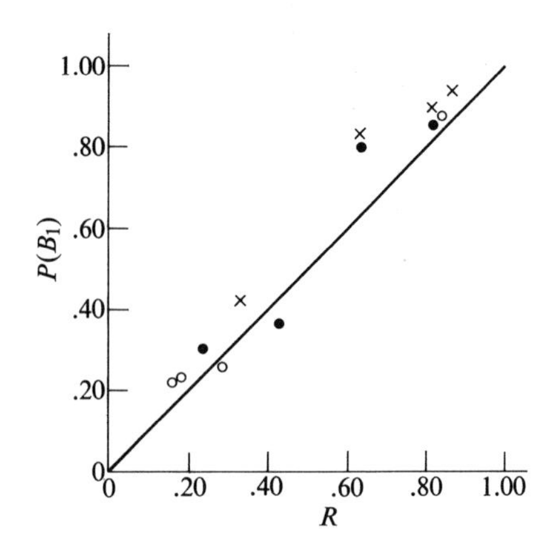

Fig. 8. Relationship between proportion of reinforcements following a response and proportion of choices of that response.

We make the further assumption that $P(B_1)$ measures the relative response strengths of B_1 and B_2; that is,

$$P(B_1) = \frac{v(B_1)}{v(B_1) + v(B_2)}.$$

We modify this equation in a familiar way:

$$P(B_1) = \frac{v(B_1)/v(B_2)}{1 + [v(B_1)/v(B_2)]}.$$

Then, using Eq. (3.4) and (3.5),

$$P(B_1) = \frac{s(E \mid B_1)/s(E \mid B_2)}{1 + [s(E \mid B_1)/s(E \mid B_2)]} = \frac{n(B_1, E)/n(B_2, E)}{1 + [n(B_1, E)/n(B_2, E)]}.$$

From the earlier equation for R,

$$R = \frac{n(B_1, E)/n(B_2, E)}{1 + [n(B_1, E)/n(B_2, E)]}.$$

But these equations show that $P(B_1) = R$, which is the result of the experiments.

The important part of the argument is Eq. (3.4), which says that the relative strengths of expectations for eating depend simply on the relative frequencies of eating following the two alternative base responses. In the discussion of *T*-maze experiments, we made this assumption of proportionality for a situation where the animal must make one of two responses on each trial. It is interesting that the same assumption seems to apply when the animal is free to respond at his own rate.

We have studied several situations where alternative responses are available, and our interest has been in the subject's expectations that the contingent response will follow the alternative base responses. In *T*-maze experiments using the correction procedure and in experiments where two alternatives are present all the time the results follow a simple pattern. In these situations, the results support the idea that a subject's expectations are proportional to the frequencies of reinforcement following the alternative responses.

3D EXPECTATIONS DEPENDING ON STIMULUS CUES

In the last section we analyzed situations where choices are influenced by expectations of a chance to perform a high-strength contingent response. In this section we consider situations where the expectation of a high-strength response is not always the same.

In the simplest situation of this kind there are two stimuli. For example, an animal may be in a box in which sometimes a light is on and other times the light is off. One of the stimuli is designated S_+ and the other is S_-. The experiment involves conditioning, so there is a base response such as a bar to press or a disk to peck. Also, a high-strength contingent response such as eating or drinking can be permitted. In the experiment, when the stimulus is S_+, the contingent response is permitted after the base response is performed. But when the stimulus is S_-, the contingent response is not permitted. For example, suppose that the subject is a rat, the base response is pressing a bar, and the contingent response is drinking. The experimenter might decide to have S_+ when a light is on and S_- when the light is off. The experimenter might turn on the light for 1 min, and then turn it off for 1 min, alternating in that way during the experiment. During the intervals with the light on, the experimenter would let the rat drink after he pressed the bar. During the intervals with the light off, the experimenter would not let the rat drink at all.

The experiment involves a simple discrimination between the two stimuli, and it can be used to study an animal's ability to see differences between lights or to hear differences between tones. If the animal distinguishes between the stimuli, the base response will be performed at a fairly high rate when the stimulus is S_+, so that the animal can obtain the opportunities to perform the contingent response. But the base response will not occur or will occur at a low rate during S_-, when the contingent response is not permitted.

The difference in response can be explained easily. The subject learns to expect the contingent response when he performs the base response during S_+, but he learns not to expect the contingent response when the stimulus is S_-. Let $s(C \mid B, S_+)$ be the strength of the expectation that the contingent response will be permitted following the base response during stimulus S_+. And let $s(C \mid B, S_-)$ be the strength of the expectation of C given B during stimulus S_-. If S_+ and S_- are easy for the subject to discriminate, then it will not be hard for the experimenter to train the subject so that $s(C \mid B, S_+)$

is high, and $s(C \mid B, S_-)$ is low. This means that the response strength for the base response will be different depending on the stimulus. Let $v(B \mid S_+)$ be the strength of B during S_+ and let $v(B \mid S_-)$ be the strength of B during S_-. For simplicity, assume that there is zero value for the base response unless it is followed by the contingent response. Then

$$v(B \mid S_+) = s(C \mid B, S_+)u(C), \qquad \text{and} \qquad v(B \mid S_-) = s(C \mid B, S_-)u(C). \tag{3.6}$$

With $u(C)$ positive, when $s(C \mid B, S_+)$ is high and $s(C \mid B, S_-)$ is low, $v(B \mid S_+)$ will be higher than $v(B \mid S_-)$; in other words, the strength of B will be higher when the stimulus is S_+ because that is when the subject expects to be able to perform the contingent response.

One use of the discrimination experiment is to study the perceptual capabilities of animals. For example, suppose that S_+ and S_- are two lights of equal intensity but different wavelength. Then if an animal can be trained on a discrimination using the lights, we know that the animal's visual system must respond differently to the two wavelengths; that is, the animal has color vision for that part of the spectrum. Or suppose that S_+ and S_- are two different patterns of tones—say, low-high-low-high and high-low-low-high. If an animal can be trained to discriminate between these stimuli, we have evidence that the animal has the ability to perceive sequential properties of auditory stimuli; that is, he can perceive simple tunes.

A more complicated kind of discrimination experiment can be done, in which we can study more complex perceptual abilities of animals—notably attention. The experimental apparatus is a T-maze or a discrimination box, such as is shown in Fig. 9. Most frequently these experiments use rats as subjects. The animal is put in the end of the box labeled "Start" in the drawing, and then goes into one of the choice compartments. The rat is hungry; if he makes the correct choice, he finds some food and can then make the high-strength contingent response of eating.

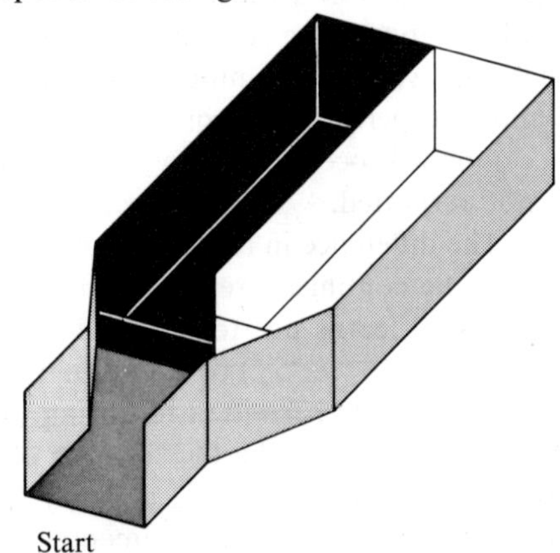

Fig. 9. An apparatus for studying discriminative conditioning.

The two choice compartments can be made different in a number of ways, involving different stimulus dimensions. In the figure, the left compartment is black and the right one white; thus, color is one of the stimulus dimensions in the situation. Another stimulus dimension is the height of a small hurdle that the rat has to step over to enter the compartment. Referring to the figure, we note that there is a low hurdle in front of the left, black compartment, and a higher hurdle in front of the right, white compartment. Other stimulus dimensions may be used, such as the texture of the floor of the compartments (smooth and rough), or the presence of a curtain made of pull-lamp chains in front of one compartment and the absence of such a curtain in the other. One dimension that always is involved is position; one compartment is on the left and the other is on the right. We will illustrate the experimental situation for a case involving three stimulus dimensions: position, color, and hurdles.

On different trials, the stimulus values are combined in different ways. For a situation involving three dimensions, there are four possible combinations. (1) The left side is black with a low hurdle, as shown in the figure, and the right side is white with a high hurdle. (2) The left side is black with a high hurdle; the right side is white with a low hurdle. (3) The left side is white with a low hurdle; the right side is black with a high hurdle. (4) The left side is white with a high hurdle; the right side is black with a low hurdle. Usually the different combinations are used equally often in an irregular schedule.

The experimenter places food in one of the compartments, using one of the stimulus dimensions to decide where to place the food. For example, one way to run this experiment would be always to place food on the white side, regardless of which side was white and regardless of whether the white side had a low or high hurdle. The dimension used to determine the correct choice is called the relevant dimension. The other dimensions are irrelevant dimensions. For instance, if food is always placed in the white compartment, then color is the relevant dimension, and position and hurdles are irrelevant. (Note that we could also have a rule of putting the food on the black side. This would still make color the relevant dimension. We could make the height of the hurdles relevant by using the rule of putting food on the side with the low hurdle, or by using the rule of putting food on the side with the high hurdle.)

The learning that occurs in this kind of experiment involves two processes. The animal learns to attend to the relevant dimension more than to the irrelevant dimensions, and he learns to choose the positive stimulus. For example, if we have color relevant and white positive, then the animal will (1) learn to attend to the colors of the compartments, and (2) learn to choose the white compartment rather than the black one. One way to describe the rat's learning is to say that he learns a strong conditional expectation $s(E \mid B_1)$, where E is the contingent response of eating and B_1 is the base response of choosing the white compartment. This is probably accompanied by a low conditional expectation $s(E \mid B_2)$, where B_2 is the base response of choosing the black compartment. Of course, if the rat is to learn to choose white rather than black, he must attend to the color of the compartments, and often the process of learning to attend is an important part of the learning process.

In one study,[22] rats were given a fairly hard discrimination problem, where color was relevant but the two stimuli were not very different. The two sides of a discrimination box were painted different shades of gray, with the darker shade sometimes on the left and sometimes on the right. The animals were hungry, and the correct choice depended on the color. (For some of the rats the positive stimulus was the darker gray and for others the positive stimulus was the lighter gray.) The experiment included two main conditions. One group of rats had to learn the discrimination between the two shades of gray. A second group began by learning a discrimination involving color, but the two stimuli were black and white. Then this second group was transferred to the hard discrimination involving the two shades of gray. The discrimination between black and white was learned more easily than the discrimination between dark and light gray, but this was to be expected. The important result was that the second group completed both their problems in fewer trials than it took the first group to learn the single discrimination between dark and light gray. The group that began with the easy discrimination apparently learned to attend to the colors of the compartments rather easily when the difference between the colors was more obvious, and this attention to the relevant dimension transferred to the harder discrimination to make the final problem much easier.

In this section we have been discussing the role of expectations that depend on stimulus cues. Equation (3.6) involves the idea that expectations, and therefore choices, may be different depending on the stimulus that applies at a given time. Our present discussion relates to the role of attention in determining what aspect of the stimulus will be effective in influencing the subject's choice. Often the stimulus that is related to opportunities to perform a high-strength response occurs along with other stimuli that are irrelevant to the reinforcement, and then a major part of the learning process may be to distinguish which aspect of the stimulus is to be used.

The final topic in this section is extinction, and we will return to considering situations that do not involve special presentations of stimuli. However, a stimulus aspect of the general situation will be involved in the discussion in an important way.

From the previous section, recall that conditioning involves learning a strong conditional expectation of a contingent response given a base

---

[22] D. H. Lawrence, "The Transfer of a Discrimination along a Continuum," *J. comp. physiol. Psychol.*, 1952, **45,** 511–516.

response. For example, a rat may be taught to expect to be able to eat after he presses a bar. To teach this to a rat we give him food after he presses the bar, and this is called reinforcement.

After an animal has been conditioned to perform some base response, an experimenter may extinguish the base response by withholding the contingent response. For example, if we have conditioned bar pressing by giving a rat food after he presses, we can extinguish the bar-pressing response if we give the hungry rat the bar to press, but do not give him food after he presses it. Before too long the animal stops making the base response. In the language we are using here, a base response will be extinguished because the subject now learns not to expect the contingent response following the base response. The value of $s(C \mid B)$ becomes low or zero. Then the response strength

$$v(B) = s(C \mid B)u(C)$$

also becomes low or zero; therefore, we know that the base response will not be performed.

An important fact about extinction relates to conditioning with partial reinforcement. We have discussed partial reinforcement based on interval schedules, where the base response is reinforced only after an interval of time has elapsed. Another type of schedule is called a ratio schedule, where the reinforcement is given only after a certain number of base responses have occurred. In either the ratio or the interval schedule, the subject can sometimes perform the contingent response after he performs the base response, but at other times he performs the base response and does not get a chance to perform the contingent response.

Intuitively, it seems as though partial reinforcement would produce a weaker expectation of the contingent response than if reinforcement were given after every base response. Recall our discussion of the relative strengths of different base responses associated with different reinforcement schedules. We used the idea that if reinforcement occurred more often following one base response, the conditional expectation of the contingent response would be stronger for that response and it would therefore be performed more often. However, it turns out that extinction following partial reinforcement is much slower than extinction following reinforcement that is given for every base response.

The slower extinction following partial reinforcement can be understood if we think about the situation in which the conditioning took place. When an animal is performing with partial reinforcement, he frequently gives the response without having an opportunity to make the contingent response. Therefore, he is frequently in a situation where he has made the base response one or more times and has not been reinforced for a while. However, in the partial reinforcement situation he will eventually be able to make the contingent response. He learns to expect reinforcement eventually, even though the base response has not been followed by reinforcement for a while.[23]

On the other hand, an animal that has been reinforced each time he has given the base response has never been in a situation where the base response has occurred without the contingent response following immediately. Therefore, by reinforcing the base response continuously we do not train the animal to expect the contingent response in a situation where it has not been allowed for a while. The result is that after reinforcement for every base response, the conditional expectation of the contingent response breaks down much more quickly.

3E EXPECTATIONS FOR DIFFERENT KINDS OR AMOUNTS OF CONTINGENT RESPONDING

In many situations there are a number of alternative base responses, and they have been associated with different contingent responses. For example, a person may have a choice between two or more restaurants when he is deciding where to go for dinner. In one of the restaurants he may have had good seafood, and in another he may have had good steak. Using the terms of our present analysis, we would say that the base response of going to the first restaurant had been associated with the contingent response of eating seafood, and the base response of going to the second restaurant had been associated with the contingent response of eating steak. Another example involves alternative family vacation trips. The base response of going to a lake resort is associated with contingent responses like swimming and boating. The base response of going to a camp in the mountains is associated with contingent responses like hiking and stream fishing.

We have a simple analysis of the idea if we consider a situation with two base responses B_1 and B_2, and two contingent responses C_1 and C_2. The response strengths for the two alternatives are

$$v(B_1) = s(C_1 \mid B_1)u(C_1) + s(C_2 \mid B_1)u(C_2),$$
$$v(B_2) = s(C_1 \mid B_2)u(C_1) + s(C_2 \mid B_2)u(C_2).$$

In the simplest case each base response will be associated with just one of

[23] Our idea here is basically the same as one used by E. J. Capaldi, although Capaldi uses different terms to express the idea. In Capaldi's statement, a situation where the base response has not been reinforced is described as a stimulus, and this stimulus is called the aftereffect of nonreinforcement. With partial reinforcement, the aftereffect stimulus often is present when the animal makes a response which then is reinforced. This means that the aftereffect stimulus becomes an S_+ stimulus, and when extinction begins, the connection between the aftereffect stimulus and response has to be extinguished. One experiment illustrating the principle is E. J. Capaldi and M. G. Senko, "Acquisition and Transfer in Partial Reinforcement," *J. exp. Psychol.*, 1962 **63,** 155–159.

the contingent responses. For example, an individual's experience might lead him to expect C_1 if he chose B_1 and to expect C_2 if he chose B_2. In the most extreme situation,

$$s(C_1 \mid B_1) = s(C_2 \mid B_2) = 1.0, \qquad s(C_1 \mid B_2) = s(C_2 \mid B_1) = 0.0.$$

In that case,

$$v(B_1) = u(C_1), \qquad v(B_2) = u(C_2).$$

The result signifies that in this kind of situation, the choice between B_1 and B_2 depends on the individual's values for C_1 and C_2. The result certainly is reasonable. If two responses lead to different outcomes, then a person will choose the response leading to the outcome he wants.

In an experimental illustration of this, rats were trained in a maze with different motives operating on different days.[24] On some days the rats were deprived of food so that the response of eating had high strength; on other days the rats were deprived of water so that drinking was at high strength. Food was always placed on one side of the maze and water on the other. The experimental result is simple: rats are able to master the task so that they run to water on days when they are thirsty and they run to food on days when they are hungry. The base response of turning one direction in the maze becomes associated with food; that is, the animal learns to expect that eating can (will) follow a turn in one direction. And in a similar way, the response of turning the other direction becomes associated with drinking. Once the two expectations are established, the strengths of the two base responses are determined by the strengths of the two contingent responses. By depriving a rat of water to drink, we raise the strength of the drinking response, hence raising the strength of the base response that leads to drinking. The situation is similar with deprivation of eating and the response that leads to eating.

We have been considering situations where different base responses lead to different contingent responses. Now we discuss some situations where different base responses lead to different amounts of the same contingent response.

One kind of experiment uses pigeons or rats as subjects. With pigeons, two keys are available; with rats, there are two levers. Each of the available responses is associated with a variable interval reinforcement schedule. The two schedules have the same average delay interval, so on the average the animal will be fed as soon for making one response as he will for the other. However, when reinforcement occurs after one of the responses, the con-

---

[24] The experimental result is called "drive discrimination." It was demonstrated in early experiments by C. L. Hull, "Differential Habituation to Internal Stimuli in the Albino Rat," *J. comp. Psychol.*, 1933, **16**, 255–273; and by R. Leeper, "The Role of Motivation in Learning. A Study of the Phenomenon of Differential Motivation Control of the Utilization of Habits," *J. genet. Psychol.*, 1935, **46**, 3–40.

tingent response is available for a longer time than it is when reinforcement occurs after the other response. For example, in one study subjects were thirsty rats, and the base responses involved two levers.[25] Each of the levers was associated with a reinforcement schedule that would permit drinking 1 min after the rat started to press a bar. On one of the bars, when drinking was permitted, the tube was available for 8 sec; and on the other bar, when drinking was permitted, the tube was available for 4 sec. In another study the subjects were hungry pigeons.[26] Each base response was pecking a disk. When the pigeon began to peck a disk, a timer started and a food bin opened after an average interval of 2 min. When eating was permitted after pecking one of the disks, the food bin was left open for 6 sec, and when eating was permitted after pecking the other disk the food bin was left open for only 3 sec.

The situation is a little like the one described in Section 3C in which there were two keys with different schedules. But in the earlier case the subject had to wait longer, on the average, before getting food for pecking on one of the keys than for pecking on the other. We said then that the pigeon probably learned a stronger expectation for eating following one response than the other.

In this case, however, there is no difference between the responses in the average delay before eating is allowed. The difference is in the amount of eating that is permitted when the food bin is opened. Then we should not anticipate a difference in the animal's expectations for eating following the two responses; instead, we should anticipate that the animal would expect different amounts of eating, and that he would have a higher value for the greater amount of eating.

Let the two amounts of contingent responding be called C_1 and C_2, and suppose that C_1 is the greater. Let B_1 be the response that is followed by amount C_1 of contingent responding, and let B_2 be the base response followed by amount C_2. For simplicity we assume again that the animal learns to expect what happens; that is,

$$s(C_1 \mid B_1) = s(C_2 \mid B_2) = 1.0.$$

In that case we have

$$v(B_1) = u(C_1), \qquad v(B_2) = u(C_2).$$

In the experiments the behavior of the subjects seems to follow a simple rule: the animals divide their choices in the same proportion as they obtain

---

[25] Miller and Premack, *op. cit.* Data are from three subjects.

[26] A. C. Catania, "Concurrent Performance: A Baseline for the Study of Reinforcement Magnitude," *J. exp. Anal. Behav.*, 1963, **6**, 299–301. Data are from three subjects.

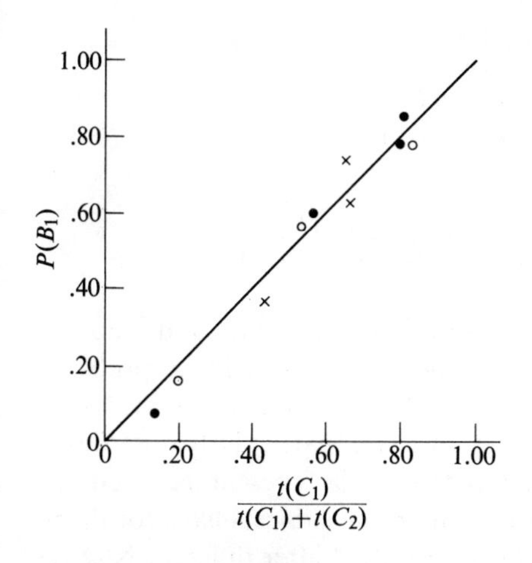

Fig. 10. Relationship between proportion of total reinforcement time following a base response and proportion of choices of that response.

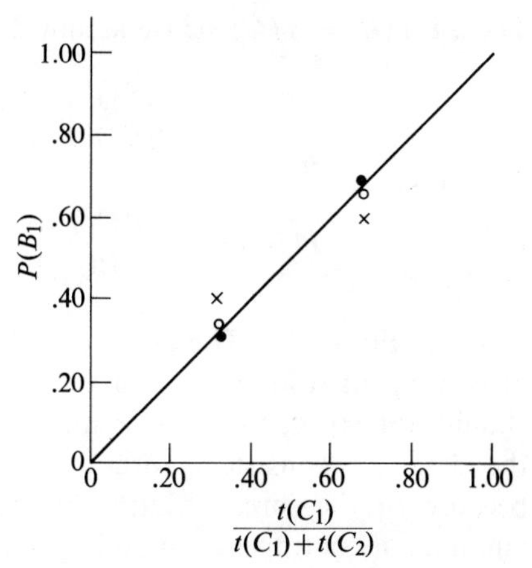

Fig. 11. Relationship between proportion of total reinforcement time following a base response and proportion of choices of that response.

food. Let $t(C_1)$ and $t(C_2)$ be the total times during the experiment that animals are allowed the contingent response following responses B_1 and B_2, respectively. And let $P(B_1)$ stand for the proportion of total responses that are responses on B_1. Then in the experiments,

$$P(B_1) = \frac{t(C_1)}{t(C_1) + t(C_2)} \cdot \tag{3.7}$$

Figures 10 and 11 show the results of the two experiments cited above: Figure 10 shows the data from the experiment with rats and Fig. 11 shows the data obtained using pigeons. In both cases the results are very close to the predicted relationship.

Equation (3.7) suggests that in these experiments there is an attractively simple relationship between the amount of contingent responding and the value the animal attaches to the reinforcer. We should expect Eq. (3.7) if the ratio of values to the subject equals the ratio of the amounts of contingent responding; that is,

$$\frac{u(C_1)}{u(C_2)} = \frac{t(C_1)}{t(C_2)} \cdot$$

It is easy to show that this relationship leads to the experimental result given in Eq. (3.7). As $P(B_1)$ is defined there,

$$P(B_1) = \frac{v(B_1)}{v(B_1) + v(B_2)} = \frac{v(B_1)/v(B_2)}{1 + [v(B_1)/v(B_2)]} \cdot$$

Then, if $v(B) = u(C)$, as we assumed earlier,

$$\frac{v(B_1)}{v(B_2)} = \frac{u(C_1)}{u(C_2)} = \frac{t(C_1)}{t(C_2)}.$$

Therefore,

$$P(B_1) = \frac{t(C_1)/t(C_2)}{1 + [t(C_1)/t(C_2)]} = \frac{t(C_1)}{t(C_1) + t(C_2)},$$

which is Eq. (3.7). The assumed relationship between values and amounts of contingent responding is a very simple one, of course, and we probably should not expect to find it in all situations. However, the situations where the data are consistent with this simple rule are particularly interesting because of the direct relationship that seems to be present between the amounts of contingent responding and the values the subjects have for them.

The amount of contingent responding permitted after different base responses is varied in a different way in experiments where rats run in *T*-mazes. Earlier we considered the simplest situation, where food is placed on one side of the maze and not on the other; rats learn to run to the side where the food is placed because they learn to expect a chance to eat following the correct base response. In similar experiments food is placed on both sides of the maze, but there is a larger amount of food on one side than the other. If the rat chooses the side with more food, he is permitted a larger amount of the contingent eating response than if he chooses the side with less food.

In one experiment the different amounts of food involved different numbers of small food pellets; for example, in one group there were four pellets on one side and two pellets on the other.[27] Call the larger amount of eating C_1 and the smaller amount C_2. Also, let B_1 be the response of choosing the side that has more food and let B_2 be the response of choosing the other side. When the animal has learned which side has the larger amount of food, then we would say that

$$s(C_1 \mid B_1) = s(C_2 \mid B_2) = 1.0,$$

as before. Then we might expect

$$v(B_1) = u(C_1), \qquad v(B_2) = u(C_2),$$

and if that were true, the frequencies of choice of the two sides would be proportional to the values of the two amounts of food. However, the experiment does not give that result. Instead, the animals eventually choose the side with the larger amount of food on every trial.

[27] K. N. Clayton, "*T*-Maze Choice Behavior as a Joint Function of the Reward Magnitude for the Alternatives," *J. comp. physiol. Psychol.*, 1964, **58,** 333–338.

There are several possible explanations of the result, but one relates to an idea we have used earlier in our discussion of choice. We considered situations where there were two choice alternatives, and all the aspects of one were also present in the other. We were interested in situations where the subject's choice depended just on the difference between the two alternatives. If the *T*-maze experiment works that way, then the response strengths might be

$$v(B_1) = u(C_1 - C_2), \qquad v(B_2) = 0,$$

where $(C_1 - C_2)$ is the difference between the two amounts of eating. In this case the probability of choosing B_1 would be

$$P(B_1) = \frac{v(B_1)}{v(B_1) + v(B_2)} = 1.0$$

which is the result obtained.

This leaves unanswered the question of why animals choose the larger reward consistently in a maze experiment, while in a bar-pressing or disk-pecking situation, the animals divide their choices in proportion to the amounts of contingent response that follow the two base responses. An exact explanation is not available, but a possible factor is the time between trials in the *T*-maze experiment. After each trial, the animal is taken out of the maze for a time before being returned to make the next choice. In the bar-pressing or disk-pecking experiment, the animal is continuously in the choice situation. As soon as one period of contingent responding is finished, the animal immediately makes another choice. The fact that animals divide their choices between the two alternatives rather than consistently choosing the larger reward may be related to the tendency for alternating between different responses when the time between choices is small.

3F CHOICES IN SOCIAL INTERACTIONS

Our analyses of choices given in Chapter 2 and thus far in the present chapter have been based on two concepts, expectations and values. In Chapter 2 we worked with various choice situations and showed how choices are influenced by an individual's expectations about what will happen if he chooses a certain action, and by his values regarding the things he thinks will happen. Thus far in this chapter we have been working with situations where contingencies between responses are set up in an experimental procedure. A subject learns the connection—he learns to expect that the contingent response will follow the base response. The result is a strengthening of the base response, at least as long as the contingency continues.

The ideas that we have used to analyze individual choice and conditioning can also be applied to situations where two or more people make choices and the outcome received by each person depends on his own choice and the choice made by the other person. As an example, consider a situation presented earlier (Problem 16, Chapter 2). The boy has a choice between going out for coffee and staying home. If he chooses to go out for coffee there are two possible outcomes: (1) meeting his girl, and (2) just having coffee. To analyze the situation completely, we also need to deal with the girl's choice situation. She may have the alternatives of going out for coffee or going to the library. If she chooses to go for coffee there are two possible outcomes: (1) meeting the boy, and (2) having coffee with other girls. If the boy chooses to go for coffee, his outcome will depend on the girl's choice in an obvious way. If she chooses to go for coffee, then the boy's outcome will be (1) meeting his girl. If the boy chooses to go for coffee and the girl chooses to go to the library, then the outcome for the boy will be (2) just having coffee. Of course, the girl is in the same kind of situation. If she decides to go for coffee and the boy also decides to go for coffee, the girl's outcome will be (1) meeting the boy. If she chooses to go for coffee and the boy stays home, her outcome is (2) having coffee with other girls.

In discussing choice situations involving one person we have used the fact that an outcome depends on the person's choice. In the choice situation where a rat is fed for turning right in a maze, we can describe the situation by showing a simple table:

Choice	Outcome
Turn right	Eat
Turn left	Not Eat

Now recall an earlier discussion where there was some uncertainty about the outcome. We discussed a situation where a person had to choose whether he would take an umbrella in the morning. There the outcome depended on something besides what the person did; namely, whether it rained or not. Then we have a more complicated table of outcomes:

Choice \ Situation	Rain	No rain
Take umbrella	Keep dry	Carry umbrella
Leave umbrella	Get wet	No problem

In situations involving interaction, each person's outcome depends on his choice and on something else, but the other factor is the choice made by the other person. In the example involving the trip for coffee, the boy's outcomes might be as follows (the numbers are hypothetical values or response strengths regarding the outcomes):

Boy's Outcomes

Girl's choice / Boy's choice	Go for coffee	Go to library
Go for coffee	Have coffee and meet girl (20)	Have coffee (2)
Stay home	Get studying done (10)	Get studying done (10)

The important new feature is that the choices made by each person affect the outcomes for the other. Therefore, we need to consider the girl's outcomes as well.

Girl's Outcomes

Girl's choice / Boy's choice	Go for coffee	Go to library
Go for coffee	Have coffee with friends and meet boy (20)	Get studying done (8)
Stay home	Have coffee with friends (15)	Get studying done (8)

It is more convenient if we can summarize all the information in a single table. Let B_1 and B_2 be the girl's alternatives (B_1: go for coffee; B_2 go to library) and let A_1 and A_2 be the boy's alternatives (A_1: go for coffee; A_2: stay home). Each combination of choices produces an outcome for each person. In the table, the boy's outcomes are in the shaded parts of the squares.

Girl's choice / Boy's choice	B_1	B_2
A_1	Girl: 20; Boy (shaded): 20	Girl: 8; Boy (shaded): 2
A_2	Girl: 15; Boy (shaded): 10	Girl: 8; Boy (shaded): 10

A two-person interaction of the kind described is like a conditioning experiment in which each person's reinforcement is controlled by the other person. If two people have many chances to interact, each one learns a great deal about what he can expect the other one to do in choice situations. Suppose that a person has to make a choice where his outcome will be affected by the choice another person makes. Then the person probably goes through something like the following decision process: Suppose the person's alternatives are A_1 and A_2. He considers the alternatives that the second person has, say, B_1 and B_2. Then the person may think, "If he (the second person) chooses B_1, then my best choice will be ______. But if he chooses B_2, then my best choice will be ______." In such a case, the person's choice depends on whether he thinks the second person will choose B_1 or B_2. In other words, the person's expectation regarding the outcome of his choice amounts to an expectation about how he thinks the second person will choose.

We can apply our earlier equations for individual choice behavior to see what the expectations and choice probabilities might be in an interaction. Remember that for each alternative available to a person, the response strength is

$$v(A_i) = s(C_1 \mid A_i)u(C_1) + s(C_2 \mid A_i)u(C_2),$$

in the case where there are two possible outcomes. The situation here is complicated because we are considering outcomes that differ for the two individuals. Let $C_{ij,A}$ be the outcome for person A if person A chooses response A_i and person B chooses response B_j. Using the example given above, $u(C_{12,A}) = 15$ and $u(C_{12,B}) = 10$. Then the response strength for choosing alternative A_i is

$$v(A_i) = s(C_{i1,A} \mid A_i)u(C_{i1,A}) + s(C_{i2,A} \mid A_i)u(C_{i2,A}).$$

Now suppose that each person's expectations about the other's choices are accurate—that is, each person knows how often the other will choose in a certain way. In that case, we can replace terms like $s(C_{i1,A} \mid A_i)$ and $s(C_{i2,A} \mid A_i)$ with probabilities of the other person's responses, obtaining

$$v(A_i) = P(B_1)u(C_{i1,A}) + P(B_2)u(C_{i2,A})$$

for the person whose alternatives are A_1 and A_2. Similarly, for the other person

$$v(B_j) = P(A_1)u(C_{1j,B}) + P(A_2)u(C_{2j,B}).$$

Example 3.2. We work out the probabilities of choice for the situation described above. First, suppose that the girl chooses B_1. If the boy chooses A_1, the girl's outcome has value $u = 20$; if the boy chooses A_2, the girl's outcome has value $u = 15$. When we assume that the girl's expectations equal the boy's choice probabilities, we get

$$\begin{aligned} v(B_1) &= 20P(A_1) + 15P(A_2) = 20P(A_1) + 15[1 - P(A_1)] \\ &= 15 + 5P(A_1). \end{aligned}$$

In the example, if the girl chooses B_2, her outcome has value $u = 8$ regardless of the boy's choice. Then

$$v(B_2) = 8.$$

Now we can write an equation about the girl's choice probability.

$$P(B_1) = \frac{v(B_1)}{v(B_1) + v(B_2)} = \frac{15 + 5P(A_1)}{23 + 5P(A_1)}. \tag{3.8}$$

We can analyze the boy's situation in the same way. First, regarding the choice of A_1,

$$v(A_1) = 20P(B_1) + 2[1 - P(B_1)] = 2 + 18P(B_1).$$

Then

$$v(A_2) = 10;$$

and

$$P(A_1) = \frac{v(A_1)}{v(A_1) + v(A_2)} = \frac{2 + 18P(B_1)}{12 + 18P(B_1)}. \tag{3.9}$$

The main idea of our analysis is expressed in Eqs. (3.8) and (3.9). Each equation gives the probability of choice by one person as a function of the choice probability for the other person. The numbers in those equations depend on the values which the two people have for the different possible outcomes in the situation. But Eqs. (3.8) and (3.9) emphasize that the choice behaviors of the two people are interdependent, and our assumptions here lead to a relatively simple analysis of the interdependence.

The solution of Eqs. (3.8) and (3.9) is not hard, but it does get a little involved and it requires solving a quadratic equation. We begin by substituting for $P(A_1)$ in Eq. (3.8), using Eq. (3.9). This gives

$$\begin{aligned} P(B_1) &= \frac{15 + 5\left[\dfrac{2 + 18P(B_1)}{12 + 18P(B_1)}\right]}{23 + 5\left[\dfrac{2 + 18P(B_1)}{12 + 18P(B_1)}\right]} \\ &= \frac{180 + 270P(B_1) + 10 + 90P(B_1)}{276 + 414P(B_1) + 10 + 90P(B_1)} \end{aligned}$$

$$P(B_1) = \frac{190 + 360P(B_1)}{286 + 504P(B_1)}.$$

Then we can obtain

$$286P(B_1) + 504[P(B_1)]^2 = 190 + 360P(B_1);$$
$$504[P(B_1)]^2 - 74P(B_1) - 190 = 0.$$

Now recall that whenever we have a quadratic equation in the form

$$ax^2 + bx + c = 0,$$

we can solve for x using the formula

$$x = (-b \pm \sqrt{b^2 - 4ac})/2a.$$

Then we obtain the solution to our equation by

$$P(B_1) = (74 \pm \sqrt{74^2 + 4 \cdot 504 \cdot 190})/(2 \cdot 504).$$

One of the roots is negative, and we are not interested in that since the desired solution is a probability. The positive root is

$$P(B_1) = .69.$$

Having found $P(B_1)$, we can easily find the solution for $P(A_1)$. We simply substitute into Eq. (3.9).

$$P(A_1) = \frac{2 + (18)(.69)}{12 + (18)(.69)} = \frac{14.4}{24.4} = .59 \blacksquare$$

Example 3.3. To understand the situation more fully, we can use the obtained results to calculate probabilities of combinations of choice. In our example, the choice by each person had to be made independently of the other. Therefore, we calculate

$$P(A_1, B_1) = P(A_1)\,P(B_1) = (.59)(.69) = .41;$$

That is, the boy and girl will both choose to go for coffee about .41 of the time. Similarly,

$$P(A_1, B_2) = P(A_1)[1 - P(B_1)] = (.59)(.31) = .18.$$
$$P(A_2, B_1) = (.69)(.41) = .28.$$
$$P(A_2, B_2) = (.41)(.31) = .13.$$

That is, about .28 of the time the girl will go for coffee and find that the boy is staying home; about .18 of the time the boy will go for coffee and find that the girl has gone to the library; and about .13 of the time neither will go for coffee. ▮

In our example, both the boy and girl have preferences for going to have coffee if they can meet each other there. The values assumed here are entirely hypothetical, but they are not unreasonable. As we have analyzed the situation, it turns out rather badly for them; they only get together about 40% of the time. The problem is that they had to make their choices independently. If they talked together before making up their minds, they could remove most of the uncertainty and behave more nearly in agreement with their preferences. We can give some analysis of situations where people communicate about their choices, but first we consider some experiments in order to apply the ideas to empirical findings.

The first experiment we consider involved a two-person interaction, and each person had two response alternatives.[28] On every trial each subject chose one of his alternative responses. After the responses, the experimenter reinforced one of the subjects by signaling that his response was correct. The other player received a signal that his response was wrong. Neither player was told the response that the other player had made. The experimenter used a random sequence to decide which player to reinforce, but the probabilities for each player were different depending on the combination of choices. Call the two players A and B; call A's responses A_1 and A_2, and call B's responses B_1 and B_2. Then, for example, on trials when A chose A_1 and B chose B_1, the experimenter reinforced A's response $\frac{1}{3}$ of the time and reinforced B's response $\frac{2}{3}$ of the time. The probabilities of reinforcing each subject's response in all four combinations are given in the following table.

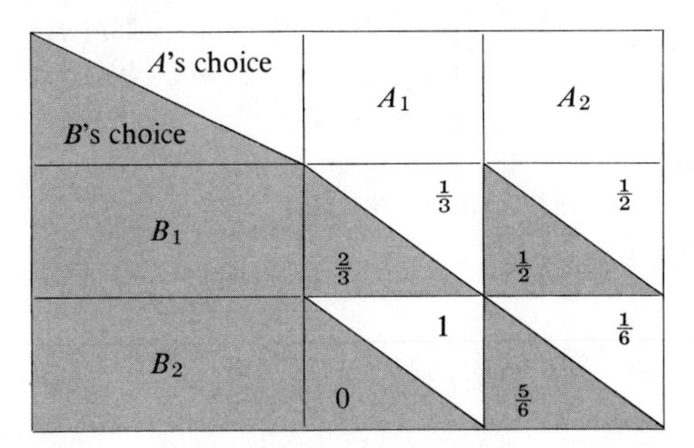

This situation is a little different from the one we used earlier; however, the same principles apply. We assume that each subject considered two possible outcomes: C_1 = correct, C_2 = wrong. Further, we assume

$$u(C_1) = +1, \qquad u(C_2) = 0.$$

[28] Reported by P. Suppes and R. C. Atkinson, in *Markov Learning Models for Multiperson Interactions*, Stanford: Stanford University Press, 1960, Chapter 3.

Finally, we assume that after many trials each subject had some steady probability of response. One subject's probabilities of response determined the other's probabilities of winning, conditional on his choices. Assume that each subject's expectations were accurate. Then

$$v(A_1) = \tfrac{1}{3}P(B_1) + P(B_2) = \tfrac{1}{3}P(B_1) + 1 - P(B_1)$$
$$= 1 - \tfrac{2}{3}P(B_1)$$
$$v(A_2) = \tfrac{1}{2}P(B_1) + \tfrac{1}{6}(1 - P(B_1)) = \tfrac{1}{6} + \tfrac{1}{3}P(B_1)$$
$$P(A_1) = \frac{v(A_1)}{v(A_1) + v(A_2)} = \frac{1 - \frac{2}{3}P(B_1)}{\frac{7}{6} - \frac{1}{3}P(B_1)}$$
$$v(B_1) = \tfrac{2}{3}P(A_1) + \tfrac{1}{2}[1 - P(A_1)] = \tfrac{1}{2} + \tfrac{1}{6}P(A_1)$$
$$v(B_2) = \tfrac{5}{6} - \tfrac{5}{6}P(A_1)$$
$$P(B_1) = \frac{\frac{1}{2} + \frac{1}{6}P(A_1)}{\frac{4}{3} - \frac{2}{3}P(A_1)}$$

By substitution,

$$P(A_1) = \frac{1 - \frac{2}{3}\left[\dfrac{\frac{1}{2} + \frac{1}{6}P(A_1)}{\frac{4}{3} - \frac{2}{3}P(A_1)}\right]}{\frac{7}{6} - \frac{1}{3}\left[\dfrac{\frac{1}{2} + \frac{1}{6}P(A_1)}{\frac{4}{3} - \frac{2}{3}P(A_1)}\right]}.$$

When we clear the fractions, we obtain

$$P(A_1) = \frac{6 - 4\left[\dfrac{3 + P(A_1)}{8 - 4P(A_1)}\right]}{7 - 2\left[\dfrac{3 + P(A_1)}{8 - 4P(A_1)}\right]} = \frac{36 - 28P(A_1)}{50 - 30P(A_1)}.$$

Then we have

$$30[P(A_1)]^2 - 78P(A_1) + 36 = 0;$$
$$P(A_1) = .60.$$

Then

$$P(B_1) = \frac{.50 + .10}{1.33 - .40} = .65$$

The data turned out to agree exactly with these theoretical values.

The last kind of experiment we discuss involves two persons making repeated choices, and after each person makes a choice, each one receives a number of points.[29] The number of points for each player depends on the

---

[29] W. K. Estes, "Theoretical Treatments of Differential Reward in Multiple-Choice Learning and Two-Person Interactions." In *Mathematical Methods in Small Group Processes*, edited by J. Criswell, H. Solomon, and P. Suppes, Stanford; Stanford University Press, 1962, pp. 133–149.

combination of choices; the situation is described in the following table:

A's choice / *B*'s choice	A_1	A_2
B_1	0 4	1 3
B_2	2 2	4 0

This situation is complicated by the fact that the subjects' outcomes are given in points. If, for example, subject A knows that B will choose B_1, he will choose on the basis that A_1's outcome is one point greater than A_2's outcome. However, A cannot know whether B will choose B_1 or B_2, so he has to consider various possible outcomes. One way for him to do this is to consider each of his alternatives, try to anticipate his outcome in each case, and then select the choice with the higher expected outcome. When A considers alternative A_1, he will have an expectation equal to $P(B_1)$ of an outcome of 0, and an expectation equal to $P(B_2)$ of an outcome to 2. When A considers alternative A_2, he will have expectations

$$s(1 \mid A_2) = P(B_1), \qquad s(4 \mid A_2) = P(B_2) = 1 - P(B_1).$$

There is some evidence that in the situation used in the experiment, subjects did not realize that the other person's choice determined the outcomes for both his choices. In that case, A would sometimes expect A_1 to be followed by 0 and A_2 to be followed by 1, but at other times A would expect A_1 to be followed by 0 and A_2 by 4. The four possibilities are given in the table below, along with the expectations that A would have for them.

Outcome of A_1	Outcome of A_2	Expectation
0	1	$P(B_1)^2$
0	4	$P(B_1)[1 - P(B_1)]$
2	1	$[1 - P(B_1)]P(B_1)$
2	4	$[1 - P(B_1)]^2$

In the first, second, and fourth cases, A chooses A_2. In the third case A chooses A_1. Therefore,

$$P(A_1) = [1 - P(B_1)]P(B_1).$$

Carrying out the same analysis for B, we have

Outcome of B_1	Outcome of B_2	Expectation
4	2	$P(A_1)^2$
4	0	$P(A_1)[1 - P(A_1)]$
3	2	$[1 - P(A_1)]P(A_1)$
3	0	$[1 - P(A_1)]^2$

The expected outcome of B_1 is higher than that for B_2 in every case. Therefore,

$$P(B_1) = 1.0$$

and when we put that result back into the preceding equation, we have

$$P(A_1) = 0.$$

The experiment lasted 200 trials, and during the last 20 trials the A subjects selected A_1 on .13 of their choices, and the B subjects chose B_1 on .92 of their choices. It seems likely that the predicted proportions of 0 and 1.0 would have been approximated even more closely in later trials had the experiment continued longer.

In another condition, different outcomes were used. They were

A's choice / B's choice	A_1	A_2
B_1	1 3	2 2
B_2	3 1	0 4

In this case, the four possibilities considered by A would be

Outcome of A_1	Outcome of A_2	Expectation
1	2	$P(B_1)^2$
1	0	$P(B_1)[1 - P(B_1)]$
3	2	$[1 - P(B_1)]P(B_1)$
3	0	$[1 - P(B_1)]^2$

The expected outcome of A_1 is higher in every case but the first. Therefore

$$P(A_1) = 1 - P(B_1)^2.$$

Considering B's situation, we have

Outcome of B_1	Outcome of B_2	Expectation
3	1	$P(A_1)^2$
3	4	$P(A_1)[1 - P(A_1)]$
2	1	$[1 - P(A_1)]P(A_1)$
2	4	$[1 - P(A_1)]^2$

The expected outcome is higher for B_1 in the first case and the third case, so

$$P(B_1) = P(A_1)^2 + [1 - P(A_1)]P(A_1) = P(A_1).$$

When we substitute back into the preceding equation, we obtain

$$P(A_1) = 1 - P(A_1)^2;$$

and when we solve the quadratic equation, we have the result

$$P(A_1) = P(B_1) = .62.$$

Two experiments were run using these outcomes. In one of the experiments each subject was informed only of his own outcome. There the obtained proportion of A_1 choices was .58 and the obtained proportion of B_1 choices was .62; the results are in good agreement with the prediction. In another experiment each subject saw both his own outcome and the outcome for the other subject after each trial. There the result did not agree with the prediction; the A subjects selected A_1 on .50 of their choices, and the B subjects selected B_1 on .69 of their choices. One possible explanation is that when the subjects saw both outcomes they sometimes interpreted them in terms of winning and losing, rather than in terms of the number of points they were accumulating individually.

In all of the situations we have dealt with so far, there is uncertainty due to the fact that the persons were not able to plan jointly what they would do. In many situations, of course, people will talk with each other and decide what to do—or at least each will tell the other what he plans to do. This kind of planning does not remove all the uncertainty about outcomes. However, it does remove the need for guessing about the other person's actions. In the case where joint planning is possible, the relevant psychological problem is to analyze the combination of actions on which the people will decide.

To carry out the analysis in a general way, we will consider a situation involving two people named A and B. A's choices for action are A_1 and A_2. B's choices are B_1 and B_2. We do not fill in precise numbers as response strengths for outcomes. Rather, we designate a preferred outcome for each person with a +, and other outcomes will be designated 0.

Using this scheme, one simple kind of matrix is

A's choice / B's choice	A_1	A_2
B_1	+ / +	0 / 0
B_2	0 / 0	0 / 0

This would correspond to the earlier example involving going for coffee. If we assume that the people plan their actions in advance and that each knows the other's preference, then it is not hard to see what they will do. A will choose A_1 and B will choose B_1.

This situation permits complete cooperation between A and B. They can agree on a course of action which is mutually satisfactory. A small difference changes the situation into one which produces competition.

A's choices / B's choices	A_1	A_2
B_1	0 / +	0 / 0
B_2	0 / 0	+ / 0

Here A does not get what he wants unless B chooses B_2, but then B cannot get what he wants. An example is a boy and girl who like each other but enjoy going different places. Suppose that the boy enjoys watching basketball games and the girl enjoys listening to jazz. On a given evening they may have to choose between seeing an important game and hearing a special concert. *A* will not enjoy the game unless *B* is there, and *B* will not enjoy going to the concert unless *A* goes along. To do what he wants, either person must get the other to give up his preferred entertainment.

A number of resolutions are possible. First, one person may simply care less than the other. Then the person who cares less about his preferred entertainment may just go along with the other for the sake of their friendship.

Another kind of resolution is more interesting psychologically.[30] The two people may develop a *trading rule*—one kind of social norm. A reasonable response in this situation is for the two people to agree to go to some basketball games and some jazz concerts—and whenever possible, to do both. In general, a *social norm* is some rule that restricts or prescribes the actions of members of a group. A trading rule is a norm that directs each person to postpone obtaining some of his personal satisfactions in order to maintain satisfaction for other persons at a reasonable level.

There are many examples of trading rules among our social norms. Our behavior at intersections when we drive cars illustrates a trading rule. It is preferable to go ahead rather than stop. But by stopping and waiting for our turn we avoid collisions.

In general, trading rules are norms which require adherence by all members of a group. If one member breaks the rule, the group must accommodate somehow—often the offender is removed from the group. The point to be emphasized here is that single choices of the kind we have been analyzing throughout this chapter are influenced by factors in addition to expectations and the attractiveness of single outcomes. In particular, they are influenced by social norms. At least in the case of trading rules, social norms can be explained with reference to the factors of value and preference. The analysis of trading rules illustrates the relationship between individual choice behavior and patterns of social interaction.

SUMMARY

In this chapter we have used the idea developed in Chapter 2, that choice probabilities are determined by response strengths. However, we have worked with situations where response strengths are changed by some feature of the situation. First, we discussed deprivation of a response, where the strength of a response increases during a time when the subject is prevented from performing it. Next, we studied simple conditioning, where the strength of a base response increases because after its performance the subject is permitted to perform a contingent response that has high proba-

---

[30] This idea, along with other interesting implications of the game-theory approach to the analysis of small group interactions, was presented by J. Thibaut and H. H. Kelley, *The Social Psychology of Small Groups*, New York: Wiley, 1959.

bility. Then we discussed situations where alternative base responses have different strengths because the subject has a stronger expectation for the contingent response following one base response than the other base response. We also discussed situations involving discriminative conditioning, where expectations for a contingent response differ in different stimulus situations. Another topic in simple conditioning involved situations where different base responses lead to different kinds or amounts of contingent responding, and the response strengths depend on the values the subjects place on the contingent responses.

In the last section we have considered simple social interaction, where the contingent outcomes of choices depend on the combination of alternatives selected by two persons. We studied two experiments in which each subject develops expectations that depend on the choices of the second person. Our analysis used choice theory to show how each person's response strengths depend on the other person's choices, as well as on the contingencies of the situation.

PROBLEMS

1. Suppose that we are feeding a hungry rat, and noting the times when he eats. Counting the time from the beginning of the session in minutes, the rat eats a pellet at each of the following times: 1.0, 1.5, 2.0, 2.5, 3.0, 4.0, 4.5, 5.0, 6.0, 6.5, 7.0, 7.5, 8.0, 9.0, 9.5, 10.0, 11.0, 12.0, 14.0, 15.0, 16.0, 18.0, 20.0. Plot a cumulative record of these responses. Plot a second graph showing the number of pellets per 5-min period.

2. Recall the data given on p. 86, regarding preferences for food rather than looking at another rat, and for food rather than playing on a hardware-cloth step. Let A_1 denote eating, let A_2 denote looking at another rat, and let A_3 denote playing on the step. Calculate the ratios $v(A_2)/v(A_1)$ and $v(A_3)/v(A_1)$ using the data given, carrying out the calculation separately for rats that had just been fed and rats that were hungry. Calculate the theoretical probability of time spent with A_2 and A_3 when these were the alternatives, again doing the calculation twice. (The actual proportions of time spent with the step rather than the other rat were .58 for rats that had just been fed, and .53 for hungry rats.)

3. Suppose that a rat with continuous access to water is in an experiment where drinking is the base response and running in a wheel is the contingent response. When the wheel is not present, the probability of drinking is found to be

$$P_0(B) = .008.$$

The animal is only permitted to run in the wheel during a one-hour session each day. During these sessions, when water is not available, the probability of running is found to be

$$P_0(C) = .091.$$

A contingency is introduced so that one second of drinking is required to permit 10 sec of running. Under this contingency, the rat drinks enough so that running is permitted during a proportion of time equal to

$$t = .30.$$

Assume that $h' = 1.50$, $b = 1.0$, and $c = .06$. Calculate the values of $v_1(C)/v(M)$ and $v_1(B)/v(M)$, and also of $P_1(B)$, the probability of drinking after conditioning.

4. Suppose that the following results are obtained in an experiment. Before conditioning, the response probabilities are

$$P_0(B) = .04, \qquad P_0(C) = .23.$$

After conditioning, the base response is performed enough so that the contingent response is available .30 of the time. Then the response probabilities are

$$P_1(B) = .13, \qquad P_1(C) = .37.$$

Calculate the values of h' and b that would lead to these results, if $c = .13$.

* 5. In the experiment described in Chapter 2, where Chicko was the subject, contingencies were tested. The following results were obtained.

Base response	Contingent response	$v_1(B)/v(M)$	t
Plunger	Door	0.14	.08
Plunger	Handle	0.18	.10
Door	Handle	0.28	.19

Assume that conditioning took place according to Eqs. (3.1) and (3.2), and calculate the values of b, c, and h'.

6. Probabilities of reinforcement (being called "right") are given below for two interaction situations. Calculate theoretical probabilities $P(A_1)$ and $P(B_1)$ for the two situations.

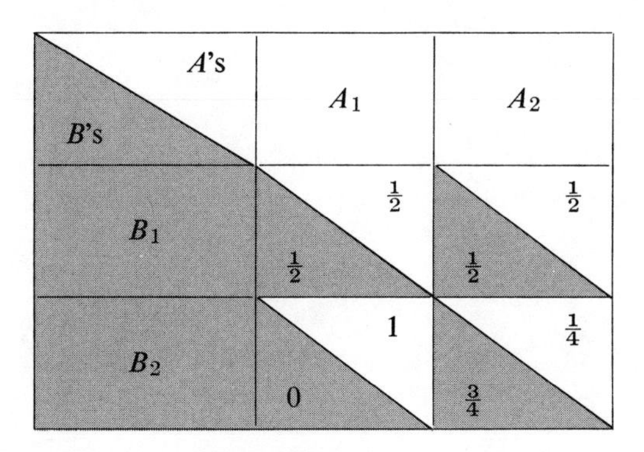

The data were $P(A_1) = .67$, $P(B_1) = .60$

A's choice / *B*'s choice	A_1	A_2
B_1	$\frac{1}{2}$ / $\frac{1}{2}$	$\frac{1}{4}$ / $\frac{3}{4}$
B_2	1 / 0	$\frac{3}{4}$ / $\frac{1}{4}$

The data were $P(A_1) = .61$, $P(B_1) = .73$. The experiments were reported by Suppes and Atkinson (*op. cit.*)

CHAPTER FOUR

Variation

The purpose of this chapter is to present the basic statistical ideas of a *distribution*, the *mean*, and the *standard deviation*. Think of giving a test to a group of people. Some number of the group will get all the answers correct, some will get one wrong, some two wrong, and so on. To write down the distribution of scores, we simply make a table listing the scores in one column and the number of individuals getting each score in the next column. The number of individuals getting a particular score is called the *frequency* of that score, and the table which lists the frequencies is called the *frequency distribution.* Sometimes it is more convenient to work with proportions of the group instead of the counted numbers. We obtain the proportions by dividing each frequency by the total number of people in the group. The proportion of individuals with a particular score is called the *relative frequency* of that score, and a listing of the proportions of all the scores is called the *relative frequency distribution.*

Table 1

Hypothetical Distribution of Scores

Score	Frequency	Proportion
10	50	.227
9	60	.273
8	40	.182
7	25	.114
6	20	.091
5	10	.045
4	10	.045
3	5	.023
2	0	0
1	0	0
0	0	0

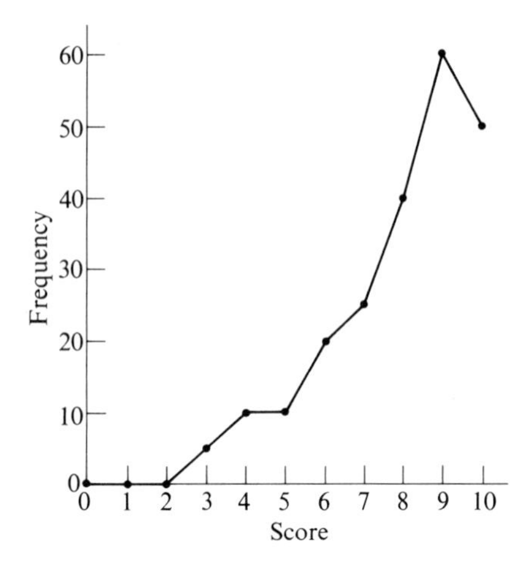

Fig. 1. A graph of the frequency shown in Table 1.

For example, consider a ten-point quiz that could be given to a class of 220 students. The possible scores are 0, 1, . . . , 9, 10. The number of students who get 10 points is the frequency of the score, 10. This frequency divided by 220 gives the relative frequency of the score. A hypothetical set of results is given in Table 1.

For many purposes, it is useful to have a graph showing what the distribution is like. Figure 1 is a graph of the frequency distribution given in Table 1. Note that the numbers along the bottom are the different test scores which can be obtained. The height of the dot above a given score corresponds to the frequency of that score. The line connecting the points is just to help in following the figure.

Table 1 and Fig. 1 each give a complete description of the distribution. Often it is useful to work with summary information. For example, we could note that most of the scores are between 8 and 10, or that the complete range is from 3 to 10.

Two of the most useful summary properties are the *mean* and the *standard deviation*. The mean indicates where the distribution is located, and the standard deviation indicates how much spread or variation there is.

The mean is just the common average of the scores. To calculate the mean, first add all the scores and then divide the sum by the number of scores.

Example 4.1. Suppose you have six quizzes in a course, and receive the grades 10, 15, 12, 15, 18, 8. Find the mean.

We add the scores and divide by 6.

$$\frac{10 + 15 + 12 + 15 + 18 + 8}{6} = \frac{78}{6} = 13. \blacksquare$$

It is convenient to have a short label, and the standard one used for the mean is μ (Greek mu). We also use a shorthand symbol to represent the method of calculation. Each score is a value of the variable, x. The Greek capital sigma stands for "sum"; therefore the notation Σx means "the sum of the scores." Let N be the number of scores (that is, the number of x's summed). Then

$$\mu = \frac{\Sigma x}{N}. \tag{4.1}$$

If it is necessary for clarity, we put a subscript after μ to show what variable we are talking about. For example, μ_x means "the mean of the x's," and μ_y means "the mean of the y's."

There is a shortcut which simplifies calculations for large sets of scores. Consider the 220 scores in the frequency distribution of Table 1. To calculate the mean, we need the sum of the 220 scores. But rather than lining up all 220 scores, we can obtain the sum by first multiplying each score by its frequency and then adding the resulting numbers together. For example, there are 50 students who received ten points. If we listed all 220 scores, the number 10 would appear 50 times. If we took those 50 scores out and added them, we would get $50 \times 10 = 500$.

Example 4.2. Find the mean of the distribution of Table 1, using the frequencies.

$$\begin{aligned}\mu &= \tfrac{1}{220}\{(10)(50) + (9)(60) + (8)(40) + (7)(25) + (6)(20) \\ &\quad + (5)(10) + (4)(10) + (3)(5)\} \\ &= \frac{500 + 540 + 320 + 175 + 120 + 50 + 40 + 15}{220} = \frac{1760}{220} = 8.0. \blacksquare\end{aligned}$$

Note that we can obtain the same result if we take each score, multiply by the relative frequency, and then add the resulting numbers. Recall that each relative frequency is obtained by dividing the frequency by the number of scores. Therefore, when we use proportions in obtaining the mean, we do not divide by the number of cases at the end.

Example 4.3. Find the mean of the distribution of Table 1, using the relative frequencies.

$$\begin{aligned}\mu &= (10)(.227) + (9)(.273) + (8)(.182) + (7)(.114) \\ &\quad + (6)(.091) + (5)(.045) + (4)(.045) + (3)(.023) \\ &= 2.27 + 2.46 + 1.46 + .80 + .55 + .22 + .18 + .07 = 8.0. \blacksquare\end{aligned}$$

Next, we consider the amount of variation in a distribution. The scores which different people obtain on a test may be fairly close to one another,

Table 2

Distributions with Different Amounts of Variation

Score	Frequency in Group I	Frequency in Group II
10	0	5
9	1	6
8	5	13
7	20	17
6	51	19
5	15	16
4	6	14
3	2	6
2	0	2
1	0	1
0	0	1

or they may be quite spread apart. The good students in a class may be far better than the poor students, or all may show nearly equal achievement.

Consider the two distributions of scores on a ten-point quiz in Table 2. Suppose that the two distributions came from two groups of students. The groups have the same number of individuals—100 in each case. And the mean scores are the same—6.0. However, the two distributions are by no means the same, as can be seen from the graphs given in Fig. 2. In the distribution for Group I, nearly all the scores are within one point of the

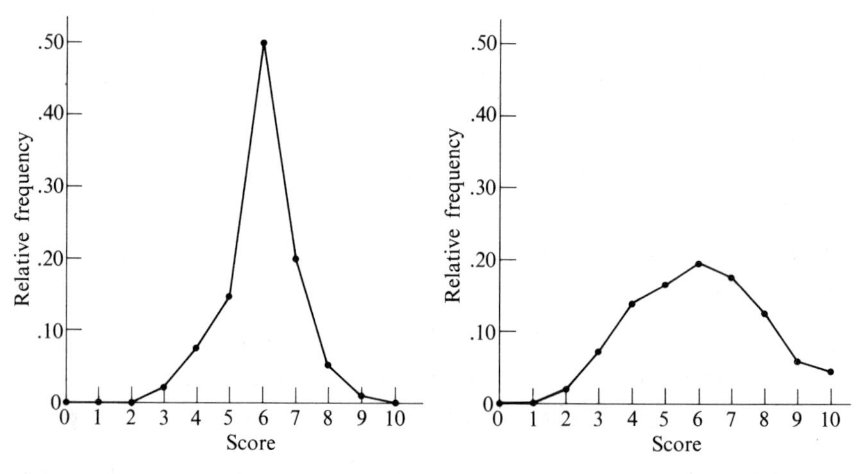

Fig. 2. Graphed distributions showing equal means and unequal variances. Frequency distributions are those given in Table 2. Group I is represented in the left panel; Group II, in the right panel.

mean. In the distribution for Group II, a substantial number of scores are farther than one point from the mean, and several scores are as far away from the mean as three points or more. We would say that the two groups of students did equally well on the quiz on the average. However, the scores obtained by Group II were quite a bit more variable than those for Group I.

There are several ways to measure the amount of variation in a population. The most widely used measures are the variance and the standard deviation, which is just the square root of the variance. The variance is based on the following idea: In a distribution where scores are spread far apart, there are many scores which are quite far above the mean, and many which are quite far below the mean. Thus if we subtracted the mean from each score, we would get many large numbers. Of course, some would be positive and some negative. However, in a distribution where scores are very close to each other, subtracting the mean from every score would result in a set of very small numbers. We take every score and subtract the mean, obtaining the *deviations* from the mean, $x - \mu$. Then we calculate the square of each deviation from the mean. This gives a set of positive numbers. If a score x is far from the mean in either direction, $(x - \mu)^2$ will be large; but if x is close to the mean, $(x - \mu)^2$ will be small.

The variance is the mean of these squared deviations. We use σ^2 (σ is small Greek sigma) to stand for the variance.

$$\sigma^2 = \frac{\Sigma(x - \mu)^2}{N} \tag{4.2}$$

Example 4.4. Calculate the variance of the scores given in Example 4.1.

First, obtain the deviation of each score from the mean.

$$10 - 13 = -3; \quad 15 - 13 = +2; \quad 12 - 13 = -1;$$
$$15 - 13 = +2; \quad 18 - 13 = +5; \quad 8 - 13 = -5.$$

Next, square each of the deviations.

$$(-3)^2 = 9; \quad (+2)^2 = 4; \quad (-1)^2 = 1;$$
$$(+2)^2 = 4; \quad (+5)^2 = 25; \quad (-5)^2 = 25.$$

Finally, calculate the mean of these squared deviations.

$$\sigma^2 = \frac{9 + 4 + 1 + 4 + 25 + 25}{6} = \frac{68}{6} = 11.3. \blacksquare$$

In Examples 4.2 and 4.3 we used shortcuts to calculate the mean of the scores listed in Table 1. The same techniques can be used to calculate the variance. This is understood when we note that the variance is itself a mean —the mean of a new set of scores. The new scores are obtained by calculating the squared deviations for each of the original scores. Each of these new scores can then be multiplied by its frequency and the results added and divided by N, or each of the new scores can be multiplied by its proportion and the results added.

Example 4.5. Calculate the variance of the scores in Table 1. Use (a) the frequencies, and (b) the proportions.

First, obtain the squared deviations from the mean which correspond to the original scores. Recall that the mean is 8.0.

x	10	9	8	7	6	5	4	3
$(x - \mu)^2$	4	1	0	1	4	9	16	25

Next, we obtain the mean of these squared deviations. First, using the frequencies,

$$\begin{aligned}\sigma^2 &= \tfrac{1}{220}\{(4)(50) + (1)(60) + (0)(40) + (1)(25)\\ &\quad + (4)(20) + (9)(10) + (16)(10) + (25)(5)\}\\ &= \frac{200 + 60 + 0 + 25 + 80 + 90 + 160 + 125}{220} = 3.36.\end{aligned}$$

Alternatively, using the proportions,

$$\begin{aligned}\sigma^2 &= (4)(.227) + (1)(.273) + (0)(.182) + (1)(.114)\\ &\quad + (4)(.091) + (9)(.045) + (16)(.045) + (25)(.023)\\ &= .908 + .273 + 0 + .114 + .364 + .405 + .720 + .575\\ &= 3.36. \blacksquare\end{aligned}$$

From the variance, it is easy to calculate the standard deviation. It is just the square root of the variance, and it is called σ.

$$\sigma = \sqrt{\sigma^2} = \sqrt{\frac{\Sigma(x - \mu)^2}{N}}. \tag{4.3}$$

The standard deviation is useful partly because it gives a number on the same scale as the scores in the distribution.

The standard deviation can be interpreted as a distance between scores expressing a "standard" amount of difference between the individual scores and the mean. In Example 4.5 we calculated the variance of the scores graphed in Fig. 1. The standard deviation of these scores is

$$\sigma = \sqrt{3.36} = 1.83.$$

Then it is possible to consider any score in relation to the mean and varia-

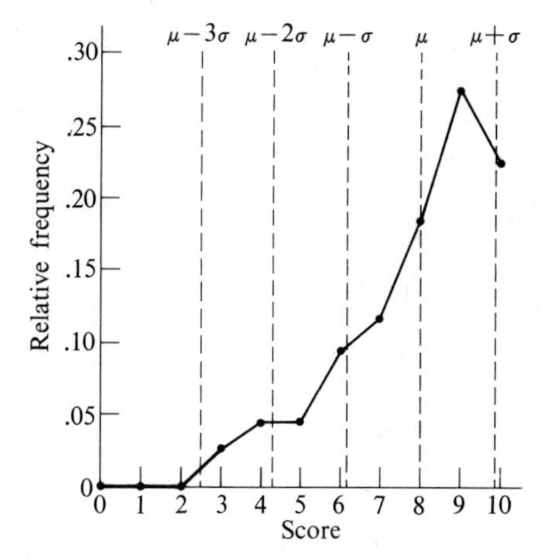

Fig. 3. Relative frequencies graphed from the scores of Table 1, with standard deviation intervals.

tion of the distribution. A score of eight is average, of course. All the scores within one standard deviation of the mean would be considered as being quite close to the mean. These are scores between

$$\mu - \sigma = 8 - 1.83 = 6.17 \qquad \text{and} \qquad \mu + \sigma = 8 + 1.83 = 9.83.$$

In the case we are considering, these "close" scores would be seven and nine.

Scores that are more than two standard deviations away from the mean in either direction would be considered as being quite far from the mean. These are scores below

$$\mu - 2\sigma = 8 - 3.66 = 4.34.$$

In other words, scores of zero, one, two, three, or four are "quite far" from the mean. Scores between one and two standard deviations away from the mean would be considered as being moderately far from the mean. These would be the scores between 4.34 and 6.17 and scores between 9.83 and 11.66. In other words, scores of five, six, and ten.

In Fig. 3 the relative frequency distribution from Example 4.1 has been drawn again. The dashed lines mark off intervals in units of one standard deviation.

Example 4.6. Consider a student who scored five points on the test whose distribution is given in Fig. 3. What is his score in standard deviation units?

First, a score of five is three points below the mean. The standard deviation is 1.83. Therefore, a score of five is equal to

$$\mu - (3/1.83)\sigma = \mu - 1.64\sigma \;\blacksquare$$

Example 4.7. What is the proportion of scores below the mean in Fig. 3? What is the proportion below $\mu - 2\sigma$?

Since the mean is 8.0, we want to know the proportion of scores at 0, 1, . . . , 6, and 7. This is

$$.023 + .045 + .045 + .091 + .114 + .182 = .500.$$

The second score in the problem is

$$x = \mu - 2\sigma = 8.0 - (2)(1.83) = 4.34.$$

To obtain the proportion of scores below $\mu - 2\sigma$, we find the proportion at 0, 1, 2, 3, and 4. This is

$$.023 + .045 = .068. \blacksquare$$

Example 4.8. What score, x, is above approximately 20% of the distribution in Fig. 3?

To find x, merely add proportions of scores from 0 until approximately 20% are obtained. The next score up the scale is the one desired.

$$0 + 0 + 0 + .023 + .045 + .045 + .091 = .204.$$

Thus the score just above 20% of the distribution is 7. ▮

As with the mean, it is sometimes necessary to add a subscript to σ or σ^2 for clarity. Then σ_x means "the standard deviation of the x's," and σ_y^2 means "the variance of the y's."

If we consider certain changes in the distribution of a variable, we can understand the mean and standard deviation more fully. First, suppose that we doubled every score in the distribution, or in general, multiplied each score by any constant k. This would move the location of the distribution, and it would also change the amount of difference between the scores, so that if k were greater than one, the distribution would be shifted higher and the amount of difference between scores would be increased. In general,

$$\begin{aligned} \mu_{kx} &= k\mu_x, \\ \sigma_{kx} &= k\sigma_x. \end{aligned} \tag{4.4}$$

Equation (4.4) gives one of the reasons for saying that σ is on the same scale as the scores themselves. For example, doubling each score would double the standard deviation. However, doubling each score would not double the variance; instead, it would multiply the variance by four.

Next, suppose that we added a constant k to every score or subtracted k from every score. This would shift the location of the distribution up or

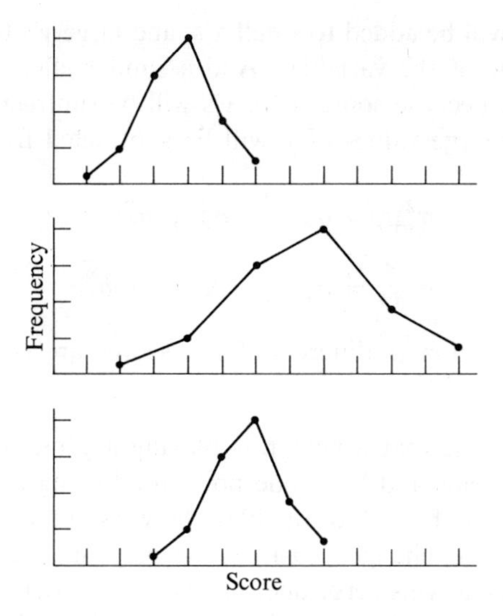

Fig. 4. Changes in a distribution produced by multiplying each score by a constant (middle panel) and by adding a constant to each score (lower panel).

down, but it would not affect the amount of difference between scores. Then

$$\mu_{x+k} = \mu_x + k,$$
$$\mu_{x-k} = \mu_x - k,$$
$$\sigma_{x+k} = \sigma_{x-k} = \sigma_x. \tag{4.5}$$

In Fig. 4, the top panel shows a distribution of scores. The middle panel shows the distribution after each score has been multiplied by a constant—in this case 2.0. The bottom panel shows the original distribution after a constant has been added to every score. Again the constant was 2.0. Note that doubling the scores spreads the distribution out, as Eq. (4.4) says it does. But adding a constant does not change the amount of variation, which is what Eq. (4.5) says.

Now, consider what would happen if we added or subtracted a variable y, instead of a constant, to every score x. Suppose that y has a distribution with mean μ_y and standard deviation σ_y. We assume here that x and y are independent. If μ_y were positive, adding a value of y to each x would increase the mean of x (and subtracting a y from each x would decrease the mean).

$$\mu_{x+y} = \mu_x + \mu_y,$$
$$\mu_{x-y} = \mu_x - \mu_y. \tag{4.6}$$

The effect on the variance is to increase it. When y and x are added, some small values of y will be added to small x's, and large y's to large x's, which increases the range of the variable. And a similar effect occurs when y is subtracted from x because some small y's will be subtracted from the largest x's, and some large values of y will be subtracted from small x's. As it happens,

$$\sigma_{x+y}^2 = \sigma_{x-y}^2 = \sigma_x^2 + \sigma_y^2,$$

$$\sigma_{x+y} = \sigma_{x-y} = \sqrt{\sigma_x^2 + \sigma_y^2}. \tag{4.7}$$

(However, the situation is different if the scores are correlated. This is discussed in Chapter 7.)

Example 4.9. Suppose that a person is playing a game where he wins one point for tossing heads and loses one point for tossing tails. Suppose that he plays 100 times, and on 50 of the plays he wins and on 50 he loses.

Now the game is changed so that one play involves two tosses. On each play, the person wins zero, one, or two points, depending on whether he throws heads neither time, one of the times, or both times. Suppose that this game is played 100 times with the results as follows: *TT* 25 times, *TH* 25 times, *HT* 25 times, *HH* 25 times. Calculate the mean and standard deviation of the scores in each game.

In the first game, there are 50 scores of one, and 50 of zero. The mean is

$$\mu = (\tfrac{50}{100})(1.0) + (\tfrac{50}{100})(0.0) = 0.50.$$

The variance is

$$\begin{aligned}\sigma^2 &= (\tfrac{50}{100})(1.0 - .50)^2 + (\tfrac{50}{100})(0.0 - .50)^2 \\ &= (.50)(.25) + (.50)(.25) = .25\end{aligned}$$

Then the standard deviation is

$$\sigma = \sqrt{\sigma^2} = \sqrt{.25} = .50.$$

In the second game, there are 25 scores of zero, 50 scores of one, and 25 scores of two. The mean is

$$\mu = (\tfrac{25}{100})(0.0) + (\tfrac{50}{100})(1.0) + (\tfrac{25}{100})(2.0) = 1.0.$$

The variance is

$$\begin{aligned}\sigma^2 &= (\tfrac{25}{100})(2.0 - 1.0)^2 + (\tfrac{50}{100})(1.0 - 1.0)^2 \\ &\quad + (\tfrac{25}{100})(0.0 - 1.0)^2 = .50\end{aligned}$$

Then the standard deviation is

$$\sigma = \sqrt{.50} = .71. \blacksquare$$

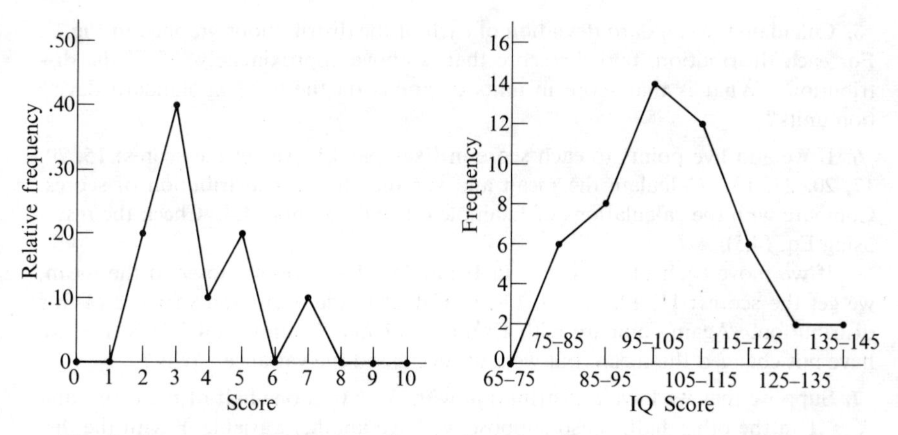

Fig. 5. Frequency distributions for use in connection with Problems 1 and 2.

PROBLEMS

1. Make up a table from the graph in the left panel of Fig. 5, listing each score and the relative frequency of that score as it is given by the graph. (Read relative frequencies to the nearest .10.) Calculate the mean and variance of the distribution. What proportion of the scores are less than $\mu + \sigma$?

2. In the right panel of Fig. 5 each point represents the frequency of scores in a 10-point interval from an intelligence test. Treat each listed interval as a score and make a table from the graph, giving the frequency and relative frequency of scores within each interval. (Frequencies to nearest 2.0). Calculate the mean and variance of the distribution. (You should use the middle score of each interval to do the calculation; that is, you have zero cases of 70, six cases of 80, etc.) What proportion of scores are below the mean? What proportion below $\mu - \frac{1}{2}\sigma$?

3. Draw a graph of the following relative frequency distribution:

Score Interval	30–40	40–50	50–60	60–70	70–80	80–90	90–100
Relative Frequency	0	.20	.10	.30	.30	.10	0

4. Twenty students took a test with fifteen points. Their scores were as follows:

8	10	9	10
11	8	9	10
7	10	13	12
10	7	10	12
12	11	11	11

a) Make a table with the frequency distribution and relative frequency distribution for the test.

b) Graph the relative frequency distribution.

c) Calculate the mean and standard deviation.

5. Calculate the standard deviation of each of the distributions graphed in Fig. 2. For each distribution, find the score that is above approximately .75 of the distribution. What is that score in units of points on the test? in standard deviation units?

6. If we add five points to each score in Example 4.1, we get the scores: 15, 20, 17, 20, 23, 13. Calculate the mean and variance for this distribution of scores. Compare with the calculations of Example 4.1 and Example 4.4. Check the result using Eq. (4.5).

If we move each of the scores in Example 4.1 one point closer to the mean, we get the scores: 11, 14, 13, 14, 17, 9. Calculate the mean and variance of this distribution. Again compare with Example 4.1 and Example 4.4. This time we have not changed the mean, but we have decreased the variance. Why?

7. Suppose that we have a distribution with $X = 0$ in one-half of the cases, and $X = 1$ in the other half. Also suppose we have another variable Y with the distribution $Y = 0$ in one-half of the cases and $Y = 1$ in the others. We select one of the X's and one of the Y's independently, and add the scores. Find the mean and standard deviation of $X + Y$ and of $X - Y$ using Eqs. (4.6) and (4.7). Explain why Example 4.9 illustrates Eqs. (4.6) and (4.7).

CHAPTER FIVE

Memorizing, Forgetting, and Transfer

This chapter presents a theory about how people learn, remember, and use simple associations. A person has learned a simple association if he knows the answer to a question. In his memory, there is an association between the question and its answer. Sometimes the material we learn is not in the form of a question and answer; therefore we shall consider associations in a more general way. We say that associations are formed between stimuli and responses. A stimulus is anything that a person sees or hears (or touches or tastes or smells). A response is anything that a person does or thinks.

Examples of stimulus-response associations abound in a student's life. If you are studying vocabulary for a foreign language course, you are learning associations between foreign-language words and their English cognates. You learn associations like "*pferd–horse*," or "*chien*–dog." If you have learned the association between *pferd* and horse, then when you see "*pferd*," you respond, "horse." "*Pferd*" is the stimulus, and "horse" is your response.

Another kind of simple associative learning occurs when you learn the date or place or some other aspect of a historical event. Examples of stimulus-response associations involving historical materials are "Napoleon's defeat–Waterloo," and "Declaration of Independence–1776." In biology, you learn the technical names of animals such as "worm–annelid." In chemistry, you learn to associate names of elements with their atomic weights such as "oxygen–16." In literature, you learn to associate authors with titles, for example, "Faust–Goethe." In each of these cases there is a stimulus (worm, oxygen, *Faust*) with which you associate a response (annelid, 16, Goethe). In formulating a theory of learning, we have the task of describing what happens when a person learns an association.

5A SIMPLE MEMORIZATION

The act of learning an association may be simple or it may involve several accomplishments. In an experiment, we may ask a subject to associate the number *4* with the word *suit.* This association is simple in several ways.

First, the number *4* is a response which the subject can perform easily with no need for training in the experimental situation. The word *suit* is familiar to the subject, and it is a simple unitary stimulus.

Compare this with the learning of an association like *Charlene Andrews*–321-4346. To accomplish this memory feat, a person must learn to perform the response 321-4346, which is a fairly complicated memorizing task in itself. The person also must avoid confusing this number with others that he knows which are similar to it. And he must remember that this number is for Charlene Andrews, not Charlotte Anderson, or anyone else with similar name or appearance.

We shall consider a theory of simple association learning which treats learning as an event which occurs in an all-or-none fashion. The theory describes an idealization of the process in a way which is common in scientific theorizing. The simple process described can be approximated by experimental conditions, but most learning situations involve complicating features which make the all-or-none assumption untrue. (Readers familiar with physics may see an analogy with the concept of an ideal gas. Only a few gases even approximate the condition assumed, but the concept is important and permits important principles to be understood.)

When we talk about the learning of an association, we have to consider the test that will be given. Consider a student working on German vocabulary. He comes to the item "*Kraft*–force," and studies that item. He may test his memory right away by looking away and trying to repeat the item. This would be a very easy test. A harder test would be to go through a number of vocabulary items—say, 10 or 20—and then try to recall all of them. Or the test might be given the next day, or the next week after the items had been studied. Of course, the longer the time between study and test of an item, the more things will have occurred that may interfere with the person's memory. Therefore, tests that occur a long time after studying generally are harder than tests that occur right away.

Another important factor is the kind of test that is given. For example, a person may be shown the stimulus and asked to say or write down the response. Or he may be shown the stimulus and two or three alternative responses and asked to pick out the correct answer. The first of these tasks requires recall of the response and usually is harder than the second, which merely requires the person to recognize the correct answer and pick it out from a set that includes some incorrect responses. The main thing that makes a test hard or easy in this second sense is the amount of information given in the question. If much information is given, as in a recognition test, then the test is relatively easy. If less information is given, as in a recall test, the test usually is harder.

Now we know better what we mean by asking, "Was this item learned?" We mean, "Was this item learned well enough so that such-and-such a test will be passed at such-and-such a time after it was studied?" In other words, we should not talk just about learning and not learning, but about learning *well enough* to satisfy a specified criterion, or not learning well enough to satisfy that criterion.

The idea of all-or-none learning is that a study trial provides an opportunity for learning an association well enough to pass a certain kind of test to be given a certain amount of time later. If the item is not learned on the first study trial, then a second study trial gives a second opportunity for learning, and the probability of learning remains the same as it was the first time. If the association is studied repeatedly, there will be some number of unsuccessful attempts, and at some point learning will occur. On any given study trial, if the item has not been learned previously, there is a fixed probability that the item will be learned at that time.[1]

If a number of associations are studied once each, ordinarily they will not all be learned, but some of them will be learned. Each time the set of items is studied some of the items in the set will become learned. Imagine yourself studying for a language exam. You have, say, 50 vocabulary items to learn. After going through the list of items three times you give yourself a test. It turns out that you know 30 of the items but haven't yet learned the other 20. The next time you go through the list will give you a chance to add some of the 20 unlearned items to the set that are learned. In our discussion here, we assume that learning is all-or-none. Therefore the probability of learning any unlearned item is a constant, regardless of the number of times the item has been studied previously. Further, we adopt the simplifying assumption that all the items being studied are equally difficult, and therefore have the same probability of learning. The letter c will be used here to stand for that constant probability.

Example 5.1. Suppose that c is equal to .20 for a list of 50 vocabulary items. On the average, how many items will become learned on the first study trial through the list?

The answer is $.20 \times 50 = 10$ items. This leaves an average of 40 items that are not yet learned.

Now, how many items will become learned on the second study trial through the list?

There are an average of 40 items which are not learned at the beginning of this trial. Each item has probability .20 of being learned. Therefore,

[1] The idea that verbal associations are learned in an all-or-none way, rather than by gradual strengthening, is due mainly to I. Rock, "The Role of Repetition in Learning," *Amer. J. Psychol.*, 1957, **70**, 186–193. The theory was developed formally and applied to new experiments by W. K. Estes, "Learning Theory and the New 'Mental Chemistry'," *Psychol. Rev.*, 1960, **67**, 207–223, and by G. H. Bower, "Application of a Model to Paired-Associate Learning," *Psychometrika*, 1961, **26**, 255–280.

Table 1

All-or-None Learning of 50 Items
where $c = .20$

Trial	Average Unlearned at Beginning	Average Learned This Trial	Average Total Learned Through This Trial
1	50.0	(.20)(50.0) = 10.0	10.0
2	40.0	(.20)(40.0) = 8.0	18.0
3	32.0	(.20)(32.0) = 6.4	24.4
4	25.6	(.20)(25.6) = 5.1	29.5
5	20.5	(.20)(20.5) = 4.1	33.6

the average number that become learned on the second study trial is $.20 \times 40 = 8$. Now, on the average, there are 32 items left to be learned. Table 1 shows these calculations carried out for a few more trials. ▮

Before we discuss the all-or-none theory at length, we need to consider whether there are learning situations in which this simple theory applies. In one kind of experiment the idea was tested by a replacement procedure.[2] A control group was shown a list of stimulus-response pairs, then shown the stimuli and asked to give the responses. This procedure was repeated with each subject until only correct responses were given. The replacement procedure was used in the experimental group, where the stimulus-response pairs were shown and tested as in the control group, but on the following trial any item which was not correct on the test was replaced by a new pair. The difference between the procedures was that the control group had a single set of stimulus-response pairs to learn, while for the experimental group a single item stayed in the list only as long as the subject gave correct responses, after which it was replaced. A subject in the experimental group had to continue with tests and study trials on a partially changing list until he had one test with no errors on the items in the list at that time.

If learning took place by a gradual process, then items that had been studied one or more times should have been partially learned, even if the subject gave a wrong response on the test. In the control group, these partially learned items were left in the list. But in the replacement group, items that were given incorrectly were replaced by new items for which no partial learning could have occurred. Therefore, a theory of gradual learning predicts that the control group should learn their lists in a shorter time than the experimental group would take to attain a perfect trial on a list with changing items.

---

[2] This was the experiment by I. Rock, *op. cit.*

The all-or-none theory makes a different prediction. According to the all-or-none theory, if an error occurs, we can tell that the item has not yet been learned. There is no partial learning, so any unlearned item could be replaced by any other unlearned item with no adverse effects on the remaining learning. Therefore, the all-or-none theory predicts that the control group and the experimental group should be equal.

The results of the initial experiments favored the all-or-none theory. In one study with letters as stimuli and numbers as responses, the mean errors per item were 1.49 in the control group and 1.43 in the experimental group. In another condition using pairs of nonsense syllables, there were 3.34 errors per item in the control group and 3.65 errors per item in the experimental group. The results quite clearly favor the prediction of equal performance made by the all-or-none theory. Further experiments have shown that if the subject is given only a short time to study and respond, or if the responses are very difficult, a sizable difference can be produced between a group with the replacement procedure and a control group. Also, the replacement procedure probably eliminates the hardest items from the list, and therefore the finding of no difference probably indicates that there is a small, real advantage from having repeated opportunities to study an item. However, the impressive fact is that the difference is very small; this indicates that the all-or-none theory is probably quite a close approximation to the learning process.

In a second kind of experiment each stimulus-response pair in a list is presented once, and then all items are tested twice.[3] If learning is approximately all-or-none, items which were correct on the first trial will have a high probability of being correct on the second trial also. But we know that items on which errors were made on the first test must not have been learned on the study trial; therefore, the only way for the subject to be correct on these items would be to make a lucky guess. The data agree with the all-or-none prediction. In one typical set of results, about one-half of the items were correct on the first test. Of the items correct on the first test, 71% were correct on the second test. Of the items missed on the first test, only 9% were correct on the second test; this latter result could easily have been produced by guessing, since there were just eight responses to choose from.

These experimental results do not prove that learning is all-or-none. The all-or-none assumption provides a powerful theoretical tool for analyzing simple learning. The fact that we can construct experiments with results which are consistent with the all-or-none assumption makes it reasonable to develop the theory more fully and test its usefulness as a tool for understanding the learning process.

---

[3] Done by W. K. Estes, B. L. Hopkins, and E. J. Crothers, "All-or-None and Conservation Effects in the Learning and Retention of Paired-Associates," *J. exp. Psychol.*, 1960, **60,** 329–339.

The calculations involved in all-or-none theory are applied from the mathematical theory of waiting times in the theory of probability. We shall discuss the general mathematical theory briefly.

Suppose that you have a coin which is weighted so that it comes up heads π of the time (π may be but is not necessarily one-half). Now you perform an experiment in which you toss the coin *until* it comes up heads. If you get heads on the first toss, then the experiment is over right away. If you get tails on the first toss, you toss again; then if you get heads on the second toss, you stop the experiment there. You always toss the coin until it comes up heads, at which point the experiment is over.

Now, suppose that we carry out the coin-tossing experiment many times, keeping a record of the number of tosses each time. Since the probability of a head on each toss is π, we find that for π of the experiments we stop after the first toss. For the experiment to last two tosses, a tail must appear on the first toss and a head on the second. $(1 - \pi)$ of the experiments will start with a tail. Then π of *those* experiments will have a head on the second toss. So the probability that the experiment lasts two trials is $(1 - \pi)\pi$. In order to last exactly three trials, we have to get tails twice and then a head. This probability is $(1 - \pi)(1 - \pi)\pi$ or $(1 - \pi)^2\pi$. There are two general formulas that develop from these considerations. First, the probability that the experiment will last longer than n trials is the probability that we have not gotten a head on Trial 1, or Trial 2, or . . . , or Trial n which is $(1 - \pi)^n$. The probability that the experiment will last exactly n trials is the probability that the experiment has not ended before the nth toss, and that we get a head on the nth toss. Thus, the probability that the experiment lasts exactly n trials is $(1 - \pi)^{n-1}\pi$.

In Chapter 4 the idea of a relative frequency distribution was discussed. The idea is that a group of individuals given a test generally have different scores. The relative frequency distribution gives the proportion of individuals that receive each score.

Now suppose that a large number of individuals each flips the same biased coin until it comes up heads, and each person's score is the number of times that he tosses the coin. If we let x stand for each score, then the formula

$$P(x = n) = (1 - \pi)^{n-1}\pi \tag{5.1}$$

gives the relative frequency distribution of the scores. In other words, if we know the value of π, we can calculate the proportion of individuals that should obtain a score of $x = n$ using Eq. (5.1). Equation (5.1) is a well-known distribution in probability theory, the geometric distribution. Figure 1 is a graph showing the geometric distribution calculated from Eq. (5.1) with $p = .20$.

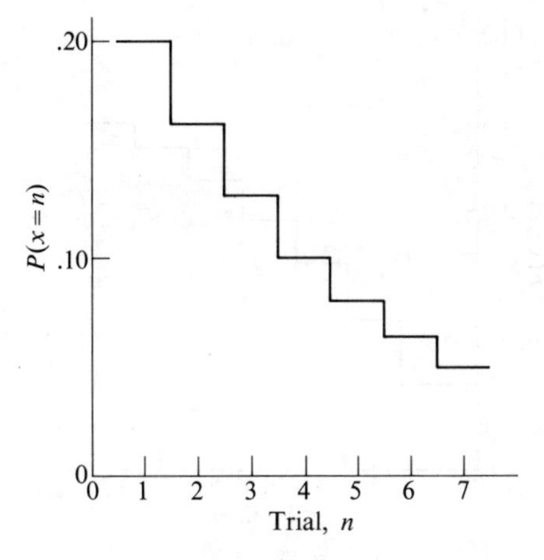

Fig. 1. Graph of relative frequency as a distribution of simple waiting times.

Equation (5.1) gives a specific theoretical distribution depending on π, the probability of ending the experiment on each trial. The mean and standard deviation also can be calculated if π is known. The mean is

$$\mu_x = 1/\pi, \tag{5.2}$$

and the standard deviation is

$$\sigma_x = \sqrt{1 - \pi}/\pi. \tag{5.3}$$

In other words, if each person in a large group took a coin with probability π of heads, and flipped it until heads came up, then the average number of tosses would be $1/\pi$, and the standard deviation of the number of tosses would be $\sqrt{1 - \pi}/\pi$.

We may ask the probability that the coin-tossing experiment ends sometime during the first n trials. In other words, we ask what the probability is that the first head occurs on the first toss, or the second toss, or the third toss, or . . . , the nth toss. We could add the probabilities for the separate trials, but there is an easier way. We know what the probability is that it will not end during the first n trials; that probability is $(1 - \pi)^n$. Therefore, the probability that it will end during the first n trials is just $1 - (1 - \pi)^n$.

The formula

$$P(x \leq n) = 1 - (1 - \pi)^n \tag{5.4}$$

is a cumulative probability distribution. It is related to the probability distribution in a simple way. Each value of the cumulative distribution is

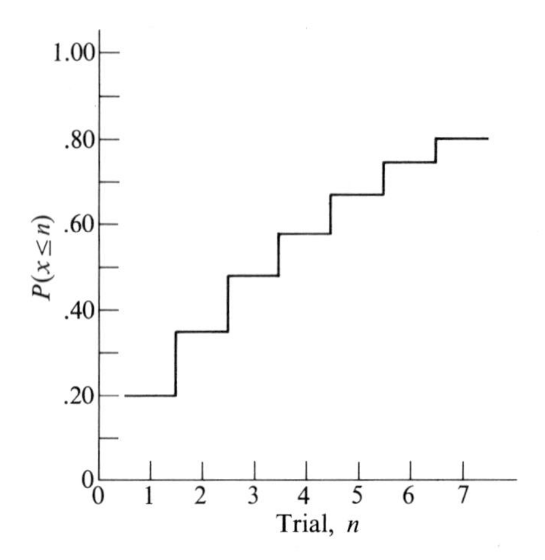

Fig. 2. Cumulative distribution of simple waiting times.

equal to the sum

$$P(x \leq n) = P(x = 1) + P(x = 2) + \cdots + P(x = n).$$

In this way, each value of $P(x \leq n)$ represents an accumulation of the values of the probability distribution. Figure 2 shows the cumulative distribution corresponding to Fig. 1.

The all-or-none theory of learning is a straightforward application of the mathematical theory of waiting times. Instead of thinking of a group of individuals each tossing a coin, think of a group of items, each being studied until it is learned. If we use c instead of π in the equations just given, we have the basic equations of the all-or-none theory of learning. Let L be the trial on which an item is learned. Then the theoretical proportion of items that become learned on Trial n is

$$P(L = n) = (1 - c)^{n-1}c. \tag{5.5}$$

The value of $P(L = n)$ equals the theoretical proportion of items that will remain unlearned through the first $n - 1$ trials, but become learned on Trial n.

Equation (5.5) gives a theoretical distribution based on an assumption about how items become learned. If the assumption is correct, the relative frequency distribution obtained in an experiment will look approximately like the theoretical distribution. The experimental results will not fit the theory exactly; however, the results of calculations based on the theory can be applied in different situations where the theory gives an approximately correct description of the learning process.

We could observe the trial of learning for each item in a large set, and then calculate the average and standard deviation. Theoretically, the mean would depend on the value of c according to the formula

$$\mu_L = 1/c, \tag{5.6}$$

and the standard deviation would be

$$\sigma_L = \sqrt{1 - c}/c. \tag{5.7}$$

Finally, consider the probability that an item becomes learned on Trial n or sooner. This is given by the cumulative distribution corresponding to Eq. (5.5)

$$P(L \leq n) = 1 - (1 - c)^n. \tag{5.8}$$

Equation (5.8) gives the theoretical average proportion of items that will be learned by the end of Trial n. If a test is given after n study trials, the proportion of correct answers will equal the proportion of items learned from the beginning through Trial n. Therefore, $P(L \leq n)$ is the average proportion of correct answers that we should expect on a test given after Trial n. In other words, Eq. (5.8) is the formula for the average learning curve when learning is all-or-none.

Example 5.2. Suppose that you are studying a list of mathematical formulas and the probability of learning a formula on a study trial is .10. What proportion of the formulas will you have learned after you have gone through the list five times?

We want to know the total number of formulas that have been learned, so we use the cumulative distribution.

$$P(L \leq 5) = 1 - (1 - c)^5 = 1 - (.90)^5 = 1 - .59 = .41. \blacksquare$$

An alternative expression of the learning curve can be translated into a logarithmic function. Consider the probability that an item is not learned after n trials. This probability is

$$P(L > n) = (1 - c)^n.$$

The value of $P(L > n)$ is the average proportion of items that remain unlearned after a lesson has been studied n times, if learning is all-or-none. If we take logarithms of both sides of the above equation, we have

$$\log P(L > n) = n \log (1 - c).$$

In an experiment, we can test a subject who has studied a list of items n times. The subject will be correct on all the items he has learned during

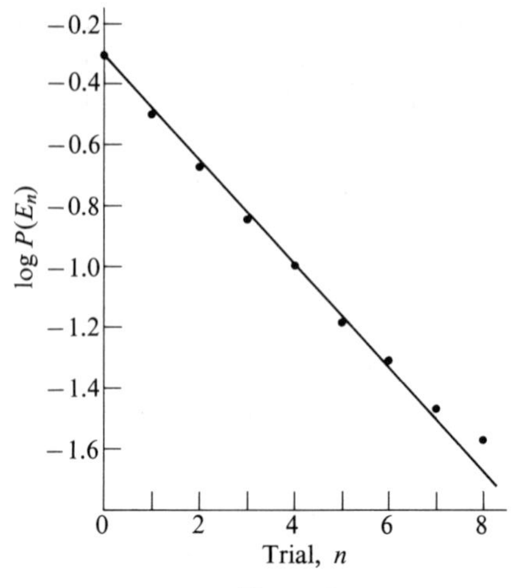

Figure 3

the n study trials. On the items he has not learned, he will make some errors. In some situations, the subject is asked to guess if he does not know the answer. Let g be the probability that the subject is correct if he has to guess. Then an error will occur if an item is not learned, and the subject fails to guess correctly. Let E_n stand for an error on a test after n study trials. Then

$$P(E_n) = (1 - g)P(L > n) = (1 - g)(1 - c)^n.$$

Now, if we take logarithms of both sides of this equation,

$$\log P(E_n) = \log (1 - g) + n \log (1 - c). \tag{5.9}$$

That is, if we plot the logarithm of the average proportion of errors against trials, we should obtain a straight line. Figure 3 shows such a plot, obtained in an experiment where subjects learned associations between two-letter stimuli and the numbers 1 and 2.[4] Subjects were asked to guess when they did not know the answers, and since there were just two responses, $g = .50$. It turned out that for these items and subjects, c was about one-third; therefore

$$\log (1 - c) = \log (.67) = -0.174.$$

The data points are very close to the theoretical straight line given by Eq. (5.9).

Thus far we have used arbitrary values of c, without considering any of the factors that influence the value of c, and without being concerned with

[4] This experiment was by G. H. Bower, "Application of a Model to Paired-Associate Learning," *Psychometrika*, 1961, **26,** 255–280.

ways of finding out the value of c in a particular experiment. Actually, a great many factors are known to influence the probability that an item will be learned.

Two of the factors influencing c were mentioned early in this section, when it was pointed out that we have to specify a test and an amount of time between study and testing before we know what we mean by "learning." If there is a relatively strict criterion of learning, due to a hard test or a long time before testing, the value of c will be relatively low.

Other factors influencing c relate to the materials to be learned and the situation in which the person studies. Generally, if there are many items to be learned, the probability of learning each item is lower than when comparable items are learned in shorter lists. A second factor involves the similarity among the items, especially among the stimuli. If the different stimuli are alike in appearance or meaning, the person has difficulty in remembering which response goes with each stimulus. A third factor involves the ease of the responses in the situation. If the responses are familiar and highly meaningful, it is easier for the person to learn and remember the associations. It was mentioned earlier that the all-or-none theory probably applies to learning situations where the learning process is relatively simple. Factors like long lists, confusions between items, and difficult responses increase the difficulty of learning partly by causing learning to take place in several stages, rather than in an all-or-none manner. However, we are not considering multi-stage learning processes in this book. To simplify discussion, variables that affect learning difficulty will be treated as just influencing the value of c.

When an experiment on memory is set up, the experimenter cannot tell in advance just how difficult the learning task will be. In fact, the point of the experiment is often to find out whether some particular factor will make learning easier or improve retention. Therefore the results of the experiment have to be used to find out about the value of c. The easiest way to do this would be to observe the trial on which each item was learned, and then calculate the mean, μ_L. Then we could use Eq. (5.6), solving for c.

$$c = 1/\mu_L. \tag{5.10}$$

Example 5.3. Suppose that in an experiment a large number of items are memorized, and we find that the mean trial of learning is 5.0. Calculate the value of c. Theoretically, what will the standard deviation be for these items?

First, we obtain a value of c using Eq. (5.10).

$$c = 1/\mu_L = 1/5.0 = .20.$$

Now we can calculate the theoretical standard deviation using Eq. (5.7).

$$\sigma_L = \sqrt{1 - c}/c = \sqrt{.80}/.20 = .89/.20 = 4.5. \blacksquare$$

Note that the last result is the theoretical standard deviation. It may or may not agree with the standard deviation found in the experiment. The agreement between the theoretical and experimental standard deviations often is used as a check to see how accurate the all-or-none assumption is for a particular experiment.

The theoretical distribution of trials before learning gives another way to test the all-or-none theory in an experiment.

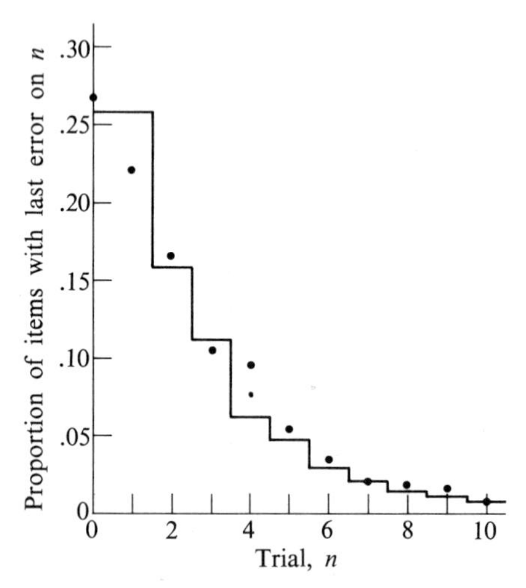

Fig. 4. A theoretical distribution of trial of last error compared with data.

We obtain evidence from a detailed statistical analysis of data from an experiment where subjects study a list repeatedly until all the items are learned.[5] The main question we consider here is whether the data agree with the geometric distribution of trials before learning that we derived earlier from the all-or-none assumption. In some cases, the agreement is quite impressive. Figure 4 shows one set of results, obtained when subjects learned 10-item lists with pairs of consonants as stimuli and the numbers 1 and 2 as responses. The distribution shown is not exactly the geometric distribution that we derived earlier, because in this experiment subjects could guess correctly when they did not know the correct answer—for example, this means that there is some chance of having no errors at all even though a test was given before the correct answer was shown even once. Therefore, we work with the distribution of the trial of the last error on individual items. This distribution, shown in Fig. 4, is closely related to the distribution of the trial of learning which we discussed earlier. And the fact that the results agree so well with the predicted distribution of this statistic gives further evidence that the all-or-none theory is a close approximation to the nature of the

[5] This type of investigation was carried out by G. H. Bower, *op. cit.*

learning process, at least in cases where the learning task is made as simple as possible.

Example 5.4. Suppose that you are studying a set of vocabulary items. In the past you have found that it takes an average of three study trials to learn a vocabulary item thoroughly. You decide that you want to study enough to get 80% correct on a test. How many times should you go through the vocabulary assignment?

First, we need to calculate a value of c, the learning probability. Using Eq. (5.10),

$$c = 1/\mu_L = 1/3 = .33.$$

Now we know that if the lesson is studied n times, the proportion of items learned will be

$$P(L \leq n) = 1 - (1 - c)^n.$$

Here, we know the value of c, and we have decided on a value of $P(L \leq n)$. Therefore, we have

$$.80 \approx 1 - (.67)^n,$$

and we want to find n. If we use $n = 3$, we obtain

$$P(L \leq 3) = 1 - .22 = .78.$$

With $n = 4$, we have

$$P(L \leq 4) = 1 - .15 = .85.$$

Therefore, to receive a score of 80%, you should go through the list four times. ▮

Example 5.5. In the situation of Example 5.4, suppose that you go through your assignment four times, and then go through once again for good measure. How many items will you learn on the fifth time through the list?

The answer comes from Eq. (5.5), since we are interested in how many items become learned on the fifth trial. With $n = 5$,

$$P(L = n) = (1 - c)^{n-1}c = (.67)^4(.33) = .05.$$

Thus, going through the assignment the fifth time should raise your score by about 5%. ▮

The student should now have an idea of how a set of items becomes learned when each item is learned in an all-or-none fashion. We have discussed the results of two experiments where learning apparently was approximately all-or-none. We have worked with the general mathematical theory of simple waiting times, and we have seen how this theory applies in simple learning situations. Finally, we mentioned a few factors that influence the value of c, the probability of learning, and we found a way to find the value of c from the results of a large experiment where learning was all-or-none.

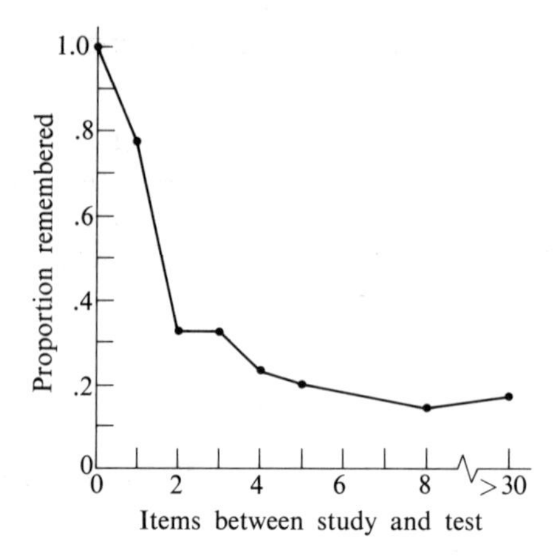

Fig. 5. Proportions of items remembered after different numbers of other items intervened between study and test.

5B FORGETTING

If a person studies a small amount of material and then is tested immediately, he almost surely will be able to pass the test. If he is tested a short time later, there is a good chance that he will have forgotten it. Figure 5 shows data obtained when a large number of simple associations were studied.[6] Each stimulus-response pair was shown for 2 sec, and then tested once at some later time. Some items were tested immediately, others were tested after some other items had been studied or tested. The data are the proportions of items remembered after each interval.

The results are typical of experiments like this one. Tests given within a few seconds after study show that a simple item like a paired associate is nearly always given correctly if it is tested right away. But forgetting is very rapid over a few seconds. Although most items are forgotten within a few seconds, some items will be remembered, and those items have a very good chance of being remembered for quite a while.

---

[6] The data are a composite of results from several studies by L. R. Peterson and others. Subjects were instructed to guess when they did not know the answer, and proportion remembered is calculated from proportion correct by the formula

$$P(R) = \frac{P(C) - g}{1 - g},$$

where g is the probability of being correct by guessing. The data are averages taken from the results of four experiments by L. R. Peterson and C. L. Brewer, "Confirmation, Correction, and Contiguity," *J. verb. Learn. verb. Behav.*, 1963, **1,** 365–371, and by L. R. Peterson, D. Saltzman, K. Hillner, and V. Land, "Recency and Frequency in Paired-Associate Learning," *J. exp. Psychol.*, 1962, **63,** 396–403.

Data like those in Fig. 5 have led to the idea that there are two memory systems. One system holds information for a short time, and the other is designed for long-term storage. Suppose that when something is studied it goes into a system where it can be retrieved easily, but where only a small amount of material can be stored at any time; therefore any one item is stored for only a short time. During the time that an item is in the short-term memory system, the person can rehearse the item or think about it in some way in an attempt to memorize it. Some of the items that are studied will be rehearsed and processed successfully. These will be memorized in a way that permits the person to remember them for a long time; we say that these items are transferred to the second memory system, which we call long-term memory. The long-term memory system can hold a great deal of material—for all practical purposes, we can consider that it has unlimited capacity. Items that are committed to long-term memory have a good chance of being retained for a relatively long time; there is some evidence that material stored in long-term memory is not lost at all. Most failures to remember information that has been stored probably are due to the person's inability to retrieve the information.

Our theory of forgetting has a structure similar to that of the theory of simple learning, presented in the last section. We shall use the theory of simple waiting times again, but this time we consider the time before an item is lost from memory, rather than the time before learning. First we consider a theory of forgetting from short-term memory. To explain the theory, we use an analogy. Suppose that there is a pan with holes in the bottom, so when marbles are placed in the pan and the pan is shaken, one or more marbles may fall out. We assume that the marbles fall out at a constant rate. Any given marble has a fixed probability of dropping out of the pan during a unit of time.

Now, suppose that a marble is put into the pan; to keep track of that marble, we might put an X on it. Now we shake the pan and look to see whether marble X is still in the pan. Then we shake the pan again and look again for marble X. We assume that if marble X is still in the pan after the pan has been shaken a few times, there is a constant probability that the marble will drop out the next time the pan is shaken. Call that probability d.

We can calculate the probability that the marble will be lost during a time when the pan is shaken a number of times. The probability that it will drop out the first time the pan is shaken is d. Therefore, the probability that it will still be there after one shake is $1 - d$. If it is still in the pan after one shake, then the probability that it will be lost the second time the pan is shaken is d. Therefore, the probability of keeping the marble during the first shake and losing it during the second shake is $(1 - d)d$. The cumulative probability that the marble will be lost during the first or the second shake is $d + (1 - d)d = 1 - (1 - d)^2$. But these are exactly the kinds of cal-

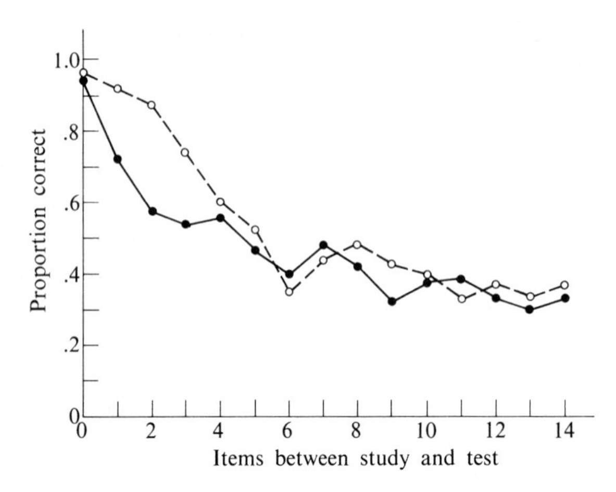

Fig. 6. Short-term retention under two different conditions.

culations we went through in Section 5A. So without further discussion, we can refer back to the previous development and say that the probability of keeping marble X for $n - 1$ shakes and then losing it the nth time the pan is shaken is just $(1 - d)^{n-1}d$. Let h_n be the probability that the marble remains in the pan when the pan is shaken n times.

$$h_n = (1 - d)^n. \tag{5.11}$$

When an item is studied and put into short-term memory, we suppose it is like putting a marble into the pan with holes in the bottom. After the item is studied, the subject has to do other things during the time before he is tested. In the experiments leading to Fig. 5 the subject had to study other items or be tested on other items. We suppose that study and test trials disrupt short-term memory and cause items to drop out. In the analogy we have made a simplifying assumption that is only true sometimes. The assumption is that after an item is put into short-term memory there is a constant probability that it will be lost during each succeeding study or test trial. The solid curve in Fig. 6 shows an experimental result where the assumption seems to have been approximately correct. The curve drops in a regular way, in good agreement with Eq. (5.11). The dashed line in Fig. 6 shows a result where the simplifying assumption apparently is not true.[7]

[7] The data are from J. W. Brelsford, Jr. and R. C. Atkinson, "Short-Term Memory as a Function of Rehearsal Procedures," *J. verb. Learn. verb. Behav.*, in press. Subjects who gave the results on the solid curve studied items silently, while subjects who gave the results on the dashed curve rehearsed the items aloud. The overt rehearsal probably had something to do with the special attention they could give to items recently put into short-term memory.

One possibility is that in some situations the subject can pay special attention to the item most recently seen, so retention after one interval is better than it should be according to the formula.

Example 5.6. Suppose that the probability of losing an item from short-term memory is $d = .60$ each time another item is studied or tested. What is the probability that an item will still be in short-term memory if it is tested after two other items are studied? How many study and test items would have to occur before the probability of holding the item in short-term memory is as low as .05?

First, we want to calculate

$$h_2 = (1 - d)^2 = (.40)^2 = .16.$$

Next we want to find a value of n so that

$$h_n = (1 - d)^n = .05.$$

If we use $n = 3$,

$$h_n = (1 - d)^3 = .064.$$

If we use $n = 4$,

$$h_n = (1 - d)^4 = .0256,$$

so the answer is 4. ▮

The value of d is the rate of forgetting from short-term memory, and it depends on a number of factors. One of the most important is the complexity of the item which is stored. If an item consists of several components or elements, it is harder to hold in short-term memory than if it holds just one or two components. For example, it is harder to remember a 10-digit telephone number than a four-digit house number. In an experiment subjects were shown items and then tested a few seconds later for recall.[8] After the subject heard an item, he was tested immediately, or he had to count backwards for 3, 6, 9, 12, or 18 sec and then try to recall the item. Items were of different kinds; some were single three-letter words, other items were sets of three short words, and still others were sets of three unrelated consonants. The experimenter's idea was that three things would be forgotten more quickly than one, but that three unrelated letters would be remembered about as well as three unrelated words. The results were consistent with the idea. Single words were retained very well; only .16 were forgotten during the 18 sec interval. Three-letter items and three-word items were forgotten rather quickly, with about .80 forgotten by the end of 18 sec; but the rate of forgetting was about equal for the two kinds of items with three elements.

---

[8] B. B. Murdock, Jr., "The Retention of Individual Items," *J. Exp. Psychol.*, 1961, **62,** 618–625.

Other important factors depend on what the subject must do in the interval between study and testing. We have been using the idea that when the subject has to study and be tested on other items, each intervening item produces an opportunity for forgetting. In some experiments, retention over short intervals has been compared when other items are presented at different rates. In one experiment subjects heard digits and tried to remember as many as they could.[9] In one condition, digits were read one per second, and in another condition they were read four per second. On test trials, a probe digit was presented, and the subject tried to recall the digit which followed the probe digit in the sequence. For example, the sequence might be

. . . 4 7 9 3 1 6 2 *7* ?,

where 7 is the probe digit. Then the correct response is 9, which is the fifth digit back in the sequence. According to the idea that each item produces a chance for forgetting, the amount of retention should depend mainly on the number of items between study and test, rather than the amount of time. For example, when the test was for the fifth item back, the number of items between study and test were the same in both conditions, but the amount of time between study and test was 4 sec in the one-per-sec condition, and only 1 sec in the four-per-sec condition. It turned out that the amount of forgetting depended almost entirely on the number of items; for a given number of items between study and test, the amount of forgetting was almost the same for the two rates of presentation.

Another factor influencing the rate of forgetting is the difficulty of the subject's task during the retention interval. If the subject has to do something simple, such as writing down digits that he hears, the rate of forgetting is relatively slow. But if the subject has to do something harder, such as counting backwards by threes or classifying digits into high or low and odd or even, more forgetting occurs.[10] A final factor that sometimes affects the amount of forgetting from short-term memory is the similarity of materials studied during the retention interval and the item to be remembered. In one study,[11] the items studied were taken from two classes; one had letters spoken with an ē sound (B, C, D, G, P, T, V, Z) and another had letters spoken with an ĕ sound (F, L, M, N, S, X). The subject heard one of the letters, and then heard eight other letters before being tested on the first one. When the intervening items had the same sound as the studied item, there

---

[9] N. C. Waugh and D. A. Norman, "Primary Memory," *Psychol. Rev.*, 1965, **72,** 89–104.

[10] M. I. Posner and A. F. Konick, "On the Role of Interference in Short-Term Retention," *J. exp. Psychol.*, 1966, **72,** 221–231.

[11] W. A. Wickelgren, "Acoustic Similarity and Retroactive Interference in Short-Term Memory," *J. verb. Learn. verb. Behav.*, 1965, **4,** 1–6.

was more forgetting than when the intervening items were taken from the opposite group.

Thus far we have theorized only about short-term memory. In earlier discussion we talked about the process of storing information in long-term memory. According to the general idea of the theory, there is a probability c that an item will be stored in long-term memory during the time it stays in short-term memory. Later we will discuss a process of interference which makes it difficult for the person to find material that is stored in long-term memory. However, the process of interference operates relatively slowly, so if we consider amounts of time longer than a few seconds, but not longer than a few minutes, we can assume that material stored in long-term memory can still be retrieved.

If an item is stored in long-term memory, then it will be remembered on a test even after it has dropped out of short-term memory. Let $r_{1,n}$ be the probability that an item will be remembered when there is one study trial and then n other items are studied before the test. Note that there are two ways for the item to be remembered; either it is stored in long-term memory, or it was not stored in long-term memory but it is still held in short-term memory. Then

$$r_{1,n} = c + (1 - c)h_n = c + (1 - c)(1 - d)^n. \tag{5.12}$$

Example 5.7 Suppose that the probability of losing an item from short-term memory is $d = .60$ each time another item is studied or tested, as before. Also assume that there is probability $c = .20$ that an item is stored in long-term memory during the time it stays in short-term memory. What is the probability that an item will be remembered after it is studied once and then tested after two other items are studied or tested? What is the probability after 10 other items are studied or tested?

In the preceding example, we calculated

$$h_2 = .16.$$

Now we need

$$r_{1,2} = .20 + (1 - .20)(.16) = .33.$$

We also need h_{10}. From Table B (p. 000),

$$h_{10} = (1 - d)^{10} = .000.$$

Then

$$r_{1,10} = .20. \blacksquare$$

It is obvious that as we increase the number of items between study and test it becomes very unlikely that the studied item will be held in short-term memory. Then the probability of remembering the item gets very close to c, the probability of storing the item in long-term memory.

Now recall our discussion of simple associative learning given in Section 5A. Remember that we assumed (with some experimental justification) that on each study trial there is a probability c that the studied item will be learned. Using the terms of our present discussion, the event previously called "learning" is what we refer to as getting an item stored in long-term memory. If the item is not stored on its first study trial, then there is another chance for it to be stored on its next study trial. On each study trial the item is stored in short-term memory and stays there for a time; during this time the item may be stored in long-term memory—that is, the item may be learned.

If an item has been studied m times, then there have been m opportunities for it to be stored in long-term memory. The item will be remembered if it was stored in long-term memory on any of the m study trials, or if it was not stored in long-term memory but is still in short-term memory. The probability that the item is remembered after m study trials with n other items between the last study and the test, is

$$\begin{aligned} r_{m,n} &= P(L \leq m) + [1 - P(L \leq m)]h_n \\ &= 1 - (1 - c)^m + (1 - c)^m(1 - d)^n. \end{aligned} \tag{5.13}$$

Equation (5.13) is the most general equation for short-term retention that we use here. Note that Eq. (5.12) is the special case of Eq. (5.13) when $m = 1$, and Eq. (5.11) simply ignores the process of storage in long-term memory.

Example 5.8. Suppose that we have an experimental situation where $d = .40$, $c = .15$. There are six paired-associate items, and the subject studies the list three times before a test is given. On the last cycle of study trials, the order of the items is *A, B, C, D, E, F*. The order of items on the test is *E, D, F, C, A, B*. What is the probability that the subject will remember the answer for item *E*? for item *C*?

Since there were three study trials, the probability of storing an item in long-term memory was

$$P(L \leq 3) = 1 - (1 - c)^3 = .386.$$

Item E is tested after just one intervening item. Therefore, for item E, we have

$$r_{3,1} = .386 + (.614)^3(1 - d) = .525.$$

However, item C was tested after there were six intervening items. Therefore, for item C, we have

$$r_{3,6} = .386 + (.614)^3(.60)^6 = .397. \;\blacksquare$$

Now, there is another simplifying assumption that should be pointed out. We have assumed that the probability of an item being stored in long-term memory is a fixed quantity, c. However, we know that some items will be held in short-term memory longer than other items, and we should expect that if an item stays in short-term memory for quite a while its probability of being stored in long-term memory should be higher than average. Thus, the assumption of a fixed value of c simplifies the situation by neglecting the differences in probability. This complicating factor is not hard to build into the theory, but it leads to relatively elaborate mathematical expressions, and is not needed to express the basic ideas of the theory.

Finally, we turn to forgetting that occurs after items are stored in long-term memory. Again, the main idea can be explained best by an analogy.[12] This time the analogy involves a large junk box, where material is stored and seldom or never drops out of the box. But, although material could stay in the junk box forever, it might not be easy to find. Items that have been put in the box recently can probably be found quite easily, since they should still be near the top. But if an item has been in the box a long time and many other items have been put in, the first item may be very hard or impossible to find.

Our idea here is that during an interval of time, a person is doing things that result in his storing information in memory. This interferes with his ability to find material that was stored earlier. For any item that has been stored, there is some probability that the person's activity during an interval of time will interfere with his ability to find the item. Again, we make the simplifying assumption that during a unit of time, there is a constant probability of interference with any stored item. Call that probability f. Actually, it would be reasonable to suppose that interference takes place more or less continuously; however, our analysis will be easier if we treat time in discrete units. Therefore we fix a unit of time, and let f be the probability that interference occurs for an item at some time during the fixed interval.

Again, our analysis takes the form of a simple waiting time. Given that an item has been stored in long-term memory, the probability that it can be retrieved after the first unit of time is $1 - f$. The probability that it can be retrieved after the second unit of time is $(1 - f)^2$. In general, the probability that an item can be retrieved n units of time after it was stored is

$$s_n = (1 - f)^n. \tag{5.14}$$

Example 5.9. Suppose that the probability of interference with an item during any 15-min period is .05. We give a person enough time to study

[12] The analogy was presented by G. A. Miller in "Comments on Professor Postman's Paper," in C. N. Cofer and B. S. Musgrave (Eds.), *Verbal Behavior and Learning: Problems and Processes*, New York: McGraw-Hill, 1963, pp. 321–329.

a lesson so that we are sure he knows all of the items in it. Then we test him one hour later. On the average, what proportion of the items should be answered correctly in the test? How long would it take before the probability of forgetting an item was at least .25?

First, we just need to calculate s_n, with n corresponding to one hour. The unit of time is 15 min, so one hour corresponds to four units of time. Therefore, we want

$$s_4 = (1 - f)^4 = (.95)^4 = .81.$$

To answer the second question, we need to know how long the value of s_n stays above .75. We have

$$(.95)^5 = .774, \qquad (.95)^6 = .735.$$

Therefore, it would take between 75 and 90 min to forget 25% of a lesson if f were .05 for 15-min periods. ▮

Equation (5.14) applies to retention intervals that are quite long. We use Eq. (5.14) when the interval between study and test is more than a few minutes. Equation (5.13) applies when there are only seconds between study and test. Equation (5.13) is used mainly to analyze retention during the time a subject is studying a set of items, and Eq. (5.14) is used to analyze forgetting during long intervals after the time when a set of items has been studied.

Another feature of Eq. (5.14) is that it applies only to items that have been stored in memory. Usually a person will stop studying a set of items before all of them have been stored in long-term memory. If a test is given some time after a lesson is studied, there are two possible reasons for missing an item: either the item was not stored in long-term memory during the study session, or it was stored but the person is unable to retrieve it from memory.

Suppose that a set of items is studied m times and then tested n units of time later. The probability that an item is stored in long-term memory during the study trials is given by Eq. (5.8). If an item is stored, the probability that it can be retrieved after n units of time is given by Eq. (5.14). Then the probability that an item is known on the test is

$$s_{m,n} = P(L \leq m)s_n = [1 - (1 - c)^m](1 - f)^n. \tag{5.15}$$

Example 5.10. In Example 5.9 we assumed $f = .05$ for 15-min periods. Now suppose that $c = .25$. What is the probability that an item will be known on a test one hour after the items are studied (a) if the items are studied once and (b) if the items are studied three times? How many times must the items be studied in order for the probability of knowing an item to be at least .70?

With just one study trial, the probability of storing an item in long-term memory is c. Therefore,

$$s_{1,4} = (c)(s_4) = (.25)(.81) = .20.$$

With three study trials, we have

$$s_{3,4} = (1 - .75^3)(.81) = .47.$$

Now we want a value of *m*, where $s_{m,n} = .70$. With six study trials, we have

$$s_{6,4} = (1 - .75^6)(.81) = .67.$$

With seven study trials,

$$s_{7,4} = (1 - .75^7)(.81) = .70.$$

Therefore, the answer is 7. ▮

The theory we have been using assumes that the probability *f* applies to each individual item stored in memory. This is a serious oversimplification, as we shall see later. However, the general idea of losing the ability to retrieve items from memory is central to the theory of forgetting, and we use our simple version of that idea to discuss some variables that affect the rate of forgetting.

The value of *f* is the rate of forgetting from long-term memory, and like the value of *d*, *f* is influenced by a number of factors. One of these factors is the amount of the subject's activity during the interval between study and test. In one experiment, subjects studied lists of nonsense syllables, and were tested later.[13] The tests were given following different time intervals, but the main variable of the experiment was whether the subjects were awake and engaging in normal activity or were asleep during the interval between study and test. After an eight-hour interval, only about 10% of the material was retained if the subjects had been awake; however, nearly 60% of the material was retained if the subjects had spent the eight hours sleeping. Another factor is the similarity between the material to be retained and other material that is studied between the time of study and test. If the intervening material is similar to the original material, the rate of forgetting will be greater than if it is different.[14]

The value of *f* also depends on characteristics of the material studied. One thing we all know from experience is that we can remember a general idea or principle longer than we can remember detailed information. We often use this fact when we have to remember a large amount of information. If we can find a way of organizing the information in some meaningful way, we have a better chance of being able to retrieve it successfully from memory.

---

[13] This frequently cited study was by J. G. Jenkins and K. M. Dallenbach, "Oblivience During Sleep and Waking," *Amer. J. Psychol.*, 1924, **12,** 605–612.

[14] Evidence on this point is presented by C. E. Osgood, "The Similarity Paradox in Human Learning: A Resolution," *Psychol. Rev.*, 1949, **56,** 132–154. The article also gives a theoretical analysis, relating general facts about interference and transfer to the ideas of stimulus and response generalization.

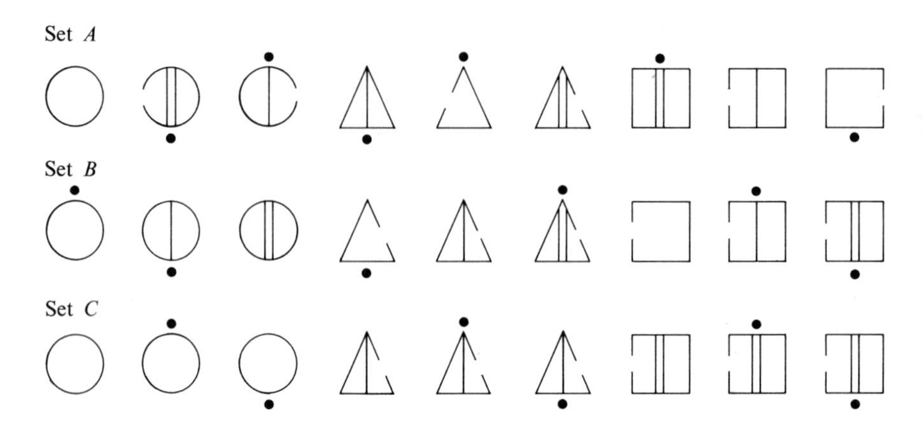

Fig. 7. Materials for an experiment concerned with organization and memory.

The advantage of being able to organize material for memory was shown in an experiment[15] where subjects looked at a series of pictures and then tried to draw as many of the figures as they could. The three sets of figures that were used are illustrated in Fig. 7. The main difference among the sets is in the simplicity of the rule that is needed to describe the overall set. In Set *C*, the subject only needs to remember three shapes (circle, triangle with vertical line broken on right, rectangle with two lines broken on left) and three variations within each set (no dot, dot above, and dot below). The figures in Set *B* can be partly generated by a simple rule (circles, triangle broken on right, rectangle broken on left; one of each set is open, one has a vertical line, one has two vertical lines; one has no dot, one has a dot above, one has a dot below), but the subject had to remember individual combinations of dot positions and numbers of vertical lines. In Set *A* there is even less information that can be generated from simple rules. The difference in ease of remembering the sets was striking; after a single exposure to all the stimuli of Set *C*, the proportion of correct responses was about .70. The proportions of correct responses for Sets *B* and *A* were about .40 and .20. After seven repetitions subjects got all of the figures in Set *C* correct; it took 19 repetitions before all subjects could remember all the figures in Set *B*; and after 20 repetitions, subjects still remembered fewer than .80 of the items of Set *A*.

Another experiment[16] was done using verbal materials. A set of 16 nonsense syllables was constructed; two groups studied sets of eight and one

---

[15] By J. R. Whitman and W. R. Garner, "Free Recall Learning of Visual Figures as a Function of Form of Internal Structure," *J. exp. Psychol.*, 1962, **64,** 558–564.
[16] W. R. Garner and J. R. Whitman, "Form and Amount of Internal Structure as Factors in Free-Recall Learning of Nonsense Words," *J. verb. Learn. verb. Behav.*, 1965, **4,** 257–266.

group studied all 16 syllables. The lists studied by the three groups are shown below:

Set *A*	Set *B*	Set *C*	
BROZ	BROZ	BROZ	PROZ
BRAJ	BRAZ	BROJ	PROJ
BLAZ	BROJ	BRAZ	PRAZ
BLOJ	BRAJ	BRAJ	PRAJ
PLOZ	PLOZ	BLOZ	PLOZ
PLAJ	PLAZ	BLOJ	PLOJ
PRAZ	PLOJ	BLAZ	PLAZ
PROJ	PLAJ	BLAJ	PLAJ

In the experiment the syllables were shown in a haphazard order, and each syllable was shown for 5 sec. Then the subject was asked to write down as many of the syllables as he could remember. Ten trials were given, and in those 10 trials subjects working on Set *C* made an average of 1.3 errors per item, subjects working on Set *B* made an average of 1.2 errors per item, and subjects working on Set *A* made an average of 4.5 errors per item.

The result is quite dramatic; usually items in long lists are harder to remember than items in shorter lists, but here the usual result is reversed. The reason for this is obvious: the items in Sets *B* and *C* can be learned in groups. In fact, the items in Set *C* can all be generated by the simple rule of making all combinations of the letters (B, P), (R, L), (O, A), and (Z, J). Again, we see that it is easier to remember a general principle and generate items than it is to remember a list of items that are not easily organized.

Now recall the formula given for forgetting from long-term memory, Eq. (5.14). That formula assumes that individual items are forgotten independently, but we have seen some cases where there are clearly relationships among the items in a list. It is reasonable to suppose that subjects find relationships and develop a structure while they are learning a list, even when the materials do not lead naturally to an organized system. Figure 8 shows the data of an experiment[17] where subjects memorized lists of nonsense syllables and were tested at different times after study. The solid curve was calculated using Eq. (5.14) with $f = .045$, counting time in units of one hour. The curve fits the data about as well as it can be fit with Eq. (5.14). Clearly, however, Eq. (5.14) is not an accurate description of the forgetting process here. Forgetting was too rapid during the time shortly after study, and too slow during the time between a few hours and two days.

One possible explanation is that subjects were able to develop a retrieval scheme that permitted them to remember some of the items very well, but

[17] By C. W. Luh, "The Conditions of Retention," *Psychol. Monogr.*, 1922, Whole Number 142.

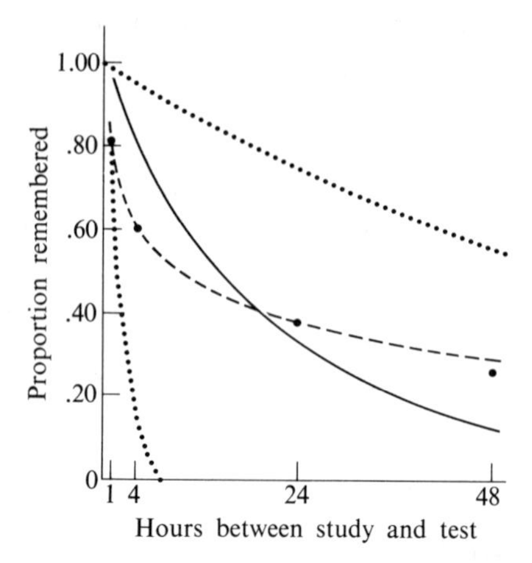

Fig. 8. Data for long-term retention compared with Eq. (5.14) (solid line) and with a theory that assumes some items are organized (dashed line).

the remaining items were forgotten quickly. Suppose that a subject had a system for remembering some of the items, but the other items were not organized and had to be remembered individually. The items that were included in the system would have a small value of f, but the unorganized items would have a much larger value of f. As an illustration of how this would show up in overall data, two dotted lines are drawn in Fig. 8: one with $f = .001$ and the other with $f = .65$. The average of these two curves is drawn as a dashed line, and it fits the data almost perfectly. The curve should be considered as an illustration; it assumes that one-half of the items were organized under a system and that the others were not. Different mixtures are possible and would agree equally well with the data. But the general idea that we can retain items that have been organized into a system, but forget quickly items that have to be held individually, apparently has merit.

We consider here one more factor influencing forgetting; this also involves what the subject does when he studies. A person may study a list of items until he barely knows them. Or he may study the items until he knows them and then study for a time after that. The extra practice is called overtraining, and overtraining causes a marked increase in retention. Figure 9 presents the data of an experiment[18] where subjects learned lists of words in a fixed serial order, and then were tested for retention 1, 2, 4, 7, 14, or 28 days later. The data are proportions of words given correctly on a test where the experimenter asked the subject for the first word, then supplied the first word if it was not given and asked for the second word, continuing in this

[18] By W. C. F. Krueger, "The Effect of Overlearning on Retention," *J. exp. Psychol.*, 1929, **12,** 71–78.

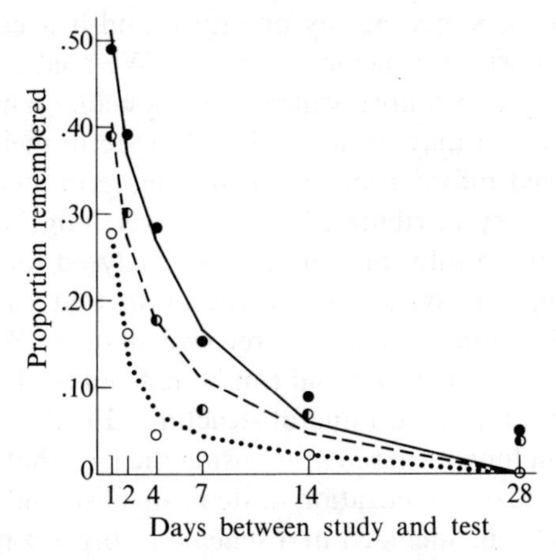

Fig. 9. Long-term retention after different amounts of overtraining.

way through the list. There were three conditions of memorizing. The open circles represent data obtained when subjects studied the list only until they had one perfect trial. The half-filled circles show the results when subjects studied the list to one perfect trial, and then had half as many additional trials as they had taken to reach the criterion. And the filled circles show the results when subjects studied to one perfect trial, and then had as many additional trials as they had taken to reach criterion.

According to the idea we are using, the overtraining groups had better retention because they had a better opportunity to organize the items in a system that could be retained for a long period. The theoretical curves in Fig. 9 were drawn using the simple idea that at each level of training some of the items were organized into systems so that they would be forgotten less rapidly. The groups are assumed to differ only in the proportion of items that are organized in retrieval systems. The quantities used were as follows: items that were organized were assumed to be forgotten at the rate of $f = .15$ per day, items that were not in organized systems were assumed to be forgotten at the rate of $f = .82$ per day. It was assumed that when practice was continued only until criterion was reached .13 of the items were organized; with 50% overtraining, .33 of the items were organized; and with 100% overtraining, .49 of the items were organized. The curve for the criterion group is given as the dotted line, the 50% overtraining condition is given as the dashed line, and the 100% overtraining group is given as the solid line. The curves fit the data reasonably well, although there is some suggestion that the overtraining condition produced retrieval systems that involved a lower value of f than was obtained in the criterion group.

In the discussion of forgetting in this section we first analyzed short-term retention. In the theory presented here, one memory system allows a small number of items to be stored at any one time, and it is easy to retrieve information in this short-term memory system. We analyzed the process of short-term forgetting as a simple waiting-time system. While an item is still in short-term memory it may be stored in a long-term memory system, and we took the view that information stored in long-term memory suffers little or no loss. The theory attributes forgetting over long intervals to loss in ability to retrieve stored information, and we analyzed long-term forgetting as a simple waiting-time system where the event that causes forgetting is interference with the subject's ability to retrieve an item. We discussed some experiments which show that material can be remembered much more easily if it can be organized into a meaningful structure. Finally, we analyzed data from experiments on long-term retention using the idea that rate of forgetting depends on the degree of organization of items in a list, and that overtraining permits more items to be included in a scheme of organization.

5C TRANSFER OF LEARNED ASSOCIATIONS TO NEW STIMULI

Consider a very young child who is still learning the names of simple objects. He has several round balls, and he has learned to say "ball" when he sees one of them. Now a friend comes to visit and brings along a football. The friend throws the ball to the child and says, "Catch the ball." The child now has to learn a new association; the elliptical thing that is thrown is a ball. This new stimulus is different in some ways from the earlier stimuli that were associated with the response "ball." In particular, the new stimulus has a different shape. But the new stimulus also has properties in common with the old stimuli. For example, the new object is something which is thrown or kicked, and it bounces when it hits the floor. In some situations like this, associations that were learned earlier will transfer to the new stimulus; in other situations they will not. In this section we consider what it is that permits old learning to transfer to new situations.

Sometimes transfer depends on aspects of a learning situation that are subtle or complicated, and we take up some relatively complicated cases in Chapter 6. Here we consider a simple kind of transfer that depends on stimulus generalization. A subject learns to give a response R to a stimulus S_1. Then he has to learn to give the same response to a new stimulus S_2. The two stimuli S_1 and S_2 are not identical, but usually they will have some properties in common. If the subject uses the shared properties of the two stimuli, the original association of the response to S_1 will transfer to the new stimulus S_2.

We shall begin with a theory about the nature of a stimulus. A subject can think of any stimulus in a number of different ways. Suppose, for example, that the stimulus is a simple word like "book." A subject could think of this as "the word starting with 'b'" or he could think "rhymes with 'look'," or he could think "something to read," or he could form a mental image of a book, or he might just recite the word "book," silently. In the theory of learning and transfer, we treat a stimulus as the collection of different ways a subject can think about it. The mathematical notion for representing a collection is a *set*. We use this notion, and we represent a stimulus as a set of different properties and ways of thinking about the stimulus.

When two stimuli are used, we represent them as two sets of properties. In the theory of transfer, the important thing about the two stimuli involves the properties that they have in common. If the two stimuli are the words "book" and "box," there are several properties that the stimuli share. For example, both of the words start with "b," and both of the words are names of things that are rectangular in shape. At the same time, each of the stimuli has properties that the other does not have. "Book" may be thought of as "something to read," while "box" would be thought of as "something to hold things." "Book" rhymes with "look," while "box" rhymes with "fox."

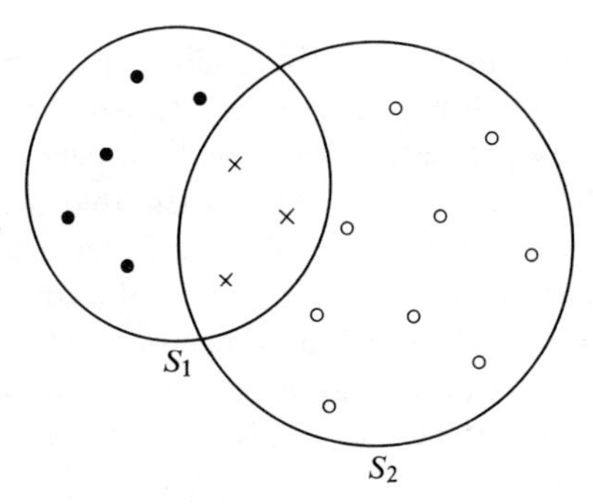

Fig. 10. A representation of the different properties and ways of thinking about two stimuli.

The situation is represented by the diagram in Fig. 10. Each large circle represents a stimulus, and the marks in each circle represent the different ways in which the subject could think about that stimulus. The black dots represent ways of thinking about S_1 that would not apply to S_2, the open dots represent ways of thinking about S_2 that would not apply to S_1, and the X's represent ways of thinking about either stimulus.

An important idea in the theory of transfer is the amount of similarity between stimuli. When we represent stimuli as sets of properties, we can think of the number of shared properties as determining the amount of similarity. In Fig. 10 the number of shared properties is smaller than the number of distinctive properties of either stimulus. Therefore, Fig. 10 represents two stimuli that are quite dissimilar. If two stimuli share many properties and each has only a few distinctive properties, then the stimuli are very similar.

The amount of similarity between two stimuli is an important factor in determining whether a response learned to one of them will transfer to the other. If a response is associated with a stimulus S_1 and a new stimulus is presented that is very similar, this means that the new stimulus has many properties that are shared with S_1 and it will be easy for the subject to transfer the response to the new stimulus. However, if the new stimulus is very dissimilar, there will be very few properties that can be used as the basis of transfer, and transfer will be less likely to occur.

The ideas presented above are the main concepts needed for a theory of transfer, but they do not describe what transfer is in a specific way. The kind of transfer process that occurs in a situation depends on the way in which learning occurs in that situation. The theory of transfer will be presented in relation to two different learning strategies that may be used by a subject, depending on the situation in which he learns the associations which can be transferred. The two learning strategies are (1) selective coding, and (2) association with patterns.

The strategy of learning by selective coding involves the idea that when a person remembers something, he does not remember everything about it. Any situation has many properties, and usually a person notices only a few things about a situation he is in. We can expect that often many aspects of a stimulus will not be stored in memory, even if they are noticed. A person may have learned an association between a stimulus and a response, but not have the "whole" stimulus represented in memory. The memory of an association may include only a part or an aspect of the stimulus—enough of its characteristics to permit the person to give the correct response, but not a complete representation.

In an experiment that illustrates selective coding,[19] subjects learned a list of associations. Each stimulus was a word and a nonsense syllable together, like RIP GEX. Each response was a number between 1 and 8. After the list was learned, there was a test on the separate parts of the stimuli. In the test, the word RIP was presented at one time, the syllable GEX was presented at a different time, and the subject was asked to give the number that belonged with each of them. In the first list there were eight pairs in all, so the transfer test involved a total of 16 items, eight with word stimuli and eight with nonsense syllables.

In one group subjects studied the first list until they had all the responses correct on one trial. In the transfer test, subjects knew the responses for more than 60% of the word stimuli, and only about 10% of the nonsense stimuli. Apparently the subjects used a strategy of associating the responses with the familiar words and ignoring the nonsense syllables that had no meaning for them for most of the items.

---

[19] By C. T. James and J. G. Greeno, "Stimulus Selection at Different Stages of Paired-Associate Learning," *J. exp. Psychol.*, 1967, **74,** 75–83.

The selective nature of learning does not always involve omitting some physical part of a stimulus. Everyone is familiar with mnemonic tricks that help us remember facts or detailed information. Children remember the notes on a musical staff with the ungrammatical mnemonic "Every Good Boy Does Fine." You may have a trick that helps you remember a telephone number that you use once in a while. Often a person will remember a fact by connecting that fact with something else that he already knows well.

In an experiment,[20] subjects learned paired associates with nonsense syllable stimuli and word responses. One of the pairs was BAC–EGGS. Some subjects were given a preliminary trial where they were shown a helpful mnemonic code. For example, these subjects were shown the item BACon. Other subjects were shown mnemonic codes that were not very helpful, such as BACk. Subjects who saw helpful mnemonic codes learned the list faster than did subjects who saw irrelevant codes. However, subjects who saw no mnemonic codes at all learned the list just as fast as the subjects who saw helpful codes. One interpretation is that subjects are very good at finding their own mnemonic codes for items like this. Showing them a set of helpful codes did not permit them to learn any faster than they could using their own efficient coding systems, although showing them irrelevant codes slowed down the process of learning.

The different mnemonic associations a person may think of, along with the different physical aspects of a stimulus and response, provide a set of codes the subject might try to use to remember an association. In studying an association, one strategy is to select one of the possible memory codes. Some of the codes that may be selected will not support memory of the association. For example, if a subject tries to remember "BACk-EGGS," he apparently has a high probability of losing the item from memory, and if he has the item "RIP GEX–5," he apparently cannot remember the item easily if he uses the nonsense syllable as his memory code. But other ways of trying to remember the items are successful and lead to good retention. When the subject selects a code that will support memory of the association and stores that code in long-term memory, he has learned the item.

When a subject uses a strategy of selective coding to memorize paired associates, learning will take place in an all-or-none fashion under some special conditions. Recall from Section 5A that the main condition for all-or-none learning is that the probability of learning is a constant, c. In selective learning, the value of c is the probability of selecting a code that will support memory of the item. In Fig. 11 the diagram represents a set of codes. Some of the codes are adequate to support memory, and these are represented by circles with plus signs. Other codes are not adequate to support memory, and these are represented by circles with minus signs. If all

---

[20] By K. M. Dallett, "Implicit Mediators in Paired-Associate Learning," *J. verb. Learn. verb. Behav.*, 1964, **3**, 209–214.

of the codes are sampled with equal probabilities, then in the situation represented by Fig. 11 the value of c would be .30. One way for the probability of learning to remain constant would be for the subject always to sample from the same set of possible codes, and always replace codes that were not successful in supporting memory.[21]

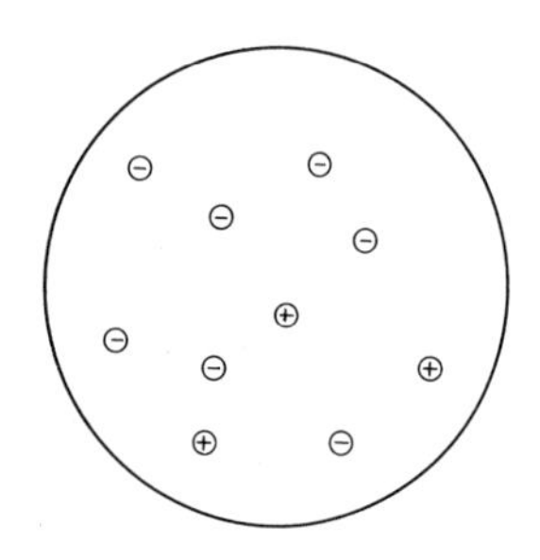

Fig. 11. Representation of adequate and inadequate memory codes.

Now recall Fig. 10, and remember the situation in which transfer can occur. A subject has already learned an association between stimulus S_1 and a response R. In learning this first association, he has selected one of the codes which support memory of the association S_1–R. In the diagram in Fig. 10 only the adequate codes are represented. Therefore, when the subject has learned the S_1–R association, he has one of the codes represented by a filled dot or by an X stored in memory.

Now the subject begins to study a new item. The stimulus for the new item is S_2, but the response is still R. Transfer will occur if the code used for learning S_1–R will also support memory of S_2–R. In Fig. 10, the X's represent codes that would support memory either of S_1–R or of S_2–R. Then if a subject learned S_1–R by selecting one of the codes represented by an X, transfer to S_2–R would occur. But if the subject learned S_1–R by selecting one of the codes represented by a filled dot, transfer to S_2–R would not occur.

Recall the example of the child learning to use the word "ball." The objects that the child already calls "balls" are round, they can be rolled, and they can be kicked or tossed, but the new object is not round and it cannot be rolled easily. The properties of round shape and easy rolling are like the filled dots in Fig. 10; they would support memory of the first association but would not apply in the second. The property of being something to kick or toss can be identified with the X's in Fig. 10. If the child associated the response "ball" with the properties of throwing or kicking, the response would transfer to the new stimulus. But if the child only associated the response "ball" with the property of round shape, then the previous learning would not transfer to the new association between a football and the response "ball."

[21] It seems more likely that if a subject tries to remember an item in a certain way and finds that the code does not work, he will be less likely to try that code again. However, it is also likely that the subject will notice new aspects of the stimulus and think of new associative codes during the experiment. If the rate of adding new codes to the set were approximately equal to the rate of removing unsuccessful codes from the set, then the probability of learning could still remain approximately constant.

The idea of selective learning and the theory of transfer based on shared codes imply that transfer will occur in an all-or-none manner. If the subject learns the first item using one of the shared codes, he will know the second item as soon as he sees it because he already has a code in memory that will support retention of the second item. If the subject learns the first item using a code that is not shared with the second item, then the first learning is irrelevant to the second item and the second item will have to be learned independently. Like all-or-none learning, all-or-none transfer is an ideal case which will only be approximated in experiments and other learning situations.[22] However, to the degree that the simple ideal is approximately correct, we can use the all-or-none assumption to understand important aspects of the psychological process of transfer.

Whenever an event occurs on an all-or-none basis, the important quantity is the probability of the event. The probability of transfer is the probability that the subject selects one of the shared codes when he learns the first item. Let b_{12} be the probability of selecting a code that is shared by the two items while studying the first item. The probability of learning the first item is c_1; this is the probability of selecting a code that will support retention of the first item. This set of adequate codes for the first item includes the shared codes as well as other adequate codes that are not shared with the second item. Let t be the conditional probability of transfer, given that the subject has learned the first item. Then

$$t = b_{12}/c_1. \tag{5.16}$$

Note that the probability of transfer depends on the probability of learning the first item c_1, but it does not depend on the probability of learning the second item, c_2. The reason is that transfer depends on the way in which the first item is learned.[23]

Example 5.11. The concept of "reinforcement" is applied to a variety of situations by psychologists. If a hungry rat is given some food after he presses

---

[22] One experiment which gave a good approximation to all-or-none transfer was by J. G. Greeno and J. M. Scandura, "All-or-None Transfer Based on Verbally Mediated Concepts," *J. math. Psychol.*, 1966, **3,** 388–411.

[23] The dependence of transfer on the nature of original learning is especially important when the two items are not equally difficult. Recall the discussion of easy-to-hard transfer in animal discrimination learning in Chapter 3. A similar situation will be presented in Chapter 6, where a quantitative analysis will be given of easy-to-hard transfer of concept identification by humans. The dependence of transfer on the first stimulus also is important when stimulus generalization is studied using stimuli of different intensities. This was discussed by F. Restle, "A Cognitive Interpretation of Intensity Effects in Stimulus Generalization," *Psychol. Rev.*, 1964, **71,** 514–516.

a bar, the food is called "reinforcement for bar pressing." If a hungry rat is put into one end of an alley that has food at the other end, we say the food is "reinforcement for running." If a person is in a conditioning experiment where an eyeblink response is conditioned to some stimulus like a tone, the tone goes on and then a puff of air causes the person to blink his eye. The puff of air is sometimes called "reinforcement for the connection between the tone and blinking."

You are studying psychology, and you have to learn numerous associations. Suppose that you learn an association, "Food after bar press–Reinforcement." We are interested in the probability of transfer to other associations, such as "Food in alley–Reinforcement," and "Air puff while tone is on–Reinforcement." Suppose that when you study the first association, the probability of learning it is $c_1 = .50$. Suppose that the codes for learning this association are as follows: With probability .08 you select a code having to do with the particular response that is learned—in this case, the bar press. With probability .30 you select a code that has to do with food being presented to a hungry animal. And with probability .12 you select a code that has to do with the fact that the thing called "reinforcement" causes some response to become more probable.

Now consider a new item, "Food in alley–Reinforcement." This situation involves food given to a hungry animal and it involves a response that becomes more probable because of something that happens after the response is performed. Therefore, the codes shared between the two items have probability

$$b_{12} = .30 + .12 = .42.$$

Then the probability of transfer between "Food after bar press–Reinforcement" and "Food in alley–Reinforcement" is

$$t = b_{12}/c_1 = .42/.50 = .84.$$

Consider the new item, "Air puff while tone is on–Reinforcement." This situation involves something that makes a response more probable. Then

$$b_{12} = .12 \qquad \text{and} \qquad t = .12/.50 = .24. \blacksquare$$

The value of t in Eq. (5.16) is the conditional probability that transfer will occur, given that the first association was learned. In many situations, transfer will be tested, but the first association will not have been studied enough to ensure that it was learned. Suppose that the first association is studied m times. Let T be the probability that transfer occurs to a second association with the same response as the first one. Transfer will occur if (1) the first association was learned, and (2) if the learning of the first association involved a code that also supports retention of the second association.

Then the probability of transfer is

$$T = [P(L \leq m)]t = [1 - (1 - c_1)^m](b_{12}/c_1). \tag{5.17}$$

Example 5.12. Suppose that a student studies the association "Food after bar press–Reinforcer" twice. Then he encounters the new items "Food in alley–Reinforcer," and "Air puff while tone is on–Reinforcer." What are the probabilities of transfer to these items?

First, we calculate the probability that the first association is learned. Since $c_1 = .50$, we have

$$P(L \leq 2) = [1 - (.50)^2] = .75.$$

Then the probability of transfer to "Food in alley–Reinforcer" is

$$T = P(L \leq 2)(.84) = .63,$$

and the probability of transfer to "Air puff while tone is on–Reinforcer" is

$$T = P(L \leq 2)(.24) = .18. \blacksquare$$

We have not yet taken into account that the first association may have been learned, but not be remembered when the second association is presented. If the first association is studied and then some time passes before the second association is presented, transfer will occur if (1) the first association was learned, (2) the learning involved a code that is shared with the second association, and (3) the first association is still remembered when the second association is presented. Suppose that the first association is studied m times, and then n units of time go by before the second association is presented. Then T, the probability of transfer to the second association, is

$$T = s_{m,n}t = [1 - (1 - c_1)^m](1 - f)^n(b_{12}/c_1), \tag{5.18}$$

where f is the probability of forgetting the first association during each unit of time.

Example 5.13. Suppose that a student studies the association "Food after bar press–Reinforcement" twice. Then, two days later, he comes to the new item "Food in alley–Reinforcement," and five days after that he comes to the item "Air puff while tone is on–Reinforcement." If the probability of forgetting the first item is $f = .05$ during each day, what are the probabilities of transfer to the two new items?

We already know that $P(L \leq 2) = .75$. We need

$$s_{2,2} = (.75)(1 - f)^2 = (.75)(.90) = .68.$$

Then the probability of transfer to "Food in alley–Reinforcement" is

$$T = s_{2,2}t = (.68)(.84) = .57.$$

The item "Air puff while tone is on–Reinforcement" is seen seven days after the first association is studied. We need

$$s_{2,7} = (.75)(.95)^7 = (.75)(.70) = .52.$$

Then the probability of transfer is

$$T = (.52)(.24) = .125. \blacksquare$$

Now we take up the effect of transfer on the learning of a new set of items. The idea is that some items will be known when the person first sees them, because of transfer. On the average, the proportion known at the start will equal T. These items will not have to be learned in the new situation. The remaining items will have to be learned in the new situation, because the way in which the person learned earlier items involved memory codes that do not apply to the new items.

Example 5.14. Suppose that a student begins working on a list of 50 vocabulary items. There is a probability of transfer $T = .24$, and the probability of learning untransferred items is $c_2 = .20$. On the average, $(.24)(50) = 12$ words will be known at the beginning, because of transfer. Therefore, an average of 38 words will be unknown on the first study trial. The probability of learning an item on the first study trial is .20. Therefore an average of $(.20)(38) = 7.6$ items will be learned on the first trial, and on the average, a total of $12 + 7.6 = 19.6$ items will be known after the first study trial. This will leave an average of 30.4 items that are unknown at the beginning of the second study trial. A table like Table 1 can be constructed for this case where there is some positive transfer.

Table 2

All-or-None Learning of 50 Items where $c_2 = .20$ with Positive Transfer where $T = .24$

Trial	Average unlearned at beginning	Average learned this trial	Average total learned through this trial
1	$(1.0 - .24)(50) = 38.0$	$(.20)(38.0) = 7.6$	19.6
2	30.4	$(.20)(30.4) = 6.1$	25.7
3	24.3	$(.20)(24.3) = 4.9$	30.6
4	19.4	$(.20)(19.4) = 3.9$	34.5
5	15.5	$(.20)(15.5) = 3.1$	37.6

Note that all the calculations here are just like those of Table 1 in this chapter, except that we start with 38 items instead of 50. The effect of transfer is simply to remove 12 items from the set that must be learned. ▮

Equation (5.5) gives the probability of learning an item on a particular trial. That probability only applies to items for which transfer does not occur. When transfer can occur, the probability that an item will be learned on trial n is less than when there is no transfer, because fewer items have to be learned. The formula for the probability of learning an item on trial n is just

$$P(L = n) = (1 - T)(1 - c_2)^{n-1}c_2. \tag{5.19}$$

Note that this is the same as Eq. (5.5), except the earlier expression is multiplied by $(1 - T)$.

Since there are some items for which learning is not necessary, the probability distribution of the trial of learning and the learning curve are different from those in Section 5A. Refer back to Fig. 1, and note that the graph starts with Trial 1. In that analysis, no items were known at the beginning. When we allow for transfer, we need only to show how many items were known at the beginning of the study session. We have a point at Trial 0, which stands for the effect of learning that occurred before this experiment started. The average proportion of items "learned on Trial 0" will equal T. An illustration is given in Fig. 12. The values of c_2 and T used in the calculations are the same as in Example 5.14.

Transfer of training affects the learning curve in a similar way. To be unknown after n trials, an item would have to fail to be known by transfer, and the item would have to remain unlearned through n study trials. Then

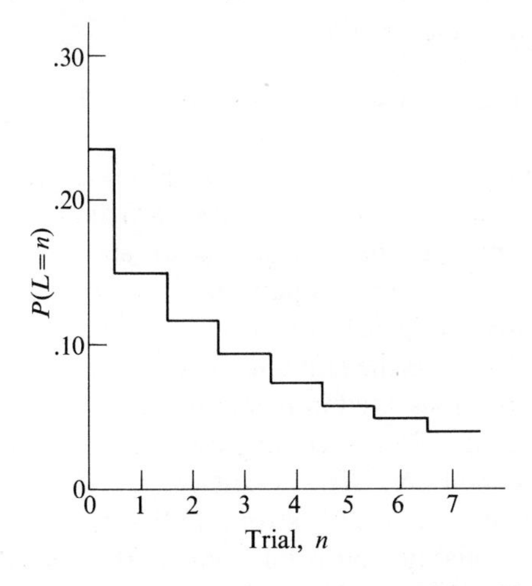

Fig. 12. Distribution of trial of learning with positive transfer.

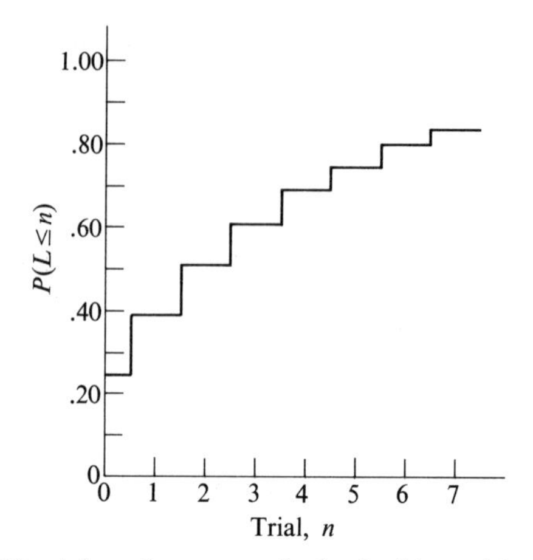

Fig. 13. A learning curve obtained with positive transfer.

the probability that an item is learned by the nth study trial is

$$P(L \leq n) = 1 - (1 - T)(1 - c_2)^n. \tag{5.20}$$

Figure 13 shows a learning curve with positive transfer, using the same probabilities of learning and transfer as in Example 5.14 and Fig. 12. Therefore, this learning curve is the cumulative distribution obtained from the probability distribution of our earlier calculations.

Example 5.15. In Example 5.13 we considered a situation where $T = .57$. Suppose that $c_2 = .35$, and calculate the probability that the second association will be known after it is studied twice.

We use Eq. (5.20) and obtain

$$P(L \leq 2) = 1 - (.43)(.65)^2 = .73. \blacksquare$$

The analysis given thus far has been based on the idea that learning is selective. However, a subject will not always learn associations by a selective strategy. An alternative is simply to memorize an association between the response and the complete stimulus pattern. If learning is by selection, then the item is represented in the subject's memory in some partial way. But if learning is an association to the stimulus pattern, then the complete pattern of stimulus aspects is represented in memory.

Like the strategy of selective coding, association to patterns can be all-or-none in certain conditions. The conditions are (1) when an association is stored in memory, it is sufficiently strong so that the subject can remember the correct response reliably, and (2) as long as the association has not yet been stored in memory, the probability of storing it in memory is a constant, c.

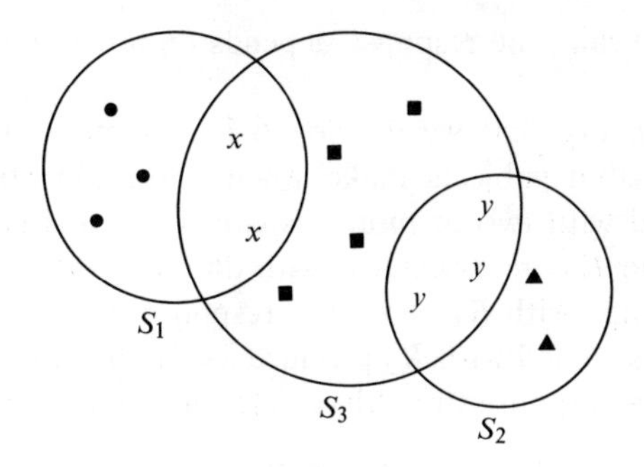

Figure 14

When learning involves association with patterns, transfer is not completely determined by what the subject has learned and remembers. Refer back to Fig. 10 and suppose that a subject has associated a response R with the pattern of stimulus aspects represented by the circle labeled S_1. Now stimulus S_2 is presented. The subject has to respond to S_2, and the question of whether he gives response R involves a decision. When S_2 is shown, there are some aspects that were part of S_1 and some that were not. The subject has to decide whether the new stimulus shares enough aspects with the first to make the old response appropriate.

In some situations where learning involves patterns, transfer follows a simple rule: subjects will decide to give the response if they notice any aspect that was part of an earlier stimulus. We call this the rule of transfer from patterns to components.[24] If the rule of transfer from patterns to components is used, a subject will be able to transfer an association to any new stimulus that shares an aspect or property with the first stimulus. All that is required is that the subject notice the shared property.

In some situations, a new stimulus pattern will be shown, and the components of the new pattern will have been associated with different responses. Figure 14 represents three stimuli. Suppose that a subject has learned to associate S_1 with a response R_1, and has learned to associate S_2 with a different response R_2. Now S_3 is presented, and S_3 has some properties in common with both S_1 and S_2.

According to the rule of transfer from patterns to components, two responses will transfer to stimulus S_3. Response R_1 will transfer because S_3 shares properties with S_1, and response R_2 will transfer because S_3 shares properties with S_2. The subject has a problem only if he is asked to give a

[24] Evidence for transfer from patterns to components has been obtained by W. K. Estes and B. L. Hopkins, "Acquisition and Transfer in Pattern-vs.-Component Discrimination Learning," *J. exp. Psychol.*, 1961, **61,** 322–328, and by M. P. Friedman and H. Gelfand, "Transfer Effects in Discrimination Learning," *J. math. Psychol.*, 1964, **1,** 204–214.

single response. Again, the response depends on a decision that the subject must make.

The choice theory that we developed in Chapter 2 has been used to analyze decisions that subjects make when a transfer stimulus has components associated with two or more responses. In a situation like Fig. 14 where both R_1 and R_2 are associated with different aspects of the stimulus, the aspects associated with R_1 produce a response strength for choosing R_1, and the aspects associated with R_2 produce a response strength for choosing R_2. If we call these response strengths $v(R_1)$ and $v(R_2)$, respectively, we have

$$P(R_1) = v(R_1)/[v(R_1) + v(R_2)]. \tag{5.21}$$

In the simplest case, $v(R_1)$ and $v(R_2)$ would be proportional to the number of aspects that had been associated with the two responses. For example, in Fig. 14, S_3 has two aspects (marked x) that were associated with R_1, and three aspects (marked y) that were associated with R_2. If the response strengths of R_1 and R_2 are proportional to the number of elements associated with each response, we would have

$$P(R_1) = 2/(2 + 3) = .40.$$

In experiments several factors have been found to produce response strengths that are not proportional to the number of aspects or components associated with the response.[25] For example, one stimulus component may have been part of several patterns in previous learning. If all these patterns were associated with the same response, then their shared stimulus component would contribute a greater response strength than other components. However, if the patterns containing the stimulus component were associated with different responses, the stimulus component would be treated as an unreliable cue, and it would contribute less response strength than other components.

In this section we have discussed conditions which lead to transfer of learned associations to new stimuli. The process of transfer depends on the way in which learning occurs. If learning involves selective coding, then the probability of transfer is the probability that a subject selects a shared code when he studies the first item. We studied a theory of selective coding and transfer in detail, including an analysis of the effect of transfer on the learning of a new set of items. Finally, we presented the main ideas in the theory of association to patterns with transfer to components, and briefly analyzed the role of a decision process that affects transfer to new stimuli.

---

[25] Experiments on this problem have been done by A. Binder and S. Feldman, "The Effects of Experimentally Controlled Experience upon Recognition Responses," *Psychol. Monogr.*, 1960, **74,** Whole No. 496, by A. Binder and W. K. Estes, "Transfer of Response in Visual Recognition Situations as a Function of Frequency Variables," *Psychol. Monogr.*, 1966, **80,** Whole No. 631, and by M. P. Friedman, T. Trabasso, and L. Mosberg, "Tests of a Mixed Model for Paired-Associate Learning with Overlapping Stimuli," *J. math. Psychol.*, 1967, **4,** 316–334.

PROBLEMS

1. Make up a table like Table 1, showing the first five trials of all-or-none learning of 60 items with $c = .30$.

* **2.** You have a bag with two white marbles and 18 black marbles. You reach in and take a marble without looking; if it is white, you stop. If it is black, you replace it, shake the bag, and draw again. What is the probability that you will draw a white marble for the first time on the tenth trial? What is the probability that the experiment will be over sometime during the first five trials?

3. If you take a deck of cards and cut them, what is the probability of drawing a spade? If you shuffle the cards and cut them until you draw a spade, how often will you have to wait more than five times before you cut a spade? What is the probability of waiting exactly five times?

* **4.** Suppose that you have to take a final exam in a biology course that involves many technical terms. You decide to select a list of important terms out of the glossary of your text—your list has 100 terms to study. Now, you go through the list once, and then test yourself later in the day. You find that you have remembered 30 of the 100 words that you studied. At this rate, how many additional words do you expect to learn on the second time through the list? How many times will you have to go through the list to learn one-half of the words? three-fourths of the words?

* **5.** Consider a teacher in a psychology course, explaining what is meant by "test reliability." For simplicity, assume that each student in the class has the same probability of understanding the concept each time the teacher explains it. Assume that the probability of learning the concept with each explanation is .50. What proportion of students will still not understand the concept of reliability after the teacher has explained it three times?

6. A student decides to study a foreign language in the following way: He buys a deck of vocabulary cards, each with a foreign-language word on one side and its English cognate on the other. Then he picks out 20 of the cards and studies them. The next day he tests himself on those 20 cards and puts aside the ones he remembers, replacing these with new cards from the deck. Each day, then, he has 20 words to study, all of which are unlearned. Suppose that the learning probability, c, is .25. On the average, how many cards will he replace each day? What will be the average number of days that a card stays in the study deck? What is the probability that a single card will stay in the deck longer than seven days?

7. In an experiment subjects memorize lists of associations and the average trial of learning turns out to be 8.0. Calculate the value of c, and calculate the theoretical standard deviation of the distribution of trials of learning. What is the theoretical proportion of items learned in the first three trials? Theoretically, what proportion of items should have been unlearned after the eighth trial?

▸ **8.** As an alternative to the all-or-none theory, assume that c is .10 on trial 1, then on each succeeding trial $(1 - c)$ decreases by a factor of .9. (That is, on trial n, $1 - c = (.9)^n$.) List the probability of learning on trials 1 through 10, and construct a table like Table 1 for 60 items showing the theoretical number of items learned on each trial. Now suppose that you obtain these data in an experiment and apply the all-or-none theory. Use Eq. (5.10) to estimate c, calculate the theoretical distribution, and compare with the "data." Also calculate the theoretical standard deviation and compare with the standard deviation of the "data."

9. Suppose that $d = .35$. What is the probability that an item will be in short-term memory after it is studied and one other item is either studied or tested? What is the probability after three other items are studied or tested? What are these probabilities if $d = .70$?

* **10.** Suppose that $d = .30$. After an item is studied, how many other items can be studied or tested before the probability of having the first item in short-term memory goes below .50? how many before the probability goes below .10?

11. In an experiment,[26] two kinds of items were studied. When single words were studied, the probability of keeping an item in short-term memory while two other items were studied was about .80. When the items were sets of three words or three letters, the probability of keeping an item in short-term memory while two other items were studied was about .25. (Count each three-element item as one item.) What were the approximate values of d for this experiment?

12. Suppose that $d = .35$ and $c = .25$. If an item is studied and then one other item is studied, what is the probability that the first item is remembered? What is the probability after four other items are studied or tested?

13. With $d = .35$ and $c = .25$, after an item is presented once, how many other items can be studied or tested before the probability of remembering an item drops below .50? below 1/3?

14. Suppose that a student is working on a lesson that contains many items of information. Assume that $c = .30$ and $d = .50$. The student studies an item of information, then studies another item, and then comes to a statement that says, "Now recall that . . ." and refers back to the first item. What is the probability that the student will remember the first item so he does not have to go back and look it up? What is the probability if there are four other items between presentation and recall?

▸ **15.** From the data in Fig. 5, it appears that $c = .15$ for the material in those experiments. Find the approximate value of d for this situation by trying out different values of d and choosing one that makes Eq. (5.12) fit the data of Fig. 5. Draw a graph showing the theoretical curve with your value of d compared with the experimental data.

▸ **16.** If you were writing a programmed textbook in social studies, you might include the following items in some form: (1) The three branches of the U. S. Government are ____________, ____________, and ____________. (2) The legislative branch consists of the ____________ and the ____________. You probably would want the students to remember Item 1 when they were working on Item 2. In your program, you want to present Item 1 once, present three other items, and then present Item 2.

[26] The experiment was by B. B. Murdock, Jr., cited in footnote 8, this chapter. The values given here are approximate, and are based partly on rough estimates that .90 of the words, and .20 of the three-letter or three-word sets were stored in long-term memory when they were presented.

Your problem is to decide whether to repeat Item 1 just before Item 2 appears, and you decide that Item 1 should be repeated if more than .25 of the students will forget it before Item 2 appears. If you assume $c = .50$ and $d = .20$, will you decide to repeat Item 1? What if you assume $c = .50$ and $d = .40$?

▶ **17.** What happens in the situation of Problem 16 if Item 1 has been presented twice, then three other items are presented before Item 2 appears with $c = .50$ as assumed before?

▶ **18.** Suppose that you are in the situation described in Problem 16, but you decide that you have to assume $c = .20$ instead of $c = .50$. If Item 1 appears twice before Item 2, how many other items can appear between Item 1's second presentation and Item 2 with the probability of remembering Item 1 still remaining above .75? Solve the problem assuming (a) $d = .20$, and (b) $d = .40$.

* **19.** In the situation of Example 5.8, calculate the probability that the subject can remember the answer for Item *D* and for Item *B*.

20. In an experiment like the one described in Example 5.8, the items were studied four times, and the order on the last study trial was *A*, *B*, *C*, *D*, *E*, *F*, as before. With the values for c and d given in the example, how early in the test sequence would Item *F* have to be tested for the probability of remembering to be at least .75?

21. Suppose that $f = .10$ with time counted in units of one day. If a lesson is studied long enough so that all the items are stored in long-term memory, how many days will it be before the probability of remembering is less than .50? What will be the probability of remembering after two weeks?

22. Suppose that while a person is asleep, the probability of forgetting an item is .05 per hour, but while he is awake, the probability of forgetting is .25 per hour. If a person studies some items until all of them are stored in long-term memory and then goes to sleep for six hours, what will be the probability of remembering an item when he wakes up? What will be the probability of remembering an item on a test that is given four hours after the person wakes up?

* **23.** Suppose that some items are studied so that all of them are stored in long-term memory. Then one group of subjects studies similar material for two hours, with $f = .10$ per hour, and a second group studies entirely different material for two hours, with $f = .05$ per hour. How much will each group remember on a test at the end of the two hours?

24. What would be the results in the experiment described in Problem 23 if the first set of items were just presented 10 times instead of guaranteeing that they were all stored in long-term memory? Assume that $c = .15$.

25. Make up a table like Table 2, showing the first five trials of all-or-none learning of 60 items with $c_2 = .30$, $T = .40$.

26. A student studies visual adaptation, and learns an association, "Increased sensitivity in the dark–Adaptation." A second association also is to be learned: "Increased judgment of warmth after exposure to cold–Adaptation." Suppose that in studying the first item, the probability of selecting a memory code that will support retention of both items is .12, and the total probability of learning the first item is .30. (a) What is t? (b) If the first item is studied four times and the second item is studied before there is time for forgetting, what is the probability of transfer? (c) If the first item is studied four times and the second item is studied five days later, what is the probability of transfer if $f = .10$ for units of one day?

27. If the probability of learning the second item in Problem 26 is .20, and the item is studied twice, what is the probability of its being known (a) if the first item was learned and is remembered when the second item is studied? (b) if the first item is studied four times and the second item is studied before there is time for forgetting? (c) if the first item is studied four times and the second item is studied five days later, where the probability of forgetting is .10 per day?

* **28.** In an experiment, a list was studied until all the items were learned. The next day, subjects were divided into two groups. Group R had a test on the items learned the previous day; they were correct on .60 of the items. Group T was shown a new set of items with the same responses as in the first list, and each response was paired with a stimulus that was similar to the one used the first day. Group T knew the answers to .25 of the new items on its first test before any answers were shown. Then Group T studied the new items twice, after which they knew .75 of the answers. Calculate the values of f (for one day), t, and c_2.

29. In social psychology and sociology, there are terms which apply to similar, but not identical situations. Suppose that a student studies social psychology first, and that he studies by selective coding. If he has probability .25 of selecting a code that will apply in both sociology and psychology, and probability .15 of selecting a code that will apply only in psychology, what is t? If he goes through his psychology material twice and then studies sociology before any forgetting occurs, what is T? If he goes through the psychology material twice and then studies sociology after he has forgotten $\frac{1}{3}$ of the terms he learned in psychology, what is T?

30. In the situation described in Problem 29 suppose that the student works on psychology first, but he learns by associating responses to patterns. Assume that there is probability .30 of associating a response to a stimulus each time the pair is studied. Also assume that the stimuli in sociology have some aspects not present in psychological situations (and vice-versa) but that none of the stimuli in sociology have aspects from more than one stimulus in psychology. Assume that transfer occurs from patterns to components. What is the probability of transferring a response from psychology to a similar stimulus in sociology (a) if the student goes through his psychology material twice and then studies sociology right away, or (b) if the student goes through his psychology material twice and then studies sociology after he has forgotten $\frac{1}{3}$ of the associations from psychology?

31. There are two associations to be learned, A–R and B–R. Either one can be presented first. First, assume that learning is by selective coding. When A–R is studied, there is probability .15 that it will be learned, and probability .10 that a code will be selected that will also support retention of B–R. When B–R is studied, there is probability .45 that the item will be learned, and probability .15 that a code will be selected which will also support retention of A–R. If A–R is studied three times and then B–R is studied three times, what is the probability that the subject will know A–R? What is the probability that he will know B–R? What are the probabilities of knowing the two items if B–R is studied first?

32. Answer the questions of Problem 31 again, except assume that learning is by associating the response to patterns and transfer occurs from patterns to components. Assume that *A–R* is learned with probability .10 when it is studied, and *B–R* is learned with probability .25 on each study trial.

CHAPTER SIX

Thinking, Problem Solving, and Understanding

People use the word "thinking" to describe several different kinds of thought processes. Sometimes thinking occurs when a person tries to remember something, or makes a judgment or a decision. In these situations, a person thinks because he wants to reduce his uncertainty about something he believes he once learned, or about a situation, or about what he should do.

A second kind of situation that involves thinking occurs when a person has to make a plan to try to accomplish some goal. In planning a sequence of actions, a person sets up a series of subgoals which he hopes will lead to the main goal he wants to accomplish.

We shall study a third kind of situation in some detail. Sometimes a person thinks to try to solve a problem. An important part of problem solving involves the use and organization of information. In the first three sections of this chapter we discuss a simple trial-and-error system of information processing that sometimes characterizes the process of solving a problem. Some important properties of the system will be examined formally in connection with one kind of problem, concept identification, and applied informally to other problem-solving situations. The fourth section deals with the question of organizing information and understanding relationships in a situation.

6A PROBLEM SOLVING

The task called concept identification can be set up experimentally and analyzed quite easily. The experimenter constructs a set of stimuli in which he varies several different properties such as the shape of a figure, its color, its size and the number of figures on a card. An illustrative set of stimuli is shown in Fig. 1. The experimenter decides on a simple rule that will be used to classify the stimuli. For example, all cards with large figures might be in category A and all cards with small figures in category B. The subject's task is to discover the rule. He sees one card at a time, with the cards presented

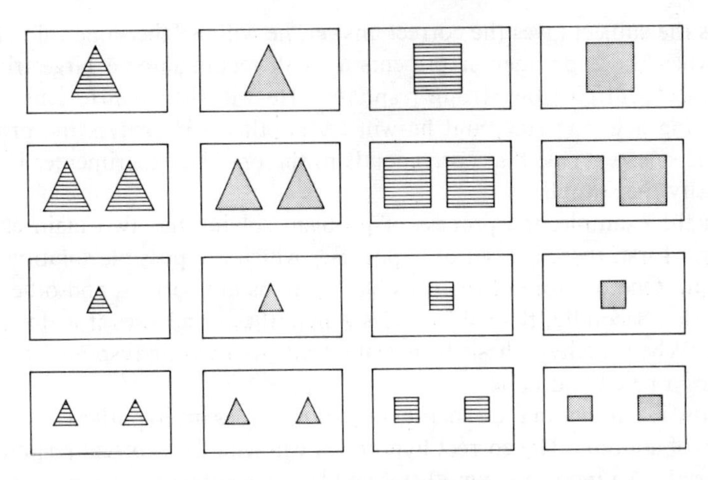

Fig. 1. Stimuli for a concept-identification experiment.

in random order. The subject responds on each trial, specifying in which category he thinks that card belongs. After the subject gives his response, the experimenter tells him the correct answer. After a number of such trials, the subject is able to give the correct response on every trial. Then the experimenter can conclude that the subject has discovered the rule for classifying the stimuli.

According to a simple theory explaining this experiment,[1] the subject finds the correct rule by a process of trial and error. The experimenter may tell the subject what dimensions of the stimuli will vary. Or, by looking at a few stimuli the subject can find out which rules are possibilities. For example, he may see that the stimuli have different shapes (rectangles and triangles), different colors (red and blue), different sizes, and different numbers of figures (one and two). Then some of the simple possible rules are: (1) rectangles are *A* and triangles are *B*, (2) red figures are *A* and blue figures are *B*, (3) large figures are *A* and small figures are *B*. Suppose that the first stimulus has two large red rectangles and the experimenter says it is in category *A*. The subject may select any of the possible rules that is consistent with the information on that trial—for example, he may try the rule that says rectangles are *A* and triangles are *B*. If the experimenter's rule is that large figures are *A*, then the rectangle-triangle rule will lead to an error when the experimenter presents a large triangle or a small rectangle. As long as the experimenter presents large rectangles or small triangles, the subject using the rectangle-triangle rule will give the correct answer. We assume that as

---

[1] By F. Restle, "The Selection of Strategies in Cue Learning," *Psychol. Rev.*, 1962, **69,** 329–343.

long as the subject gives the correct answer, he will use the same rule. However, when the experimenter presents a small rectangle or a large triangle, the subject will give the wrong response. He will then realize that he has been using a wrong rule, and he will try another. He solves the problem when he selects a rule that corresponds to the one the experimenter is using to classify the stimuli.

In the example, the process of problem solving has two main characteristics. First, there is a set of hypotheses which are possible solutions of a problem. One or more of the possible solutions are correct, and others will not work. Secondly, the subject tries a hypothesis and uses it as long as it works. When the hypothesis he is using leads to a wrong response, the subject tries a new hypothesis.

Now recall that in the experiment a subject uses his hypothesis to classify a series of stimuli. The correct hypothesis will lead to a correct response on every trial. An incorrect hypothesis will lead to a correct response on some trials and an incorrect one on other trials. For simplicity, assume that all the incorrect hypotheses lead to a correct response with the same probability, called p, and to an error with probability $1 - p = q$.

When the subject gives an incorrect response, the information from the experimenter tells the subject his present hypothesis is wrong and he will select a new one. Again, for simplicity, assume that there is a constant probability s of selecting a correct hypothesis any time the subject selects a hypothesis.[2] He solves the problem when he chooses the correct hypothesis.

The mathematical structure of this process is exactly like the structure of the processes we studied in Chapter 5—it is a waiting-time system. But here there is an interesting complication because learning can occur only when the information given to the subject is inconsistent with his present hypothesis. Therefore, the probability of learning on any trial after the first is not s, but s times the probability of an error. Assume that at the start of the experiment the experimenter shows one stimulus to the subject and gives him the correct answer for that card. The subject samples from the available hypotheses, and with probability s he finds a solution immediately. If

[2] This assumption seems unreasonable, since we expect that a subject will find that certain hypotheses do not work and use this information to increase the probabilities of selecting other hypotheses. However, when a solution is not a very obvious hypothesis, the assumption of a constant probability of the correct hypothesis seems to be fairly accurate. One reason is that subjects apparently do not eliminate wrong hypotheses permanently. After rejecting a hypothesis it can be chosen again after a few trials have gone by. This was shown by J. R. Erickson, "Hypothesis Sampling in Concept Identification," Duplicated paper, 1967. Another possibility is that subjects may think of new hypotheses to replace hypotheses they have rejected, and this process could leave the probability of the correct hypothesis approximately constant over trials.

he fails to find the solution on the first trial, he will resample on a later trial when he makes an error. The probability of solving the problem on a trial when an error is made is s. Therefore, the probability of solving on any trial after the first is qs—the probability of an error times the probability of solving when an error occurs.

We consider two questions about the waiting times in this process. The easier question is: How many errors will occur before the problem is solved? The slightly more complicated one is: How many trials will there be before the problem is solved?

First, let E be the number of errors before the problem is solved. The probability of solving with no errors is

$$P(E = 0) = s$$

If the subject selects any but the correct hypothesis on the first trial, he will make at least one error. After the first error, the probability of selecting the correct hypothesis is s. Therefore, the probability of exactly one error is

$$P(E = 1) = (1 - s)s$$

The argument can be generalized to obtain the probability of exactly j errors. For any value of j,

$$P(E = j) = (1 - s)^j s. \tag{6.1}$$

The mean of the distribution in Eq. (6.1) is the theoretical average number of errors that will be made by subjects in solving the problem. The mean is

$$\mu_E = (1 - s)/s. \tag{6.2}$$

The standard deviation of the number of errors is

$$\sigma_E = \sqrt{1 - s}/s. \tag{6.3}$$

Now, let L be the trial on which the problem is solved. We number the trials 0, 1, 2, . . . , with the initial trial called Trial 0. Then

$$P(L = 0) = s.$$

If the problem is not solved on the initial trial, the probability that it will be solved on Trial 1 is qs. (Recall that the subject will not select a new hypothesis unless he makes an error.) Then

$$P(L = 1) = (1 - s)qs.$$

The probability of failing to solve the problem on both the initial trial and

Trial 1 is $(1 - s)(1 - qs)$. So the probability of solving on the next trial is

$$P(L = 2) = (1 - s)(1 - qs)qs.$$

In general,

$$P(L = k) = \begin{cases} s & \text{for} \quad k = 0, \\ (1 - s)(1 - qs)^{k-1}qs & \text{for} \quad k \geq 1. \end{cases} \tag{6.4}$$

The mean of the distribution of L is the average number of trials needed to solve the problem.

$$\mu_L = (1 - s)/qs. \tag{6.5}$$

The standard deviation of the distribution of the number of trials needed to solve the problem is

$$\sigma_L = \sqrt{(1 - s)(1 + ps)}/qs. \tag{6.6}$$

The distributions of E and L are illustrated in Fig. 2. The quantities used in the calculations were $s = .20$, $p = q = .50$.

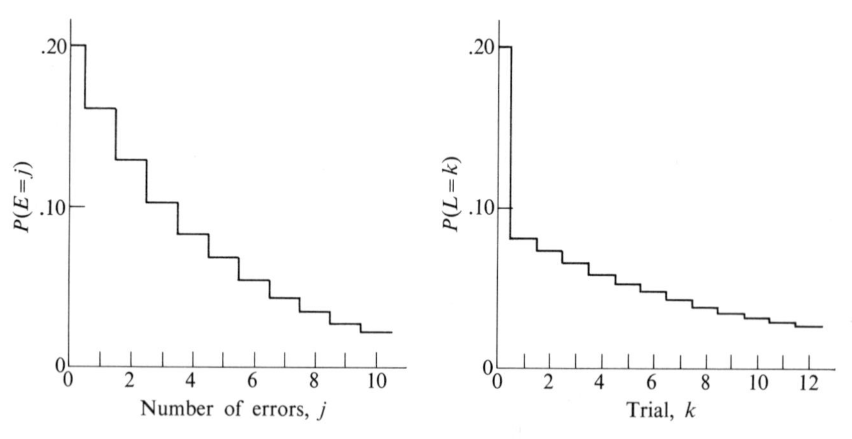

Fig. 2. Theoretical distributions of errors and trial of solution in simple concept-identification.

The cumulative distributions of both errors and trials needed to solve the problem can be obtained as cumulatives were obtained in Chapter 5. The probability that a subject makes j or fewer errors before he solves the problem is $P(E \leq j)$.

The probability of more than j errors is the probability that the subject failed to solve on the initial trial, and then failed to select a correct hypothesis

j times after making errors. That is,

$$1 - P(E \leq j) = (1 - s)^{j+1},$$
$$P(E \leq j) = 1 - (1 - s)^{j+1}. \tag{6.7}$$

The probability that the problem is solved on or before Trial k is $P(L \leq k)$. For the problem to remain unsolved after Trial k, the subject must fail to solve on the initial trial and then either give a correct response or sample an incorrect hypothesis on each of the next k trials.

$$1 - P(L \leq k) = (1 - s)(1 - qs)^k,$$
$$P(L \leq k) = 1 - (1 - s)(1 - qs)^k. \tag{6.8}$$

The function $P(L \leq k)$ is a learning curve in the following sense: If many subjects are given the same problem to solve, some will solve it right away, others will solve it after a few trials, and a few will take a long time. The value of $P(L \leq k)$ is the proportion of subjects who will solve the problem on or before Trial k on the average. In other words, if we ran an experiment for k trials, then stopped, and gave a test to see how many had solved the problem, the proportion who had found solutions would be close to $P(L \leq k)$.

Example 6.1. Suppose that a subject has probability .20 of selecting the correct rule any time he selects a hypothesis. Before he solves the problem, the probability of a correct response is .50. (a) Calculate the mean and standard deviation of the distributions of errors and trials needed to solve. (b) What is the probability that a subject will make exactly two errors before he solves the problem? (c) What is the probability that he will make more than five errors? (d) What is the probability that he will solve the problem on Trial 2? (e) What is the probability that he will not solve the problem until after Trial 5?

(a) For the mean and standard deviations of the number of errors, we have

$$\mu_E = \frac{1 - s}{s} = \frac{.80}{.20} = 4.0,$$

$$\sigma_E = \frac{\sqrt{1 - s}}{s} = \frac{.894}{.20} = 4.47.$$

The mean and standard deviation of the number of trials to solve is

$$\mu_L = \frac{1 - s}{qs} = \frac{.80}{.10} = 8.0,$$

$$\sigma_L = \frac{\sqrt{(1 - s)(1 + ps)}}{qs} = \frac{.938}{.10} = 9.38.$$

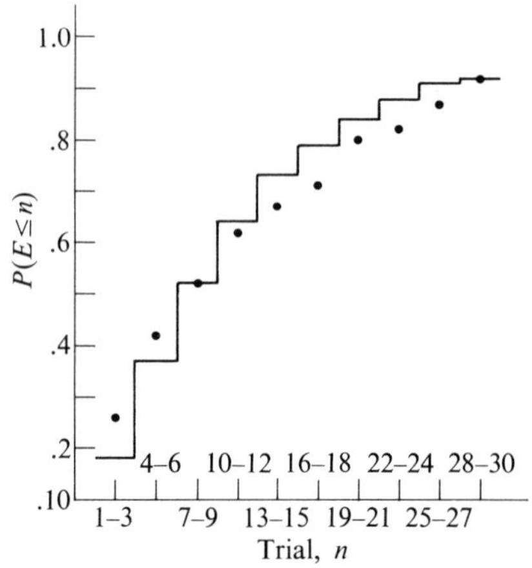

Fig. 3. Theoretical distribution of errors compared with concept-identification data.

(b) The probability of exactly two errors is

$$P(E = 2) = (1 - s)^2 s = (.80)^2(.20) = .13.$$

(c) The probability of more than five errors is

$$1 - P(E \leq 5) = (.80)^6 = .26.$$

(d) The probability of solving the problem on Trial 2 is

$$P(L = 2) = (1 - s)(1 - qs)qs = (.80)(1 - .10)(.10) = .072.$$

(e) The probability of solving the problem on Trial 5 or before is

$$P(L \leq 5) = 1 - (1 - s)(1 - qs)^5 = 1 - (.80)(.90)^5 = .53.$$

Therefore, the probability of not solving until after Trial 5 is

$$1 - P(L \leq 5) = .47. \blacksquare$$

Figure 3 shows the cumulative distribution of errors obtained in one experiment.[3] The stimuli were geometric figures with six different dimensions. The correct rule was to place red figures in one category and blue figures in

---

[3] By G. H. Bower and T. R. Trabasso, "Concept Identification," in R. C. Atkinson (Ed.) *Studies in Mathematical Learning Theory*, Stanford: Stanford Univ. Press, 1964, 32–94.

the other. The step function is the theoretical cumulative distribution obtained using Eq. (6.7).

Usually, we will have to use the data of an experiment to estimate the value of s. The most convenient statistic to use is the mean number of errors. From Eq. (6.2),

$$\begin{aligned} \mu_E &= (1 - s)/s, \\ s\mu_E &= 1 - s, \\ s &= 1/(1 + \mu_E). \end{aligned} \tag{6.9}$$

We can observe the mean number of errors made in solving a problem; then we obtain a value of s using Eq. (6.9).

Example 6.2. In the data of Fig. 3, the mean number of errors was 11.45. Calculate the value of s and assumc that $p = .50$. Calculate theoretical values of the standard deviation of the number of errors and the mean and standard deviation of trials necessary for solution.

We use Eq. (6.2) and solve for s. We obtain

$$s = \frac{1}{1 + \mu_E} = \frac{1}{12.45} = .08.$$

Then the theoretical standard deviation of errors is

$$\sigma_E = \sqrt{1 - s}/s = 12.0.$$

The theoretical mean trial of solution is

$$\mu_L = \frac{1 - s}{qs} = \frac{.92}{.04} = 18.0,$$

and the standard deviation is

$$\sigma_L = \frac{\sqrt{(1 - s)(1 + ps)}}{qs} = 19.4.$$

The obtained values corresponding to these statistics were 11.02, 22.9, and 22.4. ▌

The problem of identifying a simple concept has the main feature of many problems and puzzles. A subject has to find the solution by a process of trial and error. The trial-and-error process has a particularly simple form in concept-identification experiments, where the set of possible rules can be listed and controlled quite easily and experimental conditions can be set up in which the probability of selecting the correct rule is a constant. In these cases the process has the simple waiting-time structure we have been dealing with.

In other problem-solving situations, the subject's search for a solution does not necessarily have the simple waiting-time structure we have been considering, but the characteristic of search and selection still is important. One example is the solution of simple anagrams.[4] The subject is shown a sequence of letters, and his task is to unscramble them to form a word. The possible solutions are different arrangements of the letters. The subject arranges the letters in different orders until he arranges the letters in a sequence that he recognizes as a word in his language.

In another problem studied by psychologists, a subject solves a simple mathematical puzzle. He imagines that he has three containers of different sizes. His task is to use the containers to obtain an exact quantity which is not equal to the capacity of any of the containers.[5] Here the possible solutions are different sequences of measuring a substance with the containers. The subject tries different sequences until he happens to try one which gives the required quantity.

A third kind of problem involves accomplishing something mechanical. In one case, the subject is given some materials including a box of tacks and is asked to make a candle stand erect on a wall.[6] He can easily use the box as a candle holder, but before finding that solution he may consider other possible ways of setting up the candle, such as tacking the candle to the wall or tying it to the wall with string. These different possible solutions will not work for one reason or another, and the successful subject manages to reject these and eventually find the solution that works.

Another mechanical problem which has been studied requires that the subject tie together two strings hanging from a ceiling at some distance from each other so that neither can be reached without letting go of the other. The subject solves the problem by tying a weight to the end of one string to make a pendulum and letting it swing so it comes close to him while he holds the other string.[7] Before he thinks of the solution that works, the subject almost certainly will think of some ways to proceed that will not do, such as using different ways of holding one string while reaching for the other, or jumping into the air to try to get closer.

---

[4] An early study of anagram solution was by H. J. Rees and H. C. Israel, "An Investigation of the Establishment of Mental Sets," *Psychol. Monogr.*, 1935, **46,** Whole No. 210.

[5] This problem was used by A. S. Luchins, "Mechanization in Problem Solving: the Effect of *Einstellung*," *Psychol. Monogr.*, 1942, **54,** Whole No. 248.

[6] The candle problem was used by N. R. F. Maier, "Reasoning in Humans, I. On Direction," *J. comp. Psychol.*, 1930, **10,** 115–143.

[7] The string problem is due to K. Duncker, "On Problem Solving," *Psychol. Monogr.*, 1945, **57,** Whole No. 270. (Translated by L. S. Lees from Duncker's 1935 monograph in German.)

In this book we will deal formally only with single-stage problem solving that occurs in all-or-none fashion, and our formal analysis will apply only to situations like concept identification, where we can give test trials before the problem is solved and control the information that the subject has to work with from one trial to another. More complicated problems have been studied formally. One approach is to use the times taken to solve a problem to arrive at conclusions about how many stages are needed to reach the solution.[8] Another approach is to construct computer programs that carry out the steps of a complex problem-solving process and see whether the program gives an accurate simulation of human problem solving when subjects are given the same problem as the computer.[9] These approaches have already led to new understanding of human problem solving and thinking, and they are being used actively in current research.

6B DIFFICULTY OF PROBLEM SOLVING

We will discuss two factors which influence the difficulty of solving problems like those described in the preceding section. The first factor is the relative proportion of correct solutions in the set of possible solutions available to the subject. The second factor involves aspects of the situation that direct the subject's attention toward or away from the correct solution.

The ease of finding the correct solution clearly depends on the number of irrelevant or distracting factors present in the situation. In the candle problem, the task will be easier if the subject sees only a box with a tack or two for fastening it to the wall than if he sees a box along with string, wire, hinges, adhesive tape, pulleys, and a can opener. Irrelevant items in the situation provide possibilities for solutions which will not work. And in finding out they do not work, the subject spends time, thus delaying a solution. Similarly, long anagrams are harder to solve than short ones. The subject will probably take longer to unscramble BRTCOAA than NMA. One reason is that seven letters can be arranged in many more ways than three letters can.

The effect of irrelevant factors in the concept-identification experiment can be analyzed exactly if certain simplifying conditions are satisfied. Recall that the stimuli for this experiment are constructed by varying a

[8] J. H. Davis and F. Restle, "The Analysis of Problems and Prediction of Group Problem Solving," *J. abnorm. Soc. Psychol.*, 1963, **66,** 103–116.

[9] An important example of this approach is by A. Newell and H. A. Simon, "GPS: a Program that Simulates Human Thought." This and several other interesting investigations of cognitive processes using computer simulation are in E. A. Feigenbaum and J. Feldman (Eds.) *Computers and Thought*, New York: McGraw-Hill, 1963.

number of properties like size, number, shape, and color of figures. Each of these varied properties is called a *dimension*, and each may be relevant or irrelevant. If it is relevant, it can be used to classify the stimuli correctly. If it is irrelevant, its use for classifying the stimuli will lead to errors. In the illustration given at the beginning of this chapter, there was one relevant dimension (size) and the remaining dimensions were irrelevant.

On any trial in the experiment, the subject can form at least as many hypotheses as there are dimensions. When the subject is told that two large red triangles are in category A, his hypotheses may include: (1) stimuli with two figures are in A, (2) large figures are in A, (3) red figures are in A, and (4) triangles are in A. The subject will tend to favor some dimensions over others in forming his hypotheses. We call this tendency to favor a dimension the *weight* of the dimension, and use w_h to denote the weight of dimension h.

When the subject selects a hypothesis, the probability of using dimension h is determined by the weight of dimension h relative to the weights of the other dimensions. Specifically, the probability of selecting hypothesis h is

$$P(\text{select } h) = w_h / \sum w_j,$$

where the summation extends over all the available dimensions.

Example 6.3. Suppose that the relevant dimension in a concept-identification experiment is the size of the figures printed on stimulus cards. For one group of subjects, the shape and color of the figures are varied in addition to the size. For a second group, the size, shape, color, and number of figures are all varied. Assume that the different dimensions all have equal weight. What is the probability of selecting the (correct) size dimension for each group?

The exact number given to the weights is arbitrary—it can just as well be 1 for every dimension. The probability of selecting the size dimension for the group with varying size, shape, and color is

$$P(\text{select size}) = \tfrac{1}{3}$$

and for the group with size, shape, color, and number all varied

$$P(\text{select size}) = \tfrac{1}{4} \quad \blacksquare$$

We can use the notion of weights in an analysis of the problem-solving process. Assume that each time the subject selects a hypothesis he selects from the entire set of available hypotheses, and always selects with a constant probability for the correct solution. Then the probability of selecting the relevant dimension is equal to the value of s in Eqs. (6.1) to (6.8). Specifically, if there is a single relevant dimension with weight w_r, the probability of solving the problem after any error in a concept-identification task is

$$s = w_r/\sum w_j, \tag{6.10}$$

where the denominator is the sum of weights of all the dimensions including the relevant dimension.

Example 6.4. Calculate the mean number of errors for each of the two groups described in Example 6.3. What is the probability for each group that there will be no more than two errors made before the problem is solved?

The values of s are $\frac{1}{3}$ and $\frac{1}{4}$, respectively, for the two groups. For the group with two irrelevant dimensions,

$$\mu_E = \frac{\frac{2}{3}}{\frac{1}{3}} = 2.0.$$

For the group with three irrelevant dimensions,

$$\mu_E = \frac{\frac{3}{4}}{\frac{1}{4}} = 3.0.$$

The probabilities of two or fewer errors are

$$P(E \leq 2) = 1 - (1 - s)^3 = 1 - (\tfrac{2}{3})^3 = .70,$$

and

$$1 - (\tfrac{3}{4})^3 = .58. \blacksquare$$

The addition of irrelevant dimensions makes a problem harder, but the addition of relevant dimensions makes it easier. We say there are redundant dimensions in a concept-identification problem when there are two or more relevant dimensions. To set up redundant dimensions, some possible stimuli have to be left out of the experiment. Suppose that we want a problem with size and color relevant, and with number of objects and shape irrelevant. We may put large objects in category A and red objects in category A. But then all the large objects must be red. So small red objects and large blue objects will be omitted from this set of stimuli. Figure 4 shows a set of stimuli for which size and color are redundant. Classification by size would be equivalent to classification by color for these stimuli.

When dimensions are made redundant in this way, the subject has extra ways to classify the stimuli correctly. In the situation where color and size are redundant, the subject will solve the problem if he tries the hypothesis that size determines the category or if he tries the hypothesis that color determines the category. The effect is to increase the probability of selecting a correct hypothesis each time a hypothesis is selected.

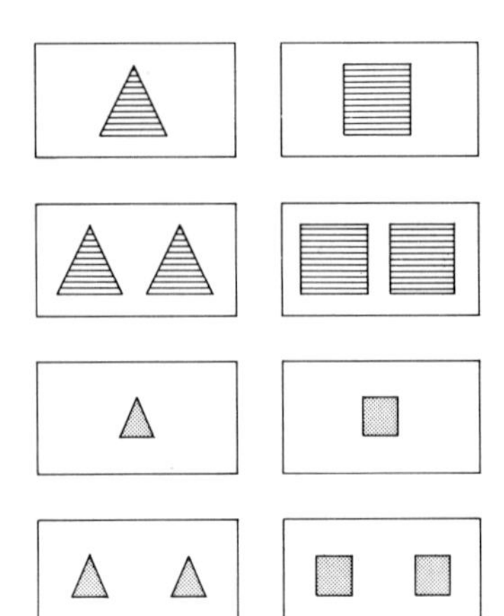

Fig. 4. A set of stimuli with size and color relevant.

In terms of stimulus weights, the probability of solving the problem is the sum of the weights of all the relevant dimensions divided by the sum of the weights of all the dimensions. Let w_r be the weight of a dimension that is relevant and w_j be the weight of any dimension in the situation. Then the probability of solving the problem on each selection of a hypothesis is

$$s = \sum w_r / \sum w_j. \tag{6.11}$$

Example 6.5. We have three groups in a concept-identification experiment. For one group, the dimensions are size, shape, and number of objects; all objects are the same color. Assume that the dimensions have equal weight and that prior to solving the problem a subject has $p = .50$ of getting a correct answer. What will be the average number of trials before solving in this group? How many trials will it take before the probability of solving is at least .90?

The value of s is .333, and $q = 1 - p = .50$. The mean number of trials to solve is

$$\mu_L = \frac{(1 - s)}{qs} = \frac{.667}{.167} = 4.0.$$

To find the second answer, we use Eq. (6.8). We want a value of k so that $P(L \leq k) \geq .90$.

$$.90 \leq 1 - (.667)(.833)^k, \qquad (.833)^k \leq .15, \qquad k = 11.$$

For the second and third groups the stimuli vary in color. For Group 2, the color is irrelevant. For Group 3, color is relevant and redundant with size. Continue with the assumptions of equal weight and $p = .50$. For these groups, calculate the mean number of trials needed to solve the problem and the number of trials before the probability of solving is above .90.

The effect of adding color changes the value of s. When color is irrelevant, the value of s drops to .25. Then

$$\mu_L = \frac{.75}{.125} = 6.0,$$

and we want

$$.90 \leq 1 - (.75)(.875)^k, \qquad k = 16.$$

When color is added and made relevant, the value of s increases to .50. Then

$$\mu_L = \frac{.50}{.25} = 2.0,$$

and we want

$$.90 \leq 1 - (.50)(.75)^k, \qquad k = 6. \blacksquare$$

For purposes of illustration in our examples, we have assumed that all the stimulus dimensions in a problem have equal weight. Of course, this is a gross oversimplification; some dimensions will be more easily noticed than others. The results of a concept-identification experiment can be used to study the amount of attention that subjects give to different aspects of the stimuli. We use the general idea that if the relevant dimension in a problem is easily noticed subjects will solve the problem easily; but if the relevant dimension has low attention value, the problem will be hard to solve.

The value of s is related to stimulus weights by Eq. (6.10). Suppose that we want to study the attention given to a dimension h, relative to a set of irrelevant dimensions. We set up a concept-identification problem using h as the relevant dimension. Then using Eqs. (6.9) and (6.10),

$$s = 1/(1 + \mu_E) = w_h/\sum w_j,$$

where $\sum w_j$ is the sum of the weights of all the dimensions. Now let $\sum w_i$ be the combined weight of all the irrelevant dimensions. Then

$$s = w_h/(w_h + \sum w_i),$$
$$s/(1 - s) = 1/\mu_E = w_h/\sum w_i. \tag{6.12}$$

Example 6.6. Suppose that in two concept-identification problems stimuli are geometric figures varying in shape, size, number, position on the stimulus cards, and color. Color is the relevant dimension in each problem. In both problems the colors are red and blue; however, in one problem the colors are saturated and in the other they are unsaturated. If the mean number of errors is $\mu_{E_1} = 4.6$ when the colors are saturated and $\mu_{E_2} = 6.9$ when the colors are unsaturated, by how much do we increase attention to colors by making them saturated?

Let w_1 be the weight of the color dimension when colors are saturated, and let w_2 be the weight when the colors are unsaturated. The irrelevant dimensions are the same for both problems. We have

$$\frac{w_1}{\sum w_i} = \frac{1}{4.6} = .217 \quad \text{and} \quad \frac{w_2}{\sum w_i} = \frac{1}{6.9} = .145.$$

Because of saturation attention to colors is increased by a factor of

$$\frac{w_1}{w_2} = \frac{.217}{.145} = 1.5. \blacksquare$$

We have seen how the difficulty of the problem is affected by adding irrelevant and relevant dimensions. Now we will look at another factor. A problem will be more or less difficult for a subject depending on how likely he is to attend to aspects of the situation which give the correct solution. A subject's readiness to attend to certain aspects of a situation is called *set*.

Set has been studied in many different problem situations. In the candle problem, the subject's attention may be directed toward using the box as a holder if hints are given. Or attention may be directed away from using the box as a holder if the box is filled with tacks. In the latter case, the box is seen as a container rather than a support. In the string-tying problem, the subject can be given a favorable set by a previous discussion about the physics of pendulums. Or he may be given an unfavorable set if the available objects for use as weights are such things as pliers, which ordinarily have a use different from that of a pendulum weight.

The factor of set affects the sampling probabilities of hypotheses. When a box is filled with tacks, it becomes less probable that the subject will think of using the box for another purpose—to support a candle. A subject will have a somewhat lower probability of thinking of tying pliers to a string to form a pendulum than he would of tying a circular weight of the kind ordinarily used in pendulum clocks. If a set produces an increased probability of sampling the correct solution, subjects will solve the problem sooner. But if the set decreases the probability of sampling the correct solution, subjects will probably take longer to solve the problem.

In concept identification, the factor of attention influences the weights of the stimulus dimensions. If we do something that sets the subject to attend to a certain dimension, we increase the weight of that dimension.

Example 6.7. Suppose that there are four dimensions which normally have equal weight, but a group of subjects is set to use the dimension of shape because a series of problems has been given where shape was relevant on many of the problems. Assume that the effect of set is to increase the weight of the shape dimension from 1.0 to 1.8 and reduce the weights of the other dimensions from 1.0 to 0.8. Suppose that we give one problem where shape is the relevant dimension, and another problem where shape is irrelevant. Assume that $q = .50$. Calculate the mean number of trials to solve in each case, and the number of trials that will be needed for the probability of solving to go above .90.

When the subjects are set to use the relevant dimension,

$$s = \frac{w_r}{\sum w_j} = \frac{1.8}{4.2} = .43.$$

Then the mean of trials needed to solve the problem is

$$\mu_L = \frac{.57}{.215} = 2.65,$$

and we want k so that

$$.90 \leq 1 - (.57)(.785)^k.$$

We have

$$P(L \leq k) = \begin{cases} .86 & \text{if } k = 6, \\ .90 & \text{if } k = 7. \end{cases}$$

Therefore, the answer is 7 trials.

When the subjects are set to use an irrelevant dimension,

$$s = \frac{.8}{4.2} = .19.$$

Then the mean of trials to solve is

$$\mu_L = \frac{.81}{.095} = 8.5,$$

and we want k so that

$$.90 \leq 1 - (.81)(.905)^k.$$

We have

$$P(L \leq k) = \begin{cases} .895 & \text{if } k = 20, \\ .903 & \text{if } k = 21. \end{cases}$$

Therefore, the answer is 21 trials. ▮

6C TRANSFER OF TRAINING

Now we look briefly at transfer of training in problem solving. Sometimes, after a subject has solved a problem by finding an appropriate rule for responding, the situation is changed in some way or a new problem is presented. We are interested in the way in which the experience of solving the first problem can have an influence on the ease of solving the second problem.

The most obvious opportunity for such a transfer comes if the subject can solve the second problem with the same rule he used in the first problem. For instance, we might set up a series of anagrams in which the letters were rearranged in the same order for all the anagrams. The words jump, rain, shoe, walk, and melt are the solutions to the anagrams UPJM, ANRI, HESO, AKWL, and ETML. In every case the anagram is solved by rearranging the letters in order 3142. The subject may solve many such anagrams without making use of the consistent order of the letters. But if he once begins to use the ordering, he will be able to solve later anagrams in the sequence with practically no effort. The process of solving the early problems makes solving the later problems much easier than it would otherwise be.

In concept identification one effect of carrying a solution across two problems is seen if an easy problem is followed by a hard problem and the two problems can be solved in the same way. For example, in one study of concept identification, the stimuli were schematic drawings of flowers, and the relevant dimension was a rather small difference in the angles between the stem and the leaves.[10] Subjects who started this problem took many trials before they noticed the stem-leaf angle and used it to solve the problem. Other subjects began with an easier version of the same problem in which a red stripe was used to emphasize the angle between the stem and the leaf, thus drawing the subject's attention to this dimension. The stimulus emphasis made the problem much easier of course. But more importantly, when the problem was changed by removing the stimulus emphasis, the subjects made very few errors on the task which had been very difficult for those subjects who did not have the benefit of the initial problem.

A theoretical analysis of this transfer is like the analysis of transfer of associations in Chapter 5. There we assumed that with two associations, if a subject memorized the first one in a way that would also support retention of the second, the second association would be known when it was first presented. Here the situation involves two problems, and we assume that if the first problem is solved in a way that also provides a solution to the second problem, the subject will know the solution to the second problem when it is first presented. If the first problem can be solved only in ways that will transfer to the second problem, the conditional probability of transfer, given solution of the first problem, is $t = 1$. Then if all subjects solve the first problem, they will all transfer to the second problem, and there will be no errors. However, if training on the first problem is not continued long enough so that all subjects solve it, the probability of transfer will be lower.

[10] By T. R. Trabasso, "Stimulus Emphasis and All-or-None Learning in Concept Identification," *J. exp. Psychol.*, 1963, **65,** 398–406.

Let T be the probability of transfer to the second problem. In general, if m trials are given on the first problem,

$$T = P(L \leq m)t, \tag{6.13}$$

as in Eq. (5.17) of Chapter 5. Of course, if $t = 1$, then the probability of transfer is just the probability that the first problem was solved during the first m trials.

We observe the effect of transfer during trials that are given on the second problem. To avoid unnecessary complications, assume that an initial trial is given on the second problem where the subject is not asked to respond, and which is called Trial 0. First we compute the distribution of E, the number of errors made on the second problem. There will be no errors if the subjcct transfers the solution from the first problem, or if the solution is not transferred but the problem is solved on the initial information trial.

$$P(E = 0) = T + (1 - T)s.$$

For a subject to make j errors ($j > 0$) he must fail to transfer, then select an incorrect hypothesis on Trial 0, select incorrect hypotheses following $j - 1$ errors, and finally select the correct hypothesis after the jth error. The complete probability distribution of E is

$$P(E = j) = \begin{cases} T + (1 - T)s & \text{for } j = 0, \\ (1 - T)(1 - s)^j s & \text{for } j \geq 1. \end{cases} \tag{6.14}$$

The mean and standard deviation of the number of errors are

$$\mu_E = \frac{(1 - T)(1 - s)}{s}, \qquad \sigma_E = \frac{\sqrt{[1 - T^2 - (1 - T)s^2](1 - s)}}{s} \tag{6.15}$$

Comparing Eq. (6.15) with Eqs. (6.2) and (6.3), we see that transfer has the effect of reducing both the mean and the standard deviation of the distribution of errors. This is because the distribution now includes a larger group of subjects who make no errors. The cumulative distribution of errors becomes

$$P(E \leq j) = 1 - (1 - T)(1 - s)^{j+1}. \tag{6.16}$$

The effect of transfer on the trial of solving is similar. Because of transfer, some subjects have the problem solved at the beginning. Then

$$P(L = k) = \begin{cases} T + (1 - T)s & \text{for } k = 0, \\ (1 - T)(1 - s)(1 - qs)^{k-1}qs & \text{for } k \geq 1. \end{cases} \tag{6.17}$$

The average trial of solving and the standard deviation are

$$\mu_L = \frac{(1 - T)(1 - s)}{qs},$$

$$\sigma_L = \frac{\sqrt{(1 - s)\{1 + ps - T[T + (1 - T)s + ps]\}}}{qs}. \qquad (6.18)$$

By comparing Eq. (6.18) with Eqs. (6.5) and (6.6), we see that transfer decreases the mean and standard deviation of the trial of solving. The cumulative distribution of trials needed to solve the problem is

$$P(L \leq k) = 1 - (1 - T)(1 - s)(1 - qs)^k. \qquad (6.19)$$

Example 6.8. Consider two concept-identification problems, one with three dimensions and the other with ten dimensions. The same dimension is relevant in both problems. Assume that all the dimensions have equal weight, and a hypothesis based on any irrelevant dimension gives correct responses with $p = .50$.

One group has an initial trial and four additional trials on the three-dimension problem, and then an initial trial and four additional trials on the 10-dimension problem. A second group has an initial trial and nine additional trials on the 10-dimension problem. Find the probability of solving the 10-dimension problem in both groups.

For the group that starts with the three-dimension problem, we have

$$P(L \leq 4) = 1 - (1 - s)(1 - qs)^4 = 1 - (.667)(.833)^4 = .68.$$

For this problem, $t = 1$, so $T = .68$. Therefore, for the second problem,

$$P(L \leq 4) = 1 - (1 - T)(1 - s)(1 - qs)^4 = 1 - (.32)(.90)(.95)^4 = .77.$$

For the group that has only the 10-dimension problem,

$$P(L \leq 9) = 1 - (1 - s)(1 - qs)^9 = 1 - (.90)(.95)^9 = .43.$$

Thus the number of subjects who solve the 10-dimension problem following training on the simpler problem is greater than the number in a group with the same number of total trials, all on the 10-dimension problem. ▮

In situations where there are different possible ways to solve a problem, it often is interesting to use a transfer task to measure the use of each solution by the subjects. We shall encounter some relatively complicated problems of this type later when we discuss productive thinking. Now we consider a simpler situation involving transfer after concept identification with redundant dimensions.

Recall the earlier discussion of redundant dimensions and Example 6.4. In these problems one of the two (or more) rules leads to correct responses on all trials. The subject tries different rules until he finds one of the correct ones. We can test to see which rule the subject used by giving him a new problem in which only one of the rules will lead to correct answers. This can be done either by making the other dimension(s) irrelevant or by removing them from the set of stimulus dimensions. When we change the problem in this way, subjects who were using the rule that is still valid should make no errors on the new task. However, subjects who solved the first problem using a rule which no longer works will have to go through the process of finding the correct rule for the new problem. Our assumption is that some subjects will use one of the redundant dimensions to solve the first problem, and other subjects will use different dimensions. The transfer task allows us to see how many subjects used each of the dimensions.

The fact that some relevant dimensions will be chosen in preference to others is expressed in the notion of stimulus weights. If all the stimulus dimensions had equal weights, a transfer task should show equal amounts of transfer regardless of which dimension is made consistent between the first and second problems. However, the redundant dimensions usually are not equal in weight, and the dimension with more weight has a higher probability of being used to solve the first problem. For example, suppose that stimuli are pictures of flowers, and there are two relevant dimensions.[11] One relevant dimension is the color of the flower; one-half of the pictures have yellow flowers and the other one-half have blue flowers. The second relevant dimension is a small difference in the angle between leaf and stem; one-half have angles of 45° and the others have angles of 30°. Under these conditions we would expect most subjects to notice the different-colored blossoms first. Suppose that after training on this problem with redundant dimensions, two different transfer tasks are given to different subjects. For one group the angle dimension is removed from the situation; all the leaves meet the stems at an angle of 38°. For this group the colors of the blossoms continue to be varied and relevant. For a second group, the angle between leaf and stem continues to be relevant but the color dimension is removed from the situation by making all the blossoms pink. If our intuition about these dimension weights is correct, then the first group (with colors continued, angle removed) should show a substantial amount of transfer. But the second group (with the strong color dimension removed and the weaker angle dimension continued) should show much less transfer.

Recall that the probability of selecting any single dimension is equal to the weight of that dimension divided by the sum of the weights of all the dimensions. It was this assumption that led us to say that the probability

[11] These conditions were studied also by T. R. Trabasso, *op. cit.*

of solving the problem equals the sum of weights for the correct dimensions divided by the sum of weights of all the dimensions. Now we are interested in the probability that the problem is solved in a particular way, given that it is solved in some way. Given that the problem was solved, we know that one of the correct dimensions was chosen. What is the probability that a particular correct dimension was the one used?

The answer is obtained by dividing the weight of the single dimension by the sum of the weights of all the correct dimensions. Let w_h be the weight of a certain relevant dimension, and let $\sum w_r$ be the sum of weights for all the relevant dimensions. The probability that dimension h is used, given that the problem is solved, is

$$t_h = w_h/\sum w_r. \tag{6.20}$$

The notation t_h is used because the probability given is the probability of transfer to a new problem in which only dimension h is relevant.

Example 6.9. In a concept-identification problem with flower stimuli, suppose that the dimension of color has weight $w_c = 3$, the dimension of angle between stem and leaf has weight $w_a = 1$, and the remaining dimensions have a combined weight $\sum w_i = 16$. The value of p is .50. The first problem is presented until all subjects have solved it. Then one-half of the subjects are given a transfer problem with color relevant and angle made constant, and the other subjects are given a transfer problem with angle relevant and color made constant. The second problem has the same irrelevant dimensions as the first problem. Find the average number of trials that will be needed to solve the first problem, and the average number of errors in each group in the transfer problem.

In the first problem, the value of s is

$$s = (w_c + w_a)/(w_c + w_a + w_i) = (3 + 1)/(3 + 1 + 16) = .20.$$

Then the average number of trials to solve is

$$\mu_L = (1 - s)/qs = .80/.10 = 8.0.$$

In the transfer problem with color relevant,

$$t_c = w_c/(w_c + w_a) = 3/(3 + 1) = .75.$$

Since the first problem is continued until it is solved, t_c is the probability of transfer. In the second problem, with color relevant

$$s = w_c/(w_c + w_i) = 3/(3 + 16) = \tfrac{3}{19}.$$

Then the average number of errors is

$$\mu_E = [(1 - T)(1 - s)]/s = [(.25)(\tfrac{16}{19})]/(\tfrac{3}{19}) = 1.33.$$

In the transfer problem with angle relevant

$$t_a = w_a/(w_a + w_c) = .25.$$

The value of s is

$$s = w_a/(w_a + w_i) = \tfrac{1}{17}.$$

Then the average number of errors is

$$\mu_E = [(.75)(\tfrac{16}{17})]/\tfrac{1}{17} = 12.0. \blacksquare$$

In these three sections we have been using the idea that problem solving is a selective process involving trial and error. When faced with a problem, a subject begins to think of possible ways to solve it. He tries one after another until he finds a way that works. One factor affecting difficulty is the relative number of hypotheses or strategies that will work. Another factor is the subject's set to attend to the hypotheses that will be successful. Another interesting problem involves transfer of training, where the experience of solving one, or a series, of problems can make it easier to solve later problems.

Simple concept identification is a problem where the set of possible solutions seems to remain fairly constant, and where the subject seems to sample randomly from the set of possibilities. These features allow a simple quantitative analysis of the factors influencing problem difficulty and transfer of training.

6D PERCEPTION AND UTILIZATION OF RELATIONS

The concept introduced in this section is from logic. It involves a distinction between two kinds of properties. Some properties are characteristics of single objects or situations. Other properties characterize sets or classes of things. When a property has to refer to more than one object, it is called a relation.

The distinction can be stated precisely in simple logical notation. Let the lower case letters *a*, *b*, *c*, . . . stand for individual objects, persons, events, or whatever. Let the capital letters *F*, *G*, *H*, . . . *R*, *S*, *T*, . . . stand for properties. We can represent sentences by the notation $F(a)$, which is read "*a* is *F*" or less briefly, "Object (or person or event) *a* has the property *F*." We may form compounds of simple sentences such as

$$F(a) \;\&\; F(b) \;\&\; F(c)$$

("*a*, *b*, and *c* have property *F*") or

$$F(a) \;\&\; G(a) \;\&\; H(a)$$

("*a* has properties *F*, *G*, and *H*").

In all these cases, the properties apply to single objects. For example, *F* might stand for being tall, *G* for having red hair, and *H* for being able to run fast. And a, b, and c might stand for three boys—John, Mike, and David. Then the two sentences above would be abstract representations of the sentences

John, Mike, and David all are tall.

and

John is tall, has red hair, and can run fast.

We can think of many ways to describe single objects. A single object may be described as having a certain height, a certain color, a certain weight, a certain shape, smooth or jagged edges, a certain temperature, or a certain taste. Height, color, weight, shape, texture, temperature, and taste are all properties of single objects.

There are other properties, however, which describe not single objects, but members of pairs or triplets or larger sets of objects. For example, think of the sentence

John and Bill are brothers.

We would not write this logically as

$$R(a) \;\&\; R(b),$$

meaning "John is a brother and Bill is a brother," because we mean to say that John and Bill are brothers of each other. The sentence does not attribute a single property to two boys separately in the same way as does "John and Bill both are tall." A relationship like "brother of" is a single property, but it applies to two persons. The proper logical form is

$$R(a, b),$$

read "a has relationship R to b." This sentence means

John is a brother of Bill's.[12]

---

[12] In this case, we could also write $R(b, a)$, since Bill is also John's brother. Some relations (for example, "cousin of") are symmetric; that is, if $R(a, b)$, then $R(b, a)$. "Brother of" is not symmetric, since, for example, John might be a brother of Mary. Other nonsymmetric relations are "father of" and "taller than." Symmetry is one of three formal properties of relations that are important for formal analyses of relational systems. The other properties are transitivity and reflexivity. If R is a transitive relation, then $R(a, b)$ and $R(b, c)$ implies $R(a, c)$. If R is reflexive, then the relation applies between an object and itself: $R(a, a)$. For example, the relation "=" in arithmetic is symmetric, transitive, and reflexive. The formal properties of relational systems are important for many purposes, and psychologists use them in the theory of measurement. They also have psychological importance in the theory of problem solving and thinking. In our discussion here, we do not discuss the formal properties of relations explicitly, because they do not affect the main point to be made here.

Relationships between members of a family or other social groups are examples of the general concept of a relation. The form $R(a, b)$ is the proper way to represent the sentences "Mary is Suzanne's cousin," or "Thomas is Willy's uncle," or "Angela's great-aunt is Elizabeth." The properties we are attributing are "brother of," "cousin of," "uncle of," "great-aunt of," and so on. Properties like these do not apply to individual persons; they apply to two people at once.

Other examples of relations are easy to think of. One object may be darker than another. The property "darker than" has to apply to an object when it is being compared with another object and we might say "a is darker than b." Another sentence describing a relation is "a is to the left of b." In this case the property is "to the left of," which must refer to an object in relation to another object or position. Sometimes a relation requires three or more objects in order to be applied. For example, the sentence "Bob is standing between Frank and Bill" is written logically

$$S(a, b, c),$$

since the property of being "between" can apply to an object only in relation to two other objects.

The logical concept of a relation clarifies a distinction between kinds of properties. Psychologically, the concept is important when we consider a person's reaction to certain kinds of stimuli and problem-solving tasks. Often a stimulus situation involves several different parts or elements. Each of the elements has certain properties. In addition, each of the elements has certain relationships with the other elements of the stimulus. For example, consider the nonsense stimulus *H X V*. We can think of this stimulus as being constructed from three elements—the letters *H*, *V*, and *X*. However, a complete description of the stimulus would include the order in which the letters are written. *H* is to the left of *X*, which is to the left of *V*. To describe the stimulus, we need to specify not only the elements which constitute it but also the relationships that exist among the elements.

Like any other property of a stimulus, a relation among parts may or may not be perceived or attended to, and it may or may not be utilized by a person as the basis for a response. One way to study responses to a relation is to set up a problem that can be solved only by using some relational property. For example, each stimulus in a concept-identification task might be made up of several figures with different shapes such as a square, a circle, a triangle, and a diamond. One way to make the solution depend on a relation is to have stimuli in one category if the square is larger than the circle and in a second category if the square is smaller than the circle. Subjects can solve problems involving a relational concept, though it is usually more difficult than solving problems involving a simple property.

When we set up a problem requiring a relational solution, we ask whether a subject *can find* a solution based on a relational property. There is another question that can be asked by using a different kind of experiment in which there are two possible solutions, one of which involves a relational property. Now we can ask whether a subject *will use* a relational property when there is also some other aspect of the situation that he might use as the basis of his response. The first question is a question about ability—can a subject develop a systematic response to a relation? The second question asks whether there is a natural tendency to respond to a relational property that is present in a situation.

This second question is formally similar to the problem of redundant dimensions in concept identification. Recall that with redundant dimensions, subjects could solve a problem in two (or more) ways. In the last section, we studied this situation from two points of view. We learned that problem solving is easier when redundant dimensions are present simply because the subject then has a larger number of ways to solve the problem and he will take less time to find one of them. Also, we studied the experimental use of transfer problems to find out which of the redundant dimensions was actually used by the subject in solving the initial problem. The question about relational properties is like the question that led us to use the method of transfer problems. There are two ways to solve a problem, one of which involves a relational property. After the subject has solved the problem, we want to see whether he used the relational property in his solution. To ascertain this, we give a new problem or test in which the subject will give one response if he solved the first problem on the basis of a relation and a different response if he solved the first problem on some other basis.

It should be noted here that we have already studied one situation which involved exactly this question. The experiments on constancy that we considered in Chapter 1 involve judgments given in two situations. In the first situation, a figure is presented with some context and the subject makes a judgment about the figure. Psychologically, the judgment could be based on two different sets of properties. One set is relational—the judgment might be based on the ratio of stimulus magnitudes between the figure and salient aspects of the context. The other is nonrelational—the judgment might be based on the stimulus magnitude of the figure itself. We find out which of these possibilities is correct by giving a new test in which each basis for judgment will lead to a different response. For instance, we change the magnitude of the background stimulus so that the ratio remains the same. If the initial judgment was based on the figure-to-background ratio, the judgment made in this new situation should be about the same as the judgment that was made originally. But if the initial judgment was based on the simple magnitude of the figure, in this test the subject should give a judgment different from his initial one. We pointed out in Section 1C that the main facts about constancy are consistent with the idea that we respond to stimulus ratios. In other words, our earlier study of perception already has provided some important examples of responses that depend on relational properties.

In the experiments on problem solving relevant to this issue, the logic is the same but the subject first solves a problem instead of making a judgment. The earliest experiments on this problem studied the question of transposition.[13] Chickens were trained on a discrimination task where on each trial the subject pecked either a white or a gray piece of paper. When the chicken pecked the gray paper, some food was given. Eventually the chicken pecked only the gray paper.

This problem seems to be one that the subject can solve using either a relation or a simple property. That is, one basis for responding correctly would be to peck on the darker piece of paper—this involves a relation. The other basis for responding correctly would be to peck at the gray paper—this involves a simple property. A transfer test was needed to show which basis was actually used, so a choice was given between the gray paper that was chosen in the first problem and a darker paper. If the initial problem was solved on the basis of a simple property, the chicken should continue to peck the gray paper in the transfer test. But if the initial problem was solved on the basis of a relation, the chicken should peck the darker paper in the transfer problem. In the experiment, most of the chickens chose the test stimulus which was new in the situation—that is, their response in the transfer problem suggested that they had solved the initial problem on the basis of a relational property.

A later analysis[14] showed that this particular result does not actually prove that the basis for the initial solution was relational. Putting the argument in general terms, it is possible that generalization of negative-response strength could occur from the white stimulus to the gray stimulus, and that positive-response strength could generalize from the gray stimulus to the black stimulus. Then the black stimulus would be chosen if the positive generalization were greater than the difference between the original response strength and the generalized negative strength attached to the gray stimulus. The argument is rather complicated and requires some special assumptions about the form of the generalization curve, but it is a valid criticism. As a result, the transposition problem became quite technical and involved. However, a somewhat different demonstration of response to relational properties has been given,[15] where the results cannot be explained on the basis of

[13] By W. Kohler, "Simple Structural Functions in the Chimpanzee and in the Chicken," in W. D. Ellis, *A Source Book of Gestalt Psychology*, New York: Harcourt Brace, 1938, 217–227. (Translated from Kohler's 1918 article in German.)

[14] By K. W. Spence, "The Differential Response in Animals to Stimuli Varying within a Single Dimension," *Psychol. Rev.*, 1937, **44,** 430–444.

[15] By D. H. Lawrence and J. DeRivera, "Evidence for Relational Discrimination," *J. comp. physiol. Psychol.*, 1954, **47,** 465–471.

stimulus generalization involving simple properties. Rats were trained to jump to one of two cards in a jumping-stand apparatus. The top half of one of the cards was lighter than the bottom half, and the top half of the other card was darker. In a series of transfer tests, most of the rats responded consistently to the relation between the two halves of the card which had applied during the initial problem. This is a situation in which a relation among different parts of a stimulus was the relevant property for responding.

The disagreements about transposition involved animals like rats; there was never any doubt that people could respond on the basis of relational properties. According to one analysis,[16] achievements in understanding relational concepts like "brother" mark important stages in intellectual development. Before a certain age—usually about six years—children typically do not know what is wrong with statements such as "Bill is Tom's brother but Tom is not Bill's brother." The difficulty apparently involves the symmetrical nature of the relationship when both children are boys. Apparently the younger child uses the term "brother" simply as a property of or a name for an individual. The older child understands that "brother" denotes a relationship, that is, a property that applies to two individuals.

Often the solution to a problem consists of discovering a relationship among some elements. Recall the candle problem and the two-string problem, mentioned in the preceding section. The solution to the candle problem is to fasten a box to an upright wall and to use the box to hold the candle. The solution to the two-string problem is to use a pair of pliers as a pendulum weight causing one string to swing closer to the other so the subject can reach them both at the same time. In both cases the critical part of the solution is perfectly evident. In the candle problem the box is easy to see. And in the string problem the pliers are placed prominently. The thing that is not "seen" is a particular way to use these objects—a relation involving these critical elements and other things that are present.

A classical analysis of problem solving and thinking[17] is based on a distinction between different kinds of solutions to problems—*A*-solutions and *B*-solutions. The distinction is not stated easily in a few words, but generally the *B*-solutions involve relatively mechanical rule-following and the *A*-solutions involve a relatively deep understanding of the problem. Typically, the distinguishing feature of an *A*-solution is that it includes an awareness of some important relation within the situation.

Now recall the analysis of transfer which was given at the end of the preceding section. Remember that we talked about problems which could

---

[16] By J. Piaget, *Judgment and Reasoning in the Child*, New York: Harcourt Brace, 1929.

[17] By M. Wertheimer, *Productive Thinking, Enlarged Edition*, 1959, New York: Harper, 1959.

be solved in several different ways. Some of the possible solutions of one problem will carry over or transfer to new problems and others will not. Whether a subject shows transfer to a second problem depends on the way he solves the first problem. If he finds one of the "good" solutions, he will have a way of solving the second problem successfully.

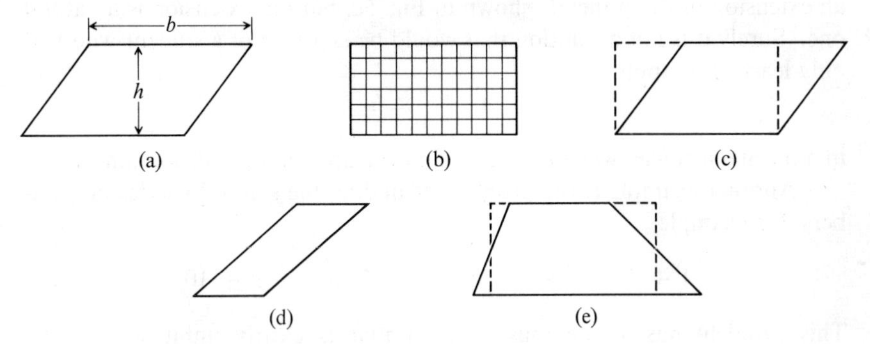

Fig. 5. Illustrations of ideas used in solving area problems.

In many problems, a solution based on a relational property will transfer to a greater variety of new problems than would a solution based on a mechanical rule. One example involves finding the area of a parallelogram. A mechanical rule for finding the area is

$$A = b \times h.$$

A student can use this rule in solving problems, such as in finding the area of the parallelogram in Fig. 5a. An alternative solution depends on the good understanding that we usually have of the area of a rectangle. It is easy to consider a rectangle as being a combination of many small squares of unit area, so that the area of a rectangle is the number of small squares contained in it (Fig. 5b). If a student understands the area of a rectangle, he can understand the area of a parallelogram since he can relate in a direct way by cutting off one corner of the parallelogram and moving it to the other end, thereby forming a rectangle with length b and height h (Fig. 5c). Finding the solution in this way involves something not involved in using the simple rule—an awareness of a relation between parts of the figure.

The importance of the distinction can be seen when certain new problems are presented. For example, consider Fig. 5d. Finding the area of this figure can be quite difficult for a student who has learned to solve the first problem using a mechanical rule. (Try measuring the "height" of the figure in its present orientation.) However, if a student has learned to solve the area problem by means of the relation, he probably will try to find a way to turn Fig. 5d into a rectangle, and this can be done quite easily.

Another advantage of the relational solution is also related to transfer of training. If a subject notices a relation or structure in one problem, he has a head start toward solving a new problem which has a similar relational property, even if he has to extend the old solution somewhat. Figure 5e shows a relational solution for finding the area of a trapezoid. It involves an extension of the principle shown in Fig. 5c, but the extension is a natural one. Surely it is not a solution that would be expected of a student who had only learned to apply

$$A = b \times h$$

in a mechanical way when he had to find the area of a parallelogram.

Another example is the problem of finding the sum of a series of numbers, for example

$$1 + 2 + 3 + 4 + 5 + 6 + 7 + 8 + 9 + 10.$$

This problem has an obvious solution that is clearly uninteresting—the numbers can be added up one by one. This solution would be unsatisfactory if the series were not very short. A more general solution uses the formula

$$S = [N(N + 1)]/2,$$

where N is the highest number in the series. Again, the formula can be applied to solve the problem, whether or not it is understood deeply.

However, there is a relation among the numbers which permits a better solution. Note that the series can be rearranged to form pairs of numbers by working in from the two ends:

$$(1 + 10) + (2 + 9) + (3 + 8) + (4 + 7) + (5 + 6).$$

The key is that each of the pairs has the same sum, so that the series is equal to the very easy sum

$$11 + 11 + 11 + 11 + 11.$$

Now the formula can be understood. Each pair of numbers is equal to $N + 1$, and the number of pairs is $N/2$. (The reader should discover why the formula also works when the highest number in the series is an odd number.)

Again, the relational solution permits transfer to a wider variety of new problems. An easy transition is to a sum like

$$15 + 16 + 17 + 18 + 19 + 20 + 21 + 22 + 23 + 24 + 25.$$

This is complicated to solve with the formula, but using the relation involving pairs we see that there are five pairs which add to 40 leaving a remaining number, 20.

The relational solution also applies directly to a sum like

$$1 + 4 + 7 + 10 + 13 + 16 + 19 + 22 + 25 + 28,$$

where the formula would be quite complicated to apply.

Writers who have considered the process of creative thinking[18] have emphasized the relational character of creative achievements. Mathematicians and others who have described their feelings while working on difficult problems report that often the solution is thought of suddenly when the person discovers a relationship within the problem that he was not aware of earlier.

In our discussion, we have emphasized simple problems where only a single idea is needed for solution. Most interesting intellectual problems are more complicated, and the discovery of a new relationship may permit only a partial solution. Also, a person may discover a new way of looking at a problem that seems promising but later turns out to be mistaken or unproductive. Another important part of creative thinking often involves reformulating the problem itself, so that the problem which finally is solved is not the same as the one the person started with. In finding new ways of thinking about a problem, a creative person often will see new aspects of the situation, and these can affect his ideas about how the different parts of the problem relate to each other.

The process of creative thinking, including reformulations of the problem, discovery of new elements that are related to the problem, investigation of trial solutions that turn out to be unsuccessful, and discovery of helpful relations, often requires a long time and much effort. When an intellectual problem is solved, the result frequently is to provide new concepts that clarify relationships among ideas and things.

PROBLEMS

For Problems 1 through 5, consider the following situation. Stimuli are constructed involving two kinds of geometric forms: three-sided and four-sided. The forms are drawn on cards at different angles: tilted to the left and to the right. Some of the forms are colored red and the others are blue; some of the cards have the forms enclosed in borders and the others have no border; and some cards have the forms on dark backgrounds and the others have light. Thus there are five dimensions: angle, border, color, darkness, and form. Assume that the weights are $w_a = 1.0$, $w_b = 1.5$, $w_c = 2.0$, $w_d = 2.5$, and $w_f = 3.0$. Assume that in concept-identification problems, irrelevant dimensions produce correct responses with $p = .50$.

---

[18] For example, J. Hadamard, *The Psychology of Invention in the Mathematical Field*, Princeton: Princeton University Press, 1945.

* 1. Subjects are given a problem with borders relevant and the other dimensions irrelevant. What is the value of s? Calculate the mean and standard deviation of the number of errors and the trial of solution. What is the probability of solving the problem before five errors are made? What is the probability of solving by Trial 10?

2. A favorable set is produced by giving a practice problem using borders. Assume that the dimension weight of the borders is increased to 2.83, and the other weights are unchanged. What will be the new value of s? Calculate the new mean number of errors, and the probability of solving by Trial 10.

3. With the original dimension weights, subjects are given a training problem in which only angles, borders, and darkness vary, with borders relevant. In the training problem, subjects have an initial information trial and then three more trials. Next a transfer problem is given with all the dimensions varying and borders relevant. What is the probability of solving the training problem in its trials? What will be the probability of solving the transfer problem by Trial 6? (Note that this gives the same number of total trials as a group starting on the final problem would have by Trial 10.) If subjects work on the transfer problem until all have solved it, what will be the average number of trials to solve the transfer problem?

* 4. Subjects are given a problem with the five dimensions varying, with borders and form relevant and redundant. What is the value of s? All subjects work on the problem until it is solved, and then are transferred to a problem with borders relevant, and form no longer varying. What is the value of t and of s for the transfer problem? What is the probability of solving the transfer problem with zero errors? What is the mean number of errors on the transfer problem?

▸ 5. A training problem has the five dimensions varying, with borders and form relevant and redundant. Subjects are given an initial trial and then four more trials. In a transfer problem, also with an initial trial and four more trials, borders are relevant and the other four dimensions, including form, are irrelevant. Calculate the probabilities of solving the training and transfer problems in the trials given.

6. In a concept-identification experiment, the mean number of errors is 5.67. Calculate the value of s and the theoretical standard deviation of the trial of solution.

▸ 7. Suppose that instead of the usual information trial at the beginning of a concept-identification experiment, the subject is asked to give an initial guess when he sees the first stimulus card. Assume that he samples from the possible hypotheses and selects the correct one with probability $\frac{1}{2}s$. The subject uses his initial hypothesis to make the first response, and holds that hypothesis if the response is correct or samples again if the response is wrong. After the first trial, the experiment proceeds according to the assumptions given in this chapter. What is the distribution of errors and the distribution of the trial of solution?

8. One concept-identification problem has size relevant, with shape and five other dimensions irrelevant; subjects make an average of 19.0 errors. In a second problem, with shape relevant and size and the other five dimensions irrelevant, the mean number of errors is 9.0. Calculate the values of s for these two problems. What will be the value of s and the mean number of errors on a problem with size and shape relevant and redundant and the other five dimensions irrelevant?

9. In the situation described in Problem 8, the group that solved the problem with size and shape relevant and redundant was divided for a transfer problem. One-half of the subjects had size relevant and shape not varied, and the other subjects had shape relevant and size not varied. Calculate the value of t for each of these transfer groups. Assume that the transfer problem had the five irrelevant dimensions that were in the first problem, and calculate the mean trial of solution in transfer for both groups.

▸ **10.** Four concept-identification problems are set up. All four problems include a set of four irrelevant dimensions. In Problem 1, color is relevant and shading is not varied. In Problem 2, shading is relevant and color is not varied. In Problem 3, shading and color are relevant and redundant. And in Problem 4, shading is relevant and color is irrelevant. Suppose that a group of subjects given Problem 1 makes an average of 8.0 errors, and a group given Problem 2 makes an average of 13.33 errors. Calculate predictions for the average numbers of errors that would be made by groups given Problems 3 and 4.

11. Two groups of subjects solve a concept-identification problem where the relevant dimension is the shading of geometric figures. Prior to solving the problem, one group was given a task where they were asked to make judgments of the aesthetic quality of shading in various figures. The other group had the concept-identification problem with no prior task. The group without a prior task took an average of 12 trials to solve the problem, and the group with the judgment task took an average of 8 trials to solve. Assuming $q = .5$, find the value of s in each group. Assuming that the weights of the irrelevant dimensions were the same in both groups, evaluate the effect of the judgment task on the stimulus weight of the shading dimension.

▸ **12.** In the situation described in Problem 11, consider two additional training conditions. Each of the additional groups solved a training problem with shading and size relevant and redundant. (Recall that in the original groups, size was irrelevant.) One of the groups had the judgment task before the training problem and the other group did not. In the new group without the judgment task, the mean number of errors in training was $\mu_E = 3.25$, and in the new group with the judgment task, the mean number of errors in training was $\mu_E = 2.22$. After the training problem, each of these two groups was divided and transfer was tested. One-half of the subjects in each group transferred to a problem with shading relevant and size irrelevant, and the remaining subjects transferred to a problem with size relevant and shading irrelevant. Except for shading and size, all the problems involved the same irrelevant dimensions. Find the values of t and s that apply to all four of the transfer groups. For all four of the transfer groups, calculate the mean number of errors and the number of trials needed before the probability of solving the transfer problem is above .75.

CHAPTER SEVEN

Normal Distribution and Correlation

In Chapter 4 we discussed frequency distributions and two summary properties, the mean and the standard deviation. The distributions considered in Chapter 4 were quite arbitrary. However, in some situations we apply a specific theoretical distribution. This happens when we have a psychological theory which tells us what distribution to expect. Then the distribution is given as a formula, derived from the theory. If the theory is correct, the frequency distribution obtained in an experiment will resemble approximately the theoretical distribution. The experimental results will not fit the theory exactly; however, we often carry out calculations using the theoretical distribution, and the results of the calculations can be applied in different situations where the theory gives an approximately correct description of the psychological process.

In Chapters 5 and 6 we used the *geometric* distribution. In the application to all-or-none learning in Chapter 5, each term of the distribution was the probability of learning after a certain trial. In general, the geometric distribution applies when we observe the waiting time for a certain event. Each trial is a chance for the event to occur, and the trials are independent. In an experiment, we have as many trials as are needed before the event occurs, and the variable that we observe is the number of trials.

The geometric distribution is a theoretical distribution, and the mean and standard deviation depend on the value of π, the probability of the event on each trial. Let x be the number of trials before the event occurs. Recall that the distribution of x is

$$P(x = n) = (1 - \pi)^{n-1}\pi. \tag{7.1}$$

The mean of this distribution is

$$\mu_x = 1/\pi \tag{7.2}$$

and the standard deviation is

$$\sigma_x = \sqrt{1 - \pi}/\pi. \tag{7.3}$$

Example 7.1. Suppose that learning is all-or-none and $\pi = .20$. What are the mean and the standard deviation of trials to learn? What proportion of the theoretical distribution is above $\mu + \sigma$?

First,

$$\mu_x = 1/\pi = 1/.20 = 5.0, \qquad \sigma_x = \sqrt{1 - \pi}/\pi = \sqrt{.80}/.20 = 4.5.$$

Next,

$$\mu + \sigma = 5.0 + 4.5 = 9.5.$$

Recall that the items with scores above 9.5 are those which are not learned during the first nine trials. Therefore,

$$P(x > 9.5) = 1 - P(x \leq 9) = (1 - \pi)^9 = .134. \blacksquare$$

Another useful theoretical distribution is the *binomial*. In this distribution, N, the number of trials, is fixed and the trials are independent. For example, we could have N tosses of a biased coin, or a test with N items which are not related to each other. The outcomes of the trials can be classified as "success" or "failure," and there is a constant probability p of success.

As an example, suppose that we define an experiment as ten tosses of a biased coin which comes up heads with $p = .60$. Each time we do the experiment we count the number of heads in ten tosses. We know we will not have exactly six heads every time. The number of heads in ten tosses will usually be between four and eight, but not always. And if we do the experiment enough times, we should expect a few occasions when all ten outcomes are heads—and a few with all ten tails.

Let y be the number of successes in N independent trials where the probability of success on each trial is p. The possible values of y are 0, 1, . . . , N. The probability distribution of y is

$$P(y = j) = \binom{N}{j} p^j(1 - p)^{N-j}, \tag{7.4}$$

where $\binom{N}{j}$ is the number of different ways that N objects can be classified into two groups with j objects in one of the groups and $N - j$ objects in the other. The equation is given here without further discussion; we merely present a few illustrations.

Figure 1 shows three cases of the binomial distribution. The upper panel has $N = 10$ and $p = .60$, the case mentioned above. The middle panel has $p = .60$, as before, but $N = 5$. Note that with the smaller number

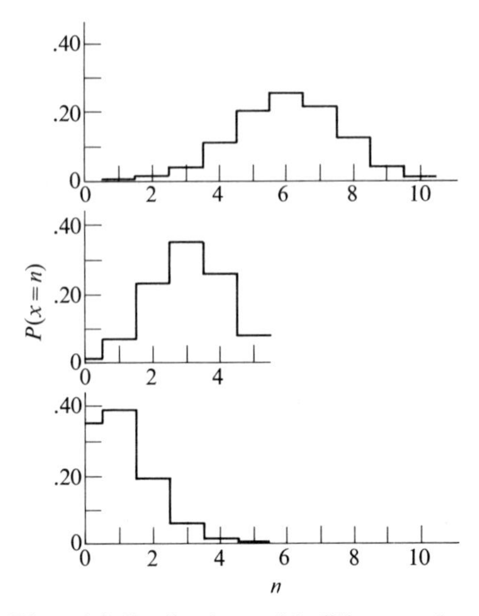

Fig. 1. Binomial distributions with different values of *P* and *n*.

of trials there will be more cases in which either all the outcomes are successes or none of the outcomes are successes. The lower panel has the binomial distribution with $N = 10$, as in the first case, but $p = .10$ instead of .60. Note that if p is far away from zero and one, as in the two upper panels, the binomial is a fairly symmetrical distribution. But if p is either close to one or to zero and N is fairly small, the binomial is very asymmetrical. (Recall that the geometric is *never* a symmetrical distribution.)

If y has the binomial distribution of Eq. (7.4), then the mean of y is

$$\mu_y = pN \tag{7.5}$$

and the standard deviation of y is

$$\sigma_y = \sqrt{Np(1 - p)}. \tag{7.6}$$

For example, with $p = .60$ and $N = 10$,

$$\mu_y = pN = (.60)(10) = 6.0;$$

$$\sigma_y = \sqrt{Np(1 - p)} = \sqrt{(10)(.60)(.40)} = 1.55.$$

Example 7.2. An experimenter presents a tone to subjects, and asks them to report whether they hear it. The tone is a little below threshold as defined in Chapter 1. Specifically, the probability of detecting this stimulus is $p = .30$.

Table 1

Binomial Distribution with $p = .30$, $N = 8$

j	0	1	2	3	4	5	6	7	8
$P(y = j)$	.058	.198	.296	.254	.136	.047	.010	.001	.000

The experimenter presents this tone 8 times to each subject, and runs 60 subjects.

Assume that the eight presentations per subject are independent trials, and that the probability of detection, $p = .30$, is the same for all the subjects. If the data correspond as nearly as possible to the theoretical distribution, what will be the mean number of detections? What will be the standard deviation of the distribution across subjects? Using the distribution as given in Table 1, find how many subjects should have scores less than $\mu - \sigma$. How many subjects should have scores higher than $\mu + 1.5\sigma$?

The mean is

$$\mu = pN = (.30)(8) = 2.4.$$

The standard deviation is

$$\sigma = \sqrt{Np(1 - p)} = \sqrt{(8)(.30)(.70)} = 1.30.$$

The point where $y = \mu - \sigma$ is

$$y = 2.40 - 1.30 = 1.10.$$

From Table 1, the proportion of scores below 1.10 is .256. Thus we expect (.256)(60), or about 15 subjects to have scores below $\mu + 1.5\sigma$.

The point where $y = \mu + 1.5\sigma$ is

$$y = 2.40 + 1.95 = 4.35.$$

Table 1 shows that .058 of the scores will be 5 or greater. Thus, (.058)(60) or about 3 subjects should have scores higher than $\mu + 1.5\sigma$. ▮

7A NORMAL DISTRIBUTION

Many psychological theories, including most theories of psychological testing, are based on the normal distribution. Unlike the geometric and binomial distributions, the normal is a *continuous* distribution. We apply the normal distribution to variables like height, weight, intelligence, and income, where a continuum of values exists.

Like the geometric and binomial distributions, the normal distribution is theoretical. A frequency distribution obtained in an experiment or by giving a test will not agree exactly with the theoretical distribution, but it may be close to it. Good approximations to the normal distribution are produced in many situations where the observed variable results from averaging a large number of quantities. In other words, we can expect the normal distribution to be approximated when we measure something which is determined in a complicated way. Physical features like height and weight are complicated, depending on heredity, diet, medical care, and several other things; the distributions of these physical features are almost exactly normal. And the scores obtained by groups of people on many psychological tests are distributed approximately as the normal. This is not surprising, since most of the things that psychologists measure, such as intelligence, aptitudes for particular jobs, and traits of personality, are determined in complicated ways.

The normal distribution is determined by two quantities—the mean and the standard deviation. By saying that the distribution is determined, we mean that from knowledge of the mean and standard deviation we can calculate the proportion of individuals below any given score. A picture of the normal distribution is given in Fig. 2 and a more complete table of the normal distribution is given in Table C of the Appendix.

The values of the mean and the standard deviation of the normal distribution are determined by whatever processes produce the variable which we observe. If we knew exactly what those processes were, we could calculate the mean and the standard deviation of the normal distribution from other quantities, as we did for the geometric and binomial distributions. However,

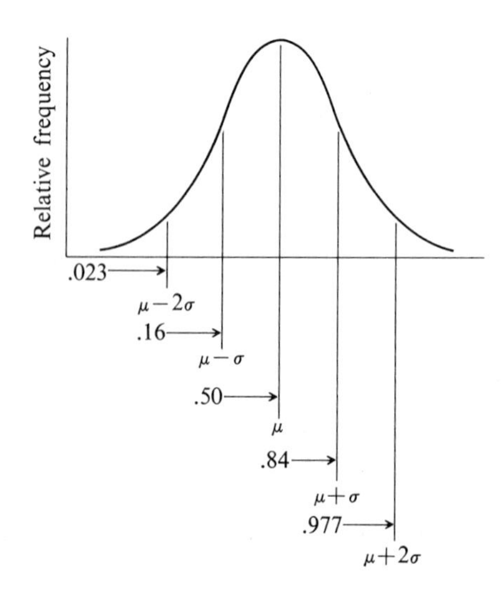

Fig. 2. Normal distributions with proportions below several scores.

in most cases where the normal distribution appears, the process is not understood very well. Then we look at the results of an experiment or a set of test scores and treat the mean and standard deviation as quantities to be obtained from data.

In the calculations that we carry out, there are four properties of the normal distribution and any one of them can be obtained from the other three. The properties are: (1) the mean μ, (2) the standard deviation σ, (3) a score x, and (4) the proportion of individuals with scores below x (or above x).

Example 7.3. Assume that $\mu = 50$ and $\sigma = 10$. What proportion of the distribution is below $x = 35$? What score x will be below about 24% of the scores?

First, the score 35 is 15 points below the mean. Since $\sigma = 10$,

$$x = 35 = 50 - 15 = \mu - 1.5\sigma.$$

Table C in the Appendix shows that the proportion below $\mu - 1.5\sigma$ is .067.

For the second part, if a score x is below 24% of the distribution, then 76% of the distribution is below x. From Table C, the score we want is $\mu + .7\sigma$. Then

$$x = \mu + .7\sigma = 50 + (.7)(10) = 57. \blacksquare$$

Example 7.4. A normal distribution has $\mu = 70$ and 90% of the distribution is below 79. What is σ?

From Table C, the score above 90% of the distribution is $\mu + 1.3\sigma$. Then

$$x = 79 = \mu + 1.3\sigma = 70 + 1.3\sigma.$$
$$9 = 1.3\sigma.$$
$$\sigma = 9/1.3 = 6.9. \blacksquare$$

Example 7.5. In a normal distribution, 31% of the individuals have scores below 38. The standard deviation is 8. Find μ.

From Table C, the score above 31% of the scores is $\mu - .5\sigma$. Then

$$x = 38 = \mu - .5\sigma = \mu - 4.$$
$$\mu = 42. \blacksquare$$

7B THEORY OF CHOICE WITH VARIABLE RESPONSE STRENGTHS

In Chapters 2 and 3 we studied a theory of choice where it was assumed that an object or stimulus produces a fixed response strength, and that choices are probabilistic. An alternative assumption is that choices are determined by response strengths, but that response strengths vary from moment to

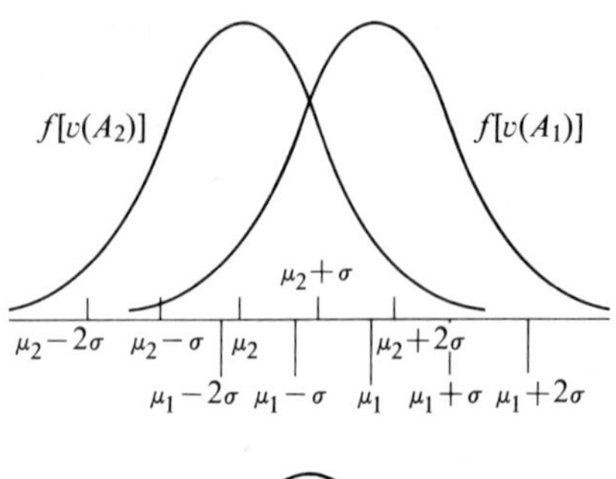

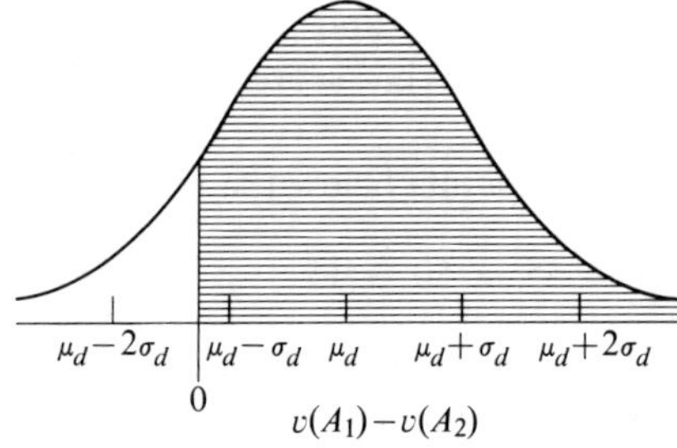

Fig. 3. Distributions of two response strengths, and the distribution of their difference.

moment.[1] According to this theory, if several alternative responses are available, the alternative with the highest response strength will be chosen with probability one. However, the same choice is not always made because the response strengths are variable.

In one common form, the theory is used to analyze choices between two alternatives, which we will call A_1 and A_2. Associated with the two alternatives are distributions of response strengths $f[v(A_1)]$ and $f[v(A_2)]$. At any specific time the alternatives have strengths $v(A_1)$ and $v(A_2)$, and if a choice is made at that time, the alternative with the higher strength will be chosen. In the simplest form of the theory, it is assumed that $v(A_1)$ and $v(A_2)$ are independent, distributed normally, with the same standard deviation σ. The difference between the means of the distributions is

$$\mu_d = \mu_1 - \mu_2. \tag{7.7}$$

An illustration is given in Fig. 3. In the illustration, μ_1 is higher than μ_2, so A_1 will be chosen more often than A_2.

When a choice is made between A_1 and A_2, the response strength of each alternative is a sample from its distribution of response strengths. In

[1] This theory was used by C. L. Hull, *A Behavior System*, New Haven: Yale University Press, 1952.

most cases, the value of $v(A_1)$ will be close to μ_1 and the value of $v(A_2)$ will be close to μ_2. But sometimes the value of $v(A_1)$ can be quite far below μ_1 and sometimes $v(A_2)$ can be quite far above μ_2. Whenever the sample from $f[v(A_1)]$ is below the sample from $f[v(A_2)]$, A_2 will be chosen.

We can analyze the choice by considering the difference between $v(A_1)$ and $v(A_2)$ when a choice is made. If $v(A_1)$ is greater than $v(A_2)$, then the difference $v(A_1) - v(A_2)$ will be positive; if $v(A_2)$ is greater, then $v(A_1) - v(A_2)$ will be negative. Therefore, we can consider the distribution of the difference, $v(A_1) - v(A_2)$. The probability of choosing A_1 is the probability that the difference is greater than zero.

$$P(A_1 \mid A_1, A_2) = P[v(A_1) - v(A_2) > 0]. \tag{7.8}$$

In Chapter 4 we considered the difference between two independent variables. Equations (4.6) and (4.7) in Chapter 4 give the mean and the standard deviation of the difference. Using those equations, we have

$$\mu_d = \mu[v(A_1) - v(A_2)] = \mu_1 - \mu_2,$$

$$\sigma_d = \sigma[v(A_1) - v(A_2)] = \sqrt{\sigma_1^2 + \sigma_2^2} = \sqrt{2\sigma^2} = \sigma\sqrt{2}. \tag{7.9}$$

The lower panel of Fig. 3 shows the distribution of $v(A_1) - v(A_2)$ corresponding to the distributions of $v(A_1)$ and $v(A_2)$ shown in the upper panel. The shaded part of the distribution is the part where $v(A_1) - v(A_2)$ is greater than zero, and thus the shaded part corresponds to $P(A_1)$.

Example 7.6. Suppose that response strengths of two alternatives have distributions with $\mu_d = \mu_1 - \mu_2 = -3.0$ and $\sigma_d = 4.0$. What is the probability of choosing alternative A_1?

With μ_d negative, a difference of zero is above the mean, and

$$0.0 = \mu_d + .75\sigma_d.$$

Using Table C, the proportion of the distribution above zero is

$$P(A_1 \mid A_1, A_2) = 1.0 - .77 = .23. \blacksquare$$

Example 7.7. In an experiment there are three alternatives A_1, A_2, and A_3, and subjects make choices between pairs of alternatives. When A_1 and A_2 are offered, the proportion of choices of A_1 is

$$P(A_1 \mid A_1, A_2) = .69.$$

When A_2 and A_3 are offered, the proportion of choices of A_2 is

$$P(A_2 \mid A_2, A_3) = .58.$$

What is the theoretical probability of A_1 when the alternatives are A_1 and A_3?

Using $P(A_1 \mid A_1, A_2)$, we can look up the difference between μ_1 and μ_2 in units of σ_d. Using Table C, we find that a probability of A_1 equal to .69 corresponds to a score of

$$0.0 = \mu_d - .5\sigma_d, \qquad \mu_1 - \mu_2 = .5\sigma_d.$$

Using the result when A_2 and A_3 are offered,

$$0.0 = \mu_d - .2\sigma_d, \qquad \mu_2 - \mu_3 = .2\sigma_d.$$

Putting these two results together, we find that

$$\mu_1 - \mu_3 = .5\sigma_d + .2\sigma_d = .7\sigma_d.$$

Then, using Table C again, we see that

$$P(A_1 \mid A_1, A_3) \doteq 1 - .24 = .76. \blacksquare$$

A closely related theory is often used to analyze forced-choice detection experiments.[2] It is assumed that the psychological magnitude of a stimulus is not fixed, but varies from one presentation to another. Suppose that there are two stimuli with physical magnitudes H_1 and H_2. Assume that their psychological effects $s(H_1)$ and $s(H_2)$ are distributed normally with the difference between the means equal to $\mu_d = H_1 - H_2$, and the standard deviation of the difference equal to σ_d. The two stimuli are presented, and a subject is asked to judge which has greater magnitude. The subject compares the psychological magnitudes produced by the two stimuli, and selects the larger one. The probability of judging H_1 to be greater than H_2 is the probability that $s(H_1)$ is greater than $s(H_2)$. That is,

$$P[\text{judge } H_1 > H_2] = P[s(H_1) - s(H_2) > 0]. \tag{7.10}$$

Example 7.8. Recall from Chapter 1 that in a forced-choice experiment the threshold (or *jnd*) is defined as the difference between two stimuli where the one with greater physical magnitude is judged greater with probability .75. In the present theory, how different must two stimuli be in units of σ_d to be separated by one *jnd*?

Appendix Table C shows that .75 of the distribution is above a score $.68\sigma_d$ below the mean. Therefore, two stimuli that are just noticeably different are separated by an amount equal to $.68\sigma_d$. $\blacksquare$

---

[2] This theory was developed by L. L. Thurstone, "A Law of Comparative Judgment," *Psychol. Rev.*, 1927, **34,** 273–286.

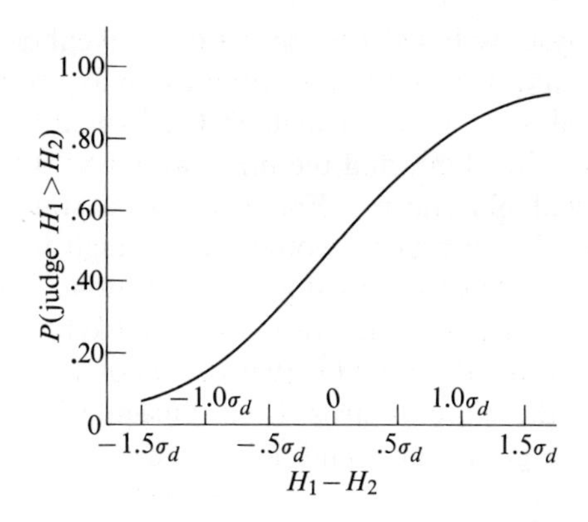

Fig. 4. Theoretical psychometric function based on assumption of normal distributions.

Figure 4 shows the psychometric function, with the probability of judging H_1 greater than H_2 plotted against the difference $H_1 - H_2$, in units of σ_d. Each point is obtained by looking up the proportion of scores above the value $\mu - x\sigma_d$, where $x\sigma_d$ is the difference between the stimuli.

A third theory is used to analyze detection performance when the signal to be detected is mixed with noise.[3] The theory's most frequent use is in analyzing the detection of a pure tone that is presented on some trials but not on others. Whether the signal is present or not, the subject hears a uniform random mixture of frequencies called white noise. During a trial, the subject either hears noise alone or the signal in noise, and his task is to judge whether or not the signal is present. The task is a little like trying to detect a weak tone, either on a radio or over a telephone, when there is a lot of static.

Because of the variability of the noise, it would be impossible to tell on every trial whether the signal was presented, even if a subject had all the information available in the physical stimulus. However, some of the stimuli that the subject hears are much more likely to be produced when there is a signal, and others are more likely to be produced when there is only noise. When the subject hears a stimulus, he can make a judgment like, "That sound is much more likely to be produced if the signal is on than if there is only noise," or, "The sound on that trial is very unlikely if the signal is on, but it is fairly likely to occur if there is only noise." The basis of the subject's response is the relative likelihood of occurrence of the stimulus he hears on the two kinds of trial in the experiment.

---

[3] A general introduction to the ideas is by J. A. Swets, W. P. Tanner, Jr., and T. G. Birdsall, "Decision Processes in Perception," *Psychol. Rev.*, 1961, **68,** 301–340.

An exact analysis is based on the ratio of likelihoods. A complete physical analysis could be made of the stimulus on any trial, and two likelihoods of that stimulus could be calculated. One would be the likelihood of the stimulus given noise alone, and the other would be the likelihood of the stimulus given signal plus noise. For example, a stimulus in which the signal seems to be clearly present would have a high likelihood given the signal plus noise, and a low likelihood given noise alone. The subject's judgment is assumed to be based on the ratio of these likelihoods, the *likelihood ratio.* We let x stand for the stimulus that occurs on a trial, and let $l(x \mid N)$ be the likelihood of the stimulus given noise alone and $l(x \mid SN)$ be the likelihood of the stimulus given signal and noise. Then the likelihood ratio is

$$LR = \frac{l(x \mid SN)}{l(x \mid N)}.$$

If the subject seems to hear the signal clearly, that stimulus will have a high value of LR; if the stimulus seems to be very different from anything that could be produced with the signal on, that stimulus will have a low value of LR.

Now consider different trials in the experiment when there is noise alone. Most of the time, a noise-alone trial will produce a stimulus that has a low value of LR, but the value of LR will not always be the same, and sometimes it will be fairly high. Similarly, on the different trials when the signal is on, the value of LR will be fairly high, but this is variable also. In other words, each kind of trial produces a distribution of values of LR. The distribution of LR associated with noise alone has a lower mean than the distribution associated with signal plus noise.

Instead of working with the distribution of LR directly, we work with the distribution of its logarithm. The value of LR can be any positive number; the value of $\log LR$ can be any number at all, and in conditions often used in experiments the conditional distributions of $\log LR$ are approximately normal.[4] Let f_N be the distribution of $\log LR$ associated with noise alone, and let f_{SN} be the distribution associated with signal plus noise. Figure 5 shows a pair of distributions, f_N and f_{SN}, that illustrate the situation a subject is in during an experiment. Note that most of f_N is below zero, and most of f_{SN} is above zero. A stimulus with $\log LR = 0$ is one for which the likeli-

[4] Exact derivations of the distributions of $\log LR$ are possible, based on theoretical analysis of the physical stimuli. If it is assumed that the subject uses all the information in the stimuli, the distributions can be shown to be exactly normal under fairly general conditions. Further, exact analyses can be given to determine the effects on the distributions that are produced by failures to use part of the information, or by introducing a filter to obtain better information in the neighborhood of the signal frequency.

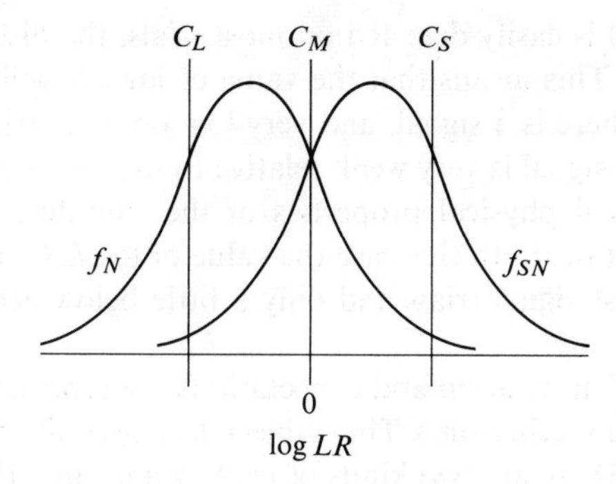

Fig. 5. Distributions of log *LR* on signal trials and noise-alone trials.

hood ratio is 1.0—that is, it is a stimulus which is equally likely on the two kinds of trial.

The information that the subject is given on a trial allows him to judge a quantity corresponding to log *LR*. If that quantity is large, then the stimulus probably came from distribution f_{SN}; if log *LR* is small, the stimulus probably came from distribution f_N. However, the subject has to choose between saying "yes" and "no" to the question, "Was there a signal?" It is assumed that he selects a criterion value of log *LR* and says "yes" if log *LR* is above the criterion, or "no" if log *LR* is below the criterion. Let C be the value of log *LR* selected by the subject as his criterion. Then the probability of saying "yes" on *SN* trials is

$$P(\text{yes} \mid SN) = P(\log LR > C \mid SN), \tag{7.11}$$

which is the proportion of distribution f_{SN} above C. And the probability of saying "yes" on N trials is

$$P(\text{yes} \mid N) = P(\log LR > C \mid N), \tag{7.12}$$

which is the proportion of f_N above C. Figure 5 shows three criteria. C_S is a strict criterion, where the subject says "yes" only when he is very sure that there was a signal. C_L is a lax criterion, where the subject says "yes" whenever he thinks that there may have been a signal. And C_M is a medium criterion.

The main use of the concepts developed in this discussion is to separate two factors in the process of making judgments. One factor is the stimulus information and the subject's sensitivity to small differences among stimuli. The other factor is the subject's motivation and expectations that also affect his decisions whether to say "yes" or "no." The factor of stimulus information and sensitivity is represented by the separation between the two distributions. If the signal is easily detected on most trials, the distributions will be widely separated. This means that the value of log *LR* will be very high on most trials when there is a signal, and very low on most trials when there is noise alone. If the signal is very weak relative to the noise, or if the subject is insensitive to critical physical properties of the stimulus, the distributions will overlap a great deal. In this case the value of log *LR* will be only a little above zero on most signal trials and only a little below zero on most trials with noise alone.

The factors of motivation and expectations are represented by the location of the subject's criterion. The subject has two alternative responses, "yes" and "no." There are two kinds of trial, *N* and *SN*. If the subject says "yes" on an *SN* trial, or "no" on an *N* trial, he is correct. These two kinds of correct response are called *hits* and *correct rejections.* If the subject says "no" on an *SN* trial, he makes an error called a *miss*, and if he says "yes" on an *N* trial, his error is called a *false alarm.* Any combination of rewards for the different kinds of correct responses, and penalties for the different kinds of errors, is possible. For example, a person might be greatly penalized for making false alarms, but only slightly for missing signals. In that case he would tend to adopt a strict criterion to avoid saying "yes" when there was no signal. Or the person might be penalized heavily for missing signals; then he would tend to adopt a lax criterion so that he would say "yes" with a high probability on signal trials. In general, we can represent the outcomes of different trials in a payoff matrix of the form

Response \ Kind of trial	*SN*	*N*
yes	R_h	P_{fa}
no	P_m	R_{cr}

where R_h is the reward for a hit, P_{fa} is the penalty for a false alarm, P_m is the penalty for a miss, and R_{cr} is the reward for a correct rejection. In general, a high value of R_h or a low value of P_{fa} will produce a lax criterion, and a high value of R_{cr} or a low value of P_m will produce a strict criterion.

The motivational factors in the subject's decisions are represented by the payoff matrix. The other factor affecting his criterion is his expectation about how often signals will occur. If the subject knows that signals occur on only a few trials, he will tend to say "yes" only when the stimulus seems to indicate clearly that a signal was present, corresponding to a strict criterion. If the subject knows that signals occur on most trials, he will tend to adopt a lax criterion.

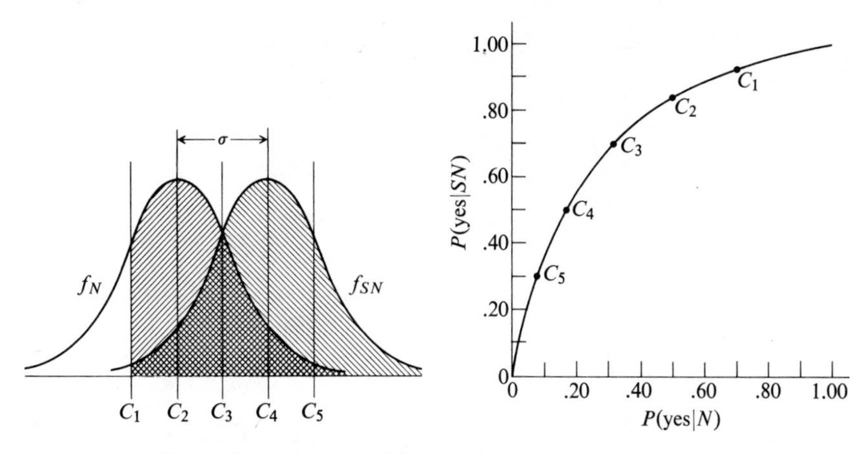

Fig. 6. Distributions of log *LR* and corresponding *ROC*.

We have discussed two concepts: the distributions of log *LR* that are associated with *N* trials and *SN* trials, and the subject's criterion for saying "yes." Now we consider how these two concepts combine in an analysis of the subject's judgments. We assume that f_N and f_{SN} are both normal, with the same standard deviation σ. In the left panel of Fig. 6 is an illustration where the difference between the means of the distributions is equal to σ. The five lines represent five criteria the subject could adopt under different conditions of payoff and expectation. The right panel shows a *receiver operating characteristic*, or *ROC*, that describes the subject's judgments in the situation represented by the distributions. The *ROC* is a graph showing the relationship between two conditional probabilities—the probability of saying "yes" on *SN* trials (or the hit rate), and the probability of saying "yes" on *N* trials (or the false-alarm rate). The dots on the *ROC* correspond to the five criteria of the left panel. C_1 is a lax criterion; it is $.5\sigma$ below the mean of f_N and 1.5σ below the mean of f_{SN}. The proportion of each distribution to the right of the criterion represents the subject's probability of saying "yes" on that kind of trial. The shaded portions of the distributions in Fig. 6 represent these conditional probabilities when the criterion is at C_1. Using Table C, we see that .69 of the distribution f_N is to the right of C_1, and .93 of f_{SN} is to the right of C_1. These are the values of $P(\text{yes} \mid N)$ and $P(\text{yes} \mid SN)$ that give point C_1 on the *ROC*. The other points are determined in the same way. Criterion C_2 is at the mean of f_N and is σ below the mean of f_{SN}. Table C says that $P(\text{yes} \mid N)$ is .50 and $P(\text{yes} \mid SN)$ is .84. Criterion C_3 is $.5\sigma$ above the mean of f_N, giving

$$P(\text{yes} \mid N) = .31 \qquad \text{and} \qquad P(\text{yes} \mid SN) = .69.$$

The discussion regarding Fig. 6 concerns the effect of the subject's criterion. An important point to remember is that all of the points on the

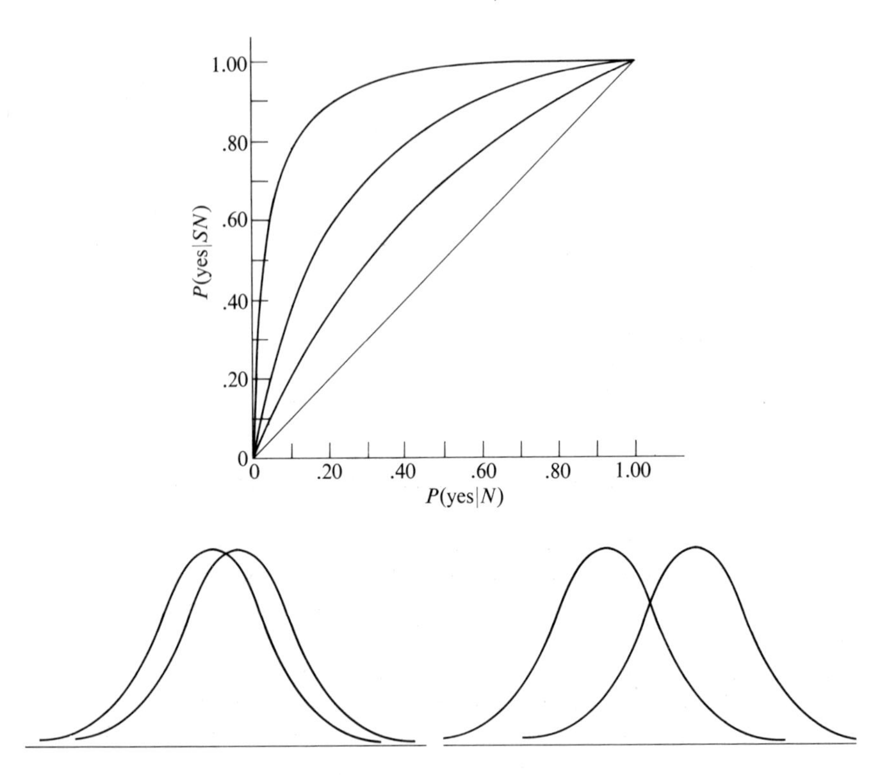

Fig. 7. Three *ROC*'s and distributions of log *LR* corresponding to the worst and best detection.

ROC represent performance in detecting the same signal relative to noise. When we take into account the subject's ability to shift his criterion, we see that detection of a signal cannot be represented by a single number. It involves an entire function.

The ability of a subject to detect the signal determines the distance between the *ROC* and the line representing chance performance. The diagonal line in Fig. 7 is called the chance line. Figure 7 shows *ROC*'s for three signals that are detectable to different degrees. The middle curve is the one shown in Fig. 6 where the means of f_{SN} and f_N differ by an amount equal to σ. The curve closest to the chance line in Fig. 7 is based on distributions whose means differ by $.5\sigma$; these distributions are drawn in the lower left panel of Fig. 7. Recall that the distributions of log *LR* that are close together indicate that the signal is hard to detect. Stimuli that are produced with the signal plus noise are very similar to the stimuli that are produced with noise alone. This produces many values of log *LR* near zero, and performance is near the chance line. The *ROC* farthest from the chance line is taken from the distributions in the lower right panel of Fig. 7, where the means of the distributions differ by 2σ. The signal is quite easy to detect in this situation. Stimuli produced when the signal is present are not likely to be confused with stimuli produced with noise alone, which means that log *LR* is usually quite far above zero on *SN* trials and quite far below zero on *N* trials. Then performance is far from the chance line, as the *ROC* shows.

Example 7.9. For distributions of log *LR* that differ by $.5\sigma$ and by 2σ, find $P(\text{yes} \mid N)$ and $P(\text{yes} \mid SN)$ when (a) the criterion is at the mean of f_N, (b) the criterion is midway between the mean of f_N and the mean of f_{SN}, and (c) the criterion is at the mean of f_{SN}.

When the means differ by $.5\sigma$, a criterion at the mean of f_N is $.5\sigma$ below the mean of f_{SN}. Then, from Table C,

$$P(\text{yes} \mid N) = .50, \qquad P(\text{yes} \mid SN) = .69.$$

A criterion midway between the two means is $.25\sigma$ above the mean of f_N and $.25\sigma$ below the mean of f_{SN}. Then

$$P(\text{yes} \mid N) = .40, \qquad P(\text{yes} \mid SN) = .60.$$

And a criterion at the mean of f_{SN} is $.5\sigma$ above the mean of f_N.

$$P(\text{yes} \mid N) = .31, \qquad P(\text{yes} \mid SN) = .50.$$

When the means differ by 2σ, a criterion at the mean of f_N is 2σ below the mean of f_{SN}. Then

$$P(\text{yes} \mid N) = .50, \qquad P(\text{yes} \mid SN) = .98.$$

A criterion midway between the means is σ above the mean of f_N and σ below the mean of f_{SN},

$$P(\text{yes} \mid N) = .16, \qquad P(\text{yes} \mid SN) = .84.$$

And a criterion at the mean of f_{SN} is 2σ above the mean of f_N.

$$P(\text{yes} \mid N) = .02, \qquad P(\text{yes} \mid SN) = .50. \blacksquare$$

In this chapter we have discussed the idea of a theoretical distribution, and we have worked especially with the normal distribution. The present section has presented a theory of choice based on the normal distribution. We have seen how this theory applies to simple choice situations, to detection of differences, and we have analyzed the effect of a response criterion due to motivation and expectations. In the next section we return to the presentation of basic statistical concepts.

7C CORRELATION

When we calculate the mean and the standard deviation of a distribution, we are working with a single set of scores or measurements. The theory of psychological testing uses the coefficient of correlation, and this involves two sets of test scores. Each individual in a group receives two scores. For example, there may be two tests given, or each person may receive a score for achievement which can be compared with his effort. Whatever the scores may represent, there are two scores, x and y, for each individual. The correlation is one measure of how much the two scores are related.

As an example, consider the number of hours spent studying for a test and the score on the test. Suppose that you studied the hours and got the test scores listed below on six psychology quizzes.

Hours studied (x)	7	11	9	6	10	5	($\mu_x = 8$)
Test score (y)	10	15	12	15	18	8	($\mu_y = 13$).

The best way to begin studying these scores is to draw a simple graph called a scatterplot. The graph is shown in Fig. 8. Each dot on the scatterplot represents a single test, with the two numbers x and y for that test determining the dot's location. Looking at the graph, we see a tendency for the scores to be near a line that could be drawn upward and to the right on the graph. This would mean that large amounts of study tended to be associated with relatively high scores on the test.

The coefficient of correlation ρ is a number that tells something about how closely two variables are associated; ρ is always between -1 and $+1$. If x and y are very closely associated, and large values of x go with large

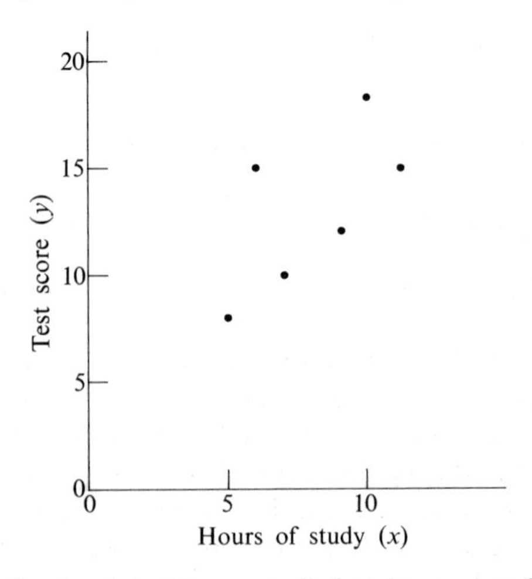

Fig. 8. Scatterplot of hours studied and scores on five tests.

values of y, ρ_{xy} will be close to $+1$. If x and y are very closely associated, but large values of x go with small values of y, ρ_{xy} will be close to -1. If x and y have practically nothing to do with each other, ρ_{xy} will be close to zero.

The first step in calculating the correlation is to obtain the covariance. Like the variance, the covariance depends on the deviations of the scores from the means of the distributions. We begin by calculating each deviation from the mean.

Hours studied $(x - \mu_x)$	-1	$+3$	$+1$	-2	$+2$	-3
Test score $(y - \mu_y)$	-3	$+2$	-1	$+2$	$+5$	-5

Now think about what should occur if the two sets of scores are associated so that large amounts of study go with high test scores. A strong positive association would mean that when the hours of study were above average, the score on that test would be above average also. And if the hours of study were below average for a test, then the score on that test would be below average. Putting this another way, if there is strong positive association between two variables, most of the pairs should give deviation scores with the same sign. If high scores on one variable go with low scores on the other, the pairs of deviation scores will tend to be of opposite sign. And if the two variables are not related at all, there will be a mixture of cases—about as many pairs with the same sign will occur as with the opposite sign.

The next step in calculating the covariance is to obtain the product of each pair of numbers. If the pairs of numbers tend to have like signs, most of the products will be positive. If the pairs of numbers tend to have opposite signs, most of the products will be negative.

The covariance is the mean of the products of the deviation scores. The notation σ_{xy} means "the covariance between x and y."

$$\sigma_{xy} = \frac{\sum(x - \mu_x)(y - \mu_y)}{N}. \tag{7.13}$$

In the small example we are considering,

$$\begin{aligned}\sigma_{xy} &= \tfrac{1}{6}\{(-1)(-3) + (+3)(+2) + (+1)(-1) + (-2)(+2) \\ &\quad + (+2)(+5) + (-3)(-5)\} \\ &= \frac{3 + 6 - 1 - 4 + 10 + 15}{6} = \frac{29}{6} = 4.83.\end{aligned}$$

Like the variance, the covariance is not on a very convenient scale, but it is easy to convert to the correlation coefficient ρ. We obtain ρ by dividing the covariance by the product of the standard deviations of the two distributions.

$$\rho_{xy} = \sigma_{xy}/\sigma_x\sigma_y. \tag{7.14}$$

For the small example we have been considering, the variance of the test scores was calculated in Example 4.4. The standard deviation is

$$\sigma_y = \sqrt{11.3} = 3.36.$$

The standard deviation of the number of hours of study is

$$\sigma_x = 2.16.$$

Therefore, the correlation coefficient is

$$\sigma_{xy} = \frac{4.83}{(2.16)(3.36)} = \frac{4.83}{7.26} = .67.$$

The correlation coefficient is always between -1 and $+1$. A correlation coefficient of $+1$ between two variables would mean that they were perfectly related by a formula like

$$y = mx + b, \tag{7.15}$$

with m a positive number so that large values of x correspond to large values of y. An example is shown in the left panel of Fig. 9, where every point is exactly on a straight line drawn upward and to the right.

In the center panel of Fig. 9 there is a scatterplot for a pair of variables which are imperfectly correlated, but which have some noticeable association.

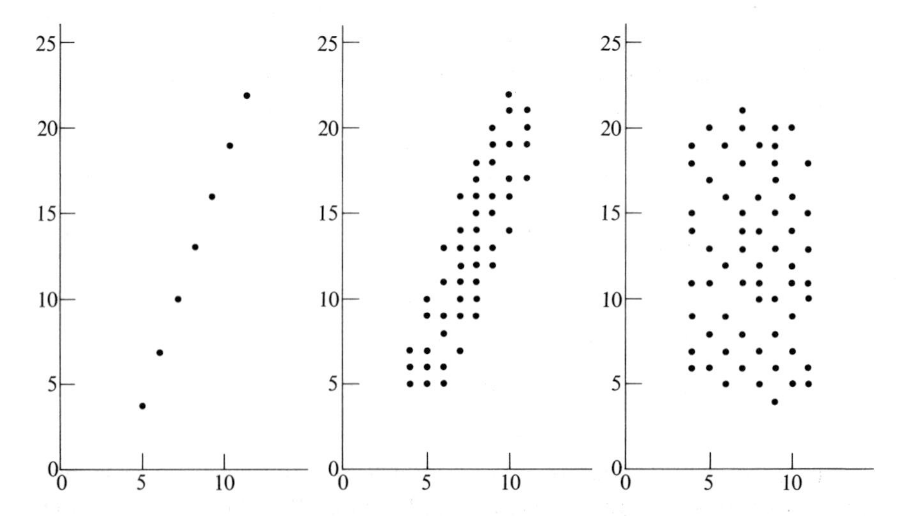

Fig. 9. Scatterplots corresponding to three degrees of correlation.

According to the center panel, if you know that $x = 5$, then you can say that y is between 5 and 10. This narrows things down somewhat, since without the information you can say only that the scores range between 5 and 22 points. However, the prediction is not certain. Another way to think about the concept is to draw or imagine a straight line through the thickest concentration of points in the center panel; this line would be quite close to all the points, but it would not lie on each point as would a comparable line in the left panel.

In the right panel of Fig. 9 the scatterplot shows no association between the two variables—a correlation of zero. In that case knowledge of x is of no help in saying what y might be. If the situation is like that depicted in the right panel, a value of x equal to 5 or 6 is just as likely to go with a high value of y as is a value of x equal to 10 or 11.

The student should realize that the correlation coefficient measures the amount of a special kind of association—a linear relationship. Any function which allowed us to calculate the value of y without error when we knew x would be a "perfect" association between the variables. For example, if x and y were related by

$$y = c \log x \qquad \text{or} \qquad y = rx^3 + sx^2,$$

we could determine y as soon as we knew x. However, to obtain a correlation of 1.0, the relationship between x and y must be a linear function, like that of Eq. (7.15). This is not a serious problem in the research where correlation is used, since the problem is usually to judge whether two variables have a substantial association, rather than to try to determine the exact formula relating the variables. The latter task requires a deeper theoretical inquiry, with attention to exact assumptions about the nature of the process being studied.

To be complete, our discussion of correlation must include one more qualification. The illustrations have involved cases where large values of x correspond to large values of y. As long as we have this condition, the values of ρ range from 0 to $+1$, and we have positive correlation. Of course, it is possible for things to go the other way. Large values of x can go with small values of y, a situation which produces a line which goes downward and to the right on a graph. The linear equation for a negative correlation has the form of Eq. (7.15), but with m as a negative number. An example would be the association between hours of study and number of *wrong* answers on a test. If the association is perfect but negative in direction, the correlation coefficient is -1. This is not an important problem, however, because we can always obtain a positive correlation merely by changing the way we score (for example, by counting the correct answers instead of the errors).

In the next chapter, we are concerned with the difference between variables, and the sum of variables, and particularly the variance of the sum or difference. At the end of Chapter 4 we noted that when we add two independent variables the variance of the sum equals the sum of the respective variances [Eq. (4.7)]. If two variables are independent, then their correlation is zero. When we add two variables which are positively correlated, the effect is to increase the variance even more. When y and x are positively correlated, small values of y probably go with small values of x, and similarly for large values. Then when we add each value of y to its corresponding x, there are many cases of adding two small scores and also of adding two large scores. Therefore there is a large frequency of extreme scores, which gives a high variance. On the other hand, if y and x are negatively correlated, most of the large y's are added to small x's, and most of the small y's to large x's, and this produces a relative decrease in the variance. The specific result here is

$$\sigma_{x+y}^2 = \sigma_x^2 + \sigma_y^2 + 2\rho_{xy}\sigma_x\sigma_y,$$

$$\sigma_{x+y} = \sqrt{\sigma_x^2 + \sigma_y^2 + 2\rho_{xy}\sigma_x\sigma_y}. \tag{7.16}$$

Note that the term $\rho_{xy}\sigma_x\sigma_y$ is just the covariance of x and y. So the variance of the sum is equal to the sum of the variances plus two times the covariance.

When we consider the difference between two variables, the effect of the correlation is the opposite. If x and y are correlated positively, large y's often will be subtracted from large x's, and small y's will be subtracted from small x's. This gives a distribution with relatively smaller variance than when small y's are subtracted from large x's and large y's from small x's.

$$\sigma_{x-y}^2 = \sigma_x^2 + \sigma_y^2 - 2\rho_{xy}\sigma_x\sigma_y,$$

$$\sigma_{x-y} = \sqrt{\sigma_x^2 + \sigma_y^2 - 2\rho_{xy}\sigma_x\sigma_y}. \tag{7.17}$$

That is, the variance of the difference is the sum of the variances *minus* two times the covariance.

PROBLEMS

1. Suppose that we have a 12-item list to be memorized, and each item is learned with probability $c = .20$. We have an experiment where each subject studies every item just once. Assuming that the items are independent, what will be the theoretical mean and the standard deviation of the number of items learned per subject? On the average, what proportion of the subjects will learn more than one-half of the items? What proportion will learn fewer than one-fourth of the items? (You will need to use Table 2 in calculating some of these answers.)

2. Regarding Example 7.2, suppose that we use the same tone as the one referred to there, but we present it to each subject until he detects it. Assume that the probability of a detection on each trial is $p = .30$, and that the trials are independent. What will be the mean number of trials per subject? What will be the standard deviation? On the average, what proportion of subjects will receive a number of trials less than $\mu - \sigma$? What proportion will receive more than $\mu + \sigma$?

Table 2

Binomial Distribution with $p = .20$, $N = 12$

k	0	1	2	3	4	5	6	7	8	9	10	11	12
$P(y = k)$	.069	.206	.283	.236	.133	.053	.015	.003	.001	.000	.000	.000	.000

* **3.** In a normal distribution, if $\mu = 45$ and $\sigma = 5$, what proportion of the distribution is below 40.0? What proportion is above 52.5? What score is above .76 of the distribution? What score is below .10 of the distribution?

4. The mean of a normal distribution is $\mu = 120$, and .16 of the distribution is below 100. What is σ? What proportion of the distribution is below 110? What score is below .90 of the distribution?

5. The standard deviation of a normal distribution is 16 and .84 of the distribution is below 116. What is μ? What proportion of the distribution is between 84 and 116? What proportion is between 68 and 132?

6. In a normal distribution, .31 of the distribution is below 7.5 and .93 of the distribution is below 9.5. What are μ and σ?

7. In the choice theory of Eqs. (7.8) and (7.9), assume that there are three distributions of response strengths, each with $\sigma = 1.414$. If $\mu_1 = 5.0$, $\mu_2 = 4.0$, and $\mu_3 = 2.0$, calculate the probabilities of choice between all three pairs of alternatives.

8. If three alternative responses are offered in pairs, and $P(A_1 \mid A_1, A_2) = .38$ and $P(A_2 \mid A_2, A_3) = .76$ calculate $P(A_1 \mid A_1, A_3)$ using Eqs. (7.8) and (7.9).

▸ **9.** The choice probabilities calculated using the theory of Eqs. (7.8) and (7.9) do not agree exactly with the theory of Chapter 2, but they are so close that it is practically impossible to tell the difference between the theories in experiments. For example, given the values of $P(A_1 \mid A_1, A_2)$ and $P(A_2 \mid A_2, A_3)$ in Example 7.7, show that the theory of Chapter 2 implies that $P(A_1 \mid A_1, A_3) = .75$ (compared with .76 obtained with Eqs. (7.8) and (7.9) of this chapter). As further examples, use values of $P(A_1 \mid A_1, A_2)$ and $P(A_2 \mid A_2, A_3)$ from Problems 7 and 8 and calculate values of $P(A_1 \mid A_1, A_3)$ according to the theory of Chapter 2.

▸ **10.** Suppose that response strengths can take only integer values, and the distributions of response strengths are geometric; that is,

$$P[v(A_i) = N] = (1 - \alpha_i)^n \alpha_i \quad (N = 0, 1, \ldots).$$

When the alternatives are A_1 and A_2, assume that a subject chooses A_1 whenever

$v(A_1) > v(A_2)$; he chooses A_2 whenever $v(A_1) < v(A_2)$; and whenever $v(A_1) = v(A_2)$, he chooses a response randomly so that $P(A_1) = .50$. Assume that $v(A_1)$ and $v(A_2)$ are independent. Show that

$$P(A_1 \mid A_1, A_2) = \frac{\alpha_2 - .50\alpha_1\alpha_2}{\alpha_1 + \alpha_2 - \alpha_1\alpha_2}.$$

Hint: use the fact from elementary calculus that if $|x| \leq 1$,

$$\sum_{i=0}^{m-1} x^i = \frac{1 - x^m}{1 - x}.$$

Calculate $P(A_1 \mid A_1, A_2)$ if (a) $\alpha_1 = .20$, $\alpha_2 = .30$; and if (b) $\alpha_1 = .50$, $\alpha_2 = .25$.

11. Suppose that when a subject lifts a weight in the neighborhood of 100 gm the psychological magnitude has a normal distribution with mean equal to the physical weight and the standard deviation corresponding to 6 gm. If judgments are made according to Eq. (7.10), calculate points on the psychometric function obtained when weights of 102, 104, 106, 108, and 110 gm are compared with a standard of 100 gm. What comparison weight is greater than 100 gm by a *jnd*?

▸ **12.** Weber's Law says that if two stimuli, H_1 and H_0, are different by a *jnd*, then we have the ratio

$$H_1/H_0 = k,$$

where k is a constant, independent of H_0. Assume the theory of difference detection given in this chapter, and show that Weber's Law is satisfied if the standard deviation of psychological effects of a stimulus in the neighborhood of H_0 is proportional to the magnitude of H_0, that is,

$$\sigma = cH_0,$$

where c is a constant. Show that if this is true, then k, the Weber ratio, equals

$$k = 1 + .96c.$$

13. In the theory of signal detectability, assume that the mean of f_{SN} and the mean of f_N differ by 1.5σ. Find points on the *ROC* corresponding to criteria from $.5\sigma$ below the mean of f_N to $.5\sigma$ above the mean of f_{SN}, in steps of $.5\sigma$.

14. Like the variance, the correlation is not affected by a constant change in either or both of the variables involved. Suppose that a student worked for three extra hours on each test and got five extra points on each test, compared with the student described by Fig. 8. Then his scores would be:

Score	15	20	17	20	23	13
Hours study	10	14	12	9	13	8

Show that the deviation scores are exactly like those on p. 245. (Since we calculate the correlation from the deviation scores, this means that the correlation will be the same, too.)

* **15.** Draw a scatterplot and calculate the correlation for each set of scores below:

(a)	x	1	3	6	8	10
	y	2	5	6	9	10
(b)	x	2	3	5	7	10
	y	3	8	5	8	7
(c)	x	1	3	6	8	10
	y	7	3	9	4	6

16. Change one pair of scores in set (a) of Problem 15, so that the correlation is between those obtained for (a) and (b) in that problem. Change a pair of scores in set (c) to yield a correlation between those obtained for (b) and (c).

17. The idea involved in Eqs. (7.16) and (7.17) can be illustrated by a simple example. Consider two variables x and y, each of which can take the values 0 and 1. If they are positively correlated, they will tend to have the same value. Suppose that

$$P(x = 1, y = 1) = .40, \qquad P(x = 1, y = 0) = .10,$$
$$P(x = 0, y = 1) = .10, \qquad P(x = 0, y = 0) = .40,$$

Calculate the variance of $x + y$ and of $x - y$.

If x and y are negatively correlated, they will tend to have different values. Calculate the variance of $x + y$ and $x - y$ if

$$P(x = 1, y = 1) = .10, \qquad P(x = 1, y = 0) = .40,$$
$$P(x = 0, y = 1) = .40, \qquad P(x = 0, y = 0) = .10.$$

The student should compare the answers with those of Problem 7 of Chapter 4.

CHAPTER EIGHT

Psychological Testing

The orientation of this chapter is quite different from that of the earlier chapters. Until now, we have been working on problems involving general processes. We have tried to understand something about what goes on when a person memorizes an association or solves a problem. We have used theories to try to describe processes that occur generally, and if our theories are correct, we understand something about the way people go about making judgments and choices and memorizing associations and solving problems. In other words, our work until now has dealt with ways in which people are alike.

When a psychological test is used, the purpose is usually to find out about differences among individuals. People may make choices in more or less the same way, but they make different choices because they have different values and goals and attitudes. Memorizing and problem solving may go on in similar ways for all people, but some people learn faster than others because individuals differ in their ability and motivation to learn.

Many practical problems make it important to measure differences among people. For example, imagine that you are in charge of the admissions office of a college or university. One of the purposes of a college is to provide education for young people, and many Americans agree that educational opportunities should be provided for as many people as possible. But we know that some people find it easy to learn and understand the things that are taught in colleges while others find it difficult or impossible. One way to find out whether a student can succeed in college is to admit him to college and see whether he succeeds. As an admissions officer, you would be happy to do that if the college had unlimited classroom facilities and plenty of teachers. However, it does not, and decisions have to be made about how to use the available facilities. If you admitted every student who applied, you would know that many students would not succeed, and the facilities used by those students could not be used for teaching more advanced students who have more ability and desire to learn and understand college material.

What you need is some way of knowing whether a student has a reasonable chance of succeeding in college before he is admitted. Then you can admit those students who have a reasonable chance of success, and the buildings and teachers can be used more efficiently. Psychological tests are used to measure college ability. The measurement is far from perfect, but it is accurate enough to be useful. Using the results of the tests, an admissions officer can select students who probably will be able to learn and understand well enough to succeed, and this results in a more efficient use of expensive resources.

College entrance exams represent just one of the many uses of psychological tests. They are one form of the aptitude test, which tests a person's ability to succeed in some kind of training program. Other organizations that use aptitude tests include industrial and commercial corporations which use aptitude tests to find out which applicants for a job are likely to succeed in training programs for the job. Military organizations use aptitude tests to find out which servicemen are likely to succeed in training programs for special technical assignments or in officer training.

Psychological tests are also used to measure characteristics other than aptitudes. In Chapter 2 we discussed two ways of testing general motivational tendencies. Other kinds of personality traits such as social adjustment, authoritarianism, dogmatism, and tendencies toward some neurotic and psychotic disorders have all been measured with varying degrees of success using psychological tests. One test[1] includes a great number of questions designed to measure a person's interests in a wide variety of activities. This test is used mainly in vocational counseling. The pattern of a person's interests can be compared with typical interest patterns of men in various occupations. The idea is that if a person is interested in most of the same things as others who are happy and successful in a certain kind of work, the chances are good that he also will be happy in that kind of work.

Our main purpose in this book is to present some general theoretical ideas about the nature of test scores. Psychological tests are widely used, widely criticized, and seldom understood. We will not try to evaluate any specific kinds of psychological test in detail. Instead, we will discuss tests in a general way and try to understand some of the ways in which specific tests can be evaluated.

8A TRUE SCORES AND ERRORS

We give a psychological test because we want to measure some aspect of a person's ability or personality. However, the score that a person gets probably will not be exactly accurate as a description of his ability or the extent

[1] The Strong Vocational Interest Blank, developed by E. K. Strong, Jr., *Vocational Interests of Men and Women*. Stanford: Stanford University Press, 1943.

to which he has the personality trait being measured. Everyone realizes that a person's performance on an aptitude test may be somewhat higher or lower than his ability would warrant. If a person takes a test when he is tired or ill, he may not be able to work as efficiently or understand as quickly as he should, and his score will probably appear to show less ability than he has. Or a person may be lucky at guessing correct answers and get a score that appears to show more ability than he really has. Scores on tests of attitudes, motives, and interests are also affected by accidental factors such as personal interpretations or misunderstanding of questions, momentary feelings, or things that have happened to the person that cause him to react in a different way than he usually would.

The theory of psychological tests is based on the ideas of a true score and an error of measurement. In a test of ability, a person's true score is his real ability to perform on the test items. It is the score the person would get if his performance had not been influenced by any accidental or temporary factors such as fatigue or luck in guessing. The true score is called t. Accidental and temporary factors produce errors of measurement. The score that a person gets may be somewhere above or somewhere below his true score. The error is called e, and it is equal to the difference between the score a person receives and his true score. Let a person's score be x; then

$$e = x - t.$$

If accidental or temporary factors produce a score that is higher than the person should have, then e is a positive number. If the person's score is below his true score, then e is a negative number, and there is a negative error of measurement. In either case, the score a person receives is

$$x = t + e. \tag{8.1}$$

That is, the person's score is somewhere above or below his true score, depending on whether the accidental and temporary factors in the situation produce a positive or negative error of measurement.

Now imagine that there are many different versions of a test of some ability, and a person takes all of these tests at different times and in different circumstances. We assume that the tests are all equally difficult, so his true score t is the same for all of the tests. But the tests vary in the exact content of the questions and the way the questions are worded, so that sometimes the person could give correct answers to questions he did not really know, and at other times he would be misled by confusing items and miss questions he really knew. Also, sometimes he would feel extremely good and work unusually efficiently and at other times he would feel tired and overlook things in the test. In addition, he would sometimes make a lot of lucky guesses and other times most of his guesses would be wrong. Because of all these factors, and others as well, the person's scores on many equivalent tests would not all be the same. He would usually receive a score quite close to his true score t, but sometimes there would be a positive error of measurement giving $x > t$, and at other times there would be a negative error of measurement giving $x < t$. In other words, the scores that a person would get on many different versions of a test would have a distribution such as the one shown in Fig. 1.

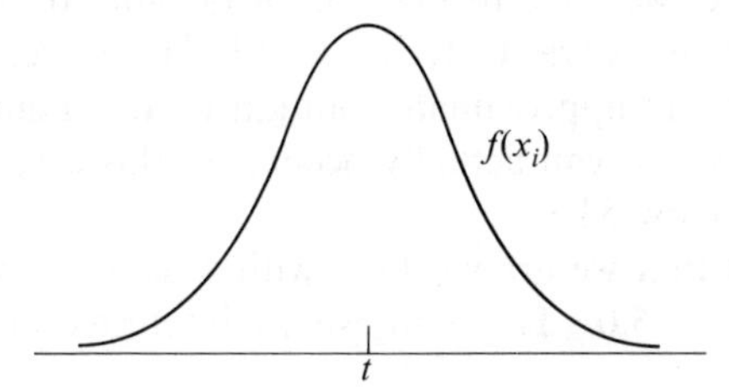

Fig. 1. Hypothetical distribution of scores for one individual on many equivalent tests.

The distribution in Fig. 1 is labeled $f(x_i)$, indicating that it is the distribution for a single individual. In many situations, we assume that this distribution is normal, with its mean equal to the person's true score t, and some standard deviation σ_e. This assumption is reasonable when the measurement error e on a particular test is probably produced by a fairly large number of accidental and situational factors. Then the value of e is probably the average of several quantities, some positive and others negative. We mentioned in Chapter 7 that when we obtain the average of a large number of random variables, we usually get a normal distribution. The assumption that the mean equals t amounts to saying that the accidental factors in the test situations are just as likely to produce a score higher than t as they are to produce a score below t.

The standard deviation σ_e is a basic quantity in test theory, and it is called the *standard error of measurement*. The value of σ_e provides one important means of evaluating a test. If σ_e is large, the scores on the test are influenced significantly by accidental and temporary factors in the situation where the test is given. If σ_e is small, accidental and temporary factors do not influence the test scores very much. Since we are interested in measuring the person's true ability or personality characteristics, we would like to use a test that has as small a value of σ_e as possible.

Example 8.1. Suppose that a person takes a test that measures his need for achievement. Suppose that his true score for this test is 60, and that the standard error of measurement for this test is 5. What is the probability that he will receive a score lower than 55? What is the probability that his score will be no more than two points different from his true score?

In this example we have to take account of the fact that only whole numbers can occur as scores. This problem will be involved in many of the examples and exercises in this chapter. The normal distribution does not apply strictly unless all scores are possible. However, when a test has a fairly large number of items, the normal distribution still can give a reasonably accurate approximation.

In the example, we have to find the probability of a score lower than 55—that is, one of the scores 0, 1, 2, . . . , 53, 54. Scores of 55, 56, . . . are in the other set. As an approximate solution we use a cutoff point halfway between two scores that can actually occur. In this case we find the probability of a score below 54.5.

Keep in mind that we are working with a distribution with $\mu_{x_i} = t = 60.0$, and $\sigma_{x_i} = \sigma_e = 5.0$. The score we are interested in is

$$54.5 = 60.0 - 5.5 = \mu_{x_i} - 1.1\sigma_{x_i}.$$

Using Table C of the Appendix, we obtain

$$P(x_i < 54.5) = .14.$$

In other words, the chance of receiving a score lower than 55 is about one in seven.

For the second question, we are interested in the scores that are different from the true score of 60 by two points or less. This set of scores is 58, 59, 60, 61, and 62. We use 57.5 and 62.5 as cutoff points.

$$57.5 = 60.0 - 2.5 = \mu_{x_i} - 0.5\sigma_{x_i}; \qquad P(x_i < 57.5) = .31.$$
$$62.5 = 60.0 + 2.5 = \mu_{x_i} + 0.5\sigma_{x_i}; \qquad P(x_i < 62.5) = .69.$$
$$P(57.5 < x_i < 62.5) = .69 - .31 = .38.$$

In other words, the chance of receiving a score as close as two points to the true score is about four in ten. ▌

To fix the idea of the standard error of measurement we consider two situations that were studied in earlier chapters. In Chapter 2 we studied measurement of a person's values for specific choice alternatives. Here we consider the measurement situation that is easiest to analyze. Suppose that we want to measure a person's relative attractions to two alternatives—they might be two kinds of food or two kinds of entertainment or any other pair of alternatives. We call the alternatives A_1 and A_2. Now suppose that the person likes A_1 four times as much as he likes A_2; that is,

$$v(A_1)/v(A_2) = 4.0.$$

Recall from Chapter 2 that we can measure the relative response strengths by observing a large number of choices from a set of alternatives.

Also recall that the measured response strengths involve an arbitrary constant, so that we measure

$$v(A_1) = KP(A_1 \mid A_1, A_2).$$

We can observe a proportion of A_1 choices; thus in this situation the true score is the true value of $P(A_1 \mid A_1, A_2)$. In the present case,

$$t = P(A_1 \mid A_1, A_2) = \frac{v(A_1)/v(A_2)}{1.0 + [v(A_1)/v(A_2)]} = .80.$$

Now suppose that we observe the person's choices between A_1 and A_2 40 different times, and we can assume that all the choices are independent. The person will choose A_1 some number of times out of these 40 choices. In this problem, we are imagining that we know the true value of

$$P(A_1 \mid A_1, A_2),$$

so we should expect about 32 A_1 choices. However, we should not be surprised if the number of choices is slightly different from 32; it could easily be 31 or 33, or 30 or 34, or even 29 or 35. As a matter of fact, the number of choices of A_1 will have the binomial distribution, discussed at the beginning of Chapter 7. Let n_1 be the number of choices of A_1; the distribution of n_1 is given by Eq. (7.4).

$$P(n_1 = j) = \binom{40}{j} (.80)^j (.20)^{40-j}.$$

The mean of this distribution is given by Eq. (7.5),

$$\mu_{n_1} = (.80)(40) = 32.0;$$

and the standard deviation is given by Eq. (7.6),

$$\sigma_{n_1} = \sqrt{(40)(.80)(.20)} = 2.53.$$

In the situation we are working with, our measurement is based on the value of n_1. But the number we actually use is the proportion of choices, $n_1/40$. The proportion will also have a distribution; its value probably will be between 29/40 and 35/40—that is, between .72 and .88. A person's score x_i is equal to the observed proportion $n_1/40$. The mean and standard deviation of the distribution of x_i can be found using Eq. (4.4) from Chapter 4.

$$\mu_{x_i} = (1/40)\mu_{n_1} = 32/40 = .80, \qquad \sigma_{x_i} = (1/40)\sigma_{n_1} = 2.53/40 = .06.$$

The distribution of x_i will be quite close to the normal. (It would not be if we had only two or three observations, but 40 observations are adequate to produce a close approximation.) Therefore, we have a situation like the one described earlier for test scores, except that here the scores are not restricted to whole numbers. The score a person attains is the proportion x_i. We know there is a true score t, but the value of x_i that we observe may be somewhat higher or lower than t. The mean of the distribution of x_i equals the true score

$$\mu_{x_i} = t = .80.$$

And the distribution of scores is approximately normal with standard deviation equal to the standard error of estimate

$$\sigma_{x_i} = \sigma_e = .06.$$

When we have observed a score x, we can transform it to units of response strength using the arbitrary constant K.

$$v(A_1) = KP(A_1 \mid A_1, A_2) = Kx.$$

This part of the problem is not important for our purposes here. Since we can let K be anything we like, we assume that $K = 1$ which means that the score x is our measure of the response strength of A_1.

Example 8.2. In the situation described above, what is the probability of obtaining a score farther than .05 away from the true score of .80? What is the probability of being within .01 of the true score?

For the first part, we are interested in the scores .75 and .85.

$$.75 = .80 - .05 = \mu_{x_i} - .83\sigma_{x_i}; \qquad P(x_i < .75) = .20.$$
$$.85 = .80 + .05 = \mu_{x_i} + .83\sigma_{x_i}; \qquad P(x_i < .85) = .80.$$

Then the probability of a score farther away than .05 is

$$P(x_i < .75) + P(x_i > .85) = .40.$$

In other words, the chances are about four in ten that the measurement of response strength would be inaccurate by more than .05.

For the second part, we are interested in the scores .79 and .81.

$$.79 = .80 - .01 = \mu_{x_i} - .17\sigma_{x_i}; \qquad P(x_i < .79) = .43.$$
$$.81 = .80 + .01 = \mu_{x_i} + .17\sigma_{x_i}; \qquad P(x_i < .81) = .57.$$

Then the probability of a score between .79 and .81 is

$$P(.79 < x_i < .81) = P(x_i < .81) - P(x_i < .79) = .14.$$

In other words, there is only about one chance in seven of getting a score within .01 of the true score. ▮

The illustration shows that even by observing a fairly large number of choices we cannot be very confident in the measurements of response strength that we obtain. The accuracy of measurement can be increased by taking a much larger set of observations. In Chapter 2 we noted that it is feasible to measure response strengths in this way if we use animals as subjects. In the experiment where rats chose between pairs of foods, the measurements were made using 120 observations per pair of alternatives. The measurements seemed to be accurate to within about .02 of the true values, based on the degree of success in predicting choice probabilities for different sets of alternatives. Of course, the problem of measuring response strengths for human subjects cannot be solved in this way; it would almost always be impossible to obtain hundreds of independent choices by one individual from the same set of alternatives. Therefore, psychologists interested in measuring specific human values have been led to develop more complicated situations, like the gambling experiments described at the end of Chapter 2.

The next situation we use here involves the all-or-none learning model developed in Chapter 5. Suppose that we have a set of 50 items that are ordinarily learned in an all-or-none manner, and we use these items to measure the learning ability of a student. The test would consist of having the person learn the items, and observing the trial on which each item was learned. Then the person's score would be a measurement of c, taken as

$$x_i = 1/\mu_L.$$

Now suppose that the person's true score on these items is $c = .25$. That is, the true probability of learning an item on each trial is .25 for this person. This means that he should have a mean trial of learning somewhere around 4.0. However, we would not expect the mean trial of learning to be exactly 4.0. We should not be surprised by a mean trial of learning as low as 3.5 or as high as 4.5.

Again, as in the case of measuring a person's response strengths, there is a distribution of scores with some mean and standard deviation. With 50 items to observe, the distribution of x_i will be nearly normal, and its mean will be quite close to the true score when $c = .25$.[2] We do not derive the standard error of measurement here; it equals

$$\sigma_{x_i} = \sigma_e = c\sqrt{(1 - c)/N}, \tag{8.2}$$

where N is the number of items.

---

[2] Actually, the mean of the distribution of measurements will not equal the true score exactly in this case. Therefore, we say that the estimate of the true score is biased. It is possible to find an unbiased estimate of the true value of c, but the complications involved are too great to go into here.

Example 8.3. Calculate the standard error of measurement for c when the true value is .25 and we observe the mean trial of learning for 50 items. Assume that the distribution of scores is normal with mean equal to the true value of c. What is the probability of a score within .05 of the true score? within .02 of the true score?

The standard error of measurement is

$$\sigma_e = (.25)\sqrt{.75/50} = .03.$$

We have

$$.20 = \mu_{x_i} - 1.67\sigma_{x_i}; \qquad P(x_i < .20) = .05.$$
$$.30 = \mu_{x_i} + 1.67\sigma_{x_i}; \qquad P(x_i < .30) = .95.$$
$$P(.20 < x_i < .30) = .90.$$

For the second question, we have

$$.23 = \mu_{x_i} - .67\sigma_{x_i}; \qquad P(x_i < .23) = .25.$$
$$.27 = \mu_{x_i} + .67\sigma_{x_i}; \qquad P(x_i < .27) = .75.$$
$$P(.23 < x_i < .27) = .50.$$

In other words, we have nine chances in ten of obtaining a score within .05 of the true score, and one chance in two of obtaining a score within .02 of the true score. ▮

Note that the standard error of measurement is considerably smaller in measuring c than it is in measuring a simple proportion. Every time an item is presented before it is learned we obtain information about c, and with 50 items needing an average of four trials to be learned, we have about 200 observations in the experiment. The standard error of measurement is smaller when we measure c by observing the learning of N items than when we measure a proportion by observing N cases, because in the learning experiment we observe each item until it is learned, thereby obtaining several observations per item. (See Problem 11.)

8B DISTRIBUTION OF TEST SCORES

In Chapter 4 we worked with distributions of scores obtained by groups of people who take a test. In this section we consider such a distribution in a situation where the individuals have different amounts of the aptitude, knowledge, or personality characteristic being tested, and in this analysis we take errors of measurement into account.

In this section, and throughout our discussion of test theory, we make considerable use of two statistical ideas, the variance of a distribution of scores, and the correlation between two sets of scores. We have already worked with both of these ideas, but before we use them in the theory of tests we need to develop a new formula for each of them. In Chapter 4 [Eq. (4.2)] the variance was defined as

$$\sigma_x^2 = [\sum (x - \mu_x)^2]/N.$$

Expanding the squared term, we obtain

$$\sigma_x^2 = \sum (x^2 - 2x\mu_x + \mu_x^2)/N.$$

Recall that there are N separate scores, giving N separate values of x. However, μ_x is a constant because we are considering a single distribution. Therefore, we have

$$\sigma_x^2 = \sum x^2/N - 2\mu_x(\sum x/N) + (N\mu_x^2)/N.$$

The last term has N in the numerator because we are summing across N terms all equal to μ_x^2. Now recall that $\mu_x = \sum x/N$. Then

$$\sigma_x^2 = \sum x^2/N - \mu_x^2.$$

A similar modification can be made of the formula for the covariance. From Eq. (7.13) of Chapter 7,

$$\sigma_{xy} = \frac{\sum (x - \mu_x)(y - \mu_y)}{N}.$$

Expanding the product, we have

$$\begin{aligned}\sigma_{xy} &= \frac{\sum (xy - \mu_y x - \mu_x y + \mu_x \mu_y)}{N} \\ &= \frac{\sum xy}{N} - \mu_y \frac{\sum x}{N} - \mu_x \frac{\sum y}{N} + N\frac{\mu_x \mu_y}{N}; \\ &= \frac{\sum xy}{N} - \mu_x \mu_y.\end{aligned}$$

Recall that the correlation between x and y is

$$\rho_{xy} = \frac{\sigma_{xy}}{\sigma_x \sigma_y}.$$

Also remember that when x and y are independent ρ_{xy} is zero. When x and y are independent, the covariance also is zero. We will use the fact that for independent sets of scores,

$$\sigma_{xy} = 0, \qquad \text{and} \qquad \frac{\sum xy}{N} = \mu_x \mu_y.$$

When a test is given to a group, we assume that each person has a true score, t. The values of t differ, so there is a distribution of the true scores. Most of the characteristics measured with psychological tests probably are quite complex. Intelligence, aptitudes for specific training programs, and personality characteristics are all influenced by many factors, and it is reasonable to suppose that in most groups of people these characteristics have distributions that are approximately normal. We assume, then, that the true scores are distributed normally with mean μ_t and standard deviation σ_t.

The true scores cannot be measured directly because of measurement errors. Recall the earlier assumption,

$$x = t + e,$$

where x is the score obtained by a person, t is his true score, and e is an error of measurement. Now we make an assumption about the errors of measurement for different individuals. We assume that for every person in the group the error of measurement is distributed normally with mean zero and standard deviation σ_e. This assumption has an important implication: the measurement error is independent of the value of the true score. If a person has a high value of t, he is no more likely to have a large or small measurement error than a person whose value of t is small. In other words,

$$\rho_{te} = \sigma_{te} = 0.$$

This means that

$$\sum te/N = \mu_t\mu_e.$$

But we assume that μ_e is zero; therefore,

$$\sum te/N = 0.$$

This equation follows from our assumption that the mean of the distribution of errors is zero, regardless of the value of t. If this assumption is true, positive and negative values of e will cancel each other, on the average, at all values of t.

Now we are ready to work with a distribution of scores. In a test, a person's score x is his true score plus a (positive or negative) error of measurement. The distribution that will be observed is the distribution of x's. This distribution will have some mean μ_x and standard deviation σ_x, and these depend on the distributions of the true scores and of the errors of measurement.

First we derive the mean of the distribution of test scores. We find that μ_x depends only on the mean of the true scores.

$$\mu_x = \sum x/N = [\sum(t + e)]/N = \sum t/N + \sum e/N = \mu_t + \mu_e.$$

But since $\mu_e = 0$, then

$$\mu_x = \mu_t.$$

This is an important result. We ordinarily give a test to each member of a group just once. Because of errors of measurement, the score that any individual receives may be quite inaccurate. But if the test is given to a large group and there are no factors causing μ_e to differ from zero, the information that we obtain about the group mean will probably be quite accurate.

Now we derive the variance and standard deviation of the observed scores. We find that these depend on both σ_t and σ_e.

$$\sigma_x^2 = \frac{\sum(x - \mu_x)^2}{N} = \frac{\sum(t + e - \mu_t)^2}{N}$$

$$= \frac{\sum(t^2 + e^2 + 2te + \mu_t^2 - 2t\mu_t - 2e\mu_t)}{N}$$

$$= \frac{\sum(t^2 - 2t\mu_t + \mu_t^2)}{N} + \frac{\sum e^2}{N} + 2\frac{\sum te}{N} - 2\mu_t\frac{\sum e}{N}.$$

According to our assumptions, $\sum te/N = 0$ and $\sum e/N = \mu_e = 0$; therefore, the last two terms equal zero. The first term equals $\sum(t - \mu_t)^2/N = \sigma_t^2$. The second term remains, but since $\mu_e = 0$, we know that

$$\frac{\sum e^2}{N} = \frac{\sum(e - \mu_e)^2}{N} = \sigma_e^2.$$

Therefore, the mean and the standard deviation of the observed scores are

$$\sigma_x^2 = \sigma_t^2 + \sigma_e^2; \qquad \sigma_x = \sqrt{\sigma_t^2 + \sigma_e^2}. \tag{8.3}$$

Equation (8.3) says that the observed distribution of scores will have more variability than the distribution of true scores because of errors of measurement, and the equation shows how this increased variability depends on the variance of the errors. If measurement is imprecise, σ_e^2 will be large and a fairly great amount of the observed variability will be produced by measurement error. However, if measurement errors are all very small, then σ_e^2 will be close to zero and nearly all of the variability that is observed will be due to differences in true scores among the individuals.

Example 8.4. If a standard test of intelligence[3] is given to a large representative group of American children, the standard deviation of the observed scores is about 16.0 and the standard error of measurement is about 5.0. Calculate the standard deviation of the true scores. If the mean score on the test is 100.0, what proportion of the group have true scores below 80.0? What proportion have true scores above 130.0? What proportion of the

[3] The Stanford-Binet Intelligence Test. A revision of the original test is described by L. M. Terman and M. A. Merrill, *Measuring Intelligence*, Boston: Houghton Mifflin, 1937.

observed scores will be below 80.0? above 130.0? If a person's true score is 120.0, what is the probability that his observed score is above 130.0? What is the probability that his observed score is between 117.0 and 123.0?

From Eq. (8.3),

$$\sigma_t^2 = \sigma_x^2 - \sigma_e^2;$$

then

$$\sigma_t^2 = 256.0 - 25.0 = 231.0;$$

$$\sigma_t = \sqrt{\sigma_t^2} = 15.2.$$

We know that the mean of the true scores equals the mean of the observed scores. Therefore, the true scores are distributed with mean 100.0 and standard deviation 15.2. In this test, scores are not restricted to whole numbers, so we need not worry about setting up artificial cut points between scores.

$$80.0 = 100.0 - 20.0 = \mu_t - 1.32\sigma_t; \qquad P(t < 80.0) = .094.$$

$$130.0 = 100.0 + 30.0 = \mu_t + 1.97\sigma_t; \qquad P(t > 130.0) = .025.$$

The observed scores are distributed with mean 100.0 and standard deviation 16.0.

$$80.0 = 100.0 - 20.0 = \mu_x - 1.25\sigma_x; \qquad P(x < 80.0) = .106.$$

$$130.0 = 100.0 + 30.0 = \mu_x + 1.88\sigma_x; \qquad P(x > 130.0) = .030.$$

These calculations show one of the effects of the variation produced by errors of measurement. About 10.6% of the population will have test scores below 80.0 and about 3.0% will have scores above 130.0. However, the percentages of true scores in these extreme ranges are somewhat smaller—9.4% and 2.5%. Of course, if the errors of measurement were larger (that is, if σ_e were larger than 5.0), the discrepancies between the distribution of true scores and the distribution of observed scores would be greater.

In the last part of this problem, we need to think about the hypothetical distribution of scores a person would get if he took a large number of equivalent tests many times. For the person in the problem, this hypothetical distribution has a mean of $\mu_{x_i} = t = 120.0$ and a standard deviation of $\sigma_{x_i} = \sigma_e = 5.0$.

$$130.0 = 120.0 + 10.0 = \mu_{x_i} + 2.0\sigma_{x_i}; \qquad P(x_i > 130.0) = .023.$$

$$117.0 = 120.0 - 3.0 = \mu_{x_i} - 0.6\sigma_{x_i};$$

$$123.0 = 120.0 + 3.0 = \mu_{x_i} + 0.6\sigma_{x_i};$$

$$P(117.0 < x_i < 123.0) = P(x_i < 123.0) - P(x_i < 117.0) = .45. \blacksquare$$

It is important to distinguish clearly among the three distributions. One is the distribution of true scores in a group of people. The mean μ_t is the average of the real abilities or real amounts of a personality characteristic as it is measured by a test, and the standard deviation σ_t depends on the amount of variability in the measured characteristic within the group being tested. A second kind of distribution applies to each individual, and describes a hypothetical set of scores that he would obtain on a large number of equivalent tests. The distribution for each individual has a mean $\mu_{x_i} = t$, his true score, and a standard deviation $\sigma_{x_i} = \sigma_e$, the standard error of measurement. Finally, there is the distribution of scores that are actually obtained, with mean μ_x and standard deviation σ_x.

8C RELIABILITY: USING EQUIVALENT TESTS TO MEASURE σ_e

We have worked with the standard error of measurement in some detail, including analysis of its effect on a distribution of test scores. It should be clear that the size of the standard error of measurement provides one important criterion for evaluating a test. If σ_e is small, the characteristic measured by the test is measured quite precisely. If σ_e is large, measurement is imprecise because scores are influenced by accidental and temporary factors to a great extent.

This section deals with the problem of measuring the standard error of measurement. In our discussion we have described σ_e as the standard deviation of a hypothetical distribution of scores a person would obtain taking a large number of equivalent tests. We do not actually give several equivalent tests to a single group of individuals for several reasons. One reason is practical; it would be hard to construct a large number of tests of equal difficulty, and it would be expensive to give them all to a single group of individuals. A second reason is that if one person took many tests of the same kind, the practice on the early tests probably would affect his performance on the later tests, so the tests would not really be equally difficult for him.

Although it is unreasonable to try to give a large number of equivalent tests to one person, it is quite reasonable to construct two equivalent tests and administer them to one person. There are several ways of setting up equivalent tests, but the following will be a sufficient illustration. Suppose that we want to measure the standard error of measurement for a certain test. We make up a new form of the test, and we give the original test (Form 1) and the new test (Form 2) to the same individuals. The new form must be as similar to the original in content and difficulty as possible, and it must be the same length. For example, if Form 1 includes problems requiring arithmetic calculations, the new form could include problems of the same kind but with different numerical values. If there were no obvious way to construct equivalent items, it would be necessary to carry out an experiment using a large number of items and select a set which turned out to be about equal in difficulty to those in the original test.

When we give both forms of the test to a large group of individuals, we obtain two distributions of scores, one for each form, and each distribution has some mean and standard deviation. If the test forms are really equivalent, the distributions will be the same for the two forms. The mean and standard deviation of the scores on Form 1 will be the same as the mean and standard deviation of the scores on Form 2. In our discussion here, we assume equivalence of the forms, and we let μ_x and σ_x stand for the (equal) mean and standard deviation of the two distributions.

Each person who takes the two forms will receive two scores x_{1_i} and x_{2_i}. We assume that the person has a single true score t for both tests, but in each test there is an error of measurement that increases or decreases his score by some amount so that

$$x_{1_i} = t + e_1, \qquad x_{2_i} = t + e_2.$$

The idea can be visualized by looking back at Fig. 1. If a person took a large number of equivalent tests, his scores would have a distribution like the one pictured with mean $\mu_{x_i} = t$ and standard deviation $\sigma_{x_i} = \sigma_e$. In the situation we are describing, he takes two equivalent tests. His scores would be represented by two points on the base line. He might get two scores near his true score t, or he might get one score above t and the other below t, or he might get both scores above t or both scores below t.

We make an important assumption about the measurement errors e_1 and e_2. We assume that they are independent. Remember that any measurement error is caused by an accident or some temporary aspect of the situation. The assumption of independent measurement errors is that the accidental features of the two test situations are independent. For example, a person's score could be increased accidentally by the wording of a few questions that made it easy for him to guess the correct answers. The independence assumption says that if this happened in Form 1, there would be no reason to expect it to happen in Form 2, but there also would be no reason to expect it not to happen.

Example 8.5. A person has a true score of 80.5 on a test where the standard error of measurement is 3.0. The obtained scores are restricted to whole numbers. The person takes two equivalent forms of the test, and the errors of measurement are independent. What is the probability that (a) both of his scores are below 80.5? (b) one score is below 80.5 and the other is above 80.5? (c) the first score is below 76 and the second is 81 or higher? (d) both scores are in the range from 78 to 83?

For (a), note that the probability of a score below the mean is

$$P(x_{1_i} < 80.5) = P(x_{2_i} < 80.5) = .50.$$

Since the two errors are independent, we find the probability of the two results by multiplying the two separate probabilities.

$$P(x_{1_i} < 80.5 \quad \text{and} \quad x_{2_i} < 80.5) = (.50)(.50) = .25.$$

The situation is just like calculating the probability of getting tails on two successive tosses of a coin.

For (b) we can get the outcome in two ways; either have $x_{1_i} < 80.5$ and $x_{2_i} > 80.5$, or have $x_{1_i} > 80.5$ and $x_{2_i} < 80.5$. We have

$$P(x_{1_i} < 80.5 \quad \text{and} \quad x_{2_i} > 80.5) = (.50)(.50) = .25,$$
$$P(x_{1_i} > 80.5 \quad \text{and} \quad x_{2_i} < 80.5) = (.50)(.50) = .25.$$

Then the probability of having either score below 80.5 and the other above 80.5 is

$$.25 + .25 = .50.$$

For (c), we need to work with the score

$$75.5 = 80.5 - 5.0 = \mu_{x_i} - 1.67\sigma_{x_i}; \qquad P(x_{1_i} < 75.5) = .048.$$

We also know that

$$P(x_{2_i} > 80.5) = .50.$$

Therefore,

$$P(x_{1_i} < 75.5 \quad \text{and} \quad x_{2_i} > 80.5) = (.048)(.50) = .024.$$

For (d), we work with the scores

$$77.5 = \mu_{x_i} - 1.0\sigma_{x_i}; \qquad P(x_{1_i} < 77.5) = .16.$$
$$83.5 = \mu_{x_i} + 1.0\sigma_{x_i}; \qquad P(x_{1_i} < 83.5) = .84.$$
$$P(77.5 < x_{1_i} < 83.5) = .84 - .16 = .68.$$

Since x_{1_i} and x_{2_i} have the same distribution,

$$P(77.5 < x_{2_i} < 83.5) = .68.$$

Then

$$P(77.5 < x_{1_i} < 83.5 \quad \text{and} \quad 77.5 < x_{2_i} < 83.5) = (.68)(.68) = .46. \blacksquare$$

We have talked about giving two equivalent forms of the same test to a group of individuals, and obtaining two scores x_{1_i} and x_{2_i} for each individual. The results of the study consist of two distributions of scores, one obtained with each form of the test. The distributions will have the same mean and standard deviation

$$\mu_{x_1} = \mu_{x_2} = \mu_x, \qquad \sigma_{x_1} = \sigma_{x_2} = \sigma_x.$$

A measurement of σ_e is obtained by finding the correlation between these two sets of scores $\rho_{x_1x_2}$.

The correlation leads to a measurement of σ_e because it measures the amount of consistency between the two sets of measurements. If σ_e is small, the two sets of scores will be very consistent, and $\rho_{x_1x_2}$ will be close to 1.0. But if σ_e is large, there will be a great deal of inconsistency, and $\rho_{x_1x_2}$ will be lower. Look back at Fig. 9 in Chapter 7, which shows scatterplots corresponding to three amounts of correlation. If every person got exactly the same score on both tests, the scatterplot would resemble that in the left panel of Fig. 9 and the value of $\rho_{x_1x_2}$ would be 1.0. However, we know that many individuals will not get the same score on both tests. A person who scored, say, 50 points on Form 1 might score a few more than 50 points on Form 2, or he might score a few less than 50 points on Form 2. This means that a scatterplot of scores on the two test forms actually would look more like the center or the right panel of Fig. 9. In general, greater influence of measurement errors on the scores will produce greater inconsistency between the two sets of scores, and hence a lower correlation.

A nonpsychological example can help in understanding the relationship here. Suppose that you had a large number of boxes and you had the job of measuring their lengths. The boxes are numbered, and you measure each box with a ruler. If you are very careful, you will have very little measurement error. But if you are careless (say, in laying the ruler across the boxes at different angles) your measurements will not be accurate. You could check the accuracy of your measurements by going through the whole set a second time, and comparing the two sets of results. First, suppose that you were very careful. Then the two measurements of each box would agree very closely, and there would be a very high correlation between the two sets of measurements. But if you were careless, there would be many cases where the two measurements of a box disagreed. Then if you made a scatterplot of the two sets of measurements, the points would not fall exactly on a straight line and the correlation would be somewhat less than 1.0.

Table 1

Two Hypothetical Tests
Each Given Twice

Person	Test *A*			Test *B*		
	x_1	x_2	$(x_1 - \mu_x)(x_2 - \mu_x)$	x_1	x_2	$(x_1 - \mu_x)(x_2 - \mu_x)$
1	20	21	380	20	29	220
2	30	29	110	30	21	190
3	40	40	0	40	50	0
4	51	50	110	51	60	220
5	59	60	380	59	40	0

Example 8.6. Table 1 shows the results of giving two forms of two different hypothetical tests to a group of five individuals. In both tests, the scores on both Form 1 and Form 2 have mean and standard deviation

$$\mu_x = 40.0, \qquad \sigma_x = 14.1.$$

Note that in Test *A* each person had two scores that were very close together, a result that would occur if the test had a very small standard error of measurement. However, the scores on Test *B* were much less consistent, and this would happen if the test had a large standard error of measurement. Calculate the values of $\rho_{x_1x_2}$ for both of these tests.

The table includes the values of $(x_1 - \mu_x)(x_2 - \mu_x)$, needed to calculate the covariance. Recall that the covariance is

$$\sigma_{x_1x_2} = \frac{\sum(x_1 - \mu_x)(x_2 - \mu_x)}{N},$$

which for Test *A* is

$$\sigma_{x_1x_2} = 190.$$

The correlation is the covariance divided by $\sigma_{x_1}\sigma_{x_2}$, but when the two standard deviations are equal we have

$$\rho_{x_1x_2} = \frac{\sigma_{x_1x_2}}{\sigma_x^2} = \frac{190.0}{199.0} = .95.$$

The correlation is close to 1.0, as we expect when the scores are very consistent.

For Test *B*, the scores are much less consistent.

$$\sigma_{x_1x_2} = 126.0; \qquad \rho_{x_1x_2} = \frac{126.0}{199.0} = .63.$$

The greater inconsistency in the scores results in a lower correlation. ▮

We have pointed out that the correlation between equivalent forms of a test is an index of the size of the standard error of measurement. Now we derive the formula that shows the relationship exactly. The covariance between the scores on the two forms is

$$\begin{aligned}
\sigma_{x_1x_2} &= \frac{\sum(t + e_1 - \mu_x)(t + e_2 - \mu_x)}{N} \\
&= \frac{1}{N}\sum\{t^2 + te_2 - t\mu_x + te_1 + e_1e_2 - e_1\mu_x - t\mu_x - e_2\mu_x + \mu_x^2\} \\
&= \frac{\sum(t^2 - 2t\mu_x + \mu_x^2)}{N} + \frac{\sum e_1e_2}{N} + \frac{\sum(te_1 + te_2)}{N} - \mu_x\frac{\sum(e_1 + e_2)}{N}.
\end{aligned}$$

The last term equals zero because $\sum e_1/N = \mu_{e_1}$ and $\sum e_2/N = \mu_{e_2}$ both equal zero. The third term equals zero because we assume that in each distribution the errors are uncorrelated with the true scores. The second term also equals zero because we assume that the measurement errors in the two forms are independent. Since

$$\rho_{e_1e_2} = 0,$$

we know that

$$\sigma_{e_1e_2} = \frac{\sum e_1e_2}{N} - \mu_{e_1}\mu_{e_2} = 0.$$

But we know that $\mu_{e_1}\mu_{e_2}$ is zero, and then $\sum e_1e_2/N$ must be zero also. It turns out, then, that only the first term is nonzero, and that term equals the variance of the true scores.

$$\sigma_{x_1x_2} = \frac{\sum(t - \mu_x)^2}{N} = \frac{\sum(t - \mu_t)^2}{N} = \sigma_t^2.$$

Now, since $\sigma_{x_1} = \sigma_{x_2} = \sigma_x$,

$$\rho_{x_1x_2} = \sigma_t^2/\sigma_x^2. \tag{8.4}$$

The correlation between the scores on two equivalent forms of a test with uncorrelated errors of measurement is equal to the variance of the true scores divided by the variance of the observed scores. The value of $\rho_{x_1x_2}$ is often called the *coefficient of reliability* of the test.

The coefficient of reliability can be used to measure the standard error of measurement. Keep in mind that we can use observed results to obtain the values of σ_x^2 and $\rho_{x_1x_2}$, but we cannot measure the value of σ_t^2 directly.

$$1.0 - \rho_{x_1x_2} = 1.0 - (\sigma_t^2/\sigma_x^2) = (\sigma_x^2 - \sigma_t^2)/\sigma_x^2.$$

But from Eq. (8.3), we see that

$$\sigma_x^2 - \sigma_t^2 = \sigma_e^2.$$

Therefore,

$$\sigma_e^2 = \sigma_x^2(1.0 - \rho_{x_1x_2}),$$

$$\sigma_e = \sigma_x\sqrt{1.0 - \rho_{x_1x_2}}. \tag{8.5}$$

Equation (8.5) says that we can measure the standard error of measurement by subtracting the coefficient of reliability from one, taking the square root, and multiplying the result by the standard deviation of the observed scores.

If a measurement of the standard deviation of true scores is wanted, it also can be obtained easily from Eq. (8.4).

$$\sigma_t^2 = \sigma_x^2\rho_{x_1x_2}; \qquad \sigma_t = \sigma_x\sqrt{\rho_{x_1x_2}}. \tag{8.6}$$

The meaning of Eqs. (8.5) and (8.6) can be seen by considering extreme cases. If there were no errors of measurement, the test scores would be completely consistent, and we would have $\rho_{x_1x_2} = 1.0$. In Eq. (8.6) we would have $\sigma_t = \sigma_x$; this is because with no errors of measurement the distribution of observed scores would be exactly the distribution of true scores. In Eq. (8.5) we would have $\sigma_e = 0$. Now suppose that the test measured only accidental or temporary factors. There would be no consistency between two forms of such a test, so we would have $\rho_{x_1x_2} = 0$. In Eq. (8.5) we would have $\sigma_e = \sigma_x$; all the variability in the observed scores would be the result of measurement error. And in Eq. (8.6) we would have $\sigma_t = 0$; the only meaning of a "true score" in this case would be the mean of the accidents, and it would be the same for all individuals.

Example 8.7. Suppose that a test of intelligence has an observed standard deviation of 16.0 and a coefficient of reliability of .90. Calculate the standard error of measurement and find the probability of obtaining a score within three points of the true score.

The standard error of measurement is

$$\sigma_e = \sigma_x\sqrt{1.0 - \rho_{x_1x_2}} = (16.0)\sqrt{1.0 - .90} = 5.06.$$

For the second part, we consider a distribution with mean t and standard deviation σ_e. A score three points below t is

$$t - 3.0 = t - 0.59\sigma_e; \qquad P[x_i < (t - 3.0)] = .28.$$

A score three points above t is

$$t + 3.0 = t + 0.59\sigma_e; \qquad P[x_i < (t + 3.0)] = .72.$$

Then we have

$$P[(t - 3.0) < x_i < (t + 3.0)] = .72 - .28 = .44.$$

In other words, in more than 50% of the cases, a person's score will be farther than three points away from his true score, in one direction or the other. ▮

Example 8.8. An instructor gives a test and obtains a distribution with mean 34.5 and standard deviation 10. He might erroneously assume that about 16% of his students knew fewer than 25 answers. However, he needs to take account of errors of measurement. Suppose that he measured reliability and found a coefficient of reliability equal to .80. What is the standard error of measurement, what is the standard deviation of the true scores, and what proportion of the students really know fewer than 25 answers?

The standard error of measurement is

$$\sigma_e = \sigma_x\sqrt{1.0 - \rho_{x_1x_2}} = (10.0)\sqrt{.20} = 4.47.$$

The standard deviation of the true scores is

$$\sigma_t = \sigma_x\sqrt{\rho_{x_1x_2}} = (10.0)\sqrt{.80} = 8.94.$$

In the distribution of true scores,

$$24.5 = 34.5 - 10.0 = \mu_t - 1.12\sigma_t; \qquad P(t < 24.5) = .13. ▮$$

Example 8.9. Suppose that a test with a standard error of measurement of 6.0 is given to two groups. The first group has a standard deviation of true scores of 10.0, and the second group has a standard deviation of true scores of 20.0. What will be the coefficient of reliability in each group?

The calculation is based on Eq. (8.4), remembering that

$$\sigma_x^2 = \sigma_t^2 + \sigma_e^2.$$

In the first group,

$$\rho_{x_1x_2} = 100.0/(100.0 + 36.0) = .74.$$

In the second group,

$$\rho_{x_1x_2} = 400.0/(400.0 + 36.0) = .92. ▮$$

The last example emphasizes that the value of the reliability coefficient will depend on the amount of variability in the group, as well as on the standard error of measurement.

We have been discussing reliability in terms of the difference between a person's test score and his true score. The true score is a theoretical quantity and cannot be measured directly unless there is no measurement error. When we measure reliability by observing the correlation between two forms of a test, we obtain two scores for each individual. The situation may be clarified further by considering the relationship between these two scores.

The problem that we take up involves predicting x_{2_i}, a person's score on Form 2, using x_{1_i}, his score on Form 1. The value of x_{1_i} gives us information about the person's true score, but we know it probably is not exactly equal to his value of t. The value of x_{1_i} is taken from a distribution with mean t and standard deviation σ_e. The value of x_{2_i} will also be from that distribution. If we knew the value of t for the individual, the best prediction for x_{2_i} would be t. It would be best because it would make errors of prediction as small as possible. If we knew the value of t for each person in a large group and predicted their scores, the values of x_{2_i} would not be exactly equal to the values of t. For each individual we could then calculate the error in the prediction, $x_{2_i} - t$. For each subject, t is the mean of his distribution of scores, so the average value of $t - x_{2_i}$ would be zero. However, the variance of these errors would be a positive number. Specifically, the variance of the errors of prediction would be

$$\frac{\sum[(x_{2_i} - t) - \mu_{(x_{2_i} - t)}]^2}{N} = \sigma_e^2.$$

The reason t is the best prediction for each individual is that t makes the variance of the errors of prediction as small as it can be. Any other rule for making predictions would lead to larger variance of predictive errors; this would indicate greater errors of prediction, on the average.

The fact that t would be the best prediction for x_{2_i} is useful, but it does not completely solve the problem. The information we obtain for each individual is his score on Form 1, x_{1_i}. We can use the value of x_{1_i} to make a guess about a person's true score, but the best guess is not generally equal to x_{1_i}. Recall from Section 8B that the variance of the actual scores is greater than the variance of the true scores. This suggests that the individuals with very high scores probably receive scores above their true scores, and individuals with very low scores probably receive scores below their true scores. It turns out that the best guess about an individual's true score, based on the score he receives, is

$$t(x_{1_i}) = \mu_x + (\sigma_t^2/\sigma_x^2)(x_{1_i} - \mu_x).$$

We use the notation $t(x_{1_i})$ to indicate that this is a guess or estimate of t based on the individual's score on Form 1. Equation (8.4) allows us to substitute for σ_t^2/σ_x^2, and we obtain

$$t(x_{1_i}) = \mu_x + \rho_{x_1x_2}(x_{1_i} - \mu_x). \tag{8.7}$$

The value of $t(x_{1_i})$ obtained by using Eq. (8.7) is the best guess we can make about a person's true score; therefore it is the best prediction we can make for his score on Form 2. Equation (8.7) shows that we need to know the mean of the scores, the reliability of the test, and the person's score on Form 1 in order to predict the person's score on Form 2.

The actual value of x_{2_i} probably will not be exactly equal to the predicted value. We should think of x_{2_i} as a score taken from a distribution. In the next section we consider the distribution around a predicted score in some detail. Here, we merely remark that the value of x_{2_i} comes from a distribution with the following mean and standard deviation:

$$\begin{aligned} \mu_{x_{2_i}} &= t_{(x_{1_i})}, \\ \sigma_{x_{2_i}} &= \sigma_x\sqrt{1.0 - \rho_{x_1x_2}^2}. \end{aligned} \tag{8.8}$$

Example 8.10. Suppose that scores on a final examination are distributed approximately normally with mean $\mu_x = 75.0$ and standard deviation $\sigma_x = 6.0$. The coefficient of reliability for the test is $\rho_{x_1x_2} = .80$. The instructor gives an examination grade of *A* to students who scored 90 or above. Suppose that you scored 88. What would be your chance of getting an *A* on a (different) equivalent form of the test? A second student's score was 86. What would his chance be of getting an *A* on an equivalent form?

First, we calculate your predicted score for the second test.

$$t(x_{1_i}) = \mu_x + \rho_{x_1x_2}(x_{1_i} - \mu_x) = 75.0 + (.80)(88.0 - 75.0) = 85.4.$$

Note that your predicted score for Form 2 is somewhat closer to the mean than your score on Form 1. Your score on Form 2 would come from a distribution with mean

$$\mu_{x_{2_i}} = t(x_{1_i}) = 85.4$$

and standard deviation

$$\sigma_{x_{2_i}} = \sigma_x\sqrt{1.0 - \rho^2_{x_1x_2}} = (6.0)\sqrt{1.0 - (.80)^2} = 3.6.$$

To receive an *A*, you would need to score at least 90. Then we consider the score

$$89.5 = 85.4 + 4.1 = \mu_{x_{2_i}} + 1.14\sigma_{x_{2_i}}; \qquad P(x_{2_i} > 89.5) = .13.$$

Therefore, you would have about one chance in seven of getting an *A* on another form of the test.

The second student has a predicted score of

$$t(x_{1_i}) = 75.0 + (.80)(86.0 - 75.0) = 83.8.$$

His score on Form 2 comes from a distribution with mean 83.8 and the same standard deviation as before. Thus, to calculate his chances of receiving an *A*, we consider the score

$$89.5 = 83.8 + 5.7 = \mu_{x_{2_i}} + 1.58\sigma_{x_{2_i}}; \qquad P(x_{2_i} > 89.5) = .06.$$

The second student's chances of getting an *A* would be about one-half as high as yours. ▮

Example 8.11. Suppose that a department uses a placement test to permit students to enter a freshman course without remedial work. Students have to pass the test with a score of at least 80 to be accepted, but anyone who gets from 75 to 79 can take an equivalent form of the test as a second try. Scores on the test are approximately normally distributed with mean

$\mu_x = 100.0$ and standard deviation $\sigma_x = 10.0$. The standard error of measurement of the test is $\sigma_\varepsilon = 4.0$. About how many students who score 75 on the first form will pass the second time with scores of 80 or better? (Assume that the students are not able to improve their true scores by studying between the two occasions of testing.)

First, we need to calculate the reliability coefficient. From Eq. (8.3),

$$\sigma_t^2 = \sigma_x^2 - \sigma_e^2 = 100.0 - 16.0 = 84.0.$$

Then from Eq. (8.4),

$$\rho_{x_1x_2} = \sigma_t^2/\sigma_x^2 = 84.0/100.0 = .84.$$

Next, we calculate the predicted score on Form 2 for students with $x_1 = 75.0$.

$$t(x_{1_i}) = \mu_x + \rho_{x_1x_2}(x_{1_i} - \mu_x) = 100.0 + (.84)(75.0 - 100.0) = 79.0.$$

Note that in this case, where x_{1_i} is less than μ_x, the predicted score is higher than the score on Form 1. The students receiving $x_1 = 75.0$ will have values of x_{2_i} distributed with mean and standard deviation

$$\mu_{x_{2_i}} = t(x_{1_i}) = 79.0,$$

$$\sigma_{x_{2_i}} = \sigma_x\sqrt{1.0 - \rho_{x_1x_2}^2} = (10.0)\sqrt{1.0 - (.84)^2} = 5.43.$$

To pass the test, a student must have a score of at least 80.

$$79.5 = 79.0 + 0.5 = \mu_{x_{2_i}} + 0.09\sigma_{x_{2_i}}; \qquad P(x_{2_i} > 79.5) = .46.$$

Then, nearly one-half of the students who score 75 points on Form 1 will pass the test when they take Form 2. ▮

8D PREDICTIVE VALIDITY: EVALUATING THE USEFULNESS OF A TEST

Psychological tests are often used to predict how well individuals will do in training programs. Tests used for such predictions are called aptitude tests. If we have an aptitude test that works, we can use it to make judgments about people, allowing more efficient use of facilities and resources. If a person is not qualified by ability or training to learn the skills needed in some job, it is cheaper to find this out in advance than to spend his time and money (or someone else's) attempting to train him only to find out by his failure that he could not learn to do the job. Aptitude tests are now used in the selection of people for training programs in the military services, in business and industry, and in government agencies, as well as in education.

You took one or more aptitude tests when you entered college. You are likely to be given an aptitude test when you apply for a job. If a person does poorly on an aptitude test, his application may not be considered further. On what grounds are psychological tests used for such purposes? How can we justify making important decisions about people on the basis of test scores?

The justification is that if a test is doing its job, it provides a dependable prediction of approximately how well a person would do if he were in the real situation. If we have a good test, we can identify some applicants in advance who would not succeed in a training program or job. The company (or government agency, or college, or whatever) administering the test can avoid wasting its resources, and the applicant can apply his efforts more usefully somewhere else.

Of course, success in a training program or job is usually a relative matter. Although success sometimes simply means not failing before the program is completed, more often the important factor is to distinguish varying degrees of success. Success in some jobs can be measured quite directly—the number of orders a given salesman sold, or the number of items a given production worker handled, or the grade average a given college student achieved. This section concerns the problem of evaluating a test's usefulness in predicting a person's performance in a training program or job situation.

The kind of situation we have in mind involves a large group of individuals who might be potential applicants for admission to a school or a specific job-training program, or applicants for a job. Each individual could be asked to take a test, and each person then would have a test score x. Any individual who was admitted to the school or training program or was hired for the job would achieve some level of performance there. The achievement of any individual in the training program or job would be his criterion score c. The important question is how accurately we can predict criterion performance using the test scores.

When a test is used to predict some criterion performance, we assume that the test scores are determined partly by characteristics that influence the criterion performance and partly by other factors. We further suppose that a person's test score is

$$x = a(r + u),$$

where r and u are theoretical quantities. The value of r represents a set of characteristics that influence the person's score on the test and also influence his criterion performance. The value of u represents a set of characteristics that influence the test score but not the criterion performance. If the value of r is high for some individual, this will contribute both to a high test score and to a high criterion performance. On the other hand, a high value of u

for a person will tend to give him a high test score, but will have no effect on his criterion performance. We include accidental factors that produce measurement errors in the characteristics that determine u. The value of a is a scaling factor that depends on the length of the test and the difficulty of the test items. The characteristics related to the criterion performance have mean μ_r and variance σ_r^2. The unrelated factors that contribute to the test scores have mean μ_u and variance σ_u^2. The mean of the test scores is

$$\mu_x = a(\mu_r + \mu_u).$$

We assume that the unrelated factors contributing to a person's score are independent of those characteristics related to criterion performance, so that

$$\sigma_{ru} = 0,$$

and therefore,

$$\sigma_x^2 = a^2(\sigma_r^2 + \sigma_u^2).$$

Now consider the criterion scores. We let c stand for the criterion performance of a person—for example, a measurement of the amount he learns in a training program or the amount of his productivity in a job. We assume that the criterion scores are produced partly by the same relevant characteristics measured in the test, and partly by other factors. We state our assumption as

$$c = b(r + v).$$

The value of r is the same as in the earlier equations, and v is the combination of other factors influencing criterion performance, including errors in measuring performance. The constant b is used to permit arbitrary units in measuring performance. The factors v that contribute to criterion performance, but are not measured in the test, have mean μ_v and variance σ_v^2. The mean of the criterion scores is

$$\mu_c = b(\mu_r + \mu_v).$$

Again, we assume that the factors not measured by the test v are independent of the measured relevant characteristics r, so that

$$\sigma_{rv} = 0.$$

Therefore, the variance of the criterion scores is

$$\sigma_c^2 = b^2(\sigma_r^2 + \sigma_v^2).$$

As an example, consider predictions of college achievement based on college aptitude tests. The tests include a wide variety of materials taken from many subject areas and tap a number of different intellectual skills. Suppose that a student takes a college aptitude test, and then goes to college and majors, say, in English. The characteristics that constitute the value of r for this student are those that influence both his test score and his performance in college. These certainly would include the student's ability to read quickly and understand written material, to grasp relationships among ideas, and to distinguish between relevant and irrelevant information in arriving at answers to questions. Some more specific characteristics would also influence his test score and his college performance, such as the level of his literary training and knowledge when he took the test.

However, there are certain other characteristics which would influence the student's test score, but probably would not contribute very much to his later success or failure in college. These might include his ability to work with mathematical concepts or the amount of his specific knowledge about chemistry and physics. In addition, the student's test score would be influenced to some extent by simple accidents of the test situation that produce errors of measurement. The value of u would be determined by the person's knowledge and skill in areas that do not affect his performance in college, and by errors of measurement. If the person had a great deal of knowledge and skill in unrelated areas, he would probably get a relatively high score on the aptitude test, and if he lacked knowledge and skill in these areas, he would probably get a lower score; but these factors would contribute little or nothing to his success or failure in college.

Now consider what happens when the student is in college. His achievement is determined partly by his ability to read and understand and so on, and partly by his specific preparation in literary subjects. Recall that these are the characteristics we originally supposed might constitute the value of r, which figures in the determination of his test score and the level of college achievement he attains. However, college achievement is also influenced by other factors not measured by the aptitude test. For example, some intellectual skills that influence college success probably do not develop until a person has received extensive specialized training in a subject field. The ability to recognize subtle aspects of literary style and to distinguish between appropriate and inappropriate uses of particular stylistic techniques influence a person's success as an English major, but these skills probably would not influence scores in an aptitude test. This is because practically no high school students receive the specialized training needed for the development of these skills, so it is not meaningful to test students on these skills. Furthermore, college achievement is influenced by factors like the student's living situation at college, whether he happens to have friends who study hard and enjoy discussing questions relating to course work, and whether the student happens to enroll in class sections where the instructors are interesting and stimulating people. None of these factors would influence the score a person received on a test he took before he entered college. The value of v represents this combination of factors that influence the student's college achievement, but were not measured in the aptitude test. These factors include accidents that produce errors of measurement when college achievement is evaluated. The student's living situation in college, the friends and instructors he has contact with, and his development of advanced specialized intellectual skills might all be highly favorable and contribute positively to his college achievement, or they might be unfavorable and produce a low level of college achievement. In any case these factors would not contribute to the person's score on a college aptitude test.

The discussion of college aptitude tests and college achievement is just an illustration. In general, for any test used to predict some later criterion performance, the test will measure some characteristics that influence performance in the criterion situation, and some other characteristics that will not. Performance in the criterion situation will be influenced by some characteristics measured in the test and by other factors not measured in the test. It is important to realize that all the factors we are discussing vary within any group of individuals we might be interested in. First, the characteristics influencing both test scores and criterion performance have some distribution in the group; this produces a distribution of the value of r. Differences in r produce variability both in test scores and criterion performance. Second, the characteristics measured by the test that do not influence criterion performance also have some distribution in the group; this produces a distribution of the value of u. The different values of u produce variability in the test scores, but do not contribute to the variability in criterion performance. Third, the factors that influence criterion performance, but not test scores, are distributed in some way in the group, giving a distribution of v. Differences in v contribute to variability in criterion performance but not in test scores.

The ideas we are discussing help us understand what is required for a test to provide accurate predictions about criterion performance. Consider two extreme cases—one where the test provides perfect predictions and the other where the test is of no use at all. In the ideal situation, all the variability in both test scores and criterion performance would be produced by characteristics that determine the values of r. In terms of our assumptions about test scores and criterion performance, perfect predictions would be possible if

$$\sigma_u^2 = \sigma_v^2 = 0.0.$$

Then every person's value of u would equal some constant k_u, and every person's value of v would equal some (probably different) constant k_v. Different individuals would have different values of r, but each person's test score would equal

$$x = a(r + k_u),$$

and his criterion performance would equal

$$c = b(r + k_v).$$

If these conditions were satisfied, then each person's criterion performance would be related to his test score in a simple way. First,

$$r = x/a - k_u.$$

Then,

$$c = b[(x/a) - k_u + k_v] = (b/a)x - b(k_u - k_v).$$

It would be easy to conduct an experiment and measure the two constants b/a and $b(k_u - k_v)$. Then every person's criterion score could be predicted exactly from his test score.

At the other extreme, we might think of a situation where none of the variability in the test scores or the criterion performance would be produced by characteristics that determined the value of r. The test would be completely useless if

$$\sigma_r^2 = 0.0,$$

which would mean that every person's value of r was equal to some constant k_r. Different individuals would have different values of u and v, and an individual's test score and criterion score would equal

$$x = a(k_r + u), \qquad c = b(k_r + v).$$

Since every person would have the same value of r, there would be no information in the test scores to help in making predictions about the criterion performance.

Of course, we can never devise a test that measures all the characteristics, and only those characteristics, that produce variability in a criterion situation. And although it would be possible to construct a test that was completely irrelevant to a criterion situation, such an outcome is certainly not probable. Therefore, we should always expect σ_r^2, σ_u^2, and σ_v^2 to be greater than zero. The extreme cases of perfect and useless prediction discussed above suggest that if σ_r^2 is relatively large and σ_u^2 and σ_v^2 are relatively small we are able to obtain rather accurate predictions, but that if σ_r^2 is small relative to σ_u^2 and σ_v^2 we are not able to predict criterion performance very accurately.

The next question we consider is how to get information about the magnitude of σ_r^2 compared to σ_x^2 and σ_c^2. We obtain this information by conducting an experiment. First, a test is given to a large number of people who are eligible to be in some training program or to hold some job. Then a sample of all the people who took the test are placed in the training program or job situation. It is important that this experimental group be representative of all the people who took the test. At this stage, we do not have enough information even to say whether the test is relevant for selection, much less to say whether a given person passed it or failed it. We obtain data on how well each person does in the training program or job, and these data provide a set of criterion scores.

After the experiment, we have two scores for each person. We have the score x that he received on the test, and we also have a measurement c of how well he did on the job or in the training program. The information we need about the test is obtained by finding the correlation between the test scores and the criterion scores, ρ_{xc}. We show that under our simple assumptions about test scores and criterion scores the square of the correlation is equal to

$$\rho_{xc}^2 = \left(\frac{\sigma_r^2}{\sigma_r^2 + \sigma_u^2}\right)\left(\frac{\sigma_r^2}{\sigma_r^2 + \sigma_v^2}\right). \tag{8.9}$$

If the variance in the characteristics that determine r is very important in producing variability in both the test scores and the criterion scores, then ρ_{xc}^2 will be close to 1.0. But if most of the variability in the test scores or the criterion scores is produced by factors other than those that determine r, then ρ_{xc}^2 will be small. The value of ρ_{xc} can be measured in an experiment of the kind described earlier. Since the value of ρ_{xc} provides information about the relative importance of factors that influence both test scores and criterion performance, ρ_{xc} is a valuable index of the usefulness of the test for making predictions. Because of this, the correlation ρ_{xc} is called the *coefficient of predictive validity*.

Now we need to show that Eq. (8.9) is correct. We begin by deriving the covariance between the test scores and the criterion scores.

$$\begin{aligned}
\sigma_{xc} &= \frac{\sum(x - \mu_x)(c - \mu_c)}{N} \\
&= \frac{\sum[a(r + u) - a(\mu_r + \mu_u)][b(r + v) - b(\mu_r + \mu_v)]}{N} \\
&= \frac{ab\sum[(r - \mu_r) + (u - \mu_u)][(r - \mu_r) + (v - \mu_v)]}{N} \\
&= ab\left[\frac{\sum(r - \mu_r)^2}{N} + \frac{\sum(r - \mu_r)(v - \mu_v)}{N}\right. \\
&\qquad \left. + \frac{\sum(r - \mu_r)(u - \mu_u)}{N} + \frac{\sum(u - \mu_u)(v - \mu_v)}{N}\right];
\end{aligned}$$

$$\sigma_{xc} = ab(\sigma_r^2 + \sigma_{rv} + \sigma_{ru} + \sigma_{uv}).$$

We have already stated the assumption that σ_{ru} and σ_{rv} are both zero. We have not explicitly assumed that σ_{uv} is zero, but that is quite a reasonable assumption. Since both u and v are assumed independent of r, it would be reasonable to expect that they would be independent of each other. Therefore, we have the result

$$\sigma_{xc} = ab\sigma_r^2.$$

Using the definition of the correlation coefficient, we see that

$$\rho_{xc}^2 = \frac{a^2b^2(\sigma_r^2)^2}{\sigma_x^2\sigma_c^2}.$$

But we can substitute for σ_x^2 and σ_c^2 using earlier equations:

$$\rho_{xc}^2 = \frac{a^2b^2(\sigma_r^2)^2}{a^2(\sigma_r^2 + \sigma_u^2)b^2(\sigma_r^2 + \sigma_v^2)},$$

and Eq. (8.9) follows directly.

Example 8.12. In a situation where college achievement is predicted using an aptitude test, suppose that the factors influencing both test scores and college grades are distributed with mean and standard deviation

$$\mu_r = 30.0; \qquad \sigma_r = 3.2.$$

The factors that influence test scores but not college grades are distributed with

$$\mu_u = 10.0; \qquad \sigma_u = 2.5.$$

And the factors that influence college grades but not test scores are distributed with

$$\mu_v = -19.0; \qquad \sigma_v = 3.9.$$

Finally, suppose that the test scores and criterion scores are determined according to

$$x = (2.0)(r + u), \qquad c = (0.20)(r + v).$$

Find the mean and standard deviation of the test scores and of the criterion scores, and calculate the value of ρ_{xc}.

For the test scores,

$$\mu_x = (2.0)(\mu_r + \mu_u) = (2.0)(30.0 + 10.0) = 80.0,$$

$$\sigma_x = \sqrt{(2.0)^2(\sigma_r^2 + \sigma_u^2)} = (2.0)\sqrt{(3.2)^2 + (2.5)^2} = 8.1.$$

The distribution of criterion scores will have mean and standard deviation

$$\mu_c = (0.20)(\mu_r + \mu_v) = 2.20, \qquad \sigma_c = \sqrt{(.20)^2(\sigma_r^2 + \sigma_v^2)} = 1.01.$$

The coefficient of predictive validity is

$$\rho_{xc} = \frac{\sigma_r^2}{\sqrt{(\sigma_r^2 + \sigma_u^2)(\sigma_r^2 + \sigma_v^2)}} = \frac{10.2}{\sqrt{(16.5)(25.4)}} = .50. \blacksquare$$

The discussion of test scores and criterion scores in terms of r, u, and v provides one theoretical basis for understanding why tests can be useful in predicting performance. In terms of our analysis here, a test is useful to the extent that the characteristics of individuals that produce variability in performance also produce variability in the test scores. Psychological tests do not give perfect predictions because test scores are influenced by factors that do not influence criterion performance, and criterion performance is influenced by factors that are not measured by the test. The student should realize that specific numerical values like those used in Example 8.12 are entirely hypothetical, although they are plausible and the value of ρ_{xc} calculated there is quite typical for the situation. In general, we do not have the kind of information needed to measure the means and standard deviations of distributions of r, u, and v separately or to determine whether the specific assumptions given here about test scores and criterion scores are correct. However, the general ideas and their relationship to predictive validity of tests probably are reasonably accurate for many situations where tests are used to predict performance.

Now we consider the practical problem of predicting criterion performance using test scores. First we consider what would happen if we had direct measurements of r—that is, suppose that we could measure the characteristics influencing both the test scores and the criterion performance. Also suppose that we could know the mean of the unmeasured factors μ_v and the value of the scaling factor b. We do not assume that we have any information about an individual's value of v, apart from what we can conclude from knowing the group average.

In the situation described, with b, r, and μ_v known, the best prediction we could make about a person's criterion performance would be

$$p(r) = b(r + \mu_v).$$

We use the notation $p(r)$ to indicate that this would be a predicted value of c based on knowledge of r. Since we would not know the value of the unmeasured factors for an individual, the best we could do would be to predict his performance using the mean of those factors. Of course, there would be errors of prediction produced by the unmeasured factors and related to the varying values of r. A single individual with a known value of r would have some criterion score

$$c_i = b(r + v),$$

and the error of prediction would be

$$c_i - p(r) = b(v - \mu_v).$$

If there were several individuals for whom r was known, then there would be different errors of prediction for the different individuals. The mean of the errors of prediction would be

$$\mu_{[c_i - p(r)]} = 0,$$

and the standard deviation would be

$$\sigma_{[c_i - p(r)]} = \sqrt{\frac{\sum [c_i - p(r)]^2}{N}} = \sqrt{\frac{\sum b^2(v - \mu_v)^2}{N}} = b\sigma_v.$$

We cannot obtain a direct measurement of r for an individual. Instead, we have the individual's test score x_i. The situation is like the one described at the end of Section 8C, where we presented a formula for estimating a person's true score from his score on one of the forms of a test. In the present case we have a formula that could be used to estimate the value of r for an individual, based on his test score x_i:

$$r(x_i) = \mu_r + a\left(\frac{\sigma_r^2}{\sigma_x^2}\right)(x_i - \mu_x).$$

The student may notice the close similarity between this and the equation directly preceding Eq. (8.7). Here we use the notation $r(x_i)$ to indicate that the estimate is made using the test score x_i.

If we knew the values of μ_r, σ_r^2, and a, we could use the equation for $r(x_i)$ to actually estimate an individual's value of r. We usually cannot obtain values for μ_r, σ_r^2, and a; to get this information, we would probably need a theory about the characteristics being measured in a test and some special experimental procedures for investigating their distribution in a group of people. However, we do not need this information to obtain predictions about criterion performance. Recall that if we knew the value of r for each individual we would predict criterion performance using the formula

$$p(r) = b(r + \mu_v).$$

We substitute using the formula for $r(x_i)$;

$$p(x_i) = b[r(x_i) + \mu_v] = b(\mu_r + \mu_v) + ab\left(\frac{\sigma_r^2}{\sigma_x^2}\right)(x_i - \mu_x).$$

This formula has quantities we can obtain from the distributions of test scores and criterion scores. First, recall that

$$b(\mu_r + \mu_v) = \mu_c,$$

the mean of the criterion scores. Then we only need a value for $ab\sigma_r^2$; but we showed earlier that

$$ab\sigma_r^2 = \sigma_{xc}.$$

Therefore, we have

$$p(x_i) = \mu_c + \frac{\sigma_{xc}}{\sigma_x^2}(x_i - \mu_x),$$

or, since $\rho_{xc} = \sigma_{xc}/\sigma_x\sigma_c$,

$$p(x_i) = \mu_c + \rho_{xc}\left(\frac{\sigma_c}{\sigma_x}\right)(x_i - \mu_x). \tag{8.10}$$

Equation (8.10) is a formula used to predict an individual's criterion performance using his test score x_i. Note that to calculate the predicted criterion score for a person, we need to know the mean and standard deviation of the test scores, the criterion scores for the group, and the correlation between the test scores and the criterion scores.

The criterion performance an individual achieves will give him some criterion score c_i, and c_i will probably be somewhat higher or lower than the predicted score $p(x_i)$. In other words, the value of c_i comes from a distribution. The mean of the distribution is equal to the predicted criterion score for the individual; that is,

$$\mu_{c_i} = p(x_i).$$

And the difference between the predicted value of c_i and the value achieved by an individual is the *error of prediction* for that individual. That is,

$$c_i - p(x_i) = c_i - \mu_c - \rho_{xc}\left(\frac{\sigma_c}{\sigma_x}\right)(x_i - \mu_x).$$

When predictions are made about all the individuals in a large group, the error of prediction will be different for different individuals. The mean of the errors of prediction will be zero and the distribution will have some standard deviation σ_{c-p}.

At this point, it may be useful to study a picture of the situation. Figure 2 shows a distribution of test scores $f(x)$ at the bottom. The mean of this distribution μ_x is shown and the distribution of test scores has some standard deviation σ_x. There is also a distribution of criterion scores $f(c)$, shown at the left. The mean of the criterion scores is μ_c and their distribution has standard deviation σ_c. A few particular test scores are shown; they are labeled x_1, x_2, x_3, and x_4.

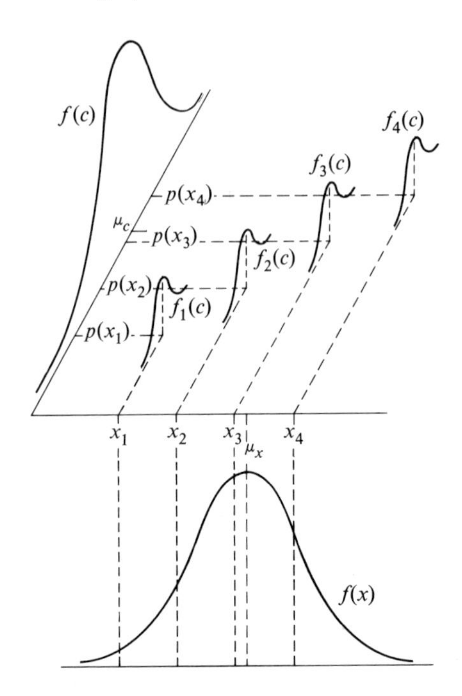

Fig. 2. Illustration of concepts involved in predictive validity.

For each individual who takes the test, we can predict the criterion performance using Eq. (8.10). For example, the criterion score shown as $p(x_1)$ is the predicted score for individuals with test score x_1. The picture shows that each test score corresponds to a distribution of criterion scores. For example, $f_1(c)$ shows the distribution of criterion scores we would obtain from a large group where every individual in the group had a test score of x_1. The mean of each of these distributions is a predicted score. For example, the mean of $f_1(c)$ is $p(x_1)$. Each individual receives a test score x_i and a criterion score c_i. When we know a person's test score, we know from which of the small distributions his criterion score comes. If a person has a test score of x_1, we know his criterion score comes from the small distribution $f_1(c)$. The particular value obtained for c_i can be compared with the prediction for that person, and the difference will be the error of prediction for that person. In other words, a person with a test score of x_1 will receive some criterion score c_i that will come from $f_1(c)$. The error of prediction for that person is equal to $c_i - p(x_1)$.

Now we are ready to derive a formula about the errors of prediction. Our main concern is whether the errors tend to be large or small. If there are many large errors of prediction, then the distributions $f_1(c)$, $f_2(c)$, . . . in Fig. 2 will be highly variable. That is, large standard deviations for those distributions would indicate that many of the criterion scores obtained by individuals were much higher or lower than the predictions made about those individuals. On the other hand, if almost all the errors of prediction were very small, then the distributions $f_1(c)$, $f_2(c)$, . . . would have very small standard deviations.

Because of our assumptions of independence among r, u, and v, all of the distributions like $f_1(c)$, $f_2(c)$, . . . are identical. Therefore, we need only consider a single quantity, the *standard error of prediction*, σ_{c-p}. This quantity is equal to the standard deviation of each small distribution shown in Fig. 2. The value of the standard error of prediction is obtained from the variance,

$$\sigma^2_{c-p} = \frac{\sum(c - p - \mu_{c-p})^2}{N}.$$

The mean error of prediction is $\mu_{c-p} = \mu_c - \mu_p = 0$. Therefore,

$$\sigma^2_{c-p} = \frac{\sum(c - p)^2}{N} = \frac{\sum[(c - \mu_c) - \rho_{xc}\left(\frac{\sigma_c}{\sigma_x}\right)(x_i - \mu_x)]^2}{N}$$

$$= \frac{\sum(c - \mu_c)^2}{N} - 2\rho_{xc}\left(\frac{\sigma_c}{\sigma_x}\right)\frac{\sum[(x_i - \mu_x)(c - \mu_c)]}{N}$$

$$+ \rho^2_{xc}\left(\frac{\sigma^2_c}{\sigma^2_x}\right)\frac{\sum(x_i - \mu_x)^2}{N};$$

$$\sigma^2_{c-p} = \sigma^2_c - 2\rho_{xc}\left(\frac{\sigma_c}{\sigma_x}\right)\sigma_{xc} + \rho^2_{xc}\left(\frac{\sigma^2_c}{\sigma^2_x}\right)\sigma^2_x.$$

When we use the fact that $\rho_{xc} = \sigma_{xc}/\sigma_x\sigma_c$, we obtain

$$\sigma^2_{c-p} = \sigma^2_c(1.0 - \rho^2_{xc}).$$

Therefore, the standard error of prediction is

$$\sigma_{c-p} = \sigma_c\sqrt{1.0 - \rho^2_{xc}}. \tag{8.11}$$

Recall Eq. (8.9), which showed that ρ^2_{xc} measures the relative importance of the characteristics that influence both test scores and criterion scores. Equation (8.11) shows how the value of ρ^2_{xc} can be used in practical situations to measure the standard error of prediction. Using Eq. (8.11) we can determine the accuracy of predictions based on the test scores. Note that if ρ_{xc} is large, the standard error of prediction is close to zero; that is, a high value of ρ_{xc} shows that predictions based on the test scores are very accurate. On the other hand, if the value of ρ_{xc} is very low, the standard error of prediction is high. If ρ_{xc} is close to zero, the standard error of prediction is nearly as large as the standard deviation of the criterion scores, and in this case the test gives little or no information about the criterion scores.

Remember that to evaluate a test's usefulness we conduct an experiment, giving the test to a representative group of people and observing their performance in the criterion situation. The results of the experiment give a measurement of ρ_{xc}. With this result it is possible to decide whether the test is useful for whatever purpose it is intended. The person interested in using the test needs an idea of how accurate the predictions should be for the test to be useful. If the value of ρ_{xc} indicates that the predictions are sufficiently accurate, the test probably will be used in the future for selecting individuals. On the other hand, if the value of ρ_{xc} shows that the predictions are too inaccurate, then further work on the test is needed, or there will be a decision not to use the test at all.

In the rest of this section, we are concerned mainly with examples to clarify the concepts involved in evaluating predictive validity and using tests to make predictions. However, a few comments are needed before we do that. The assumptions we used about test and criterion scores have some features that are needed for the applications we consider, and other features that were introduced simply for convenience. For example, the assumptions that u and v are both independent of r and of each other are needed to derive Eq. (8.11), used to measure the standard error of prediction. If there were a high correlation between u and r, or between v and r, the results we have obtained would not apply.

Another important aspect of our assumptions is that if $x = a(r + u)$ and $c = b(r + v)$, then, on the average, c will be a linear function of x. This fact is used in deriving the expression showing the best guess that can be made about r when we know a person's test score and the correlation ρ_{xc}. Other assumptions about x and c that could be made would also imply a linear relationship. Therefore, the specific assumptions made for our analysis are not required. However, if other assumptions were made, the results given here would not follow. For example, if we assumed that

$$c = ar + br^2 \qquad \text{or} \qquad c = k \log r,$$

then Eq. (8.10) which uses ρ_{xc} would not give optimal predictions. On the other hand, the results derived here may give a reasonably accurate approximation even if the relationship between x and c is nonlinear. In most cases, psychological tests are developed with little or no attention given to psychological assumptions about the characteristics influencing test scores and criterion performance. This is regrettable, since it limits the information we can obtain from research using tests. However, as a practical matter, the main purpose of an investigation is often just to see whether a certain test permits the user to make reasonably accurate predictions about people. In such cases, the coefficient of predictive validity probably provides a fairly accurate index of the test's usefulness even when the assumptions are not satisfied exactly.

Example 8.13. College aptitude tests typically have a correlation of about .50 with college grades. Assume that the distribution of grade-point averages for freshmen is approximately normal with mean 2.20 and standard deviation 1.01. Also assume that the distribution of scores on a college aptitude test has mean $\mu_x = 80.0$ and standard deviation $\sigma_x = 8.1$. Find the linear equation that will give the most accurate predictions of grade averages, based on the test scores, and find the standard error of prediction.

The prediction formula is from Eq. (8.10).

$$\begin{aligned} p(x_i) &= \mu_c + \rho_{xc}(\sigma_c/\sigma_x)(x_i - \mu_x) = 2.2 + (.50)(1.01/8.1)(x_i - 80.0) \\ &= 2.2 + 0.06(x_i - 80.0) = 0.06x_i - 2.60. \end{aligned}$$

The standard error of prediction is

$$\sigma_{c-p} = \sigma_c\sqrt{1.0 - \rho_{xc}^2} = 1.01\sqrt{1.0 - (.50)^2} = 0.87. \blacksquare$$

Example 8.14. Suppose that an industrial firm measures job success by counting the number of items produced by a worker per hour. The present workers have a mean production of 70.0 units per hour, and a standard deviation of 12.0. If the company were to require an aptitude test with a standard error of prediction of 6.0, how high a coefficient of predictive validity would be required? If the test scores had a mean of 40.0 and a standard deviation of 8.0, what would be the linear formula that would give the best predictions about production based on test scores?

First, we substitute in Eq. (8.11) and solve for ρ_{xc}.

$$\sigma_{c-p} = \sigma_c\sqrt{1.0 - \rho_{xc}^2}, \qquad 6.0 = (12.0)\sqrt{1.0 - \rho_{xc}^2},$$

$$\rho_{xc}^2 = 1.0 - (.50)^2 = .75, \qquad \rho_{xc} = .87.$$

Then the prediction formula is

$$\begin{aligned} p(x_i) &= 70.0 + (.87)\left(\frac{12.0}{8.0}\right)(x_i - 40.0) \\ &= 1.30x_i + 17.8. \blacksquare \end{aligned}$$

If the results of an experiment indicate that a test gives predictions that are sufficiently accurate, then the test can be used to select applicants who have good chances of success. This is done by fixing a *critical score* which an applicant must achieve on the test before he can be accepted in a training program or job. The critical score might be selected simply on the basis of the predicted performance in the criterion task; for example, a college might accept as students only applicants whose predicted grade averages were *C* or better. However, this method of fixing a critical score does not take into account the most important features of the situation. The important considerations usually involve the chances of success for individuals who are rejected because of the test, and the chances of failure for individuals who are accepted.

We assume that when a person takes a test and we use Eq. (8.10) to predict his criterion performance, his actual criterion performance will come from a normal distribution with mean equal to the prediction and standard deviation equal to σ_{c-p}. This allows us to evaluate the person's chance of success or failure with respect to some definition of success in the criterion task—for example, getting a certain grade average in college or producing a certain amount in a job. That is, we select some criterion score as a definition of successful performance. The person's chance of success or failure depends on where the definition of success is located in the distribution with mean $p(x_i)$ and standard deviation σ_{c-p}. To find the probability of success, we find out how far the definition of success is above or below $p(x_i)$ in units of σ_{c-p}, and look up the probability in Table C of the Appendix.

Example 8.15. Consider the test for college aptitude described in Example 8.13, and use the results obtained there. Suppose that a student gets 85 points on the aptitude test. What are his chances of having a grade point average below 1.8?

First, we calculate the prediction for this student.

$$p(x_i) = 0.06x_i - 2.60 = (0.06)(85.0) - 2.60 = 2.50.$$

The prediction is the mean of a distribution with standard deviation

$$\sigma_{c-p} = 0.87.$$

The definition of success here is a grade average of 1.8. Recall that $\mu_{c_i} = p(x_i)$, and $\sigma_{c_i} = \sigma_{c-p}$.

$$1.80 = 2.50 - 0.70 = \mu_{c_i} - 0.80\sigma_{c_i}; \qquad P(c_i < 1.80) = .21.$$

That is, this student's chance of getting a grade average below 1.8 is about one in five. ▮

Example 8.16. Continue the discussion of Example 8.14. Suppose that the firm decided it could not tolerate production by any individual of less than 65 units per hour, and it was decided that no person would be hired unless he had at least a .80 chance of exceeding this minimum level of performance. What would be the lowest score a person could get and still be hired?

To solve this, we first have to calculate the predicted performance that corresponds to a .80 chance of success. From Table C,

$$P(c_i > 65.0) = .80; \qquad 65.0 = \mu_{c_i} - 0.84\sigma_{c_i}.$$

Since $\sigma_{c_i} = \sigma_{c-p} = 6.0$,

$$p(x_i) = \mu_{c_i} = 65.0 + (0.84)(6.0) = 70.0.$$

Now we need to see what test score corresponds to a prediction of 70.0. The prediction formula is

$$p(x_i) = 1.30x_i + 17.8.$$

Therefore,

$$x_i = \frac{p(x_i) - 17.8}{1.30} = \frac{52.2}{1.30} = 40.1.$$

The company would decide to hire only people who scored at least 40 points on the aptitude test. ▮

This last example shows the method of deciding on a critical test score. Note that we used a definition of success (in this case, 65 units per hour) and a specified chance of success that a person had to have to qualify for the job. From these two specifications, we calculated the critical score of 40. If the company adopts the policy of hiring only individuals who score above the critical score, every employee will have at least an 80% chance of succeeding on the job.

8E CONSTRUCT VALIDITY: USING TESTS TO TEST THEORIES

Often a theory about a personality trait or a motive will be related closely to the development of a psychological test for measuring that trait or motive. When this happens, questions about the validity of the test cannot be separated from questions about the validity of the theory of the trait or motive the test measures. If we find that the test provides accurate predictions about some relevant criterion performance, we thereby obtain evidence favoring the theory.

There are many situations in the study of personality where psychological tests are used to test ideas and theories. An especially nice example is the study of achievement motivation. Recall our earlier discussion of the test for need achievement; subjects are shown pictures and tell stories to describe what might be going on. Subjects whose stories have frequent references to success, getting things done, and excelling in challenging tasks receive high scores on this test, and they are considered to have strong needs for achievement.

The test is based on an assumption about the nature of achievement motivation—that people with strong needs for achievement will tend to suppose that people pictured in ambiguous situations are probably thinking about or engaged in some achievement-related activity. Another assumption about achievement motivation is that people with strong needs for achievement will probably try harder to succeed in mildly challenging tasks, even if the tasks are presented in an experimental situation with no obvious rewards given for success. If both of these assumptions are correct, then there should be a correlation between two scores—the score a person receives on a test for achievement motivation and the score he receives on a task given to him in an experiment.

Note that the situation here is of the same general kind as the one we discussed in the preceding section. We have a test we are interested in, and we want to see whether scores on the test correlate with scores on some criterion task. But in the last section we dealt mainly with practical questions about validity. Now our interest is at least partly theoretical. We are interested in checking the validity of the test for achievement motivation, but our interest is not just in the test; we also want to evaluate a theoretical idea or a construct of the motive the test measures. Thus we are studying construct validity in addition to predictive validity.

In a study of construct validity for need achievement[4] the test for achievement motivation was given to 40 college students who were asked to work on a scrambled-words test for 20 minutes. A person's score on the achievement-motive test plays the role of a test score, and could be used to predict performance on the scrambled-words problems. The performance on scrambled words by subjects who scored above the group mean on the test was compared with the performance by subjects with test scores below the group mean. The subjects with above-average need achievement solved an average of 5.8 scrambled-words problems per minute, and the subjects with below-average need achievement solved an average of 4.9 problems per minute. From these data we cannot calculate the exact validity coefficient, but we can see that the two sets of scores must be correlated. This supports the idea that the thing being measured in the test for achievement motivation really is what we think it is, and that the test really does measure it.

In another validation experiment for the test of need achievement,[5] two groups were selected. The groups were made up of students selected on the

---

[4] E. L. Lowell, "A Methodological Study of Projectively Measured Achievement Motivation," reported by D. C. McClelland, *Studies in Motivation*, New York: Appleton-Century-Crofts, 1955.

[5] E. G. French, "Effects of the Interaction of Motivation and Feedback on Performance," in J. W. Atkinson (Ed.), *Motives in Fantasy, Action, and Society*. New York: Van Nostrand, 1958, pp. 400–408.

basis of their scores on two tests—one for need achievement and the other for need affiliation. The test for need affiliation is like that for achievement motivation, except that high scores are obtained by people who refer frequently to friendship and warm feeling between people, and to people helping one another. One of the groups in the study had subjects with high achievement scores but low affiliation scores; the other group had low achievement scores but high affiliation scores. The members of each group were divided into teams of four students, and they were asked to work on a problem of making a story out of some phrases and sentences which were on separate cards. The subjects were not permitted to show each other the cards they had, but had to get information from each other by talking.

The experimental task was not necessarily the sort of problem in which a person would be expected to excel if he was strongly motivated to achieve. In fact, the students with high need achievement did a little better than those with high need affiliation, though the difference was small. However, the experimenter did something else which led to the appearance of a marked difference between the two groups. Twice during each team's work the experimenter came into the room and gave the team feedback about their progress. For one-half of the teams, the experimenter gave feedback relating to achievement, saying "This team is working very efficiently," while for the other teams, the feedback was related to the affiliative feelings of the group members, saying, "This team works very well together." The idea was that the achievement-related feedback would be a more effective form of encouragement than the affiliation-related feedback to the teams whose members had high scores for need achievement; but that the affiliation-related feedback would work better for the teams whose members had high scores for need affiliation. The idea turned out to be correct. For the teams with high achievement motivation, the average performance was about eleven points better with achievement feedback than with affiliation feedback. But for the teams with high need affiliation, performance turned out to be about nine points better with affiliation feedback than with achievement feedback.

These studies of need achievement are only two of many experiments which have been conducted to clarify the notion of achievement motivation. And experiments like these have also been conducted to test many other ideas about personality and motivation. Without giving an extensive listing of these various studies and research problems, we can see the basic nature of this kind of work. A concept is developed—in this case the concept is "achievement motivation." One important question is how to measure achievement motivation. Another important question is what the concept of achievement motivation really is about. Both of these questions are involved in experiments like those discussed here. The question about measurement is most directly involved in the development of a psychological test for the motive. And the question of what the concept really is about is most directly involved in the selection of an experimental situation, including a task for subjects to perform. Then we study, as in the first experiment, whether scores on the test correlate with performance in the experimental situation as we expect them to. This kind of study is exactly like the general kind of validation experiment we talked about before, except that the criterion performance is observed in an experimental situation rather than in some practical situation. Or we study, as in the second experiment, whether certain experimental variables will affect subjects differently depending on their scores on the test. In either case the idea is to use a test along with the results of an experiment to test a theoretical idea.

PROBLEMS

* **1.** Suppose that you take a college aptitude test with a standard error of measurement of 3.6. If your true score is 60.0, what is the probability of getting a score less than 55? What is the probability of a score between 58 and 62?

2. In a course examination, there are 50 points. The instructor gives grades on the following scale: 42 or above, *A*; 35 to 41, *B*; 25 to 34, *C*; 19 to 24, *D*; below 19, *F*. The standard error of measurement on the test is 4.0. Suppose that your true score is 38.0—that is, you should score in the middle of the *B* range. What are your chances of getting a *B*? of getting an *A*? of getting *C* or lower? Now consider a student whose true score is 18.5—that is, he is on the borderline between passing and failing. What are his chances of failing? What are his chances of getting a *C* or better?

3. Think of a football game as a measurement of the difference in ability between two teams. The obtained score is the difference in points between the two teams; let us say

$$x = (\text{points for home team}) - (\text{points for visiting team}).$$

Suppose that the measurement errors are normally distributed with a standard error of estimate of about seven points. If the home team is really not as good as the visiting team, and the real difference in ability is about five points, what is the probability that the home team will win?

4. A man likes steak about $1\frac{1}{2}$ times as much as roast beef. Suppose that you can observe his choices between steak and roast beef 40 times in different situations where he is on an expense account so that cost does not affect his choice. You decide to measure his response strength for choosing steak as the proportion of choices he makes of steak. (That is, let $K = 1$.) What is the true score? What is the standard error of measurement? What is the probability of obtaining a score that is within .05 of the true score? What is the probability of obtaining a score farther away than .02 from the true score? Repeat the calculations assuming that you have 400 observations instead of 40.

▸ **5.** The man in Problem 4 likes steak nine times as much as hamburger. What is the true probability of choosing steak rather than hamburger? What value of *K* should be used so that the person's liking for steak in this situation has the same numerical value as it does when he chooses between steak and roast beef? Using this value of K to measure response strength, what is the true score? If you observe his choices between steak and hamburger 40 times, what is the standard error of measurement? What is the standard error of measurement if you have 400 observations?

▸ **6.** For the man described in Problems 4 and 5, what is the true probability of choosing roast beef when the alternatives are roast beef and hamburger? What is the standard error of measurement if you measure the proportion of choices by observing his choice 40 times? Suppose that you measured his choices between steak and roast beef and between steak and hamburger by observing 40 choices from each pair of alternatives. Denote the alternatives as A_1: steak; A_2: roast beef; A_3: hamburger. Consider the following possibilities: (a) Your measurement of $v(A_1)$ is one standard error of measurement above the true value in both situations. (b) Your measurement of $v(A_1)$ is one standard error of measurement below the true value in both situations. (c) Your measurement of $v(A_1)$ is σ_e above the true value in the situation with roast beef and σ_e below the true value in the situation with hamburger. What theoretical value would you calculate for $P(A_2 \mid A_2, A_3)$ based on each of the results? In each case, calculate the probability of obtaining a measurement of $P(A_2 \mid A_2, A_3)$ that is as far away from the true value (in either direction) as the one you would calculate. Repeat the whole set of calculations, assuming that you have 400 observations in each of the three situations, instead of 40.

7. In the data analyzed in Example 2.8, in Chapter 2, the following results were obtained:

$$P(A_1 \mid A_1, A_2) = .62, \qquad P(A_1 \mid A_1, A_3) = .95, \qquad P(A_2 \mid A_2, A_3) = .91.$$

The measurements were obtained by observing 120 choices per pair of alternatives. Now suppose that the true response strengths had the following relationships:

$$v(A_1) = (2.0)v(A_2), \qquad v(A_1) = (20.0)v(A_3).$$

Calculate the true probabilities of choice for the three pairs of alternatives, based on these assumed response strengths. Calculate the error of measurement for each of the obtained values, and calculate the difference between the true scores and the obtained scores in units of σ_e.

Table 2

Points on Theoretical Psychometric Function

Difference between stimuli	P(judge $H_1 > H_2$)
$-1.0\sigma_d$	.16
$-0.5\sigma_d$	.31
0.0	.50
$0.5\sigma_d$	.69
$1.0\sigma_d$	.84

8. Consider the theory of detection of differences between stimuli given as Eq. (7.10) in Chapter 7. Some of the points in Fig. 4 in Chapter 7 are given in Table 2. Suppose that measurements were made by taking 100 observations for each pair of stimuli listed in the table. Calculate the standard error of measurement for each data point. Copy Fig. 4 (Chapter 7), and draw curves one standard error of measurement above and below the theoretical curve. What is the probability that a measurement of one of the probabilities would be between the curves that you have drawn in?

9. Calculate the standard error of measurement of c when the true value of c is .30 and when we observe the mean trial of learning for 50 items. Refer back to Example 8.3, involving a student for whom $c = .25$. What is the probability that the measurement for a student with $c = .30$ would be lower than the measurement for a student with $c = .25$ if that student's score is $1.0\sigma_e$ above his true score?

10. The value of c can be measured by giving a single study trial on a set of items, and then testing some time later to see what proportion were learned. Suppose that 50 items are studied once each. What is the standard error of measurement if the true value of c is .25? if the true value of c is .30?

▸ **11.** In measuring the value of c using the mean trial of learning, we can consider each study trial of each item before the item is learned as an observation. In other words, each study trial before an item is learned is an opportunity for learning to occur, and the measurement of c is the proportion of these observations on which learning occurs. Theoretically, the number of observations will equal the mean number of trials before learning multiplied by the number of items. According to this idea, the standard error of measurement should equal

$$\sigma_e = \sqrt{\frac{c(1 - c)}{N\mu_L}}.$$

Show that this result agrees with Eq. (8.2).

* **12.** Consider a hypothetical test that measures an individual's social adjustment. Suppose that when the test is given to a representative group of American college students the mean score is 75.0 and the standard deviation is 10.0. The standard error of measurement is 5.0. Calculate the standard deviation of the true scores, the proportion of true scores between 64.5 and 85.5, and the proportion of observed scores between 65 and 85. (Assume that the observed scores have to be whole numbers.) Consider a well-adjusted person whose true score is 85.0. What is the probability that his observed score will be less than 80? What is the probability that his observed score will be less than the mean of the population?

▸ **13.** Suppose that we measure preferences between two alternatives A_1 and A_2. The measurement for each person uses just two choices, so the measured values of $P(A_1 \mid A_1, A_2)$ must be .00, .50, or 1.0. There are 300 individuals in the study. For 100 individuals, the true value of $P(A_1 \mid A_1, A_2)$ is .40; for 100 individuals, the true value of $P(A_1 \mid A_1, A_2)$ is .60; and for 100 individuals, it is .80. (a) Calculate the variance and standard deviation of the true scores. (b) For each value of the true score, find the theoretical frequency distribution of the measurements.

[The number of A_1 choices will be distributed binomially, so that

$$P(n_1 = 0) = (1 - t)^2, \qquad P(n_1 = 1) = 2t(1 - t), \qquad P(n_1 = 2) = t^2,$$

where t is the true value of $P(A_1 \mid A_1, A_2)$.] Show that the overall mean of the measurements equals the mean of the true scores. Find the overall variance and standard deviation of the measurements. (c) Translate each score into a measurement error. Show that $\mu_e = 0$ and $\sum te = 0$. Find the overall variance and standard deviation of the errors of measurement. (d) Show that $\sigma_x^2 = \sigma_t^2 + \sigma_e^2$.

14. Consider a student whose true score is 65.0 on the test for social adjustment described in Problem 12. If this student takes two equivalent forms of the test, what is the probability that (a) both of his scores will be less than 70? (b) one score is less than 70 and the other is 70 or greater? (c) both scores are in the range from 65 to 70?

▸ **15.** Suppose that a preference test is given to 200 individuals. Each measurement is based on two choices between A_1 and A_2. The true value of $P(A_1 \mid A_1, A_2)$ is .40 for 100 of the individuals and .80 for the other 100 individuals. The test is administered twice, giving two measurements of $P(A_1 \mid A_1, A_2)$ for each individual. There are nine possible combinations of scores: x_{1_i} may be .00, .50, or 1.0 and so may x_{2_i}. Calculate the theoretical frequency of each combination for each of the true scores. Find the value of $\rho_{x_1x_2}$ using the scores from all 200 individuals. Note that the value of σ_e depends on the true score in this situation. What is the relationship between the two values of σ_e and the quantity that would be calculated using the value of $\rho_{x_1x_2}$ and Eq. (8.5)?

16. What is the coefficient of reliability of the test described in Problem 12?

* **17.** In an examination, the mean score is 44.2 and the standard deviation is 9.0. If the reliability coefficient for the test is .75, what is the standard error of measurement? What are the mean and standard deviation of the true scores? If a student has to get a score of 35 to earn a *C*, what is the probability of earning a *C* if a student's true score is 38.6?

18. Two psychologists develop tests for reading readiness. Each reports that his test has a coefficient of reliability of .90. However, one of them studied his test using a group with a standard deviation of 5.0, and the other used a group with a standard deviation of 12.0. Calculate the standard error of measurement for both tests, and comment on the relative precision of the two tests. Can you think of any reasons for thinking that the less precise test might be better, even though it has a larger standard error of measurement?

▸ **19.** Suppose that reliability is measured using situations where errors of measurement are correlated. (For example, if errors of measurement are partly caused by the way instructions are given, then if both tests were taken with exactly the same instructions, the errors caused by instructions probably would cause a positive correlation between measurement errors.) Find the formula for $\rho_{x_1x_2}$ that is more general than Eq. (8.4), showing how the correlation depends on σ_t^2, σ_x^2, and $\sigma_{e_1e_2}$.

20. Use the situation described in Example 8.10, and suppose that the instructor gives a grade of *B* to students who scored in the range from 81 to 89. What proportion of the students would receive *B*'s? Consider the two students with scores on

Form 1 of 88 and 86. For each of these students, what is the chance that he would get a *B* on an equivalent form of the same test?

21. Suppose that a college admits only students who score 50 points or above on an entrance examination. The examination scores are distributed approximately normally with a mean of 48.7 and a standard deviation of 8.7. The test has a standard error of measurement of 2.9. If a student wants to, he can take two equivalent forms of the test. If a student scores 40 points on his first try, what is his chance of getting at least 50 points on the second try? What if a student scores 47 points on his first try?

22. Suppose that an aptitude test is being considered as a possible means of predicting success in a training program for salesmen. The test is given to a group of applicants, and all these applicants are given the training program. The mean and standard deviation of the test scores is

$$\mu_x = 60.0, \qquad \sigma_x = 9.5.$$

Performance in the training program is measured on a point system, and the criterion scores have mean and standard deviation

$$\mu_c = 270.0, \qquad \sigma_c = 27.9.$$

The coefficient of predictive validity is measured and the result is

$$\rho_{xc} = .40.$$

Now suppose that the psychologist conducting the study has a theory about what characteristics contribute to test scores and criterion performance in this situation. On the basis of additional tests and experiments, he decides that the distribution of characteristics that influence both test scores and criterion performance has mean and standard deviation

$$\mu_r = 120.0, \qquad \sigma_r = 10.0.$$

The mean of those characteristics that influence tests scores, but not criterion scores, is

$$\mu_u = -30.0.$$

And the mean of those characteristics that influence criterion scores, but not test scores, is

$$\mu_v = 48.0.$$

Calculate the standard deviations σ_u and σ_v. (*Hint:* Use the values of μ_r, μ_u, and μ_v to find the values of *a* and *b*. Then use these along with σ_r^2 to find σ_u^2 and σ_v^2.)

▸ **23.** Suppose that there are three tests giving scores *x*, *y*, and *z*, determined according to

$$x = a(r + u), \qquad y = b(r + v), \qquad z = c(r + w).$$

We could use values of *x* to predict values of *y* and *z*, and we could use values of *y* to predict z. Show that if u, v, and w are all independent of r and of each other, then

$$\frac{\sigma_r^2}{\sigma_r^2 + \sigma_u^2} = \frac{\rho_{xy}\rho_{xz}}{\rho_{yz}}.$$

Also find ways of measuring the ratios $\sigma_r^2/(\sigma_r^2 + \sigma_v^2)$ and $\sigma_r^2/(\sigma_r^2 + \sigma_w^2)$.

▸ **24.** The best estimate of $r(x_i)$ was given without proof, because elementary calculus is needed in the derivation. However, students who know simple differential calculus can carry out the derivation quite easily. We let

$$r(x) = \alpha x + \beta,$$

and we will select α and β to give predictions that are as accurate as possible. What we want to do is minimize the mean square error of prediction, defined as

$$\frac{\sum[r(x) - r]^2}{N} = \frac{\sum(\alpha x + \beta - r)^2}{N}.$$

We find the optimal values of α and β by expanding the second term, differentiating with respect to α and with respect to β, and then setting each of the partial derivatives equal to zero. Show that this procedure leads to the results

$$\beta = \mu_r - \alpha\mu_x, \qquad \alpha\frac{\sum x^2}{N} = \frac{\sum xr}{N} - \beta\mu_x.$$

Next, show that these equations have the solution

$$\alpha = \frac{\sigma_{xr}}{\sigma_x^2}, \qquad \beta = \mu_r - \left(\frac{\sigma_{xr}}{\sigma_x^2}\right)\mu_x.$$

Finally, find the value of σ_{xr} and verify the equation for $r(x_i)$ given in the text.

25. For the test described in Problem 22, find the formula for predicting criterion performance from test scores, and calculate the standard error of prediction. If an applicant has a test score of 63, what is his chance of obtaining at least 270 points in the training program? Suppose that a score of 250 points is needed to pass and be qualified as a salesman. If the company wanted every man in the program to have at least a .50 chance of passing, what critical score would be chosen?

* **26.** A school system tried an accelerated reading program for all its students. At the end of the program an achievement test was given. The mean score on the achievement test was 42.6 and the standard deviation was 12.5. Because of the cost of the program and the extreme variability of performance, the school decided to continue the reading program only with students of high ability. A test for selecting the students is needed, and the school officials want a test with a standard error of prediction at least as low as 10.0. What coefficient of predictive validity will be needed? If the mean and standard deviation of scores on the selection test are 28.8 and 8.3, what critical score will be needed to ensure that every student in the program has at least a .75 chance of achieving a score of at least 50 points in the achievement test?

Appendix

Basic Equations

(1.1) J = judged magnitude, H = physical magnitude;

$$J = cH^p,$$

where p is an experimental result and c is arbitrary.

(1.3) D = scale value where units are equally discriminable, H = physical magnitude;

$$D = b \log H,$$

where

$$b = \frac{1}{\log k} = \frac{1}{\log (H_1/H_0)},$$

and H_1 and H_0 are separated by one *jnd*.

(2.1) $\mathcal{A} = \{A_1, \ldots, A_k\}$, a set of choice alternatives. The response strength for choosing A_x is $v(A_x)$. The probability of choosing A_i from the set $\mathcal{A}$ is $P(A_i \mid A_1, \ldots, A_i, \ldots, A_k)$.

$$P(A_i \mid A_1, \ldots, A_i, \ldots, A_k) = \frac{v(A_i)}{\sum_{A_x \epsilon \mathcal{A}} v(A_x)}.$$

(2.10) The amount of a person's liking for outcome O_j is $u(O_j)$. The person's expectation that outcome O_j will occur if he chooses alternative A_i is $s(O_j \mid A_i)$. The number of possible outcomes considered is n.

$$v(A_i) = \sum_{j=1}^{n} u(O_j)s(O_j \mid A_i).$$

(3.1) The initial strength of a base response is $v_0(B)$; $v_1(B)$ and $v_1(C)$ are the strengths of the base response and a contingent response after an animal has adjusted to a contingency.

$$v_1(B) = bv_0(B) + cv_1(C),$$

where b and c are empirical constants.

(3.2) The initial strength of a contingent response is $v_0(C)$, and t is the proportion of time the contingent response is available.

$$v_1(C) = v_0(C) + h(1 - t),$$

where h is an empirical constant.

(4.1) The mean of a distribution of scores is μ. Each score is a value of x and there are N scores.

$$\mu = \sum x/N.$$

(4.2) The variance of a distribution is σ^2.

$$\sigma^2 = \sum(x - \mu)^2/N.$$

(5.5) The trial of learning an association is L, and c is the probability of learning on each trial.

$$P(L = n) = (1 - c)^{n-1}c.$$

(5.8) The probability of learning on Trial n or sooner is $P(L \leq n)$, in other words, the average learning curve.

$$P(L \leq n) = 1 - (1 - c)^n.$$

(5.10) To find the value of c, the probability of learning, when μ_L, the mean trial of learning, is known,

$$c = 1/\mu_L.$$

(5.11) The probability of holding an item in short-term memory for at least n trials is h_n. The probability of losing the item on any trial is d.

$$h_n = (1 - d)^n.$$

(5.13) The probability of remembering an item after it is studied m times, and then n other items are studied or tested is $r_{m,n}$.

$$r_{m,n} = 1 - (1 - c)^m + (1 - c)^m(1 - d)^n.$$

(5.14) The probability that a stored item can be retrieved after n units of time is s_n.

$$s_n = (1 - f)^n.$$

(5.15) The probability that an item is stored during m study trials and can still be retrieved after n units of time is $s_{m,n}$.

$$s_{m,n} = [1 - (1 - c)^m](1 - f)^n.$$

(5.16) The probability of transfer from a known association to a new association is t. If learning occurs by selective coding,

$$t = b_{12}/c_1,$$

where b_{12} is the probability of selecting a code that will support retention of both associations while studying the first association, and c_1 is the probability of selecting a code that will support retention of the first association.

(5.18) T is the probability that a subject will know the response for a new association when an earlier association is studied m times and n units of time elapse before the second association is presented.

$$T = [1 - (1 - c_1)^m](1 - f)^n t.$$

(6.1) The number of errors made in a simple concept-identification problem is E. The probability of solving after each error is s.

$$P(E = j) = (1 - s)^j s.$$

(6.2) The mean number of errors is μ_E.

$$\mu_E = (1 - s)/s.$$

(6.4) The trial of solution in simple concept identification is L. The probability of an error on each trial before solution is q.

$$P(L = k) = \begin{cases} s & \text{for } k = 0, \\ (1 - s)(1 - qs)^{k-1}qs & \text{for } k \geq 1. \end{cases}$$

(6.5) The mean trial of solving is μ_L.

$$\mu_L = (1 - s)/(1 - qs).$$

(6.9) To find the value of s when μ_E is known,

$$s = 1/(1 + \mu_E).$$

(6.11) The sum of the weights of relevant dimensions is $\sum w_r$, and $\sum w_j$ is the sum of all the dimension weights.

$$s = \sum w_r / \sum w_j.$$

(6.14) In a transfer problem, where T is the probability of positive transfer,

$$P(E = j) = \begin{cases} T + (1 - T)s & \text{for } j = 0, \\ (1 - T)(1 - s)^j s & \text{for } j \geq 1. \end{cases}$$

(7.8) If we assume that response strengths are variable and that the individual chooses the response with the greatest momentary strength with probability one,

$$P(A_1 \mid A_1, A_2) = P[v(A_1) - v(A_2) > 0].$$

(7.13) The covariance between two variables x and y is σ_{xy}.

$$\sigma_{xy} = \frac{\Sigma(x - \mu_x)(y - \mu_y)}{N}.$$

(7.14) The correlation between x and y is ρ_{xy}.

$$\rho_{xy} = \frac{\sigma_{xy}}{\sigma_x \sigma_y}.$$

(8.1) A person's test score x is

$$x = t + e,$$

where t is the person's true score and e is an error of measurement.

(8.3) The standard deviation of a distribution of test scores is

$$\sigma_x = \sqrt{\sigma_t^2 + \sigma_e^2},$$

where σ_t^2 is the variance of the true scores and σ_e^2 is the variance of the errors of measurement.

(8.4) Scores on two equivalent forms of a test are x_1 and x_2. The coefficient of reliability of the test is $\rho_{x_1x_2}$.

$$\rho_{x_1x_2} = \sigma_t^2/\sigma_x^2.$$

(8.5) The standard error of measurement of a test is σ_e.

$$\sigma_e = \sigma_x\sqrt{1.0 - \rho_{x_1x_2}}.$$

(8.9) If we assume that a person's test score is $x = a(r + u)$ and his criterion performance is $c = b(r + v)$ where r, u, and v are independent, then the square of the coefficient of predictive validity is

$$\rho_{xc}^2 = \left(\frac{\sigma_r^2}{\sigma_r^2 + \sigma_u^2}\right)\left(\frac{\sigma_r^2}{\sigma_r^2 + \sigma_v^2}\right).$$

(8.10) If an individual has a test score x_i then the prediction of his criterion performance is

$$p(x_i) = \mu_c + \rho_{xc}\left(\frac{\sigma_c}{\sigma_x}\right)(x_i - \mu_x).$$

(8.11) The standard error of prediction is

$$\sigma_{c-p} = \sigma_c\sqrt{1.0 - \rho_{xc}^2}.$$

Table A

Logarithms (Base 10)

	.0	.1	.2	.3	.4	.5	.6	.7	.8	.9
1	.000	.041	.079	.113	.146	.176	.204	.230	.255	.279
2	.301	.322	.342	.362	.380	.399	.415	.431	.447	.462
3	.477	.491	.505	.518	.532	.544	.556	.568	.580	.591
4	.602	.613	.623	.634	.644	.653	.663	.672	.681	.690
5	.699	.708	.716	.724	.732	.740	.748	.756	.763	.771
6	.778	.785	.792	.799	.806	.813	.820	.826	.832	.839
7	.845	.851	.857	.863	.869	.875	.881	.886	.892	.898
8	.903	.908	.914	.919	.924	.929	.934	.940	.945	.949
9	.954	.959	.964	.968	.973	.978	.982	.987	.991	.996

	0	2	4	6	8
1.00	.0000	.0008	.0017	.0026	.0035
1.01	.0043	.0052	.0060	.0069	.0078
1.02	.0086	.0094	.0104	.0111	.0120
1.03	.0128	.0137	.0145	.0153	.0162
1.04	.0170	.0179	.0187	.0195	.0204
1.05	.0212	.0220	.0228	.0237	.0245
1.06	.0253	.0261	.0269	.0278	.0286
1.07	.0294	.0302	.0310	.0318	.0326
1.08	.0334	.0342	.0350	.0358	.0366
1.09	.0374	.0382	.0390	.0398	.0406

Table B

$(1-p)^k$

$(1-p)$	$(1-p)^2$	$(1-p)^3$	$(1-p)^4$	$(1-p)^5$	$(1-p)^6$	$(1-p)^7$	$(1-p)^8$	$(1-p)^9$	$(1-p)^{10}$
.05	.002	.000							
.10	.010	.001	.000						
.15	.022	.003	.001	.000					
.20	.040	.008	.002	.000					
.25	.062	.016	.004	.001					
.30	.090	.027	.008	.002	.001	.000			
.35	.122	.043	.015	.005	.002	.001	.000		
.40	.160	.064	.026	.010	.004	.002	.001	.000	
.45	.202	.091	.041	.018	.008	.004	.002	.001	.000
.50	.250	.125	.062	.031	.016	.008	.004	.002	.001
.55	.302	.166	.092	.050	.028	.015	.008	.005	.003
.60	.360	.216	.130	.078	.047	.028	.017	.010	.006
.65	.422	.275	.178	.116	.075	.049	.032	.021	.013
.70	.490	.343	.240	.168	.118	.082	.058	.040	.028
.75	.562	.422	.317	.237	.178	.134	.100	.075	.056
.80	.640	.512	.410	.328	.262	.210	.168	.134	.107
.85	.722	.614	.522	.444	.377	.321	.272	.232	.197
.90	.810	.729	.656	.590	.531	.478	.430	.387	.349
.95	.902	.857	.815	.774	.735	.698	.663	.630	.599

$(1-p)$	$(1-p)^{11}$	$(1-p)^{12}$	$(1-p)^{13}$	$(1-p)^{14}$	$(1-p)^{15}$	$(1-p)^{16}$	$(1-p)^{17}$	$(1-p)^{18}$	$(1-p)^{19}$
.50	.000								
.55	.001	.001	.000						
.60	.004	.002	.001	.001	.000				
.65	.009	.006	.004	.002	.002	.001	.001	.000	
.70	.020	.014	.010	.007	.005	.003	.002	.002	.001
.75	.042	.032	.024	.018	.013	.010	.008	.006	.004
.80	.086	.069	.055	.044	.035	.028	.023	.018	.014
.85	.167	.142	.121	.103	.087	.074	.063	.054	.046
.90	.314	.282	.254	.229	.206	.185	.167	.150	.135
.95	.569	.540	.513	.488	.463	.440	.418	.397	.377

$(1-p)$	$(1-p)^{20}$	$(1-p)^{21}$	$(1-p)^{22}$	$(1-p)^{23}$	$(1-p)^{24}$	$(1-p)^{25}$	$(1-p)^{26}$	$(1-p)^{27}$	$(1-p)^{28}$
.70	.001	.001	.000						
.75	.003	.002	.002	.001	.001	.001	.001	.000	
.80	.012	.009	.007	.006	.005	.004	.003	.002	.002
.85	.039	.033	.028	.024	.020	.017	.015	.012	.011
.90	.122	.109	.098	.089	.080	.072	.065	.058	.052
.95	.358	.340	.323	.307	.292	.277	.263	.250	.238

Table C

The Normal Distribution

x	Proportion below x	x	Proportion below x	x	Proportion below x
$\mu - 3.0\sigma$	.001	$\mu - .9\sigma$	.184	$\mu + 1.1\sigma$	.864
$\mu - 2.9\sigma$	.002	$\mu - .8\sigma$	.212	$\mu + 1.2\sigma$	.885
$\mu - 2.8\sigma$	.003	$\mu - .7\sigma$	.242	$\mu + 1.3\sigma$	.903
$\mu - 2.7\sigma$	.004	$\mu - .6\sigma$	.274	$\mu + 1.4\sigma$	.919
$\mu - 2.6\sigma$	.005	$\mu - .5\sigma$	.309	$\mu + 1.5\sigma$	.933
$\mu - 2.5\sigma$	.006	$\mu - .4\sigma$	.345	$\mu + 1.6\sigma$	.945
$\mu - 2.4\sigma$	.008	$\mu - .3\sigma$	.382	$\mu + 1.7\sigma$	.955
$\mu - 2.3\sigma$	.011	$\mu - .2\sigma$	.421	$\mu + 1.8\sigma$	.964
$\mu - 2.2\sigma$	.014	$\mu - .1\sigma$	.460	$\mu + 1.9\sigma$	.971
$\mu - 2.1\sigma$	.018	μ	.500	$\mu + 2.0\sigma$	.977
$\mu - 2.0\sigma$	.023	$\mu + .1\sigma$	.540	$\mu + 2.1\sigma$	.982
$\mu - 1.9\sigma$	.029	$\mu + .2\sigma$	.579	$\mu + 2.2\sigma$	.986
$\mu - 1.8\sigma$	.036	$\mu + .3\sigma$	.618	$\mu + 2.3\sigma$	.989
$\mu - 1.7\sigma$	.045	$\mu + .4\sigma$	.655	$\mu + 2.4\sigma$	.992
$\mu - 1.6\sigma$	.055	$\mu + .5\sigma$	.691	$\mu + 2.5\sigma$	.994
$\mu - 1.5\sigma$	.067	$\mu + .6\sigma$	.726	$\mu + 2.6\sigma$	.995
$\mu - 1.4\sigma$	.081	$\mu + .7\sigma$	.758	$\mu + 2.7\sigma$	.996
$\mu - 1.3\sigma$	.097	$\mu + .8\sigma$	.788	$\mu + 2.8\sigma$	.997
$\mu - 1.2\sigma$	.115	$\mu + .9\sigma$	.816	$\mu + 2.9\sigma$	.998
$\mu - 1.1\sigma$	.136	$\mu + 1.0\sigma$	.841	$\mu + 3.0\sigma$	.999
$\mu - 1.0\sigma$	.159				

Table D

Squares of Numbers

N	N^2	N	N^2	N	N^2
01	0001	34	1156	67	4489
02	0004	35	1225	68	4624
03	0009	36	1296	69	4761
04	0016	37	1369	70	4900
05	0025	38	1444	71	5041
06	0036	39	1521	72	5184
07	0049	40	1600	73	5329
08	0064	41	1681	74	5476
09	0081	42	1764	75	5625
10	0100	43	1849	76	5776
11	0121	44	1936	77	5929
12	0144	45	2025	78	6084
13	0169	46	2116	79	6241
14	0196	47	2209	80	6400
15	0225	48	2304	81	6561
16	0256	49	2401	82	6724
17	0289	50	2500	83	6889
18	0324	51	2601	84	7056
19	0361	52	2704	85	7225
20	0400	53	2809	86	7396
21	0441	54	2916	87	7569
22	0484	55	3025	88	7744
23	0529	56	3136	89	7921
24	0576	57	3249	90	8100
25	0625	58	3364	91	8281
26	0676	59	3481	92	8464
27	0729	60	3600	93	8649
28	0784	61	3721	94	8836
29	0841	62	3844	95	9025
30	0900	63	3969	96	9216
31	0961	64	4096	97	9409
32	1024	65	4225	98	9604
33	1089	66	4356	99	9801

Table E

Square Roots

N	$\sqrt{N}$	N	$\sqrt{N}$	N	$\sqrt{N}$	N	$\sqrt{N}$
1.0	1.00						
1.1	1.05	5.6	2.37	11	3.32	56	7.48
1.2	1.10	5.7	2.39	12	3.46	57	7.55
1.3	1.14	5.8	2.41	13	3.61	58	7.62
1.4	1.18	5.9	2.43	14	3.74	59	7.68
1.5	1.22	6.0	2.45	15	3.87	60	7.75
1.6	1.26	6.1	2.47	16	4.00	61	7.81
1.7	1.30	6.2	2.49	17	4.12	62	7.87
1.8	1.34	6.3	2.51	18	4.24	63	7.94
1.9	1.38	6.4	2.53	19	4.36	64	8.00
2.0	1.41	6.5	2.55	20	4.47	65	8.06
2.1	1.45	6.6	2.57	21	4.58	66	8.12
2.2	1.48	6.7	2.59	22	4.69	67	8.19
2.3	1.52	6.8	2.61	23	4.80	68	8.25
2.4	1.55	6.9	2.63	24	4.90	69	8.31
2.5	1.58	7.0	2.65	25	5.00	70	8.37
2.6	1.61	7.1	2.66	26	5.10	71	8.43
2.7	1.64	7.2	2.68	27	5.20	72	8.49
2.8	1.67	7.3	2.70	28	5.29	73	8.54
2.9	1.70	7.4	2.72	29	5.39	74	8.60
3.0	1.73	7.5	2.74	30	5.48	75	8.66
3.1	1.76	7.6	2.76	31	5.57	76	8.72
3.2	1.79	7.7	2.77	32	5.66	77	8.78
3.3	1.82	7.8	2.79	33	5.74	78	8.83
3.4	1.84	7.9	2.81	34	5.83	79	8.89
3.5	1.87	8.0	2.83	35	5.92	80	8.94
3.6	1.90	8.1	2.85	36	6.00	81	9.00
3.7	1.92	8.2	2.86	37	6.08	82	9.06
3.8	1.95	8.3	2.88	38	6.16	83	9.11
3.9	1.97	8.4	2.90	39	6.24	84	9.17
4.0	2.00	8.5	2.92	40	6.32	85	9.22
4.1	2.02	8.6	2.93	41	6.40	86	9.27
4.2	2.05	8.7	2.95	42	6.48	87	9.33
4.3	2.07	8.8	2.97	43	6.56	88	9.38
4.4	2.10	8.9	2.98	44	6.63	89	9.43
4.5	2.12	9.0	3.00	45	6.71	90	9.49
4.6	2.14	9.1	3.02	46	6.78	91	9.54
4.7	2.17	9.2	3.03	47	6.86	92	9.59
4.8	2.19	9.3	3.05	48	6.93	93	9.64
4.9	2.21	9.4	3.07	49	7.00	94	9.70
5.0	2.24	9.5	3.08	50	7.07	95	9.75
5.1	2.26	9.6	3.10	51	7.14	96	9.80
5.2	2.28	9.7	3.11	52	7.21	97	9.85
5.3	2.30	9.8	3.13	53	7.28	98	9.90
5.4	2.32	9.9	3.15	54	7.35	99	9.95
5.5	2.35	10.0	3.16	55	7.42	100	10.00

Answers to Selected Problems

Chapter 1

4. When $H = .05$ lamberts, $J = 3.5$.
When $J = 2.5$, $H = .025$ lamberts.

6. Let H' be weight in pounds. Then $J = 830(H')^{1.4}$.
When $H' = .125$, $J = 45$.
When $H' = 1.0$, $J = 830$.

10. When $H_0 = 100$ dynes/cm^2, $H_1 = 109$ dynes/cm^2.
When $H_0 = 10^{50}$ dynes/cm^2, $H_1 = (1.09)10^{50}$ dynes/cm^2.

11. When $k = 1.09$, $H = 24.4$.
When $H = 100$ dynes/cm^2, $D = 49.8$.
When $H = 10^{50}$ dynes/cm^2, $D = 1221$.

Chapter 2

3. $P(A_1 \mid A_1, A_2, A_4, A_6) = .30$.

4. (a) $a = \{A_4, A_5,\}$ or $\{A_4, A_6, A_7\}$.

11. See graphed points in Fig. 3.

13. See Table 1.

Chapter 3

5. $b = .60$, $c = .41$, $h' = .07$.

Chapter 4

2. $\mu = 103.6$, $\sigma^2 = 223$, $\sigma = 14.9$.
$P(x \leq \mu) = .56$ when we include the group of scores 95–105.
$P(x \leq \mu - .5\sigma) = .28$ when we let $\mu - .5\sigma \approx 95$.

Chapter 5

2. Let X be the trial on which a white marble is drawn.
$P(X = 10) = .04$, $P(X \leq 5) = .41$

5. $P(L > 3) = .13$

10. 2 items, 7 items

19. For D, $r_{3,3} = .52$; for B, $r_{3,9} = .39$.

23. .81, .90

28. $f = .40$, $t = .42$, $c_2 = .42$

Chapter 6

1. $s = .15$, $P(E \leq 5) = .62$, $P(L \leq 10) = .61$

4. In training, $s = .45$
In transfer, $s = .21$, $t = .47$, $P(E = 0) = .47$, $\mu_E = 2.52$

Chapter 7

3. $P(x < 40) = .16$, $P(x > 52.5) = .07$, $P(x < 48.5) = .76$, $P(x > 51.5) = .10$

15. .98, .49, $-.06$.

Chapter 8

1. $P(x < 54.5) = .06$, $P(57.5 < x < 62.5) = .51$

12. $\sigma_t = 8.66$, $P(64.5 < t < 85.5) = .77$, $P(64.5 < x < 85.5) = .71$
If $t = 85.0$, $P(x_i < 79.5) = .14$, $P(x_i < 74.5) = .02$.

17. $\sigma_e = 4.50$, $\mu_t = 44.2$, $\sigma_t = 7.79$
If $t = 38.6$, $P(x_i > 34.5) = .82$.

26. $\rho_{xc} \geq .60$. If $x_i = 66.7$, $p(x_i) = 66.24$ and $P(c_i > 59.5) = .75$.

Index

ABCDE698